The SCREENWRITER *in* British Cinema

JILL NELMES

palgrave
macmillan

A BFI book published by Palgrave Macmillan

First published in 2014 by
PALGRAVE MACMILLAN

on behalf of the

BRITISH FILM INSTITUTE
21 Stephen Street, London W1T 1LN
www.bfi.org.uk

There's more to discover about film and television through the BFI.
Our world-renowned archive, cinemas, festivals, films, publications and learning resources are here to inspire you.

Palgrave Macmillan in the UK is an imprint of Macmillan Publishers Limited, registered in England, company number 785998, of Houndmills, Basingstoke, Hampshire RG21 6XS. Palgrave Macmillan in the US is a division of St Martin's Press LLC, 175 Fifth Avenue, New York, NY 10010. Palgrave Macmillan is the global academic imprint of the above companies and has companies and representatives throughout the world. Palgrave® and Macmillan® are registered trademarks in the United States, the United Kingdom, Europe and other countries.

Cover image: *Night Train for Inverness* screenplay (Ernest Morris, 1960), BFI National Archive
Designed by couch

Set by Cambrian Typesetters, Camberley, Surrey & couch
Printed in China

This book is printed on paper suitable for recycling and made from fully managed and sustained forest sources. Logging, pulping and manufacturing processes are expected to conform to the environmental regulations of the country of origin.

British Library Cataloguing-in-Publication Data
A catalogue record for this book is available from the British Library
A catalog record for this book is available from the Library of Congress

ISBN 978-1-84457-365-3 (pb)
ISBN 978-1-84457-366-0 (hb)

CONTENTS

ACKNOWLEDGMENTS

This book would not have been possible without access to the Special Collections held at the British Film Institute and its ever helpful library staff. I am especially indebted to Nathalie Morris and Jonny Davies who worked with me patiently for more than three years on the project and have always been ready and willing to give information and advice, despite their busy workloads. I am extremely grateful to the British Academy for funding my initial research on the Janet Green Collection and to the AHRC for awarding a Fellowship which allowed me to take a much needed sabbatical to complete the monograph. I received invaluable feedback from my colleagues, particularly Jule Selbo, Ian Macdonald, Robert Murphy and Andrew Spicer, while the Screenwriting Research Conferences in Helsinki, Copenhagen and Brussels allowed me to test my research.

I would also like to thank those I interviewed while undertaking research for the book, particularly Paul Laverty, Lord David Puttnam and Thelma Schoonmaker. Barry McCormick kindly regaled me with stories about his stepmother, Janet Green, that I promised not to publish and Leo Box, Muriel and Sydney Box's grandson, agreed without hesitation to the publication of screenplay extracts and notes from their diary. My thanks to the David Lean Foundation for allowing me to use extracts from letters and unpublished screenplays.

The generosity of the production companies who have consented to the publication of extracts from letters and screenplays is greatly appreciated; this includes Studio Canal for *A Canterbury Tale*, *A Matter of Life and Death*, *The Lavender Hill Mob* and *Passport to Pimlico*; ITN Source for *Victim*, *Carry on up the Khyber* and *The Seventh Veil*; Goldcrest Films for *Local Hero* and *The Killing Fields*; Sixteen Films for permission to quote from *The Wind That Shakes the Barley*; Columbia Pictures for permission to quote from the screenplays of *The Long Arm* and *The Lawbreakers*.

Intellect Publishing has given permission to use extracts from two articles published in the *Journal of Screenwriting*, 'Collaboration and Control in the Development of Janet Green's screenplay *Victim*' vol. 1 no. 2, 2010 and 'Re-writing Paul Laverty's Screenplay – *The Wind That Shakes the Barley*' vol. 2 no. 2, 2011.

Finally I would like to thank BFI Publishing for commissioning and publishing the book, in particular Rebecca Barden, Sophia Contento and copy editor, Belinda Latchford.

This book is dedicated to my daughter, Corrina, my sisters Claire and Sarah and last but not least to Robert Murphy for his wisdom, advice and encouragement.

INTRODUCTION

Neither the screenwriter nor the screenplay in British cinema has received the academic attention either deserves; yet it would be impossible to make the majority of films without a screenplay. Historically, the screenplay has been viewed as having value solely as the blueprint for a
film, without literary or artistic merit in itself, rather than as a crucial part of the production
process, which also has a separate existence. This indifference has meant that few writers have
left traces of their work; Charles Bennett, for instance, wrote more than sixty-five films, some
of his most famous for Alfred Hitchcock, but hardly any of his screenplays survive, while the
Ealing Collection of screenplays was rescued from a skip before being donated to the British
Film Institute (Morris 2010: 197).

    This book highlights the contribution of the screenwriter to British cinema, while drawing
attention to the screenplay development process and discussing some of the screenplays available for study, from early sound cinema to the present day. Each of the eleven chapters refers to
a selection of the archival content held in the Special Collections at the British Film Institute,
the major archive collection of film and television in the UK and the focus for this research. The
Special Collections hold film treatments, screenplays, correspondence, film budgets and many
other items relating to film production. A wealth of material is available but not all of it meets
the criteria for inclusion in this book; in particular, a range of screenplay drafts and correspondence needed to be available for study, representing each writer's body of work and shedding
light on his or her relationship with others involved in the screenplay development process.[1] All
of the writers discussed have collaborated closely with a producer or director, though some
relationships were, or are, more harmonious than others. The producer and director as well as
the actors may all have a say in the screenplay, which can change while the film is being shot and
edited, or even in the dubbing room.

    Despite the fact that film-making is a collaborative process, the auteur theory, centring on
the director has become pervasive in academia and diverted attention from an understanding of
the true nature of film-making. In the early years of cinema the writer was considered the creator of the film, the director merely the person who followed the shots laid out in the script, but
the rise of the Hollywood Studio System brought about a change of focus, with the producer
becoming the most powerful person on the film, with a similar approach spreading to Britain.
The transfer of emphasis to the director began in France with the *Cahiers du cinéma* critics in the
1950s while in the US, Andrew Sarris's book *The American Cinema: Directors and Directions
1929–1968* (1968) was influential in establishing the director's predominance. As independent
production companies took over from the studios, the director's role continued to be significant,
with directors' names serving more recently as marketing tools. This shift has resulted in the
writer receiving less attention than he or she deserves. It is not the intention of this book to

argue for the screenwriter as auteur, rather to suggest that both the role of the screenwriter and the contribution of the screenplay have been sidelined and are worthy of academic scrutiny.

The screenplay, as a text, has two main functions: first, to help plan the film, which includes attracting funding and securing a producer, director and actors; second, as the shooting script once filming has begun. The first stage is often protracted because the screenplay is often more open to discussion and to change during its development than other written forms and this may involve the writing of many drafts.

A consequence of considering the screenplay a stage in an industrial practice, with the director as its creative head, has led to the dismissal of the screenplay as a literary text. Steven Maras has examined the issue of the unstable screenplay text, referring to the 'object problem' in screenwriting and the difficulty in defining the screenplay and deciding whether it can exist independently from the film (2009: 11). These concerns have been questioned by genetic theory, which argues that there is no one stable text, all texts being important in the creative process.[2] Indeed, the screenplay is not usually an autonomous work, although many unfilmed or unrealised screenplays exist which could fit into this category; Robert Bolt and David Lean's work on *The Lawbreakers* and *The Long Arm* for example, which is discussed in Chapter 8. The fact that the screenplay 'disappears' once filmed, having played its part, has constituted an argument for the exclusion of the screenplay as an area of study, yet it is the very existence of these records which make it stand out as a different form.

Further to this, the screenplay has artistic and literary qualities which can be usefully compared to other forms; the most obvious comparison is with the play text, where scene, description and dialogue are separated in a similar way (O'Thomas 2011: 237–49). Many writers and academics have compared the screenplay to poetry because of its condensed form and the often strict guidelines regarding layout and structure. Steven Price cites Kevin Boon's argument that a screenplay has similar qualities to the work of the Imagist poets such as William Carlos Williams (2010: 34). The ballad form also has much in common with the screenplay, as an oral medium relating a narrative (Ganz 2010: 225–36), while Marja-Ritta Kiovumaki has explained how the screenplay can be likened to a plan for a performance, comparing it to a musical score interpreted by a conductor (2010: 27–30).

Examining the screenplay in British cinema requires some historical context. From the first short film reels produced in 1895, films have needed written plans. Until the coming of sound, these plans were called scenarios, with the writers dubbed scenarists. By the late 1920s and the arrival of sound, scenarists were supplanted by screenplay writers. Director Adrian Brunel's instructive book, *Filmcraft*, published in 1936, discusses writing for both silent and sound film, advocating that a scenario or shooting script should be 'as nearly as possible, a description in detail and in technical language of the film you shoot' (1936: 14), an element of advice still appropriate for any contemporary screenplay writer.

Historically, the film writer has been neglected in favour of the director and by the advent of sound, the status of the screenwriter had considerably diminished, as Ian Macdonald explains:

> By the end of the silent period, however, the British screenwriter was less of the lead collaborator or 'author' behind the film and more of a supplicant making suggestions … screenwriters in the 1910s may have had some hopes of creating a new art of screenwriting, but by 1930 they were located rather more firmly in their industrial place as craftsmen and craftswomen. (2010: 62)

The first scenarists had to adapt to the transition from silent film to sound and many did not survive. Some writers, like Harry Fowler Mear, successfully spanned the two eras, penning over 100 films, including the adaptation of Hitchcock's *The Lodger* (1932); likewise, Angus MacPhail, went on to become a key writer and script editor for Ealing Studios. But Eliot Stannard, who had authored many of Hitchcock's scenarios, did not and, although respected as a silent film writer, he disappeared into obscurity after the transition to sound, his last film credit being in 1933 for *To Brighton with Gladys*. Stannard's importance as an early scenarist is often unrecognised although Michael Eaton describes him as the 'patron saint of British screenwriters'.[3]

By the 1930s the writer's status in the film industry had declined considerably. Indeed, Charles Bennett, author of some of Hitchcock's most acclaimed films, including *The 39 Steps* (1935), received little recognition, even though he was respected in the industry. In the 1930s story writers and separate dialogue writers often worked together on a screenplay: Ian Hay, for instance, is credited for the dialogue on *The 39 Steps*. Some studio heads at that time, such as Michael Balcon, at Ealing, did appreciate the importance of the writer, as did film-makers like Michael Powell, who knew the difference a great storyteller like Emeric Pressburger could make to a film. The status of the screenwriter has remained much the same to the present day, with a few exceptions such as Robert Bolt and, more recently, Richard Curtis, whose international hits with *Four Weddings and a Funeral* (1994), *Bean* (1997) and *Notting Hill* (1999) gave him the freedom to write and direct his films.[4] Generally, though, writers in the film industry work in stark contrast to those in television and theatre, who are considered pivotal to a production.

The screenwriters discussed in this book are presented in chronological order, from the 1930s to the present day, offering some sense of the changing landscape for the writer in British cinema. Although this is not intended to be an historical overview of the subject, the working practices of the writer in different periods are revealed as a result of the findings in the archives.

The first section of each chapter provides a background to the screenwriter and his or her relationship with the producer or director they have worked with; the second section draws from the material selected from the Special Collections. Each chapter then takes a slightly different approach, dependent on the writer and the material available; either discussing aspects of the writing process, referring to the development of a screenplay or analysing the screenplay or screenplay drafts in further detail. This includes the study of single texts, multiple texts and unrealised texts, as in some instances the screenplays were never produced: projects frequently fall through no matter how respected the writer.

Chapter 1 discusses Jeffrey Dell, who wrote three screenplays for Sydney Box, when the latter was a contract producer at Two Cities, and worked on numerous projects with the Boulting brothers, producers who enjoyed many popular successes. While Dell's screenplays may have lacked the quality of those from such luminaries as Emeric Pressburger or Robert Bolt, they are entertaining and well written. Dell was rarely allowed to write to his best ability because of the demands placed on him by producers, who required a particular type of entertainment film. The chapter focuses on an analysis of three screenplays in the collection that are representative of his very different styles: two comedies, *Don't Take It to Heart* (1944) and *A French Mistress* (1960) and the stylish thriller, *The Dark Man* (1951).

Emeric Pressburger and Michael Powell's film-making partnership was one of the most artistically and creatively successful in British cinema. Pressburger was an accomplished writer whom Powell greatly admired for his sense of story and character. Chapter 2 outlines

Pressburger's early career as a writer for Ufa, the German-based studio, his meeting Powell and how their great collaborative partnership took off before focusing on two screenplays in the Pressburger Collection. The beginning of an early handwritten draft is compared to a later version of *A Matter of Life and Death* (1946), and the screenplay structure, and narrative and character development of *A Canterbury Tale* (1944). The latter is one of the most overlooked of Pressburger's scripts yet the one he liked the most; indeed, it is an example of a screenplay that can be likened to poetry, in its use of metaphor and intensity of expression.

Chapter 3 looks at the writers at Ealing Studios and their relationship with the studio head, Michael Balcon, who recognised the importance of the writer to his producer–director teams in developing original screenplays. The key studio writers are discussed, including the only woman credited with writing for Ealing, Diana Morgan. The Brunel and Balcon Collections offer an insight into the career of Angus MacPhail, whose pivotal role as script editor has often gone unrecognised; the T. E. B. Clarke Collection holds screenplays for some of Ealing's best-known films as well as editing notes, which outline the development of *Passport to Pimlico* (1949) and allow a study of the writing of Clarke's Academy Award-winning screenplay, *The Lavender Hill Mob* (1951).

Muriel Box's writing partnership with her husband, Sydney, was prolific, producing many films over a period of more than thirty years, from their days penning documentary shorts in the 1930s to their last film *Too Young to Love* in 1960, but the quality of their work often suffered because of the need to fulfil studio output demands. Chapter 4 discusses Muriel Box's career as a writer and script editor and her interest in writing films for women with a feminist perspective such as *Street Corner* (1953), a moving and cleverly structured film about women police officers. The chapter then examines the draft screenplays held in the Muriel and Sydney Box Collection of two of her films, the Oscar-winning melodrama, *The Seventh Veil* (1946), and a light comedy, *The Truth about Women* (1957), the latter of which Muriel also directed.

Chapter 5 looks at another accomplished female writer, Janet Green, who had a very successful career, co-writing with her husband the three social issue films, *Sapphire* (1959), *Victim* (1961) and *Life for Ruth* (1962), for which she is best known, all discussed here. Green had the foresight to preserve her work, safeguarding for us one of the most detailed accounts of the screenplay development process of a film available. The letters in the collection reveal a chronological breakdown of the development of the screenplay for *Victim* and much about Green's working relationship with producer Michael Relph and director Basil Dean. The chapter concludes with an analysis of the changes to the draft screenplays of *Victim*, Green making many of these because of pressure from the producer, Michael Relph, and the British Board of Film Censorship.

In contrast, Mark Grantham was a prolific writer of 'B' movies, working for the Danziger brothers, who were noted for their ability to produce films quickly and cheaply. Chapter 6 discusses the producer/writer relationship along with Grantham's creative process, in which he was expected to complete a screenplay in two weeks. Ironically, this time constraint allowed Grantham a degree of autonomy as the screenplays would often be shot as written. Many of Grantham's screenplays were not of high quality but a few stand out for being well structured despite the haste in which they were turned out. The chapter focuses on three screenplays in the Mark Grantham Collection, examining the structure, narrative and stylistic content of the murder mystery *Feet of Clay* (1960), the suspenseful *Night Train for Inverness* (1960) and the less successful comedy *She Always Gets Their Man* (1962).

Chapter 7 looks at the *Carry On* screenplays which, apart from the last four, were the work of two men: Norman Hudis wrote the first six films after which Talbot Rothwell took over, continuing in this role until *Carry on Dick* in 1974. The popularity of the early films was such that *Carry on Nurse* (1959) ran in one cinema in Los Angeles for more than a year. Though the *Carry On* films were made on a low budget, their production values were much higher than those on the Danzigers' films and Peter Rogers, having once been a writer himself, knew the value of a good screenplay, paying the writers more than the actors. The collection, donated by Gerald Thomas, the director of all the *Carry On* films, holds draft screenplays for each of the films. The quality of the screenplays produced was very variable, the history cycle and the parodies being better received by the critics. This chapter focuses on two of the best in the series, discussing the genesis of the screenplay for *Carry on Sergeant* (1958), then analysing the screenplay for *Carry on up the Khyber* (1968), comparing the two drafts in the collection.

Robert Bolt began his career writing for the stage and BBC radio, taking up screenwriting when he was asked to rewrite *Lawrence of Arabia* (1962) for David Lean, who much admired Bolt's work. The collaboration prospered and Bolt went on to pen the screenplays for *Doctor Zhivago* (1965), winning an Academy Award for the adaptation, and *Ryan's Daughter* (1970) which was poorly received. Bolt also worked on other projects with Lean that were not realised, including screenplays about the mutiny on the Bounty and *Nostromo*. The second part of Chapter 8 looks at the development of the two screenplays for the Bounty story, *The Lawbreakers* and *The Long Arm*, which were eventually filmed by another director, Roger Donaldson, as one film, *The Bounty* (1984). The revealing letters, script notes and draft screenplays in the David Lean Collection are discussed, including feedback Lean sent to Bolt about the screenplays, and Bolt's style and technique are examined.

Producer David Puttnam was known for his ability to build a good relationship with his production team and for finding talented writers, whose decisions he supported, even when under pressure to make changes to a script. Chapter 9 discusses three screenplays and correspondence in the David Puttnam Collection, tracing their development. The section on *Local Hero* (1983), written and directed by Bill Forsyth, looks at an early treatment of the film before comparing two drafts of the screenplay. Despite recourse to a number of different writers, including Robert Bolt, a project entitled *The October Circle* (screenplay 1979) never came to fruition. Letters offer a revealing account of the difficult writing process and how respected writers like Tom Stoppard were approached to 'improve' the script. *The Killing Fields* (1984) was written by Bruce Robinson, with whom Puttnam took a measured risk in employing someone new and untried, but the film proved a great critical success, with Robinson nominated for an Academy Award for his adaptation of Sydney Schanberg's article.

John McGrath's early roots were in theatre and then television, where he worked with Ken Loach and Ken Russell in the 1960s, going on to write *Billion Dollar Brain* (1967) with Russell, *The Virgin Soldiers* (1969), *The Bofors Gun* (1968, an adaptation of his stage play) and *The Reckoning* (1969). The latter two films were directed by Jack Gold and starred Nicol Williamson. Chapter 10 explores McGrath's writing and how it was influenced by his socialist convictions and desire to move away from realist narratives. McGrath was able to adapt to a range of styles, from the playfulness of *Billion Dollar Brain*, to *The Reckoning*, an underrated and coruscating attack on greed and the consumer society. The chapter compares two short outlines of *Billion Dollar Brain*, and the draft screenplays of *The Reckoning*.

In common with McGrath, political convictions have also been central to Paul Laverty's writing and, coincidentally, both he and McGrath have worked with Ken Loach, Laverty having authored all of Loach's films bar one, since *Carla's Song* in 1996. With some serendipity, Laverty contacted Loach at a time when he was looking for a new collaborator finding in Laverty someone in tune with and sympathetic to his working methods. Chapter 11 discusses Laverty's screenplays and his writing relationship with Loach, featuring a breakdown and analysis of two very different drafts of *The Wind That Shakes the Barley* (2006), which show how the revised draft changed to focus more on the central character and the narrative flow, at the expense of historical and expositional detail.

NOTES

1. For more on the content of the Special Collections, see Nathalie Morris's 2010 article in the *Journal of Screenwriting*.
2. Genetic criticism arose out of the French structuralist movement, arguing that all the stages in the development of the text are as important as the 'final version'. Genetic criticism is particularly relevant for the screenplay, which often goes through many drafts, as it pays attention to the developmental stages of a work, an aspect of film yet to receive much recognition from academics, attaching value to tracing the life of a screenplay. See Jed Deppman *et al.*, *Genetic Criticism: Texts and Avant-Textes* (2004) for a more detailed breakdown of genetic criticism. See Anna Sofia Rossholm's 2012 article discussing the Ingmar Bergman Archive and the notion of avant-texte, and Rosamund Davies's (2012), examining the genesis of the film *Don't Look Now* (1973). Both articles appear in the *Journal of Screenwriting*.
3. See http://old.bfi.org.uk/sightandsound/feature/49173.
4. See Andrew Spicer's article 'The Author as Author: Restoring the Screenwriter to British Film' (2007), which discusses Curtis's career as a screenwriter and the amount of creative control he is able to exert.

01

JEFFREY DELL

SATIRE, SOCIALISM AND SUSPENSE

Jeffrey Dell, born in 1904, was a highly respected screenwriter, whose career spanned more than thirty years, from the first sound films in the early 1930s through to the late 1960s. He is credited as writer or contributor on at least twenty-seven films and as director on five. He studied and practised law before realising that he was in completely the wrong line of work and becoming a playwright. He quickly achieved success, his first play, *Payment Deferred*, being bought by a Hollywood studio and filmed in 1932.[1] Two further plays were subsequently optioned in Hollywood but not produced. Alexander Korda, film producer and head of London Films, took note of Dell's abilities and asked him to write for his studio. Dell's first screenplay for Korda and probably his best-known film, *Sanders of the River*, was adapted from an Edgar Wallace novel in 1935; the story, a celebration of British colonial rule, was a triumph, performing exceptionally well at the box office. After writing for Korda, Dell suffered a lean period during which he penned *Nobody Ordered Wolves* (1939), a satire about the workings of the film industry and his time with Korda. Mirroring Dell's own experience of the industry, the increasingly cynical hero of the book talks to a starlet, who asks him,' I suppose you have dreams of writing something terrific and seeing it on the screen?' To which he replies:

> No I realise that's too much to ask. My ambitions have grown more modest. I'd like to write something before I die but I've no illusions about recognising what I've written when it's put on the screen. That would be too much to hope for. (1939: 163)

Despite Dell's cynicism about the film industry, he continued to be in demand in the 1940s, writing and directing comedies such as *Don't Take It to Heart* (1944) and adapting *Thunder Rock* (1942), a play by Robert Ardrey, whose allegorical subject matter and anti-isolationist theme regarding World War II won it many accolades.

Dell first began working for Sydney Box, a producer at Two Cities Films, in the early 1940s, contributing dialogue to the screenplay for *Freedom Radio* (1941), and going on to write and direct two further films, *The Flemish Farm* (1943) and *Don't Take It to Heart*. Dell often worked with his third wife, Jill Craigie, with whom he co-wrote *The Flemish Farm*, about the search for a Belgian Army flag which had been buried to keep it safe from the Nazis during World War II. They authored at least one play together, *The Judge* (1938), which they also intended to become a film. Other projects were in development with the Boxes, including Dell's own novel, *The Hoffman Episode* (1954), but none were produced. Dell's relationship with the Boxes ended when Sydney Box left Two Cities because he had little creative freedom there (Spicer 2006: 46).

It was Dell's association with the twin brothers, John and Roy Boulting, which was to be his most long-lived collaboration. Their twenty-four-year relationship began with *Thunder Rock* in

Screenwriter Jeffrey Dell on set (right) with director Roy Boulting

1942 and ended with Dell's contribution to the screenplay for *The Family Way* in 1966. The script is credited to the play's author, Bill Naughton, though Dell had fleshed out the adaptation into suitable film material by extending the opening sequence and introducing subplots (Aldgate 2000: 240). Dell completed many screenplays for the Boultings, usually in conjunction with one of the brothers, and was adept at improving scripts and developing dialogue. He is credited with adding scenes and dialogue to the adaptation of Kingsley Amis's *Lucky Jim* (1957) and for additional dialogue on *Cone of Silence* (1960). Dell worked on other screenplays for the Boultings, for which he is not credited, such as *Suspect* (1960) and they held him in high regard for his writing and collaborative skills. Roy Boulting notes how well they worked together:

> when you're working on a movie script, it's important to have somebody with whom you are in
> accord – that is vital. If you're not in accord, it will never work and I've had experience of that. But
> to have somebody with whom you're on some sort of wavelength, then to have writers like Frank
> Harvey or Jeffrey Dell is a great benefit. (Burton *et al.* 2000: 261)

Dell first teamed up with the Boultings on *Thunder Rock*, at a time when the brothers believed the cinema had a duty to educate and inform. Raymond Durgnat describes the Boultings' early films as 'earnest evangelicals' (1970: 234), while Laurie Ede points out their belief in linking art to education, 'The Boultings were similarly convinced of their dual role as protectors and disseminators of good art .... They wrote that art should be thought of "in

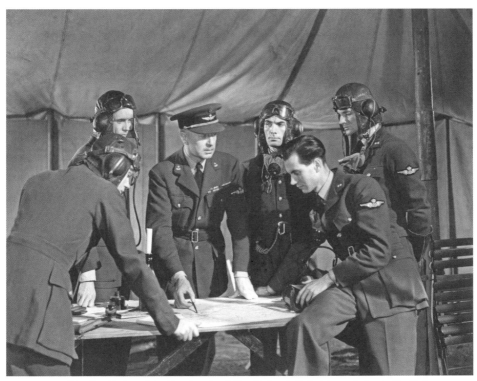

A scene from *The Flemish Farm* (1943), written by Jeffrey Dell and Jill Craigie, and directed by Dell

terms of education", and should "illuminate the function of living"'(2000: 37). Yet, by the late 1950s, the Boultings were better known for satire and comedy, their post-war idealism compromised by changes in British culture and society and the need to attract an audience.

Dell wrote a number of comedies for the Boultings in the late 1950s, often combining humour with light satire. This included the entertaining *Brothers in Law* (1957), also credited to Frank Harvey and Roy Boulting as writers; *Happy Is the Bride* (1958), adapted from a play by Esther McCracken and co-written with Roy Boulting; and *Carlton-Browne of the F.O.*, which Dell co-wrote and directed with Roy Boulting; *Carlton-Browne* was released in 1958, starring Peter Sellers and Terry-Thomas and, while a hit at the box office, received mixed reviews. The film pokes fun at British foreign policy and, although more farce than satire, boasts many amusing moments, as Tony Whitehead explains:

> The Boultings' mixture of satire and broad comedy in this context was not universally well received: the *Monthly Film Bulletin* thought their position 'invidious' and the comedy 'uncomfortable'. The topicality having faded, however, the film can more readily be enjoyed as a timely lampoon of outmoded imperialist attitudes and bureaucratic ineptitude.[2]

Alan Burton more or less agrees, describing the film as 'A clever, surer return to satire' (2012: 82), but points out that the Boultings' comedies had become dated and their satire muted in comparison with the new television comedies like *That Was the Week That Was* (1962–3).

Dell's last few screen credits were co-written with Roy Boulting, including *A French Mistress* (1960) and the mildly engaging crime comedy, *Rotten to the Core* (1965), also credited to two other authors.

Dell penned some very effective thrillers for other producers. For instance, *The Dark Man* (1951), a cleverly plotted film, written and directed by Dell, was produced by Julian Wintle of Independent Artists, responsible for many films from the 1950s to the early 1970s, as well as the *Avengers* TV series (1961–9) in the 1960s. Dell also wrote *The Saint's Vacation* (1941) for RKO Radio British Productions while his play *The Treasure of San Teresa* was adapted for film in 1959.

Dell's screenplays may not have the sharpness of observation and characterisation of, for example, the best Ealing films, but he worked in markedly different conditions, with little importance placed on rewriting and with a contrasting type of editorial and producer input. Most of his films credit him as co-writer, possibly indicating that he did not have the creative freedom to write as he would like. Dell's screenplays could be accused of being bland and clichéd but the producers he worked with, particularly Sydney Box and the Boulting brothers, failed to push him to write to the best of his abilities. Even so, his output is often amusing and, in the case of dramas such as *The Dark Man*, tautly effective.

THE JEFFREY DELL COLLECTION

The collection holds nine of Dell's realised screenplays, all part-credited to Dell apart from *Woman Times Seven* (1967), on which it seems likely that he did some rewriting. Only one draft of each screenplay is available, although there are also an early typescript draft and shooting script for *Thunder Rock*. Six unrealised screenplays also feature in the collection, including an adaptation of Dell's novel, *The Hoffman Episode*. The film was attached to Two Cities Films, further evidence of his close working relationship with Sydney Box. A shooting script of the renamed *The Hoffman Case* is also held here, dated 1949, suggesting that the film was only pulled close to production, at a very late stage of development.

The earlier screenplays such as *Thunder Rock* and *It's Hard to Be Good* (1948) conveyed a clear social message. *Thunder Rock*, produced by the Boulting brothers, about a lighthouse keeper who will not leave his lighthouse, can be interpreted as a metaphor for the isolationism which had kept America out of World War II until Pearl Harbour. The script is based on a play by Robert Ardrey, a left-wing American author, which had a successful run in London. Quite popular with the critics, the film was less well received by the general public, possibly because the screenplay gives away its theatrical roots, the action often static and the dialogue stilted. *It's Hard to Be Good* is a drama with some comic moments, written and directed by Dell for Sydney Box at Two Cities Films. The screenplay follows a man adapting to civilian life at the end of World War II as he struggles to maintain his principles and accept that others do not always agree with him. The screenplay impresses to begin with but the narrative, once set back in England after the war, becomes static with little character development. The script suggests we should not forget the spirit of co-operation engendered during the war, yet the ending shows a man still at odds with the world. There are some amusing scenes and certain parallels with *Thunder Rock* when James's mission for peace is shown to be unrealistic and his idealism unsuited to the world around him. The more he interferes and tries to help, the worse things get and, in the last section of the story, when he speaks at a meeting to proclaim the need for co-operation, chaos ensues:

>   JAMES
>   Listen! If the people of one little town can make up their minds to
>   sink their petty differences, to help one another and work
>   together as a community if they really put their backs into it …

He suddenly sees Mary (his wife) and nearly dries.

>   We might be able to show that goodwill is not to be confined to
>   one day in three hundred and sixty five – it is not just something
>   you give the kids pennies not to sing about. If we could do that –
>   there's no limit. It could spread to other towns, other countries
>   even. It might involve some adjustments; but so would the atom
>   bomb! There's got to be a beginning somewhere and I'd like it to
>   begin right here. (JED/3)

James's speech triggers off a mini-riot; his good intentions are ignored; and he is accused of being a Communist, after which a fight breaks out.

Despite a few entertaining moments, the characters remain underdeveloped; the muddled narrative lacks a clear focus; while the ending is unsatisfying, suggesting the script needed more work.

Don't Take It to Heart

Don't Take It to Heart is a comedy that again has an underlying message of social change. Made towards the end of World War II, the film anticipates the class changes in society that occur after the war. Andrew Spicer describes the film as a 'mildly socialist satire thrown into confusion by the war' (2006: 46). Dell wrote and directed the original story for Sydney Box at Two Cities Films. The screenplay is theatrical in style but often entertaining, poking fun at the nouveau riche, playing with class reversal and incorporating some light discussion of left-wing politics. Poverty-stricken Lord Chaunduyt lives in a grand house that is falling apart, which he has to open to visitors to make ends meet. The plot shows what happens when a ghost, locked in the walls of the manor house for hundreds of years, is unexpectedly released and reveals that the true Lord of the Manor is actually the local poacher, Henry.

The screenplay begins by setting up the scene for conflict while introducing an element of humour when the stately home is thrown into the twentieth century. A witty change of mood occurs, moving from serenity to a bomb falling onto the ancient hall, the event that frees the ghost:

>   Untouched by passing centuries, the historic home of the Earls of Chaunduyt stands
>   in the moonlight a symbol of peace and security.
>
>   Title FADES OUT. MUSIC ENDS. There is the SCREAM OF A BOMB FALLING.
>   We see the explosion. (JED/2: 1)

When the ghost explains that the wrong Lord of the Manor is in place, he appears in court to give evidence, generating some lighthearted scenes:

CONSTABLE (to the ghost)
Now then Court's sitting.

GHOST
But I want to give evidence.

CONSTABLE
Well you'd better come on then.

(Ghost enters – sound of screams) (ibid.: 10)

The script makes a clear divide between 'old money', represented by Lord Chaunduyt and 'new money', represented by the wealthy but heartless Pike, who is presented as a spoiler of fun, opposed to 'the old traditions'. When Henry, one of Lord Chaunduyt's tenants, is accused of poaching, he takes the crime none too seriously while Pike is determined to prosecute:

PIKE
Property must be protected, m'Lord, we landowners must stick
together. If we don't the whole country will go to pot.

LORD CHAUNDUYT
I must say I sometimes rather envy Henry. It must be fun to do a
little poaching. Don't you think?

PIKE
No, I don't. I'm a law-abiding man.

LORD C
Ah, yes. The Law. (ibid.: 16)

The scene continues as Pike refuses to be sidetracked from his mission:

PIKE
Do I take it then that you refuse to prosecute?

LORD C
Well, I've known Harry for a very long time. And I like to think of
his children having a rabbit.

PIKE
But I keep saying it wasn't a rabbit, it was a hare.

LORD C
Well that can be very nice too with a little redcurrant jelly.

> PIKE
>
> Well I tell you that they won't get away with it. If they want a fight
> they can have it and before I've done with him Harry Bucket will
> wish … (ibid.: 17)

Socialist themes are brought into the story and dressed up as comedy, with Mary, Lord Chaunduyt's daughter, acting as the voice for this point of view. There is some playful political debate as Mary argues with Aunt Harriet about preparations for a ball for the tenants, professing herself a socialist who does not agree with patronising the tenants:

> HARRIET
>
> I hope you realise you have to help me with the arrangements for
> the ball.
>
> MARY
>
> Yes, so long as it's understood that I don't approve. You know
> my views on that sort of thing.
>
> HARRIET
>
> I've heard them but I don't understand them.
>
> MARY
>
> Well it's just that it's obsolete. Its sole purpose is to reduce the
> tenants to a proper state of humility.
>
> HARRIET
>
> I've never heard anything so preposterous. You talk like … er …
> a socialist.
>
> MARY
>
> I am a socialist Auntie.
>
> HARRIET
>
> That sort of thing comes from not having a mother. (ibid.: 23)

Aunt Harriet's character represents the snobbish and entrenched version of the aristocracy. She criticises Mary's intentions to marry her fiancé, George Bucket, the son of the poacher, because he is not gentry, to which Mary retorts:

> MARY
>
> … . Just because hundreds of years ago somebody knocked
> somebody else off a horse, George Bucket's not good enough
> to speak to us … . But he's good enough to fight for us. And
> when he comes back if he still wants me to I intend to marry
> him. (ibid.: 25)

The narrative may project socialist ideas but order is finally restored when Mary discovers that George Bucket, whom she has not seen since he joined the army, is no longer interested in her while the man she eventually falls for, Peter, will become a baronet when his father dies.

The screenplay inverts society's values in the Bakhtinian sense;[3] the rulers are taken over by the ruled and the fun-loving lawbreakers win the day over the pious puritans. The aristocracy is sympathetically portrayed throughout while Pike is the wrecker of 'carnival', who tries to destroy the happy and balanced coexistence of aristocracy and villagers. As revenge against the villagers, Pike intends to dig up the cricket pitch and takes the poacher Harry to court. If found guilty, Harry would lose his home and be unable to support his large family. Pike upsets the locals and loses the case, vindictively attempting to oust Harry from his land:

> PORTER
>
> Why Pike. He's gone and bought the land where Harry's got his
> brickfield and 'e give old Harry notice to quit. Reckon it'll about
> finish 'im. (ibid.: 39)

Pike serves as a device to emphasise the denial of pleasure and kindness in a community, having no consideration for the poacher who has to feed seven children. When Peter organises for a lorry full of farm animals to be delivered to Pike's house as revenge for Harry, the furious Pike takes the men involved to court. But Peter offers to represent them, arguing that the land is common land so the villagers have the right to graze their animals. In court the legal process is ridiculed when Pike's lawyer quotes from past legal cases and Peter retaliates by going back even further in time and creating false cases as evidence.

> MAID
>
> Why do they keep going back?
>
> BUCKET
>
> That's the law. It's a question of which can go back furthest.
> (ibid.: 54)

When Harriet asks a policeman how far they have got with the case, he replies: 'When I came out ma'am they'd just got back to Ethelred the Unready' (ibid.: 57).

The screenplay features many witty and mildly satirical jibes at different aspects of society, the court system included. When the court case is decided in Peter's favour, Pike complains: 'It's a scandal, there's one law for the rich, and another for the – aristocracy' (ibid.: 57).

Peter reveals the real Lord's identity in court, but when further evidence is needed, the ghost is called to the stand, causing a sensation when he enters the witness box and testifies:

> GHOST
>
> I swear by Almighty God … that the evidence I shall give shall
> be the truth … the whole truth and nothing but the truth.
> Arthur Bewketty – that's the proper way to pronounce it …
> late of Chaunduyt Court … commonly known as the 'Terror of
> Chaunduyt'. (ibid.: 66)

Once Harry is instated as the rightful Lord of Chaunduyt, the theme of accepting social change becomes much more focused. Bucket the butler laments the fact that his relative Harry Bucket will be the new Lord and his view of the new world is negative:

> BUCKET
>
> That's it, another world. My world ended this morning, there in court. Harry Bucket an Earl! What sort of a world is that? And all the old estates being sold up to pay death duties. When I think of the old days. (ibid.: 71)

A maudlin Bucket describes what he'll have inscribed on his gravestone, a memorial to an earlier age:

> Here lies Alfred Bucket, butler and valet for five and fif …
> No, I've got it. 'To the memory of Alfred Bucket the last of the Gentlemen's gentlemen.' (ibid.)

Lord Chaunduyt tries to soften the blow by telling the butler:

> LORD C
>
> Don't take it to heart, when this war is over, I don't suppose it'll matter very much, how our names are pronounced. Personally I think it's just as well. (ibid.: 72)

Lord Chaunduyt is phlegmatic about the changes, as is his daughter Mary. The reader is reminded about the effects of the war and how it will alter British society though, ironically, Bucket is less able to accept the upheaval:

> LORD C
> Does this mean you're leaving me Bucket?
>
> BUCKET
> No m'lord, I'm too old to make a change. I shall remain in your service.
>
> LORD C
> Even in a cottage?
>
> BUCKET
> At least m'lord it would be warmer, but it's all very regrettable. (ibid.)

Harriet, Lord Chaunduyt's sister, is also finding adapting to the new order problematic; she keeps fainting and becomes confused:

HARRIET

I'm perfectly alright – or am I? Charles, tell me at once – who
am, what am I?

LORD C

Well my dear Harriet, for the moment you're one of the
Bouquets, but it rather looks that very shortly you'll be just an old
bucket. (ibid.)

The screenplay ends with an amusing reversal of the beginning in which the new Lord
shows visitors around the stately home while collecting money for the 'Chaunduyt Benevolent
Fund', as Lord C watches:

HARRY

How am I doing m'Lord?

LORD C

Very well indeed m'lord. But just between ourselves it was
Worcester not Waterloo, And it was oak, not a beech.

HARRY

Oh, they don't know the difference m'lord.

LORD C

Oh, you mustn't call me m'lord, m'lord (ibid.: 73)

The often witty screenplay suggests there will be an embracing of post-war social change
with not too many regrets. Dell creates an enjoyably rounded ending in which the old world has
been turned upside down and Harry the poacher becomes Lord of the Manor, while the ex-Lord
is happily resigned to his new role in life and Mary, the socialist, is to be married to a future
baronet.

A French Mistress

This comedy farce was co-written by Dell with Roy Boulting, adapted from the play by Sonnie
Hale. Receiving only lukewarm reviews, *Monthly Film Bulletin* notes that the story is full of
clichéd characters and presents a view of a Britain which no longer exists:

A mildly amusing, quintessentially English farce, with stock material and jokes. But its stage origins
give the plot some shape and its characters some consistency … . Given more wit or a wilder series
of complications, given above all some relation to contemporary English life … so the reservations
creep in. It is time surely that we pensioned off even in farce, these phoney English public schools,
fire-eating colonels, bird watching vicars … and all the other dearly loved images of 'the English as
they see themselves'. (Anon 1960: 142)

Paternal and filial confusion in *A French Mistress* (1960), written by Jeffrey Dell and Roy Boulting

Indeed, the characters and story appear just as clichéd fifty years on, though more positively, critic Paul Wells describes the film as 'an overlooked satire' arguing, 'Essentially the Boultings chart the shift from quasi-Victorian values to the new sexual openness, focusing along the way upon the guilt and confusion attendant in the transition' (2000: 62). But, as the earlier review notes, the film is more farce than satire, and in reality a hackneyed story capitalising on early 1960s interest in sex comedies, tagging on an updated ending to this adaptation of a play written in the mid-1950s. Alan Burton wryly notes that Dell and Boulting seem 'dogged in their determination to succeed with this style of humour' (2012: 80)

The final draft screenplay features some amusing moments, the dialogue flows naturally and it is a light and easy read. The plot though is forced and highly implausible, revolving around the problems arising when an attractive French mistress, Madeleine, enters a nearly all male environment, the boys' school. It is her sexual attractiveness that causes this disorder, a new order only being reinstated at the end of the script by her acceptance into the masculine world. Much of the screenplay describes the French mistress in a voyeuristic way and the *Carry On*-cum-*Doctor in the House*-style of writing reveals a confusion and awkwardness about male/female relations.

The first eighteen pages of the screenplay concentrate on an overlong building-up of suspense to the entrance of the French mistress, involving much curiosity from boys and staff as to what she will be like. Her arrival is heralded by the boys singing the 'Marseillaise' as Edmonds, the head boy, enters:

HEAD
Yes, Edmonds?

EDMONDS (away in a starry dream)
Oh, yes sir!

As he answers, MADELEINE LAFARGE enters. She is young, very attractive and her clothes, though quiet, have an air of French chic. The Head and Martin both gape at her in astonishment.

MADELEINE
Good afternoon, m'sieur !

HEAD
Good … heavens! … Let me see, you're … er …

MADELEINE
Madeleine Lafarge, monsieur.

HEAD
Really?

Looks at Martin, shocked.

MADELEINE
You were not expecting me?

HEAD
Certainly not! … I mean, but of course we were! Er … please …
Come in!

MADELEINE
Thank you. (JED/9: 19)

The entry of Madeleine causes consternation and the head boy becomes flustered and unable to concentrate because of the effect she has on him:

EDMONDS
Edmonds, you'd better go.

Edmonds is still in a daze, and keeping his eyes on Madeleine.

EDMONDS
Yes, sir … whatever you say, sir.

He does not move.

HEAD
Well, that's what I <u>did</u> say !

EDMONDS
I beg your pardon, sir.

HEAD
It's over there!

EDMONDS
What, sir?

HEAD
The door, Edmonds!

EDMONDS
Oh … yes, sir.

He goes to the door and stops for a last look at MADELEINE.

HEAD (thundering)
Go! (ibid.: 20)

The description of Madeleine is particularly voyeuristic, emphasising her sexuality, as the boys look on:

A reverse angle shows Madeleine in vigorous and graceful action, dressed in the briefest tennis shorts. Her drive carries beyond the baseline. The crowd cheers and applauds. Colin, surprised, looks at the boys level with the line.

COLIN
Wasn't that out?

BOYS
Oh no, sir. Well in, sir!

COLIN
Oh. (ibid.: 37)

The voyeuristic description continues almost to the halfway point and, while it emphasises the effect Madeleine has on the boys, each incident enhances the visual comedy: the more the boys obsessively watch her, the greater the chaos:

EXT. DRIVE. DAY

Close on Madeleine's legs pedalling. Camera pulls back to show her and Colin on
bicycles. A great many boys also on bikes pass them going in the opposite direction.
Madeleine's skirt suddenly blows up in the wind, and as the couple pass camera the
boys' eyes all come round following Madeleine, resulting in a chain reaction of
collisions and spills. (ibid.: 38)

The boys spy on Madeleine in the swimming pool and from the classroom; one boy with binoculars
gives a blow-by-blow account of the couple's movements, with a great deal of innuendo, until
he is interrupted by a member of staff in a witty reveal:

MILSOM
Well, <u>she's</u> still stretched out … I must say she looks in beautiful
shape lying there, by the pool, with a shaft of sunlight playing on
her … her …

BOY
Shoulder?

MILSOM
Her shoulder – thank you. Hullo, What's happening now? He's
getting up. Yes! He's getting up. Now he's bending down – (with
mounting excitement) and I think they're going to … . Yes, they
are! She's getting up! Oh, this is terrific – I wish you could be
here!

PEAKE'S VOICE (offside – acid)
I am here! (ibid.: 40)

Although the screenplay is initially repetitive, with too much space devoted to introducing
Madeleine, the story then evolves into an often entertaining read. Plot complications add dramatic interest when it is revealed that the headmaster thinks he may be the father of the French
mistress, having had an affair with her mother in France twenty-five years before. This problem
is compounded by the fact that his son, Colin, has fallen in love with Madeleine, provoking
numerous misunderstandings. This revelation takes place about halfway through the script,
although the prelude to what we eventually find out is the wrong conclusion is somewhat prolonged, taking more than ten pages. In this extract the head reveals his worries to another teacher:

HEAD
Don't you <u>see</u>? She's twenty-six!

They look at each other.

MARTIN
Now wait a minute ! You can't jump to conclusions like that. Just
because she's twenty-six …

>   HEAD
> I've got to know, Bob! I've got to be sure!

>   MARTIN
> All right! Quite simple! Ask her about her father.

>   HEAD
> Bob, I don't think I could! I've got a horrible feeling in my bones …

>   MARTIN
> Now, don't start panicking … All right! Leave it to me! A few well-chosen questions, put with my customary tact, and we'll soon set your mind at rest. In any case, you've nothing to worry about. She couldn't possibly be a relative of yours.

>   HEAD
> Really? Why not?

>   MARTIN
> My dear fellow, she's much too good-looking! (ibid.: 61)

The scene is carefully crafted to finish on an amusing punchline.

Once the major plot point has been introduced, further consequences, complications and misunderstandings ensue. The head has to tell his son, Colin, that the woman he is in love with is actually his half-sister:

>   COLIN
> Madeleine and I love each other. We're going to get married.

Head wheels round.

>   HEAD (loudly)
> But that's just it! You can't!

>   COLIN
> Why ever not?

>   HEAD
> Because it's … positively … illegal!

>   COLIN (incredulous)
> Illegal? (he laughs) Are you feeling alright?

>   HEAD
> No! … I mean, yes! I'm just telling you … (ibid.: 82)

The revelations may be drawn out, but Dell extracts as much tension, drama and humour from the situation as possible:

>   COLIN
> All right, so you were half-way up a mountain with Madeleine's
> mother.

>   HEAD
> Please stop prompting me! … A mist came down ! … We were
> stranded! (ibid.: 83)

The complications escalate and the head is accused of having designs on Madeleine himself and being a sex maniac.

The last act is triggered by Peake, the deputy head, informing the school governors of the chaos Madeleine is causing. An emergency meeting is called at which the head decides Madeleine will have to go, but without explaining why. Some entertaining dialogue surrounds this confusion, with Madeleine asking why she has to leave:

>   COLIN
> No, no! You've got it all wrong! He means like a daughter.

>   MADELEINE
> Oh, yes! I have heard that excuse from nasty old men before!

>   COLIN
> Listen! I promise you, he only loves you as a father, and it's
> because he loves you as a father that I must love you as a brother!

>   MADELEINE
> Oh, mon dieu! What is this madness? Because he loves me as a
> father you must love me as a brother! I suppose if he loves me
> as an Arab you must love me as a camel?

>   COLIN
> I can't explain …

>   MADELEINE
> Nobody can! It is impossible to understand you English! (ibid.: 90)

Male reaction to Madeleine's beauty is used again to add dramatic contrast when the chairman of the board of governors first meets her; he disguises his surprise with some dexterity as he had assumed her to be a brazen temptress:

HEAD
I will willingly resign <u>now</u>?

COLONEL
Well, you can't. Not till after our meeting. But first I'm going to
deal with this Madame Pompadour. I'm going to make sure she
stops pestering my boy …

The door opens and Madeleine comes in.

MARTIN
Colonel … this is Mademoiselle Lafarge!

As the colonel turns –

COLONEL
Ah! … Now you just listen to … (he stops and goggles at her)
Ah … my dear !

MADELEINE
You wanted me?

COLONEL
Why … er … yes. I … er … just wanted to say, I … er … do
hope my boy hasn't been pestering you? (ibid.: 110)

Now won over, the colonel overrides the other governors' concerns, suddenly becoming a supporter of equal rights for women:

A GOVERNOR
Well, Colonel … I – er … a … er – woman …

COLONEL
Exactly! They've got 'em in Parliament! Got 'em in medicine!
Got 'em in the law courts! Why not here? No use being stick in
the mud! Got to keep up with the times! She's lively, intelligent,
and healthy. Be a great asset. I think Crane's to be
congratulated. (ibid.: 117)

The colonel, rather conveniently, undergoes a complete change of opinion, recommending that
Madeleine stay. The final revelation resolves all the complications, the fact that Madeleine lied
about her age and is only twenty-four, meaning that she cannot be the head's daughter.

The screenplay is entertaining, despite the story being incredible. This is partly because the
complications are set up well and the reader wants to see how the characters will get out of the
situations they find themselves in. The narrative, though, 'wants to have its cake and to eat it',

the voyeuristic description and focus on the attractiveness of Madeleine drive the story while the narrative concludes that women should be accepted in a male world. Yet the problem really is the acceptance of sexually attractive women in this male world, as the cook and matron are already quite at home here.

Dell's writing was perhaps at its most fluent in the thriller and detective genre, one in which he had considerable experience, from the effective play *Payment Deferred* through the engaging *The Saint's Vacation* to *The Treasure of San Teresa*, a light thriller adapted from his own play. Set in Germany, it involves the disappearance of stolen diamonds after World War II and tells how the hero, Brennan, an American adventurer becomes implicated in their theft. The lively, plot-led story is told mostly in flashback after Brennan has been arrested for the theft. There are many involving twists and turns, some not very convincing, and the characters are stock types, boasting little depth or complexity. The major conceit, revealed late in the story, is that the German police who have followed and questioned Brennan are really criminals in disguise. The plot though becomes confused as the story moves towards a conclusion and the characters' motivations are not clear: Zena, the woman Brennan has helped, appears to double-cross him with no reason in a rather out-of-character development.

The Dark Man

The Dark Man, written and directed by Dell for Independent Artists, is a much more effective and suspenseful thriller. The shooting script is, at times, a riveting read. It tells the story of Molly, an actress, who is witness to a murder, and the murderer's subsequent quest to kill her. Unusually, we often see events from the murderer's perspective, which partly aligns us to him, yet we also feel concern that Detective Viner catch 'The Dark Man' before he gets to Molly. This well-written story contains some vivid description as well as moments of great tension. Although rather two-dimensional, with little in the way of a dramatic arc, the characters are interesting enough to generate in us some anxiety about the outcome. The obstacles in the narrative are well constructed and, although the plot conveniences are large, there is plenty of dramatic interest.

The story begins with the Dark Man stealing money from a safe and shooting the safe's owner, before making his escape by taxi. The reader starts to worry for the safety of the taxi driver who can now identify the Dark Man. Note how in the following extracts the shooting script gives shot details whereas earlier draft scripts would not usually do so.

EXT. POYNINGS LOCATION. DAY

B.C.S. of mirror cutting in DRIVER'S head. In mirror he can see Dark Man's hand. It is bringing a gun from his pocket.

CUT TO EXT. POYNINGS LOCATION. DAY

C.S. DRIVER, astounded at what he has seen, wrinkles up his forehead, puzzling it out. He stares along the road ahead and is very conscious of that gun behind him. He stares at road ahead but gives quick glances at the mirror.

DARK MAN
Pull up by those trees.

The gun suddenly assumes a personal significance. DRIVER is terrified. He has
difficulty in speaking.

                                     DRIVER
                          Pull up ? … What … what for ?

                                    DARK MAN
                                  I'm getting out.

Driver moistens his lips and swallows. He glances fearfully out of corner of his eye to
see what the Dark Man is doing. Then looks ahead. (JED/4: 7)

The scene description is economical but powerful, putting the reader in the position of the
driver as we see and hear events from his point of view. The driver glimpses the gun, but the
sense of fear is not fully developed until the Dark Man asks the driver to pull over, at which
point he realises his life is in peril.

By chance, Molly sees the Dark Man's car in the distance while riding her bike. The
description cleverly uses sound to build up a three-dimensional and more filmic image of the
scene:

EXT. POYNINGS LOCATION. DAY

A little further up the road a girl comes into sight on a bicycle. On the bar is a
shopping basket. She is free-wheeling down a gentle slope.

CUT TO EXT. POYNINGS LOCATION. DAY

A nearer view of the girl. It is very peaceful, the only sounds being the click of the
bearings and the grating of the tyres on the road. The peace is suddenly shattered by
the sound of a shot. The girl's head whips up and she looks toward the wood. There
is a second shot. She stops, resting a foot on the bank. Then she looks at something
above the tree tops.

CUT TO EXT. POYNINGS LOCATION. DAY

Her view of a colony of rooks flying above the trees with their usual babel of protest.
(ibid.: 8)

While the screenplay may not always be a riveting 'page turner', it does feature moments of
great intensity. Dell generates dramatic interest and tension by applying the conventions of the
thriller to the story and asking questions at different stages of the script, the central one being
'Will the Dark Man get to Molly?'[4]

Dell's characters are often quite bland but likeable. Even the Dark Man is presented in a neutral
way, rather than as evil. Molly's character has little complexity, mainly acting as a vehicle for the
Dark Man to pursue, though her character arc does become important later in the story.

Our introduction to the heroine is a diverting and lively one, as she talks with her dresser, Carol, in the theatre, the latter disclosing that the police are looking for her:

> CAROL
>
> Molly! Listen! The police are anxious to interview a young woman who was cycling yesterday morning on the Waltham Bay Anstead road and who may have passed the car near Beacon Wood. The young woman made a purchase of fruit and honey at Lower Anstead Farm and is believed to have come from Waltham Bay. That's you!

Carol swings around on her stool. They stare at each other.

> MOLLY
>
> Yes, but … I couldn't tell them anything. I didn't …

She stops, appalled.

> Yes, I did. There was a car. and a man. He came out of the trees.

> CAROL
>
> The murderer! Fancy actually seeing him. It's terrific! You must tell the police at once … and the press!

Carol is round-eyed with excitement.

> MOLLY
>
> Don't be ridiculous. How can I? I'm on in a few minutes …

> CAROL
>
> Sheila will have to play for you … . Did he have blood on him?

Molly is distracted.

> MOLLY
>
> I don't know. It was miles away. I hardly saw him. (without conviction) It may not have been the man at all.

> CAROL
>
> Of course it was. It's the most marvellous publicity. If only he'd threatened you! Or dragged you into the woods …

> MOLLY
>
> Don't be horrible.

CAROL (reflectively)
It must have only been just after he shot the taxi-man.

MOLLY
Shot?

CAROL
Yes. He shot him twice. In the back … What's the matter?

Molly has sat down abruptly, staring in front of her. (ibid.: 11–12)

The wide-eyed Carol, enjoying the gruesome murder details, makes a nice contrast to the worried Molly. The scene is entertaining while revealing a major plot point – Molly was too far away to see anything. We also find out more about Molly's character, partly by the contrast with Carol: Molly is not a gossip, she is shocked at the revelation, doesn't like violence and reacts thoughtfully, whereas her friend is excited by the dramatic news.

The dashing Detective Viner is assigned to protect Molly from the Dark Man. His role in the story is emphasised by the Assistant Commissioner, establishing the potential for romance, who tells him: 'We must avoid a third tragedy. She's your responsibility, you understand. Don't leave it to the local force. Look after her yourself …' (ibid.: 14).

The script details many elegant links from scene to scene. For instance, when Molly and Viner are eating in a restaurant, he tells her she will need protection to ensure her safety. The danger she is in is emphasised by a cut to a sinister shot of the Dark Man, who has been watching them, and who will be even more difficult to recognise because he has changed his disguise.

MOLLY
But … it just isn't practical. I mean, there won't always be
someone to see me home.

VINER
There will, only you won't always know it.

He takes his hat.

MOLLY
Oh! And when does this begin?

She gives a nervous smile. He takes her arm.

VINER
It's begun.

CUT TO: EXT. RESTAURANT. NIGHT

> M.C.S. From the shadows on the opposite side of the road the Dark Man watches
> them until they turn the corner. He is now clean shaven. It changes his appearance
> completely. (ibid.: 22–3)

The developing romance between Viner and Molly helps to increase the tension, as Viner has
started to care more about what happens to her.

The Dark Man follows Molly and breaks into her flat. The screenplay imbues this scene with
palpable tension but, interestingly, the focus is as much on the Dark Man as Molly, engendering
an unusual degree of intimacy, if not sympathy, with the character. Events are described from
the Dark Man's point of view and we are privy to his reactions as he waits for Molly to arrive.
Suspense is built up in a Hitchcockian manner, with time drawn out from the antagonist's point
of view, as the audience is made to wait in 'real time' to see what happens.[5] On entering her flat,
Molly finds the lights don't work:

> Puzzled she (Molly) crosses to the standard and presses the stud-switch. Again no
> result. At this moment the door of the opposite flat opens and the YOUNG MAN who
> went down for the bottle looks across the landing and calls back over his shoulder –
>
> > YOUNG MAN
> > Her door's open.
>
> Carol comes past him and crosses the landing. The young man follows. Seeing the
> room is dark Carol says –
>
> > CAROL
> > Is that you Molly?
>
> > MOLLY
> > Oh, hullo … the lights seem to have fused. (ibid.: 50)

One of the young men at the party, in the opposite flat, offers to help but Molly demurs, saying
she wants an early night. The scene thus cleverly stokes the reader's anxiety, as we witness Molly's
chances of rescue diminishing, and she is alone with the Dark Man in the flat. When the Dark Man
strangles her, Dell introduces a mirror image to increase the reader's alignment with his reaction:

> The movement of her hands becomes feeble. Her eyes turn up. Her hands drop, she
> slips down. There is a soft thud. In the mirror the Dark Man can be seen standing
> quite still, looking down. He is breathing rather fast. He suddenly springs into action.
> (ibid.: 51)

We become complicit in the murder as the Dark Man checks that all traces of his identity are
erased from the scene. Tension accrues when he realises he has lost a button from his coat, evidence that he can't risk leaving behind:

> He is sweating. Something on the carpet catches his eye. He peers closer. He lifts
> the candle near his face. Candle-grease drips from his glove on to the carpet.
> He rubs the spot with his other hand. He stares at it wildly, rubs again. Caution is
> going. Assurance has already gone. We can see what he is feeling – urgency, fear,
> exasperation. The carefully worked-out plan is going to pieces, all because of a
> button. There is a distant crash and some shouting and laughter. He stands up and
> replaces the candle on the mantelpiece. As he does so there is a faint metallic sound.
> He looks down. The button, which he has kicked against the fender, rolls a little way,
> then drops. He exhales sharply, snatches it up and jabs it in his pocket. He blows out
> the candle and walks swiftly to the door. As he reaches it the phone rings. (ibid.: 52)

The relief on finding the button is dissipated by the phone ringing, raising a new question – will Molly's friends wonder why she doesn't pick up? The Dark Man lifts the receiver and places it down before leaving the room, co-opting the reader as an accomplice, involved as we have become with his actions and reactions.

Molly, however, survives the strangulation. The Dark Man's presence becomes much more malevolent as he watches his prey sunbathing on a beach, Molly growing more and more agitated as the beach empties and:

> The last of the family party are disappearing over the crest and the beach is deserted.
> The only sounds are the sea-birds and the approaching footsteps. She is really
> frightened. Her breathing is rapid. Her hands clutch the book tightly but she is not
> looking at it. The footsteps come nearer, slow and deliberate. Suddenly she can
> stand it no longer. She jumps to her feet, grabs towel and bag, leaving her writing
> case still on the ground. (ibid.: 38)

In the plot the Dark Man makes three attempts on Molly's life and the reader is caught up in the relentless nature of his pursuit. His final attempt eventually fails but the confrontation between the two is direct and dramatic when he poses as a police constable taking Molly to see Inspector Viner. Once in the car she realises this is a ploy and sees her chance to escape when a lorry blocks the road:

> INT. CAR. DAY
>
> Molly tries to open the door. It won't open. The car has backed and starts forward
> with a jerk throwing her back. She gets up, leans over and presses horn on steering
> column. The Dark Man knocks her hand away violently.
>
> CUT TO EXT. CAMBER. DAY.
>
> The lorry driver comes round his lorry to see what is happening.
>
> CUT TO INT. CAR. DAY
>
> Dark Man leans out of the window to see how far he's got and Molly leans over and
> pulls steering wheel with all her might.

CUT TO EXT. CAMBER. DAY

Rear wheel of camber goes into ditch.

CUT TO INT. CAR. DAY

Dark Man swings round and throws Molly back. He puts car into gear, roars engine.

CUT TO EXT. CAMBER. DAY

Back wheel spins, sliding further into the rushes.

CUT TO INT. CAR. DAY

Dark Man's mouth tightens as he realises he's stuck.

CUT TO EXT. CAMBER. DAY

From twenty yards away the lorry driver is astonished to see a police officer there. He
is still more amazed when a girl screams from inside of the car. (ibid.: 85)

Now fighting on equal terms, the girl and her pursuer confront each other; no longer an object
of the Dark Man's predatory voyeurism, Molly has taken control of the situation, transforming
herself from a passive to an active protagonist. Her character arc concludes with her as victor
rather than victim.

With Molly free, Inspector Viner is shown pursuing the Dark Man in an overlong final
sequence extending to almost twenty pages. The dramatic question changes from 'Will the Dark
Man catch Molly?' to 'Will Viner catch the Dark Man?'. Even though the final chase is well
written and dynamic, the question of whether the Dark Man will kill Molly remains more interesting. The story so far has focused on the Dark Man getting to Molly, rendering the denouement between the Dark Man and Inspector Viner rather anticlimactic because we do not feel the
same investment in Viner as we do in Molly.

CONCLUSION

Jeffrey Dell was an extremely able and consistent writer whose forte was light satirical comedy,
alongside entertaining thrillers. His stories may have been predicable and plot-bound, with often
two-dimensional and underdeveloped characters, yet the screenplays displayed fluent dialogue
and effective description. Commanding respect in his profession, Dell improved many screenplays, some credited, and some not. The Boulting brothers were particularly appreciative of his
rewriting skills, as seen in a letter about his work on the screenplay *Lucky Jim*, for which he
added scenes and dialogue:

Here is the balance of the money due to you for your most invaluable and highly appreciated services
on 'Lucky Jim'. Without you to laugh with we should have gone round the bend. Without your wit
and talent we should not have a good script now. We are very, very grateful … . (JED/27)

A fitting compliment for a writer whose ability to entertain with words is evident and who had worked with some of the most influential film producers in Britain.

As a screenwriter, Jeffrey Dell's skills may not seem exceptional when compared to those of Emeric Pressburger, discussed in the next chapter, but then, their working relationships could not have been more different. Pressburger found a creative partner in Michael Powell, who was able to bring his stories to life. They formed their own production company, The Archers, sharing equal film credits, as producer, writer and director. Pressburger could be considered an artist whereas Dell was a talented writer and fixer of screenplays, an entertainer rather than an artist.

NOTES

1. The film starred Charles Laughton and was based on a C. S. Forester novel which Dell had adapted for the theatre.
2. See http://www.screenonline.org.uk/film/id/444355/index.html.
3. See Bakhtin (1984) and Brottman (2005) for a discussion of carnival and the temporary reversal of hierarchies and restoration of order.
4. For further reading on the conventions of the thriller genre, see *Writing the Thriller Film: The Terror Within* by Neill D. Hicks (2002).
5. See *Marnie* (1964) when Tippi Hedren is waiting in the toilets for the office to empty.

02

EMERIC PRESSBURGER

ARTIST, WRITER, COLLABORATOR

> Today I saw your picture which in this country is called *The INVADERS*. What a picture! I am proud of you ... this is one of the finest pieces of writing I have ever seen ... this is the first picture of this kind which faces the issue and does not try to ridicule the enemy.[1]

The film credits, 'Written, directed and produced by Michael Powell and Emeric Pressburger', suggest an equal partnership in the film production process but Pressburger's contribution as screenwriter has been overshadowed by Powell's reputation as director. Ian Christie argues that Pressburger is possibly the greatest screenwriter in British cinema and his contribution has gone largely unrecognised: 'For even now, when The Archers' films have been widely rediscovered and reassessed, Pressburger's individual reputation remains shrouded in obscurity' (1984: 318). Indeed, Pressburger's abilities as a screenwriter were internationally acknowledged at the time, the head of the script department at Paramount Studios choosing *I Know Where I'm Going* (1945) as an example of a perfectly written screenplay (Macdonald 1994: 249).

The collaboration between Powell and Pressburger represented an innovative and creative partnership spanning more than three decades, but Pressburger was already an experienced screenwriter when the two first met. Over the duration of his career, more than seventy screenplays were filmed, a substantial number when compared to Robert Bolt, for instance, who had only seven screenplays produced. Pressburger's first film, *Abschied/Farewell* (1930), was made in Germany in 1930 and his last, *The Boy Who Turned Yellow*, in 1972, marked his final collaboration with Powell. He was nominated for three Academy Awards for Best Original Screenplay: *49th Parallel* (1941), *One of Our Aircraft Is Missing* (1942) and *The Red Shoes* (1948), winning the Academy Award for *49th Parallel*.

Pressburger was born in Hungary in 1902, attending a Jewish lycee where he excelled, before studying in Prague and eventually moving to Germany, where he managed to survive for some time on very little money. He decided to try writing after reading a friend's work and thinking he could do better. He was talented enough to have a number of short stories published, explaining that 'I became one of those very few young writers who could live on their earnings. I wrote short stories but my heart was lost to films' (EPR 2/9/3). He regularly submitted scripts to the German film studio Ufa, famous for the films it produced between the two World Wars, but received many rejections. The head of the scenario department at Ufa eventually commissioned him to adapt a novel into a screenplay, for which he was paid 220 marks. Pressburger's work was impressive enough to secure him a job initially in the scenario department and then in Dramaturgy, liaising between the literary and production end of film-making.

Here he learnt about film structure and the technical side of film writing. Between 1930 and 1933, Pressburger penned more than fourteen screenplays at Ufa, collaborating with very experienced writers and directors such as Max Ophuls and Robert Siodmak.

Pressburger left Ufa in May 1933, when the Nazi Party forced all Jews out of employment. He was reluctant to leave Germany and remained there as long as possible, before eventually deciding it was no longer safe and fleeing to Paris. While there, Pressburger gained some writing work, with two of his films enjoying a positive reception, the comedy *Incognito* (1934) and *La Vie Parisienne* (1936), a romantic comedy directed by Siodmak. But he was not earning enough to live on so in July 1935 left for England in the hope of getting more work.[2]

Pressburger did some uncredited writing in the UK, including *The Great Barrier* (1937) for Gaumont British, but struggled to make a living. His fortunes improved after he made contact with a group of Jewish Hungarian émigrés escaping Nazi persecution, and he began writing for the producer Arnold Pressburger, who had made many films in Germany and Austria. Film composer Miklos Rosza put Pressburger in touch with producer and head of London Films, Alexander Korda, who took Pressburger on but it was two years before he achieved a screen-writing credit. The resulting film, *The Challenge* (1938), about the race to climb the Matterhorn, became his calling card.

Pressburger impressed Korda enough to be asked to improve the script for *The Spy in Black* and to create a more interesting part for the star, Conrad Veidt (Macdonald 1994: 149). *The Spy in Black* was released on 12 August 1939, not long after war was declared, garnering positive reviews and performing well at the box office. More crucially, this is when Pressburger first met Powell, who had been taken on to direct the film. The pair got on immediately and Powell's assessment of Pressburger's qualities makes it clear how pivotal this meeting was:

> a screenwriter who could really write. I was not going to let him go in a hurry. I had always dreamt of this phenomenon: a screenwriter with the heart and mind of a novelist, who would be interested in the medium of film, and who would have wonderful ideas, which I would turn into even more wonderful images, and who only used dialogue to make a joke or clarify the plot. (2000: 305)

Korda next asked Pressburger to look at a screenplay that had been in development since 1934 but which had been shelved: it was *The Red Shoes*, the original story and screenplay written by novelist G. B. Stern. Korda disliked the latest draft, suggesting to Pressburger that he dispose of it: 'The whole of this wad of material; the result of much hard work ... is a mess. ... The dialogue is awful. The characterisation is non-existent ... I should throw it away' (EPR 1/28/1). Pressburger was asked to supply a completely new story and undertook a vast amount of research, watching ballet rehearsals for many weeks. Korda liked the resulting script but the war halted production and he left England to work in Hollywood, agreeing to sell Powell and Pressburger the rights to the film in 1946. The resulting screenplay was radically different, with the art-versus-life theme elevated to a more central position, more in line with the interests of writer and director.[3]

49th Parallel was the first Powell and Pressburger film to attract the attention of an international audience when it won the Academy Award for Best Screenplay in 1942. The film, about a damaged German U-boat landing in Canada, and the survivors' attempt to reach the neutral US, was intended to act as an incentive to the US to join the war. Macdonald argues that, in this period, Pressburger became 'the single most important person in Britain's film propaganda war' (1994: 166). Pressburger believed that the US needed a reminder that the Nazis represented a

Emeric Pressburger with Michael Powell on location for *The Red Shoes* (1948)

danger to freedom and democracy worldwide. He realised that the Americans, being neutral, would not allow a propaganda film to be made in the US and came up with the idea of filming in Canada, geographically on the 49th Parallel. Anticipating that the Americans would understand that a Nazi invasion could take place as easily in the US as Canada, the Ministry of Information funded a £2,500 research trip for Pressburger.[4]

Pressburger was closely involved with the whole film, from the writing, to choosing the actors, to organising the finances. He wrote the first treatment on the boat back to England. It had four acts, which he thought could each feature a star in a cameo role (ibid.: 169). Letters between Pressburger and Powell reveal how the story was developed as well as Pressburger's willingness to take criticism. For instance, with some modesty, he agrees with Powell that a sequence does not work:

> I understand from your letters that you do not like very much any of the suggestions for the final
> sequence. I must say I entirely agree with you. So I have tried to find an entirely new way, keeping
> everything I thought worthwhile … . (EPR 1/19/6)

49th Parallel did extremely well in the UK and the US, where it was called *The Invaders*. Pressburger's mentor from Ufa, Reinhold Schunzel, wrote to him, declaring: 'This is one of the finest pieces of writing I have ever seen and it puts you in the front rank of story tellers and rightly so' (Macdonald 1994: 182). David Lean was the film editor and remembers that, when he first read the script, he could not put it down, deeming it 'fabulous', although pointing out that 'ultimately the film did not live up to the script' (ibid.: 180).

Macdonald argues that the film is an indication of Pressburger's future talents:

> As such it is perhaps the last of Emeric's films which could, conceivably, have been written by somebody else. But the film also contains signs of things to come … . Stylistically the film seems to be bursting at the seams. The narrative moves unapologetically from one style to another … . (ibid.: 194)

COLLABORATING WITH MICHAEL POWELL

Powell and Pressburger formed their own production company, The Archers, in 1942, sharing financial and creative responsibility. Their collaboration reached its creative peak between 1942 and 1950, when Pressburger wrote *One of Our Aircraft Is Missing*,[5] *The Life and Death of Colonel Blimp* (1943),[6] *A Canterbury Tale* (1944), *I Know Where I'm Going*, *A Matter of Life and Death* (1946), *The Red Shoes* and *Black Narcissus* (1950), all original screenplays, with the exception of *Black Narcissus*, an adaptation of the bestselling novel by Rumer Godden.

Because of their collaborative working relationship, it is not always easy to separate Powell and Pressburger's roles in the development process and they sometimes give slightly conflicting accounts. Powell agrees that Pressburger mostly conceived the story ideas and wrote the first draft, after which they would both develop the script further, as he explains:

> Emeric's working out in script form, from then we worked together and I would take over the direction, but every decision that was of any importance, including, of course the editing particularly … was all [sic] made by the two of us together. (ibid.: 189)

The film was then directed by Powell with Pressburger generally supervising the post-production stage, being especially interested in the editing which he saw as a continuation of his role as the screenwriter.

Powell did contribute to the screenplays at a later stage, making notes, rewriting sections and amending dialogue, while on occasion suggesting more substantial changes. Kevin Gough-Yates suggests that Powell was very dependent on Pressburger's creative input in the initial story development and writing:

> Without him, he never rose above the quota-quickie in which he started his directing career. Some of the major themes of their joint films, unless you ignore the tensions of the visual are more Pressburger than Powell. Of the films they made separately, Pressburger's are clearly his own, whereas those of Powell alone are frequently characterless. Powell, sometimes a brilliant visualiser, displays all his weaknesses without a strong script to discipline his waywardness. (1998: 61)

Powell acknowledges how much he learnt from Pressburger and clearly prized his abilities, recalling, 'Working with Emeric I learned a great deal. He was a born dramatist and writer, and he didn't learn as much from me as I did from him' (Lazar 2003: 70). Yet Powell brought his own perspective to the scripts, rewriting drafts, and emphasising the need for economy of expression. In an undated letter to Pressburger regarding a draft he was working on for *A Matter of Life and Death*, Powell reiterates this point:

I shall try and finish my draft by the time you join me. I have given some thoughts to the sets and particularly to economy in telling the story. I was going to discuss these ideas with you and so I wrote a long letter & notes and list to Alfred to guide him in his preliminary work ... and we have such a grand story and conception here that we can afford to tell it as economically as possible. (Macdonald 1994: 271)

Thelma Schoonmaker, whom Powell was married to until his death in 1990, points out that Pressburger often needed help with dialogue because his spoken English lacked fluency:

Michael Powell wrote much more than most people realize. Perhaps Emeric couldn't capture the flavour of English dialogue in the way Michael Powell could because he just hadn't been in the country long enough. It is clear that if Michael wasn't working with Emeric, another writer would be hired to help Emeric with dialogue (Rodney Ackland on *49th Parallel*, for example). Even much later in their collaboration, Michael Powell notes that Emeric needs some help with dialogue.

However, the beautiful original ideas for the films were Emeric's and Michael helping him in no way takes away from that. Emeric's brilliant sense of story was critical to the films of The Archers. (email to the author, 12 May 2012)

Pressburger suggests their success was partly because they were so critical of each other at every stage of the film-making process:

When I am writing the script Michael always says, 'Do we need that? ... Don't you think we could get rid of that scene? Do we really need this dialogue?' And I really begin to resent him. Then he goes off and shoots and shoots and shoots and I have to say, 'Michael do we need that? Why don't we pull out this bit, or join these two scenes together?' And he hates *me* for it – but that's really why we work so well together. (Macdonald 1994: 247)

Although the men emerged from very different backgrounds, they had similar ideas about film and the empathy between them produced a highly creative working partnership, which Powell described as a 'marriage without sex' (ibid.: 155). This extract from a letter to Pressburger, written while looking for locations for *A Matter of Life and Death*, demonstrates how much he values their closeness:

Emeric Pressburger and Michael Powell inside Canterbury Cathedral when filming *A Canterbury Tale* (1944)

> This is almost the first time that I have been able to consider our friendship. How lucky we have
> been! What struggles we have shared and what happiness it has been to struggle and succeed together
> at just the time when we can do our best work. (EPR 1/25/3)

The collaboration was driven by a mutual respect, both admiring the qualities the other brought
to their films, with Pressburger explaining how nothing was 'as important as for me to transfer
to Michael how I feel about an idea, who on the floor made it into what it was finally' (Gough-
Yates 1995: 30).

Their films displayed a European sensibility very different to the 'realism' of many of the
British films produced in the same period. Pressburger brought with him the working methods
and ideas he had developed at Ufa and had also been greatly influenced by German expression-
ism, which at least partly accounts for the often poetic and fantastic nature of The Archers'
stories. The combination of Powell's interest in Romanticism and the spiritual and anti-realist
side to Pressburger's writing produced some exceptionally crafted and inspired films. As
Schoonmaker notes,

> Great partnerships, like that of Powell and Pressburger are mysterious. One would have had to be
> there to really know how it worked. Michael told me they couldn't work in the same room because they
> would argue too much. So Emeric would do a draft, send it to Michael and then Michael would rewrite
> and send it back to Emeric, and this would go on until they got it done. I assume that at some point they
> had to get into a room together to do the final work on the script. (email to the author, 12 May 2012)

PRESSBURGER'S APPROACH TO WRITING

Pressburger learnt how to craft screenplays during his time in the Dramaturgy department at
Ufa, 'which found subjects, wrote treatments, doctored scripts, and made contact with writers,
before handing material on to the production units' (Macdonald 1994: 57). His first commission
at Ufa was a screenplay for Robert Siodmak, *Abschied*, a critically acclaimed comedy, and he was
taken on as Lektor and Dramaturg. Pressburger learned about all aspects of film-making,
including editing, while working with highly skilled directors, actors and technicians. At Ufa he
was taught about the importance of collaboration and that the screenwriter was as important to
the film as the director, a conviction of Pressburger's that Powell readily accepted.

Macdonald believes that some of the ideas in the screenplays of this period, such as *Emil
and the Detectives* (1931), for which he is not credited, and *Dann schon lieber Lebertran/I'd
Rather Have Cod Liver Oil* (1931), directed by Max Ophuls, prefigure Pressburger's later scripts.
Emil and the Detectives features a dream sequence rather like the one on the train in *I Know
Where I'm Going*, while *I'd Rather Have Cod Liver Oil* involves a representation of heaven com-
parable to that depicted in *A Matter of Life and Death* (ibid.: 75–7).

When Pressburger came to the UK, he had not only to learn a new language but also to
understand a different culture if he were to succeed as a writer. In his spare time, Pressburger
studied the society, etiquette and geography of Britain in detail, amassing knowledge about the
people, their language and behaviour. While his spoken English was not fluent, his written
English was more correct though, when dictating scripts to the secretaries, he would ask their
opinion if not sure of the right word (ibid.: 231).

When developing a script idea, Pressburger preferred to have a structure worked out, with
a rhythm and theme embedded in the narrative before putting pen to paper:

When you have done as many scripts as I have, you work out a sort of method. With me – I can't do it any other way – I like to work out the whole structure of the script, but if I don't succeed and yet know I'm on the right track, I start writing and suddenly, it is as if the characters take over, and they bring me so far that I can stop again and set up the whole structure. But if I can help it, I never sit down to write the real script until I know where I'm going and I've worked out the rhythm and so on beforehand. I'm very musical and that might have something to do with it. But I cannot work on anything until I have a certain rhythm in myself about it. So I write down the theme of it again and again and again and soak it up. (ibid.: 231)

Pressburger thought that good writing was a result of 'inspiration and perspiration', believing the process to be partly rational and partly a case of tapping into the emotions, and that being able to combine the two aspects was essential. He compares the creative process to a parent nurturing a child,

Each time you create something – and I don't mean 'each time you make something', it will live. 'Creating' is when you give it something from yourself. Parents give their children something from themselves. Their youth, their vivaciousness. Something that is their special own. In time the child has more, the parent less of it. If I spoke to you about a subject the next time I speak to you again I'd have the urge to say something different to you. And the day will come when I'll have nothing new to communicate and I'll be sorry for myself. (ibid.)

The first draft of a screenplay would be written in longhand and given to Powell for comment. Powell would write his own version, correcting the dialogue, adding detail but never changing the basic shape of the story. The script would go back to Pressburger, possibly up to a dozen times but, once typed and bound, further alterations were rare. The two men would spend many hours talking about their ideas, although 'Emeric himself thought that about 80 per cent of the time things were realised on the screen as he had visualised them' (ibid.: 233). Interestingly, Pressburger's scripts became less technically detailed during his partnership with Powell because there was less need to explain every point with the result that his screenplays began to read more fluently (ibid.: 214).

Pressburger's stories often contain an autobiographical element relating to his earlier life and exile from Hungary. The theme of an outsider entering a new world with a different culture and customs permeates his work. Charles Barr points out, 'The dominant structural element in the Powell–Pressburger films is the entry of a leading character into a strange land' (1999: 96).[7] Pressburger inserted his life experiences into his screenplays: from the German Captain Hardt in *The Spy in Black*, as the outsider struggling with English, to Theo the German soldier in *Colonel Blimp*, to the US sergeant in *A Canterbury Tale*, or Joan Webster visiting remote Scottish isles in *I Know Where I'm Going*, and the nuns trying to settle in exotic India in *Black Narcissus*. During World War II, Pressburger, like Theo in *Colonel Blimp*, was registered as a possibly dangerous alien and his movements were restricted. Also like Theo in his relationship with Blimp, he finds a true friend in Powell. Pressburger acknowledges this connection to his own experiences and, when discussing why the three women in the different stages of Colonel Blimp's life are all played by Deborah Kerr, he notes, 'I think that many people have a certain type that they are always chasing through their lives, trying to find in their lives again and again and again.' Sometimes he was aware of the autobiographical component; sometimes it crept in 'involuntarily'. 'Everybody', he said, 'has something in his make-up which recurs without him being conscious of it' (Gough-Yates 1995: 30).

THE EMERIC PRESSBURGER COLLECTION

The following analysis relates to the screenplays and correspondence held in the BFI Special Collections, first examining the beginning of two early drafts of *A Matter of Life and Death* and then looking at the structure and style of a draft of *A Canterbury Tale*.

Pressburger seized on the idea of *A Matter of Life and Death* because it allowed him to write a film that was part serious and part comedy and which would make full use of Technicolor. The story concerns a pilot, Peter, whose plane is shot down and who miraculously survives the fall without a parachute. Peter believes he should be dead and that he has to argue his case for survival in heaven. His need to win is galvanised by the fact that he has fallen in love with June, the radio operator who tries to rescue him and who he then meets after his descent.

The handwritten first draft script, with its many amendments and crossings out, demonstrates Pressburger's approach to rewriting. The differences between the beginning of the handwritten script (EPR 1/25/1: D1) and the shooting script (S14828: D2)[8] are not major but the writing in the early draft exhibits a rawness and the introduction is shorter, while the shooting script is more polished with a detailed foreword. The handwritten draft begins:

> A casual voice commentates:

> > 'this is the system of the sun, the Planet rotating towards us is
> > the Earth,
> > Over Europe there's night … this tiny pinpoint of light is a burning city.
> > It had an air raid a few hours ago …'
> > And this is what is called a pea-souper that started to descend
> > on England/I hope all our planes are home and safe …
> > Can you hear the fog horns? Even the big ships are frightened …
> > The air is full with radio messages,
> > Instructions, distress signals …

> Then slowly a girl's voice emerges out of the jumble of noises. It is an American voice.
> The girl's name is June.

> > June's voice – Norfolk West XIV –aerodrome
> > Calling – visibility nil – I repeat. Nil
> > No aerodrome open North of 52 Parallel
> > Repeat no aerodrome open North of 52 Parallel
> > Emergency landing possible South 52 Parallel
> > Emergency landing possible South of 52 Parallel
> > Request your position – request your position
> > Come in Lancaster – come in Lancaster –
> > (D1)

D1 is sketchlike, setting the tone and atmosphere. D2 develops this further, featuring much of the dialogue from D1 but with individual word changes such as 'Even the big ships are scared', rather than 'frightened' in D1. D2 elaborates on the radio messages and is more specific:

> Radio messages, orders, distress-signals – there's an S.O.S. –
> bits of news, even part of a statesman's speech … (The growl of
> Churchill is here for a moment.) Listen – Listen …! (D2: 2)

In D2 the scenes are described more imaginatively; the solar system is a two-page scene in itself. Some of the voiceover is very similar but in D2 the wording is more charming and intimate, encouraging the audience: 'Let's go closer'(ibid.). Both scripts cut in at this stage to June answering a distress call. In D1 we hear June first whereas in D2 we hear Peter's slightly surreal dialogue, the spiritual and metaphysical element emphasised by his recitation of Marvell's rousing poem as a way of readying himself for death.

The account of the action inside the Lancaster in D2 is more detailed, creating a heightened atmosphere: 'The wind howls and whistles through them. The fog streams in and out, torn by the wind. The lights, those that function, flicker on and off strangely' (ibid.: 3).

Peter is described much earlier in D2, and we are informed of his state of mind: 'his eyes are gleaming with a strange light … he talks like a man, already dead, treading among the stars as if that was his rightful place'(ibid.).

The two screenplays afford a rare glimpse into how Pressburger added layers to his stories. The spine of the story is outlined in his handwritten draft while the screenplay has been developed over a number of drafts into a final script, which increases the clarity and intensity as well as character detail.

A Canterbury Tale

A Canterbury Tale was Pressburger's favourite screenplay and yet it was the least successful of The Archers' films upon release. Originally conceived as a version of *Pilgrim's Progress*, the project was supported by ardent Methodist J. Arthur Rank. After trying out various possibilities, Pressburger was not sure if this would work so suggested he write his own version, set around Canterbury Cathedral with Chaucer's *Canterbury Tales* as its basis. Pressburger sought to create an anti-consumerist film concerned with the moral values of society, while Powell was keen to make a film about the area where he grew up, Kent, and to incorporate facts from his mother's books on the history of the area.

Powell realised the film's potential: Emeric had imagined a rather complicated story, but very delicate and enthralling' (Lazar 2003: 50). The premise of the film, which revolves around the hunt for a man who has been throwing glue on women's hair, had sexual connotations. Powell commented:

> We had some rather important things to say in *A Canterbury Tale*, so when he proposed this almost
> sexual idea of a man pursuing girls in the blackout and dropping glue on them, I thought, 'Oh,
> Christ, this is going to stop the British in their tracks.' I thought I'd better not tell Emeric because he
> might abandon the idea. (Fuller 1995: 34)

Emeric Pressburger's notes for an introduction to a
1978 screening of *A Canterbury Tale*

Introducing a screening of *A Canterbury
Tale* in 1978, Pressburger explains why the film
is so special:

> What we have in *A Canterbury Tale* is I think
> some magic. … You can only prepare a few tiny
> soft nests for it and hope for the best. …
> There's such a nest in the first five minutes of
> *A Canterbury Tale*. (EPR 1/23/3)

Pressburger explains how the story took on
greater significance as it developed:

> Originally it was meant to be an exercise in
> values of tradition. A fine beginning. A slender
> story-line that seemingly could lead to anything
> more significant than a tiny window with a poky
> little back-yard behind it. But when we open the
> window … . (EPR 1/23/3)

During the early stages of writing, Powell
wrote to Pressburger about the locations, building up a picture of the Kent countryside and
intimating what the Colpeper character and his
background might be like:

> I have been reading up Canterbury etc in mother's books. I think that Chartham or Chilham is the
> village we need. It may give you an idea if I tell you that Chartham has the big Canterbury Lunatic
> Assylum [sic] dominating the landscape, while Chilham has the castle (inhabited). Both are about 4
> miles from Canterbury and on the hills which look down at the city. Chartham Assylum is the most
> prominent landmark on Canterbury's western horizon, it stands up with an odd shaped tower like a
> pointing finger. The local magnate would most probably be a hop-grower, if he was a farmer; he
> would be a J.P. (Justice of the Peace) and would sit on the bench for minor crimes at least once a
> week, in Canterbury. He would also meet other hop-growers and cattle-dealers. Canterbury
> Barracks are on the east side of the town … . The River Stour is of course a great feature of the
> whole valley … I am longing to come back and start work. (EPR 1/23/1)

Powell's knowledge of the area, its people and their way of talking suffuses the screenplay, yet
the construction, the structure, the development of the characters and how they interact is
surely the work of Pressburger. It is the collaboration of ideas that makes this one of their
greatest films.

On release, *A Canterbury Tale* meet with a mainly puzzled reception from both audiences and critics, but not all reviews were negative; *Time and Tide* (January 1945) liked it, commenting, 'this film, despite the doolally plot, happens to be the most memorable produced in 1944' (EPR 1/28/8). On the whole, though, the film was too poetic for audiences of the period, who failed to grasp what it was trying to say and considered it too continental. In notes held in the collection, Pressburger explains why he still likes the story so much and how the film has, despite the slender storyline, stood the test of time:

> I saw *A Canterbury Tale* five weeks ago. But until then I have never seen it for 33 years. I remembered what I never ceased to love about it; the beginning when it changes over to modern times (although once seen the surprise has gone, I always tremble a little before it happens) ... the short scene between an old wheelwright of Kent and a young American soldier about how to season wood, especially the old man's last line: 'You can't hurry an elm!' I now love the rather slender story line which seemingly doesn't lead anywhere except perhaps to a dusty old caravan but in fact it leads to the majesty of Canterbury Cathedral when the central characters suddenly realise that they are really pilgrims themselves. (EPR 1/23/5)

5–11.

CHILLINGBOURNE STATION, NIGHT, continued.

BOB: I heard you with my own ears calling out 'Canterbury!'
            After we started to move.

PETER: (a voice in the darkness, a confident, positive,
            tough Londoner's voice) He called out 'Canterbury
            next stop!'

BOB: But I'm going to Canterbury, darn it!

PETER: The train is going to Canterbury: you're stopping
            here, at Chillingbourne!

By now SERGEANT PETER GIBBS has loomed up into the
lantern-light.   He belongs to a British Rifle Regiment.
He has his kit-bag on his shoulder.

BOB: Well, fan my brow!   (to Duckett)   What time is the
            next -

DUCKETT: (without waiting for the question) 8.57.

BOB: (an octave higher) 8.57!!

DUCKETT: A.M. (his light plays over Skoots and shows the
            three stripes on his sleeve) What do those stripes
            mean?

BOB: Sergeant.

DUCKETT: They're the wrong way up. (His light plays on
            Peter's arm) He's a Sergeant.   See?

BOB: (wearily) Turn the page, brother, turn the page!
            Sergeant Kelly is far from home and in no mood for
            Quiz Questions.   What kind of a place is this, with
            no train all night?

DUCKETT: This is the kind of place where people sleep at
            night.   (He turns to Peter) You all right, Sergeant?

PETER: Yes.   I'm for Chillingbourne Camp.

DUCKETT: O.K.   Ticket please.

PETER: Here.

DUCKETT: (to Bob) You can keep yours.   Both of you follow me!

They get going, following Duckett and his lantern.
They cross the platform and plunge into the station
vestibule.
We would like to emphasize here, particularly to Alfred
Junge and Erwin Hillier, that the Railway Station and
Chillingbourne Village at night are only described thus
prosaically because, in daylight, that is what they
really are.   But at night they loom, awful and
mysterious, of dimensions unknown, of potentialities
undescribable, full of strange shapes, stranger sounds,
menacing shadows and hard corners.
As the little party moves through this nightmare decor
the two soldiers talk to Thomas Duckett, genius loci.

BOB: Say, Pop! where's the hotel?

DUCKETT: They'll tell you at the Town Hall.

The undated screenplay of *A Canterbury Tale* referred to is 120 pages long and divided into forty-four sequences.[9] This use of sequences to break down the structure of a screenplay is not that common, though it has some adherents; Pressburger adopted this system in other early drafts of screenplays such as *Black Narcissus* and probably learnt the method at Ufa.[10] In *A Canterbury Tale*, a change of location generally signifies a new sequence, although a sequence is typically defined as a group of scenes with a common factor in driving the narrative.

The story is framed around the detective genre but elements of other genres are evident, particularly the journey motif in the central characters' pilgrimage to Canterbury. Although the desire to identify the 'Glue-Man' dominates the film, the conventions of the detective genre are turned on their side when the Glue-Man is revealed and the characters decide not to expose him. The story is much more complex than a conventional 'Who done it?' geared towards a final revelation. Colpeper is clearly the culprit, from early on in the story, once

An extract from Emeric Pressburger and Michael Powell's screenplay *A Canterbury Tale*

Alison has found the clothes he's changed out of hidden in the closet, but confirmation of this fact is postponed. As a search for the truth, the story is not really strong enough to engage the reader; we never sense that anyone is in physical danger and the fearless Alison is not at all worried about the Glue-Man. The interest lies in the unravelling of how the three outsider characters react to the new world they have entered and to Colpeper. The story strands are carefully woven into the screenplay, gradually building up to the emotional finale in Canterbury Cathedral.

The film structure enables conflict to develop naturally because there is so much thematic opposition: new versus old, town versus country, English versus American, modernity versus traditional values, male versus female, outsiders and those steeped in the local landscape such as the blacksmith, the wheelwright and, of course, Colpeper. We are continually reminded of the need for us to connect to our historical and cultural heritage, a fact exemplified by Colpeper and his lectures.

The story is unconventional, the pacing slow, with little in the way of dramatic tension. The attack on Alison and the reveal of Colpeper as the likely culprit are left hanging for much of the film. There is often no attempt to make events rational but this is also where the screenplay includes elements of the poetic; events take place without seeming to develop the narrative. For instance, the army convoy that descends upon Alison has no obvious dramatic function, apart from reintroducing Alison to Peter. But the sequence does illustrate the intrusion of man and his machinery into the natural world; it is invasive and threatening, and more so in the screenplay than the film, because the former contains an extra sequence showing the soldiers preparing to attack their mock target – Alison and her horse and cart. The wheelwright sequence is a long aside that only obliquely touches on the hunt for the Glue-Man, in which the cutting of timber is presented as a complex metaphor for links to the past, to nature and other nations.

Yet many conventional techniques are evident in the screenplay. All the main characters demonstrate wants and needs. They repeatedly state that they want to find the Glue-Man. We discover that Bob wants to get letters from his girlfriend; Alison wants to go to her caravan, a reminder of the boyfriend she believes dead; Peter wants to be back in London away from the countryside; while Colpeper wants to shake people up and make them think about the past. They all need to go on a pilgrimage to Canterbury, including Colpeper, who needs to become less led by doctrine, more understanding and to seek forgiveness.

The characters affect and change each other in a classical way.[11] All four characters have developmental arcs and are shown to be significantly affected by events at particular moments.

- Alison is in many ways an inspirational figure, bringing 'common sense' to the world. She displays great strength of character and a love for the country despite having lived and worked in London. Her arc of change is about gaining an understanding of Colpeper; first, she is suspicious of him, believing him a misogynist and suspecting that he is the Glue-Man. When she sees him working in the garden of what she describes as the 'perfect' home, she begins to question her assumptions. At the lecture she begins to understand his motivations, with the final change in her arc occuring when they meet in the Kent fields and she realises 'You have to dig to find out about people …' (S13976: 95).
- Bob, the American soldier, loves the movies and this blinkers his outlook, preventing him from seeing the beauty of the landscape around him or appreciating the history of Kent.

He is changed when encounters with the locals teach him that they do things the same way in Kent that they do at home. Colpeper's lecture also makes him see things differently. Like Alison, he is rewarded in Canterbury with a minor miracle, the news that his girlfriend's letters have arrived.

- Peter is the most cynical of the characters in the script and the one who changes the most. He dislikes being outside London and has corrupted his talent for the organ by playing one in the cinema. He tells Bob and Alison, 'I wouldn't spend my leave in Canterbury' (15) and is critical of village life. Peter is the one who wants to tell the police that Colpeper is the Glue-Man, the one who visits his house, takes the fire watch rota as evidence and confronts Colpeper on the train. Finally, he is beguiled by the atmosphere of the cathedral and allowed to play the organ.

- Colpeper is most noticeably changed by Alison. His negative views about women are confounded by Alison's strength, dignity and understanding of history. He is surprised when she reveals that she possesses the old coins he would like to trace and by her knowledge of the area. Late in the story they meet accidentally in the fields outside the village, when he acknowledges that he has misunderstood her. Colpeper is an enigmatic character and made the more interesting because of this: he hovers in the background, appears and disappears in unexpected places while his desire to connect with the past has a mystical significance in the narrative.

Structure of *A Canterbury Tale*

The structure of the film is unusual. The first half of the screenplay sets up the situation in a leisurely way, and it is only in the second half that the search for the Glue-Man begins in earnest. Once it is certain that the Glue-Man is Colpeper, Peter confronts him, yet this is not the end of the story; the final part is not about the Glue-Man but about Alison, Bob and Peter as pilgrims in Canterbury receiving their miracles. The revelation that Colpeper is the Glue-Man becomes a device to link the characters together; more important are the concluding personal revelations and the effect that the cathedral has on the characters.

The following beat breakdown of the script yields a detailed insight into the story structure. This method is often adopted by screenwriters to chart the changes in a story. A 'beat' refers to every time there is a change that has an impact on the narrative:

Prologue – Chaucer's pilgrims are on their way to Canterbury when we cut to the twentieth century.

1   The three central characters arrive by train at night in a new world, the village of Chillingbourne in Kent. The local magistrate, Thomas Colpeper, has decreed that 'No girl must go out alone at night.'
2   Alison is escorted by two soldiers, Peter and Bob, from the US, when she is attacked by the 'Glue-Man'. (16)
    (*This is the event that triggers or determines the rest of the story.*)
3   The Glue-Man is chased to the town hall where he disappears.
4   Alison and Bob go inside the town hall while Peter goes to his barracks. (20)
5   Alison and Bob are introduced to some of the locals who have their own preconceptions about Americans. Bob is told, 'This is Chillingbourne, Sergeant Johnson, not Chicago.' (21)
6   We see Colpeper for the first time and it is evident that he is respected in the community (22)

7   As Alison's hair is washed, they find out that eleven other women have been victims of the Glue-Man. (23)

8   Alison and Bob meet Colpeper, who advises Bob against watching films: 'People may get used to looking at the world from a sitting-position … and then, when they actually do pass through it, they can't see anything.' (24)
    (*The message or heart of the film – taking part in life.*)

9   Colpeper seems pompous and self-righteous but when on his own we see him smile and are told that 'It is as if he said to himself in reproof: "Colpeper! Colpeper!" There is nothing sinister about his smile; on the contrary he seems rather to enjoy it.' (25)

10 Alison explains she's come to work as a farm labourer. But Colpeper won't take her on because she's a girl.

11 Alison hears a noise in the cupboard. When Colpeper opens the door a coat hanger swings, just as if clothes have been hurriedly put away. Alison's suspicions about Colpeper are aroused. (26)
    (*End of first section. This is an important turn in the story and the first clue.*)

12 Back at the army camp, Peter discovers that they know about the Glue-Man. He tells them the Glue-Man has been caught and they celebrate. (27–30)

13 Alison reveals she has been to the village before and knows about 'the Bend' that was part of the road the pilgrims travelled on. (31)

14 Alison and Bob stay the night in a pub/hotel. Peter arrives with his army friends to be informed that the Glue-Man is still at large. Peter resolves to catch him. Alison has suspicions about Colpeper because he 'has no use for girls'. (36–8)
    (*Building up to the hunt for the Glue-Man.*)

15 Bob meets the locals. He gets on with them all, unlike Peter, who finds them hostile. Bob and Alison decide to stay another day to help Peter. (38–9)

16 Bob goes to see Alison at the wheelwrights, where she is getting a wheel repaired. She declares that she will go out every night until she catches the Glue-Man. (44–6)

17 Bob gets on well with the wheelwright, finding they have much in common and speak the same language about wood. (49)
    (*Beats 16 and 17 diverge from the story trajectory but forge links between the two nations.*)

18 Bob and Alison ride in the cart past a perfect house in the village and see that Colpeper lives there. Alison is shaken because he looks just 'right' there even though she suspects he's the Glue-Man. (50)
    (*A major question mark for Alison's character.*)

19 Bob tells Alison he hasn't had a letter from his girlfriend for seven weeks. (51)

20 Alison mentions to Bob that her boyfriend was lost in enemy action. (52)
    (*The above two beats reveal important personal information.*)

21 As Alison drives the horse and cart back to the farm, she is surrounded by an army convoy on manoeuvres. Peter is in one of the vehicles. (56–7)

22 Peter informs her that Colpeper is giving a talk in the town hall, saying, 'In detective work every clue is important.' (58)
    (*Halfway – the investigation kicks in fully here.*)

23 Alison is taken on as a farmworker and declares herself unafraid of the Glue-Man. (60)
    (*This comment undermines the tension and threat in the story – no one seems to mind him – there's no danger!*)

24   Bob gets to know the local children, telling them he's on the trail of the Glue-Man and asking for their help.

25   Alison realises that the Glue-Man is someone in the village who is trying to stop girls going out with the soldiers. She begins her detective work by finding out the names of other women attacked by the Glue-Man. (68)

26   Bob, Alison and Peter go to Colpeper's lecture. (70)
     (*A turning point as they get to hear Colpeper's ideas and begin to like him.*)

27   Colpeper talks about local history, the pilgrims' journey and how the landscape links the past to the present. (71)

28   When Alison reveals that she has some ancient coins that Colpeper would like to trace, he begins to see her in a different light. (73)
     (*This is an important turn in the story as Colpeper changes his attitudes.*)

29   Suspicions about Colpeper are compounded as Bob, Alison and Peter go looking for evidence. But by now Alison can't believe he's the Glue-Man. (76–7)
     (*The investigation now begins in earnest.*)

30   Alison talks to some more of the women attacked. (78–9)

31   The three meet up and compare notes, trying to work out if there is a pattern to the attacks. (80)

32   Peter reveals that he plays the organ in a cinema and that his girlfriend's left him. (81)

33   Alison, Peter and Bob meet up again to feedback their findings while the children bring Bob the accounts book from the general store to check if any glue has been sold. It hasn't.

34   Peter goes to see Colpeper. They talk about the attacks. Peter takes the fire watch rota when Colpeper is out of the room. (85–8)

35   While Peter is with Colpeper, the boys Bob has befriended ask to collect the waste from Colpeper's house. (89)

36   The three work out when Colpeper was on fire watch duty – every eighth day – which coincides with the attacks. (91)

37   At the salvage hut, Peter and Bob uncover the final piece of evidence they need: Colpeper's rubbish contains wrappings from a stationer who sells glue. The three don't seem in any hurry to do anything with this knowledge. (92–3)
     (*The final revelation/confirmation that Colpeper is the Glue-Man takes the script to the last section. The new question is what they will do with this information. The revelation is undercut by the fact that they fail to react.*)

38   Alison goes for a walk in the country where she meets Colpeper. They realise they were mistaken about each other and she observes, 'You have to dig to find out about people.' (94–5)

39   Alison tells Colpeper about her caravan in Canterbury. (95a)
     (*Colpeper becomes her confidant.*)

40   Alison and Colpeper overhear a conversation between Bob and Peter which discloses the fact that they know the Glue-Man is Colpeper. They both confess that they like Colpeper. (96–8)
     (*The earlier revelation is again undercut – they all like Colpeper.*)

41   When Alison, Bob and Peter meet on the train to Canterbury, Peter says he will tell the police about Colpeper; then Colpeper gets into their compartment.
     (*Confronting the culprit.*)

42   Peter confronts Colpeper, who, explains that he did it to 'pour knowledge into people's heads'. The soldiers were too busy chasing the local girls and so he came up with the glue idea. (102)

(The confrontation scene is typical of the detective genre but undercut here because Colpeper's explanation is so peculiar.)

43   Alison suggests he should have invited females to the lectures. Colpeper admits he hadn't thought of this. (103)

(The final section/the three pilgrims get to Canterbury/the three miracles.)

44   Bob says the three are pilgrims to Canterbury. The sunlight around Peter's head looks like a halo – a miracle.

45   The four separate and Peter goes to the police station, only to learn that the sergeant has gone to the cathedral.

46   Peter takes in the majestic cathedral and talks to the organist, who knows his old teacher. Peter plays the organ at the service for his squadron who are leaving for duty – a miracle. (108–10)

47   Bob enters the cathedral as Peter practises – he's astounded by its magnificence. (111)

48   Bob meets an army friend who gives him the letters from his girlfriend that have been held up – a miracle. (113)

49   Alison walks through the parts of Canterbury city centre devastated by the bombs.

50   Alison arrives at the garage where the caravan is stored. She turns to see Colpeper there. He's come to support her. (115–16)

51   The garage owner informs Alison that her fiancé has been found in Germany. She's joyful – another miracle. She turns around to find Colpeper has disappeared. (116–17)

52   The soldiers arrive at the cathedral. Peter plays the organ and Bob and Alison stand in different parts of the nave, content and at peace. Colpeper stands on his own: 'His penance is a lonely one.' (119)

53   Outside the cathedral the bells ring and a new battalion of American soldiers enters the camp at Chillingbourne. (120)

The beat breakdown shows the bones of the story. At its heart is the investigation into the Glue-Man. The key events are based on the step-by-step unravelling of the clues as Alison, Bob and Peter try to identify him. The investigative structure is undermined by the anodyne nature of the crimes and the lack of suspense around the need to find the culprit. Because the initial evidence points so clearly towards Colpeper being the offender, the narrative focuses on the confirmation of this fact, unlike a conventional detective story, which is driven by the imperative to uncover the offender and to prevent further incidents. After Alison's attack, there are no more and this decreases the tension. Anticipation around the denouement is diffused, because this is more of a reaffirmation and thus almost bathetic; the ultimate discovery that Colpeper probably buys his glue from Ryman's in London is not a very dramatic one.

In the case of this film, the detective structure serves as a convenient frame to hang the story on and invoke some dramatic interest. Indeed, Peter and Bob refer to the husband-and-wife detective partnership of William Powell and Myrna Loy in *The Thin Man* (1934), Bob responding to Peter, ' "I'm no William Powell. And he has Myrna Loy." (He looks at Alison, who smiles and shakes her head)' (p. 38). The narrative is more concerned with the characters, their revelations and how they interact with and affect each other. It builds to the finale when the miracles occur for the three friends, while Colpeper is left isolated, ironically the outsider looking on, as they stand in Canterbury Cathedral.

Writing style in A Canterbury Tale

A Canterbury Tale has a lyrical style, enlisting description to create the visual and aural experience of a film. The writing is measured, almost leisurely and the introduction links the past to the present, a key theme of the film:

> This is a tale of four modern pilgrims, and of the Old Road which runs to Canterbury and of the English countryside, which is eternal.

The beginning foreshadows the fact that the journey will have religious and spiritual qualities, with bird imagery engaged to suggest the exhilarating upwards momentum of flight. The vivid description of the falcon and the characters are brought to life by touches of detail, as if in a film close-up:

> The peregrine on the gloved wrist of the SQUIRE is unhooded. It ruffles its head and its fierce eyes open wide and glare about it. The Squire casts off the bird. It mounts swiftly into the sky, higher – higher – higher –

> His hand shading his eyes, the SQUIRE watches. We are so close to him that we can see the veins on his forehead, the bones of his nose; his curled locks, his wide embroidered sleeves – 'Embroidred was he, as it were a Mead' – no longer seem important: we see instead his brown face, his intent gaze, as he watches the hawk.

> We hear a distant humming, strange and yet familiar, as it grows louder and louder. It is the sound of an aircraft engine: a fighter.

> High in the summer sky, the hawk has become a Spitfire.

> We see again the Squire, as he watches the Spitfire. His curly hair is cropped, his helmet is steel, he wears battledress; but the brown face, the intent gaze are the same; the background of the English countryside is the same:

> We are in the twentieth century. (ibid.: 2)

The dissolve, as the falcon soars into the sky to then become a fighter plane, is a stunning visual image, while the cut to the man in army uniform is a surprising turn, neatly informing us that it is wartime.

Pressburger's writing allows the reader to see and hear the events almost as if they were viewing a film. For instance, in the sequence when Alison is attacked by the Glue-Man, the description of the torch creates light and movement; the image of Bob, Peter and Alison 'silhouetted' is strongly visual; the lovely simile of Alison dashing 'off like a hare' suggests speed; while the sounds of the cock crowing and the dogs barking build up the scenario:

> The huge beam of Bob's torch suddenly flashes down the street after their quarry. The three stand silhouetted against it. At the far end of the street a soldier in battledress is running.

> BOB (bellows)
> Hey! You!
>
> PETER
> A soldier! Can you run miss?
>
> ALISON
> Watch me!
>
> She is off like a hare, the others after her. BOB keeps his torch pointing ahead.
> ALL THREE are hindered by their bags and coats. They reach the corner and stop,
> panting, as BOB flashes his torch. By this time the dogs are barking. Even a cock
> starts to crow. (ibid.: 17)

This visual sense is constant throughout the screenplay and functions in different ways: to surprise, to tease playfully and to develop the narrative, as when Bob's view from his room upstairs at the inn defies belief:

> Finally he turns round and gets a horrid shock.
> A seeming miracle faces him.
> A short distance from the big window, seemingly in mid-air, a little boy is sitting,
> LESLIE.
>
> LESLIE
> Hello!
>
> BOB
> Hello, there. What are you doing?
>
> LESLIE
> Sitting.
>
> Bob walks to the window and looks out.
> The miracle is explained. Leslie is sitting on the top of a load of hay, in the wagon,
> which has stopped outside 'The Hand of Glory'. (ibid.: 42)

The description, besides the revelation, also foreshadows the concept of the 'miracle', planting the word in the reader's mind as to what might happen later in the story.

Possibly the most referenced part of the film and one that Pressburger particularly liked is the moving and skilfully written 'wheelwright sequence', set just before halfway through the screenplay (pp. 44–8). The sequence begins with Alison being teased by the suspicious locals as an outsider while she is determined to prove herself and her skills as a horsewoman. The writing conveys the awkward atmosphere and the dialogue wittily projects their dry country humour as Alison brings up the subject of the Glue-Man:

ALISON
Did you hear last night's news, Mr. Horton?

JIM
There was nothing on the wireless.

ALISON
I didn't mean that sort of news – I mean what happened here
last night.

SMITH
We get all our local news here at 6, miss.

BOB
You got a local newspaper?

SMITH
No. That's when the pub opens. (general guffaw)
What happened? Your Glue-Man was on the war-path. Nobody
seems very excited.

JIM
Who was he after this time?

ALISON
Me.

Everyone stops and looks at her.

SMITH
I suppose that'll learn you not to run around at night!

ALISON
On the contrary. I shall go out every night until I catch him.

Everyone stares at this girl.

Alison's strong response and determination to catch the Glue-Man confuses the men; she
continues to defy their negativity as she capably backs the horse into the cart while they watch
her. Smith replies to Alison's bravado:

SMITH (finally)
Well, it aint likely.

This opinion delivered, everyone feels the matter can be left in abeyance. By now the wheel is on. Alison brings the horse and backs it into the shafts, which are propped horizontally on their stands. Nobody offers to do it for her, or steady the shafts. They all wait to see if she can do it or not. Except BOB, always chivalrous.

BOB
Can I give you a hand, ma'am?

ALISON (she knows she is on trial and is quite confident)
Thanks BOB, but I'd sooner do it alone.

She backs the horse skilfully in and starts to harness up. (ibid.: 46)

The following extract, from the end of the same sequence, is a subtle and gently moving propaganda passage where not only does Bob the GI prove himself to be a knowledgeable out-sider, but links between Britain and America are forged by his experience with and understand-ing of wood. The dialogue is superb, showcasing Powell's familiarity with the local dialect. Bob and Jim the wheelwright's lines ping-pong back and forth rhythmically to emphasise their like-mindedness.

They walk on towards the sheds, where there are stacks of boards.

BOB
Do you get much sweating in your elm planks?

JIM
Average.

BOB
At home we build two stacks at a time. For steadiness. Side by side.

JIM
So do us; to tie they longer strips together.

The boards have strips nailed across each end. Bob points to them.

BOB
I see they were sown last winter.

JIM
Is that how you do it in America?

BOB
It's how we do it in my part of America. But we take off the strips when we put the planks away in stock.

JIM
So do us. How much do you count for seasoning timber?

BOB
A year to every inch of thickness.

JIM
Same here. You can't hurry an elm.

BOB
No. But some folk try to hurry it all the same.

JIM (darkly)
Capitalists.

BOB
Can't stand to see their money lie idle a piece.

JIM
And the war!

BOB
Why the war?

JIM
Folks go mad. They cut oak in midsummer!

BOB
No!

JIM
I'm telling you, yes!

BOB
Oak should be cut in winter … or spring.

JIM
That's right.

BOB
And beech in the Fall.

JIM
And opened into quarters at Christmas.

<pre>
                              BOB
            At Christmas. That's how my Dad taught me.

                              JIM
        Ah! You was well brought up. In the timber-business was you?
        (ibid.: 47)
</pre>

By the end of the scene Jim and Bob are getting on so well that they almost talk in unison. The antipathy of the locals towards the outsiders has gone; Alison and Bob have proven themselves, so much so that Jim invites Bob to dinner.

The next sequence is important to the narrative because it shows Alison's reaction to seeing where Colpeper lives. The mix of specific detail and explanation as to how she responds to the house as she and Bob drive past is cleverly handled:

> On the near side of the village-green is a good square house, honest-looking, white-painted with green shutters. There is something so right about its proportions, so homely about its atmosphere, so perfect about its setting …

<pre>
                        ALISON (sighs)
            What a perfect place! I wonder whose it is and what it's like at
            the back.
</pre>

The description of an English idyllic country house continues:

> Behind the house is a garden, informal and sheltered, with a lawn and flowering trees. An old white carriage-gate leans permanently open. A short gravel drive skirts the house and ends in a stable-yard. Beyond lie the farm-buildings.

> A smooth lawn ends in a tree, around which the grass has been allowed to grow long, while the daffodils bloomed. A man in shirt-sleeves is scything the grass. Alison stops the cart to look enviously at the perfect picture.

<pre>
                        ALISON (whispers)
            'O more than happy countryman!' What wouldn't I give to grow
            up in a place like that!
</pre>

> The man with the scythe stops to whet his blade. He hasn't heard the cart and they are screened by the leaves. As he sharpens the blade with his whetstone he turns to get a good grip. It is THOMAS COLPEPER. ALISON cracks her whip and the old horse starts off with a jerk of surprise. (ibid.: 50)

The prelude to the revelation, with the scene described from Alison's point of view, guides the reader as to what to see and how to interpret this knowledge. Alison's reaction is initially strongly positive and she seems almost envious of the occupier only for the scene to turn once she recognises the owner as Colpeper. The mood created is not quite as gently pastoral as it seems: the character of Colpeper possesses darker connotations and the scythe is wielded expressively, evoking the grim reaper and Freudian imagery; it is a complex description, qualified by the last lines in the sequence: 'Thomas Colpeper continues to sharpen his scythe, carefully and expertly, as a countryman should' (ibid.).

Often the most effective screenplay creates a sense of being 'in the film', and this applies to much of Pressburger's work. The sequence when Alison meets Colpeper in the fields outside the village is poetic and economically expressed yet brings the fields of Kent to life.

> Here, on the top, a little wind blows, mingling with the song of the birds, the chirp of the crickets and the hum of insects and all the thousand sounds of the Kentish countryside; and the strangest thing of all is that all these noises together result in a glorious silence. Then, suddenly coming from nowhere, she hears the thrumming of horses' hooves, distant chatter and laughter and a simple melody, played on a wind instrument: just as we hear the sound of the pilgrims in the prologue, only less distinct. She turns around but nothing is there; only the Old Road and the grass bending in the wind. At that very moment she hears Colpeper's voice. (ibid.: 94)

The magical atmosphere, where past and present meet, is captured in the writing and it is notable how many references there are to sound, from the insects, to the horses' hooves, to Colpeper's voice.

The final page parallels the beginning of the script, building up to a finale in the cathedral, cutting to the outside, then pulling out to show the countryside and the Spitfire in the sky:

> THE FINAL SEQUENCE
>
> The bells of Canterbury Cathedral are ringing. We see the bells, great and small, shaking the timbers of the roof with their clamour. We see the towers of the Cathedral, the Angel Steeple, the mass of the building. The bells are still ringing. There is no sign to show whether the time is 600 years ago or today.
>
> We see the Cathedral, far away across the valley of the Stour, the houses of Canterbury huddled around it. The bells sound faintly, but the organ is still playing.
>
> High up white clouds are sailing in the wind. A small black speck appears in the sky. Its familiar hum breaks through the organ music. It is a Spitfire. (ibid.: 120)

The script then cuts to Chillingbourne camp, where a new battalion of soldiers has arrived. We are told: 'Here our story ends' and, as the end credits appear, the script finishes on:

> Here is the 'Colpeper Institute'. There is a poster up, advertising a series of lectures. And – believe it or not! – soldiers and girls are going in. (ibid.: 120)

The postscript tells us that Colpeper has now paid his penance, understood the error of his ways and has invited both men and *women* to his lectures.

Comparing the script to the film

Only one undated draft of the screenplay is held in the collection, although there would have been a number of drafts and a final shooting script. Comparing the screenplay to the film is an interesting exercise; the screenplay is similar to the film, despite structural changes to the story and some changes to the dialogue. These are mostly minor but occasionally more substantial. A few sections have been cut or rearranged; for instance, when Alison, Bob and Peter enter the village at night, at the beginning of the film, some lines of dialogue have been deleted, most likely to speed up the flow of action. Sequences have occasionally had their dialogue cut to tighten the ending and add emphasis to the lines spoken.

Some sequences in the screenplay have been deleted or reordered in the film. For instance, sequence 9, set in Chillingbourne army camp, has been cut because, though it shows Peter with his army friends, the scene provides no new story information. Later in the film, there is some more rearranging of the army convoy sequences when Alison is attacked. The three consecutive sequences (14, 15, 16) in the screenplay are changed and the first one deleted, most probably because the two-page sequence slowed the pacing and did little to develop the narrative, mainly serving as an introduction to the convoy as it appears over the horizon.

In the film, the pivotal sequence when Bob, Alison and Peter complete the final part of their journey to Canterbury and Peter confronts Colpeper, includes more than a page of additional dialogue. In this section, Colpeper admits that he is the Glue-Man and the three friends question him about his motives. The movement of the scene in the script and the film is almost the same but the film's extra dialogue allows for further discussion of Colpeper's crime and makes him easier to understand. The new section follows Colpeper's admission that he had never considered inviting girls to his lectures. Peter questions him further:

> PETER
> What beats me is that a man in your position, a Magistrate, somebody whose job it is to judge other people. I wonder what sort of sentence you would pass if the Glue-Man was brought before you and your friends on the bench?

> COLPEPER
> It would depend upon the findings of the court. I would try to find out the truth. I never pass sentence without doing that. I should try to discover the motives of the accused. I should question every witness.

The rest of Colpeper's speech is cut out by the whistle of the train.

> PETER
> But you know that every witness would be against him.

> COLPEPER (To Peter)
> Are you against him?

ALISON
Fee Baker said that a lot of people in the village were not against him.

COLPEPER
Are you against him?

BOB
He meant well.

The new dialogue emphasises that most of the villagers, including Alison and Bob are 'not against' Colpeper. The extra section ends with Colpeper accepting that he should pay for his crime if he has harmed anyone and that God will decide if he is guilty or not.

COLPEPER
In any case Sergeant Gibbs if harm has been done I shall have
to pay for it.

PETER
In order to make you pay somebody must denounce you. I want
to make that quite clear.

COLPEPER
There are higher courts than the local bench of Magistrates.

The religious emphasis in the above lines segues pleasingly into the end of the scene as the three pilgrims arrive in Canterbury and a discussion about the purpose of a pilgrimage ensues.

From then on the screenplay and the film are almost identical, though the final scenes are hidden by the film titles and end credits.

CONCLUSION

After *The Red Shoes*, Pressburger continued to write but his screenplays were nearly all adaptations of novels such as *Gone to Earth* (1950) or opera, *The Tales of Hoffman* (1951), although he did script *The Battle of the River Plate* (1956) with Powell and wrote the novel and screenplay for *Miracle in Soho* (1957), directed by Julian Amyes. Macdonald suggests that:

Emeric's films began to retreat from politics and ethics and busied themselves with an alternative world of music, colour and art. He stopped writing original stories. Perhaps he found it too painful to confront his inner life – at least in so public a medium.

Emeric said,

If you are looking for something new, something interesting then why start reading up books? It is certainly very difficult to take a book and suddenly subjugate your own talent, which cannot be exactly the same as the talent of the writer of this book has been, so it will be a compromise … .
(Macdonald 1994: 265)

Pressburger turned to writing novels, publishing *Miracle in Soho* and *Behold a Pale Horse*, adapted by J. P. Millar and directed by Fred Zinnemann in 1964 but was to have one last collaboration with Powell, *The Boy Who Turned Yellow*, a fifty-five-minute film supported by the Children's Film Foundation in 1972.

Pressburger's ability as a screenwriter may have been undervalued, but Powell certainly appreciated his skill as a writer. Despite their many disagreements, Pressburger and Powell's collaboration was one of the longest-lasting partnerships and produced some of the most interesting and provocative films in British cinema. Although Pressburger did write screenplays without Powell, the resulting films lacked the imagination and artistry of the films they made together. Their working relationship generated exceptional stories and screenplays. Now that auteur theory is under scrutiny as a realistic appraisal of the film-making process, perhaps Pressburger's contribution as writer can be appreciated more fully and his screenplays studied as works of great literary merit.

The autonomy that Powell and Pressburger enjoyed as 'The Archers', allowed them a great deal of artistic freedom, something that few film-makers could hope for. Yet producer Michael Balcon, head of Ealing, accorded his writers a sort of freedom too, encouraging the development of many original stories. The next chapter discusses how the writers at Ealing Studios such as Angus MacPhail and T. E. B. Clarke were vital to the studio with 'the team spirit'.

NOTES

1. Letter to Pressburger from Reinhold Schunzel in Beverly Hills, California, 15 April 1942 (EPR 1/19/13).
2. For more on Pressburger's early life, see Macdonald (1994) and Christie (2002), both of which give further detail of Pressburger's family background and schooling.
3. Both the Pressburger and Powell Collections at the BFI contain details about the planning and making of *The Red Shoes*.
4. When developing the script for *49th Parallel*, Pressburger faced a number of difficulties: the Ministry of Information (MOI) had to intervene to prevent him being deported as an undesirable alien and then interest in the project waned as the Battle of Britain waged. But Powell showed the treatment to the new minister at the MOI, Duff Cooper, who was so impressed that he decreed: 'Finance must not stand in the way of this project.' A letter from Kenneth Clark, head of MOI Films Division, to the Home Office, emphasises the importance eventually allocated to Pressburger's contribution to the war effort as a writer. The letter confirms that he is to visit Canada solely for the purpose of making the film under the auspices of the MOI. 'It is essential to the interests of said picture that Mr Pressburger returns with his associates to England and that he be given a permit for that purpose' (10 April 1940).

   A letter to Powell from Pressburger, on 5 September 1940, contains detailed notes about how he tackled the script. Pressburger explains the problems he had persuading Mr Deutsch and Mr Bamford from the MOI that a second Canadian trip was necessary but, after two meetings, he finally convinced them that he needed 'to be present at the final shaping of the script and especially the last sequences'. Unfortunately, after this agreement the Home Office lost his passport, precluding further travel (EPR 1/19/6).
5. *One of Our Aircraft Is Missing* resulted from Pressburger's resolve to make films to help the war effort. Inspired by the planes that failed to return from battle and the older men who insisted on volunteering to fight, the story was turned down by Rank but supported by the MOI, which, while

not giving financial help, did allow access to secret military details. Macdonald argues that the British characters could only have been written by a non-native as they display no recognition of class, a point they share with most Pressburger scripts. This film is concerned with the portrayal and opposition of old and young, farmer and townie, artist and sportsman (1994: 192).

6. Ian Christie's *The Life and Death of Colonel Blimp* is probably the most written about Powell and Pressburger film. Ian Christie has published notes on the development of the screenplay, including a treatment, a draft of the script and letters about content which are fascinating to read (1994).

7. In the same article, Barr outlines the thematic patterns that occur in their films (1999: 96).

8. Shooting script of *A Matter of Life and Death* (S14828 BFI Screenplay Collection).

9. Screenplay of *A Canterbury Tale* (S13976 BFI Screenplay Collection).

10. There are some recent exponents of the sequence structural breakdown. For instance, see Paul Gulino's *Screenwriting: The Sequence Approach* (2004).

11. See Bordwell *et al.* (1988) and Bordwell (2006).

03
EALING
THE STUDIO WITH THE TEAM SPIRIT

Michael Balcon, head of Ealing Studios from 1937 to 1959, understood the vital contribution of the screenplay to the success of a film, encouraging an atmosphere in which writers, directors and producers could collaborate and develop their own projects overseen by him.

Balcon took over Ealing Studios after many years' experience as a head of production, first founding Gainsborough Pictures in 1924, then becoming director of production for Gaumont-British in 1932 and going on to 'two frustrating years in charge of production at MGM-British' (McFarlane 2003: 40). Balcon needed a base for his newly formed independent production company and Ealing functioned as both a studio and a production company until 1955, when the studio was sold to the BBC. Ealing Films, financed by MGM, continued to make pictures at Borehamwood studios until 1959.

Ealing was termed 'the studio with the team spirit', though it was rather an exclusive team and almost solely male, as writer and publicist Monja Danischewsky notes, 'All of us young fellows were given our break in Mr. Balcon's Academy for Young Gentlemen' (1966: 133). Only one female writer was regularly employed, Diana Morgan, best known for *Went the Day Well?* (1942) and *Pink String and Sealing Wax* (1945).

Balcon made nearly 100 films at Ealing over a twenty-year period, averaging between four and seven films a year. The films ranged from serious drama to comedy, with writers frequently working in more than one genre; T. E. B Clarke, for instance, although best known for his comedies, also penned popular dramas such as *The Blue Lamp* (1949). Michael Relph, producer of many Ealing pictures, explains that Balcon had a clear idea of the type of story he wanted to develop, insisting that they should be 'socially responsible and that they should be trying to say something which was positive … . I don't think he would have wanted to make a film which really pulled one of our institutions to pieces' (Drazin 1998: 107). Charles Drazin argues that Balcon's desire to produce 'safe', conservative films resulted in stories which often seemed forced and undramatic in their construction, avoiding discussion of more dangerous or contentious subjects, particularly sexuality (ibid.). Paradoxically, it was Balcon's preference for films embedded in reality that allowed the writers to create some of Ealing's most enjoyable tales, particularly with regard to the comedies about unlikely or fantastical happenings.

The continuity of output at Ealing was made possible because Balcon brought with him many of his team from Gaumont-British, including scenario editor and writer Angus MacPhail. Drazin suggests, 'The studio drew its strength from the resulting bond of loyalty and friendship, and the continuity these qualities fostered' (ibid.: 106). The success of Ealing was at least partly due to the excellence of the scenario department and its script supervisors, in particular MacPhail. Although many writers passed through Ealing, three developed and wrote by far the most scripts: MacPhail, credited with twenty-three scripts between 1939–49; John Dighton, credited with seventeen scripts between 1940–51 and T. E. B. Clarke, with fifteen scripts between 1944–57. In addition, well-known and respected authors such as H. E. Bates, Kenneth Tynan and Monica Dickens also worked for short periods at Ealing, developing, writing and advising on different projects.[1]

Clarke explains how Balcon encouraged creativity in his staff and, while not always easy to work with himself, respected their opinion even when not entirely sure about a project:

> if he was 'over-possessive and a hard bargainer, he had a sagacity, courage and forbearance to a degree almost unique among film producers. Mick regarded his creative staff as experts in their own line and relied on them to bring in the raw materials of movie-making. Headmaster he may have been but he was no dictator: a subject about which he personally had misgivings would nevertheless get the go-ahead if the consensus of opinion was in its favour. (1974: 141)

The importance that Balcon assigned to developing a story, combined with a willingness to take a risk on original ideas, made him stand out as an exceptional producer, as Clarke remarks:

> He deserves the thanks of writers for his readiness to acknowledge that the story was a film's most important ingredient – and, what was more, to act on that belief. The average producer, in choosing a subject needs the reassurance of knowing it has already succeeded as a book, a play or a TV series. Not so Balcon: if he could 'see' a film in a suggestion that might cover only half a page of typescript, then its instigator would be authorised to develop it until its worth could be fairly judged by himself and others. (ibid.: 141–2)

Whether Balcon was always quite so democratic is questionable, as Drazin notes: 'the best way to prosper at Ealing was to choose a subject that was contemporary and uncontroversial' (1998: 109). Selecting topics that met Balcon's criteria for subject matter lent a project a much greater chance of getting off the ground and the most successful partnerships and writers at the studios understood that.

Balcon points out a number of factors to be taken into consideration when deciding on a subject, such as the type of story, how it fits into the production programme and its audience appeal:

> In the selection, the producer must bear in mind, not only the individual merit of the stories, but also their relation to the effect upon his proposed production programme. This must be carefully planned to ensure that one particular style of subject does not predominate. He must also consider the selling organisation through which his films pass to the exhibitor …. . They must suit his contract artistes to ensure their constant use. They must be subjects which his resident writers and directors can best handle. And, above all, they must be subjects which coincide with his forecast of public taste at the time of their release to the cinemas. (1945: 6)

Balcon places himself at the centre of the decision-making process; even after a project has been allocated a production team, his approval is required at each stage of the script development:

> Once the producer has made his selection of story, he then assigns to it the personnel he thinks most suited to it. This unit originally consists of writers, associate producer and director, and they carry the

development of the story through its various stages of synopsis, treatment and scripting, always submitting the results of the various stages of progression to the producer for his overall approval. (ibid.)

At Ealing, eight associate producers, eight directors and six scriptwriters were usually working on different projects at the same time, with a few key senior editors, cameramen and art directors also on long-term contracts. Clarke notes how this method of retaining key staff not only ensured their loyalty but facilitated collaboration and cross-pollination of ideas:

> All of us were on a permanent salary, which left us free of worry between productions … . Not that security meant a lot to us in our comparative youth; what we appreciated far more was the fact that we were a working community rather than a heterogeneous collection of individuals brought together for one job and then summarily disbanded. This made it possible for us to get really well acquainted; to recognise who might best be approached for help with a problem foxing one's own particular team knowing it would be given willingly and conscientiously. (1974: 140)

At a weekly 'round table', the producers, writers and directors would discuss new ideas and the progress of projects in development in a very open way, with ideas either rejected or selected for further work. According to Monja Danischewsky,

> The committee system worked well. Generally we all liked each other, were mostly good friends outside the studio and various projects were not regarded as competitive; so we read each other's scripts and kicked in with our suggestions and contributions to all the films. (1966: 135)

He relates how the crew would frequent the local pub the Red Lion, without Balcon, often to let off steam and complain about the boss, exclaiming, 'I'm going to tell Mick tomorrow – straight to his face – if that's what he wants, he can find himself another boy' (ibid.: 136). Clarke notes the importance of the pub as a place to debate, away from Balcon, and to further develop ideas: 'Many an Ealing film was influenced by the candid exchanges of opinion which took place out of working hours in the bar of the Red Lion opposite the studio gates' (1974: 140).

Ealing, unlike the majority of studios, developed many original stories; only about 25 per cent of its films were adaptations of novels or plays. Most screenplays went through at least four drafts before the final shooting script and would be thoroughly analysed by Balcon and MacPhail 'for points of characterisation, dialogue, motivation and clarity of development' (Ellis 1975: 96). All the senior staff at Ealing would take part in the development of ideas; director Henry Cornelius, for example,

The round table at Ealing Studios, used for meetings and frequently referred to by writers and directors who worked there originally thought of the idea for *Hue and Cry* (1946) as a vehicle for the actor Harry Fowler; Clarke then wrote the script which went on to be directed by Charles Crichton.

THE WRITERS AT EALING

This section looks at the most prolific writers at Ealing, focusing on Angus MacPhail and T. E. B. Clarke, with reference to the screenplays and correspondence held in the T. E. B. Clarke and Balcon Collections, concluding with discussion of the development notes on *Passport to Pimlico* (1949) and an analysis of the screenplay of *The Lavender Hill Mob* (1951).

Charles Barr argues that the writers at Ealing were not as important to the studio ethos as the six main directors, with the sole exception of T. E. B. Clarke, who helped to create the post-war image of Ealing, his films such as *Passport to Pimlico* and *The Blue Lamp*, assisting in Ealing's transition from World War II to post-war England (1998: 82). Yet other writers, particularly Angus MacPhail and John Dighton, were also vital to the studio and their contributions made a significant stamp on the films produced there.

John Dighton was an established playwright as well as being credited with seventeen scripts while at Ealing, though very little is known about his background. Dighton had worked for Gaumont-British and Warner, penning films for comic actors Will Hay and George Formby in the 1940s as well as the screenplays *Kind Hearts and Coronets* (1949) and *The Man in the White Suit* (1952) for Ealing. He received an Academy Award nomination for both *The Man in the White Suit* and *Roman Holiday* (1953) the following year before moving to Hollywood.

Roger MacDougall is credited with six screenplays for Ealing; not including the uncredited *The Foreman Went to France* (1942). Often collaborating with his cousin, director Alexander Mackendrick, the two set up their own production company in 1942, specialising in propaganda shorts. MacDougall wrote many other screenplays besides those scripted at Ealing and enjoyed a successful career as a playwright, moving into television in the mid- 1950s.

Diana Morgan is credited with six Ealing scripts. She was the sole female writer based there and, although women were occasionally employed on a short-term basis, she was the only one to stay as a house writer. Houston reflects that the studio cultivated an anti-female atmosphere and Morgan recalls that they 'used to say "We'll send in the Welsh bitch to put in the nausea"' (Houston 1992: 33). She relates how some women left the studio in tears, put off by the boys' school atmosphere in which women were just about tolerated (ibid.).

Morgan is perhaps best known as one of the writers credited with *Went the Day Well?*, a film about a British village that is taken over by the Nazis during the war. The film is very loosely based on a short magazine story by Graham Greene, originally only a few columns long. There were rumours that Greene had also worked on the script and Penelope Houston surmises that Greene and director Alberto Cavalcanti may have collaborated on story ideas but that the project was probably shelved in its early stages (ibid.). The Ealing house writers Angus MacPhail and John Dighton inherited the screenplay, retaining the basic idea but constructing a new narrative that portrayed the villagers in a more positive way. Brought in to improve the characters, Morgan considered MacPhail good with ideas but not with dialogue:

> I went over and found this script which was almost ready to be done … and it was unplayable … .
> They knew it was, and that's why they sent for me. It was all a fearful muddle. The story was there, the action was there, but the people weren't. They were just names. And what I really did was make them into parts for the actors and make them actable scenes. (ibid.: 1992: 18)

Angus MacPhail (left), head of the scenario department at Ealing Studios, with the studio head, Michael Balcon

Morgan was also called on to rewrite a number of scenes during shooting but points out that Ealing's script credits were often inaccurate: 'Sometimes you got a credit for something you hadn't done, or you had written most of the picture and didn't get a credit. We didn't worry about things like that' (Houston 1992: 33).

Monja Danischewsky is credited with authorship of four films at Ealing between 1943 and 1954, while also working on other scripts that were shelved. Originally employed as head of publicity, Danischewsky wanted to try scriptwriting and Balcon gave him the chance to work on a film called *Undercover* (1943), with the far more experienced John Dighton. He researched the story, about guerrilla fighters in Yugoslavia, passing the facts on to Dighton, who then created the screenplay. Script development was difficult due to changes in politics and, as Danischewsky explains, 'It was an assignment the completion of which drove me back gratefully to my publicity desk' (1966: 151).

Angus MacPhail worked for Balcon for more than twenty-five-years, first at Gainsborough in 1926, then moving with Balcon to Gaumont-British and finally, Ealing. Little has been written about MacPhail, apart from Charles Drazin's chapter in *The Finest Years* and Martin Stollery's useful short outline of his career on Screenonline.[2] Letters in the Adrian Brunel and Michael Balcon Collections held at the BFI reveal MacPhail's complex and, at times, difficult relationship with the producer.

MacPhail's career in the industry began under the pioneering director Adrian Brunel from the early to mid-1920s, when his talent for comedy and inventing jokes and puns became apparent. Brunel sums up these powers in the introduction to MacPhail's short article, 'Film Writing':

> As a scenario editor Mr. MacPhail is the perfect listener, an executive who knows what he is talking about (and says it brilliantly), and, above all a skilled diplomat. Occupying one of the most important positions in the British film-production industry, he has had much occasion for exercising this rare combination of qualities, plus his rich sense of humour as you will observe. (Brunel 1936: 194)

MacPhail's sense of humour is evident in the following extract from the article, in which he wittily, and cynically, describes the role of the scriptwriter with regard to original screenplays:

> An original screen story is the work of a man who is too idealistic, too stupid or too lazy to realise that he could make more money – and, incidentally, secure a more faithful communication of his ideas – by writing his story as a novel or a play: afterwards selling the film rights at an immensely exaggerated figure. (ibid.)

Many Ealing films were improved by MacPhail's sense of story and knowledge of plot and structure. Martin Stollery argues that MacPhail's contributions frequently went unacknowledged, citing the fact that he received no credit for the screenplay of Hitchcock's *The Man Who Knew Too Much* (1934). MacPhail worked on a number of other scripts for Hitchcock including the adaptation of *Spellbound* (1945) and it is likely that he devised the term 'Maguffin' usually attributed to Hitchcock (Drazin 1998: 89).

As head of the scenario department at Gainsborough, MacPhail had an influential role on the type of films developed. Letters between the two men in the Balcon Collection yield a fascinating account of his time there, and provide examples of his acerbic critiquing of a story, as in this example of an idea that interested Hitchcock: 'I cannot understand why Alfred Hitchcock should be keen on either this subject or 'Sally Who?' when there is such a large number of potential vehicles for Miss Mathews' (Balcon 28/6/33).

In his role as story editor MacPhail would often consider whether a script would be suitable as a star vehicle: in a letter to Balcon he comments, 'You asked me to report on "Juggernaut" .... This story is certainly worth consideration as a possible vehicle for Boris Karloff' (Balcon 30/3/33).

MacPhail expected Balcon to be involved in the decision-making process regarding which scripts should be developed: 'Herewith Mr. Macfarlane's draft outline for the story "Men without Work". I thought you would wish to read it in this form so that we may know whether in general it expresses the idea you had in mind' (Balcon 19/6/33).

The occasional friction in the relationship between the two can be seen in a letter to MacPhail, in which Balcon deplores the fact that the studio did not present a united front:

> You would do me a great favour if you did not write such letters in the future. I can never quite make out what your idea is – are you trying to prove to other people that you can never be wrong? … I know how satisfactory your judgement is … I am not concerned as to what Mr. Rowson thinks of studio matters, but your letter must lead him to believe that there are serious differences of opinion between us. From my own point of view this does not matter but I think you are being unfair to others. (Balcon 30/3/33)

Later, while at Gaumont-British, MacPhail indicates he lacked confidence in his ability to produce what Balcon wanted, thinking it time to strike out on his own. His letter to Balcon elucidates:

> I wanted to write and tell you how very much I've appreciated your arranging for me to have a trial with MGM. The sorry truth is that I know now I am unable to supply the kind of work you require …. Incidentally it's high time I stopped sheltering behind you from the stormy blast. Getting along on my own may teach me a thing or two. (Balcon 31/5/37)

MacPhail often felt under-appreciated and dissatisfied with his position in the studios, keen as he was to be a writer rather than scenario editor. He complains to Balcon about others receiving preferential treatment:

> If by any chance the firm wants to retain my services beyond this date, I'd like to negotiate as a writer and not as a so-called Scenario Editor. Since you clearly consider Sidney worth better treatment and

more money than myself, it's absurd that I should have to shoulder the responsibility for what he writes; the situation made doubly absurd by the existence of Mr Gordon as Super Scenario Editor at a, no doubt, enormously higher salary. (ibid.)

Despite MacPhail's unhappiness in the position of scenario editor, he exercised a great deal of influence during his time at Ealing, with Barr arguing he was as important as the director Cavalcanti (1998: 43). Rarely given sole credit as writer, MacPhail worked with others developing ideas, improving the story and adding dialogue to many more screenplays than he is credited on. Described by T. E. B. Clarke as looking more like an Oxbridge don than a screenwriter, MacPhail's input was invaluable:

His filmic knowledge was encyclopaedic and his memory so good that he could find a parallel in almost any suggested story situation. This made him, as a writer, rather too prone to rely on film clichés, but it equipped him to be a marvellous scenario editor. (1974: 149)

Another colleague assesses MacPhail's extraordinary skills:

Every story Angus read fell into that sharp, well-stored mind as a collection of technical scripting problems that had to be solved, more or less expertly, in a number of previous movies. It was of course disconcerting, not to say humbling, to find that a story-line one had conceived as distinctly, exquisitely one's own had a film-ancestry reaching back to the industry's earliest days. (Drazin 1998: 94)

MacPhail though could be hard on those with less talent, as Clarke notes, 'Angus was severe on slipshod work by a writer. A bad line or a fatuous suggestion would make him clutch his head and bawl for his mother' (1974: 150).

MacPhail's output at Ealing was wide-ranging, from comedy such as *The Goose Steps Out* to drama in *Went the Day Well?*, both made in 1942; the first a vehicle for the popular comedian, Tommy Trinder, the latter written with Diana Morgan. *Champagne Charlie* (1944) is an entertaining and popular musical credited to three writers, including MacPhail, featuring sharp, witty dialogue, a particular hallmark of his style. MacPhail's last writing credits at Ealing were in 1949, for the comedy *Whisky Galore* and a drama in four parts, *Train of Events*, the former proving a big hit both in the UK and abroad, going on to become Ealing's most successful film.

MacPhail's talents as a script editor and advisor were in great demand throughout his life and his contribution to the story and style of Ealing's films unquestionable. He was full of contradictions; he was a talented gag writer yet gleaned little satisfaction from his work as a scenario editor. MacPhail had a drink problem and retired early, leaving Ealing in 1949. He only worked occasionally after that and was employed by Hitchcock to develop the screenplay for *The Wrong Man* (1955), where he was apparently often too drunk to work. He died in 1962 aged only fifty-nine.

T. E. B. *'Tibby' Clarke* began his career as a journalist in Fleet Street, writing humorous features, before joining the police force in World War II, where he gained the experience that made his screenplay for *The Blue Lamp* so convincing. The film was a huge success and, when adapted for television as the series *Dixon of Dock Green* (1955–76), ran for twenty years.

T. E. B. Clarke, writer of many of the most popular Ealing comedies

Clarke joined Ealing in 1943 on a three-month trial at £15 a week. While there, he developed a close working relationship with directors Basil Dearden and Charles Crichton; of the fifteen films he wrote at Ealing, six were directed by Dearden and seven by Crichton. Clarke authored two of the studios' most famous films, *Passport to Pimlico*, nominated for an Academy Award for Best Screenplay and *The Lavender Hill Mob*, which won the Academy Award for Best Screenplay. Indeed, Barr considers the body of work produced by Clarke while at the studios to be so influential as to afford him the status of an auteur (1998: 98).

Clarke's original screenplays made up a significant part of the group of films termed 'Ealing comedy' after the release of the three major triumphs, *Passport to Pimlico*, *Whisky Galore* and *Kind Hearts and Coronets*. The Ealing stable boasted a number of talented comedy writers besides Clarke, including John Dighton, William Rose, Michael Pertwee, Robert Hamer and Henry Cornelius, making the fifteen comedies produced in the post-war period not such a surprising output.

Balcon believed that the secret to the popularity of the Ealing comedies was that the 'unconventional characters went about their daily tasks against a realistic background' (1969: 158), and that the films were reflective of post-war society:

> The country was tired of regulations and regimentation, and there was a mild anarchy in the air. In a sense our comedies were a reflection of this mood … a safety valve for our more anti-social impulses. Who has not wanted to raid a bank (*The Lavender Hill Mob*) … make the bureaucrat bite the dust (*Passport to Pimlico* and *The Titfield Thunderbolt*). (ibid.: 159)

As Balcon noted, the stories followed a particular pattern:

> Our theory of comedy – if we had one – was ludicrously simple. We took a character – or group of characters – and then let him or them run up against an apparently insoluble problem, with the audience hoping that a way out could be found, which it usually was. The comedy lay in how the characters did get around their problem … .(1969: 158)[3]

Indeed Tim O'Sullivan describes the Ealing comedies as 'conservative daydreams, suggesting Clarke's scripts contained narratives of 'relatively gentle, comic disruption and disorder …' (2012: 71).

The first film Clarke worked on was *The Halfway House* (1944), a script-doctoring assignment at which he did well enough to gain Balcon's trust and be asked to do script rewrites on other films. The first comedy Clarke penned for Ealing was *Hue and Cry* (1947). The director, Henry Cornelius, had asked that Clarke help develop the story idea. Clarke submitted a fifteen-page outline that impressed both Cornelius and Charles Crichton but it was eventually given to Crichton to direct. Balcon judged the film risky and unconventional, insisting it be made on a low budget (Barr 1974: 156). In fact, the film, about a group of children who foil the plans of a master criminal, was a box-office success and easily recovered its production costs.

THE T. E. B. CLARKE COLLECTION
Passport to Pimlico

Henry Cornelius was keen to collaborate with Clarke again, with the writer developing ideas for him to direct. The resulting screenplay tapped into the zeitgeist of a people who had had enough of rationing and post-war restrictions. Cornelius mentioned to Clarke that out-of-date statutes and laws might produce some interesting comedy for their next film. Clarke was further inspired after reading a news item about Princess Juliana of the Netherlands:

> Exiled in Canada after the occupation of the country, she was expecting a baby; had this been a
> boy he would have become heir to the throne of Holland, yet there would inevitably have been a
> constitutional crisis, for according to Dutch law the heir had necessarily to be born on Dutch soil.
> (1974: 159).

The Dutch government resolved the problem by passing an act of parliament decreeing that the room where the birth took place was to become Dutch soil. Clarke's continued research revealed that it was quite common for an exiled monarch to have his or her residence declared part of their kingdom. He then transferred the story to the restrictions of post-war London, realising any extraterrestrial rights would mean that the land was foreign soil and its citizens could not be rationed. His research also found that 'the old state of Burgundy met my requirements almost to perfection' (ibid.: 160), because its last ruler, Charles the Bold, had fled to England and been granted asylum in what is now part of Pimlico.

Cornelius liked the story and pushed for a realistic treatment, pointing out:

> if it were suddenly discovered that these studios had been technically part of Burgundy for the last
> five centuries, some people might try to be funny by visiting the wardrobe department and coming
> out dressed in medieval costume. I don't believe we'd laugh would we? What would make us laugh
> would be an emergency meeting of the works committee to sort out whether the union was still
> responsible to the TUC. (ibid.)

Balcon was initially critical of the script for *Passport to Pimlico*, pointing out that it was 'too long, uneconomical and overwritten' (Drazin 1998: 110). But Clarke declares of the film, 'I personally believe it was the best plot I ever invented' (1974: 160). Interestingly, Barr believes that *Passport to Pimlico* is most typical of Ealing, but not the best 'because its writer, Clarke, is so completely the film's author. To an unusual extent, the film is *there* in its script, not least in the very rich and full descriptions ... of how each character looks, thinks and behaves' (1998: 98).

The archive content on *Passport to Pimlico* includes a six-page story outline, a detailed treatment of ninety-seven pages and a shooting script (S202) as well as detailed notes relating to script revisions, which lend a fascinating insight into the screenplay development process.

The script notes, probably by Balcon, include references to writers besides Clarke involved in the script development; author Monica Dickens, for instance, is often mentioned. The author begins with a point about the purpose of the notes, 'I have collated them in script order as they may be useful to all sorts of people in the course of production and a reminder to myself.'

Suggestions for changes are made scene by scene, focusing on strengthening the story, tightening the script and enhancing the visual aspect, while developing comedy and character. The first page asks for changes to

> the main descriptions of the characters in the new Draft Script which will give it a feeling of freshness. They should be mainly based on the agreed conception of characters as discussed after the suggestions made by Monica Dickens.

The involvement of other writers such as Dickens does question Barr's notion of Clarke as an auteur, though there is no indication as to what the suggested changes were or indeed if they were incorporated into the screenplay.

There are numerous references to trimming and tightening the script to avoid repetition, for instance, the 'Town Hall' section is marked for deletion and the library scene for editing, with the explanation that 'The whole scene should be trimmed considerably and we should rigidly avoid making points which would then again be repeated in the Coroner's Court.'

The notes comment on instances of overwriting, and of the scene with the general meeting, advise 'We should lose almost one half.' Also emphasised is the need for scenes to be more tightly paced and more visual; for example, 'Faster and *more visual*. I think we could forget the somewhat pedantic idea that each person's actions must be directly caused by his having heard the previous person.'

The structure of the film comes under discussion, but in less detail than might be expected; though page numbers are referred to as a way of breaking down and keeping track of the story, which indicates that target times were set for certain events: 'I have a strong feeling that we should arrive at this point of the film with no more than 35/40 pages.'

Character development is a regular subject; the character of Burrows, the academic who declares Pimlico to be part of Burgundy, becomes female, played by Margaret Rutherford in the film: The notes suggest:

> She should be a Dame e.g. Dame Gertrude Burrows, D.B.E. M.A. (History) ... I think she should wear very masculine clothes, porkpie hat, brogue shoes, tweeds etc. Refer to herself and introduce herself always as 'Burrows is the name' never as 'Dame Gertrude'.

There is also an example of how she might behave and talk:

> She might arrive late and out of breath for the inquest with profuse apologies and this line: I was delayed – an exhumation in Biggleswade, so tiresome. Remains of a Plantagenet Courtier and a very slipshod job at that. They only sent for me after they'd messed it up themselves, but then they always do. Now, about this matter etc ... .

Changes are proposed to the pompous bureaucrat played by Basil Radford, who is characterised as 'anxious to have as much contrast as possible between official jargon (recited parrot fashion) and racy, private-life conversation'. The notes include some possible lines of description and dialogue:

> He holds his hand over the mouthpiece and speaks to an unseen colleague.
>
> GREGG
> He said 'Don't talk bilge', old man! (into phone) But my dear sir,
> don't you read your White Papers? I should advise you to get in
> touch with Mr. Pringle of the Law Officers' Department.
> Telephone number? My dear sir, how should I know?

The need for realism is often stressed, 'we should contrive the feeling that the realism of "this is Burgundy" once it has started is carried on right into the snowball and to the pub'.

There is advice on how to create a clearer visual picture and make the scene description more vivid, for instance: 'Outside Arthur's shop; A garden hammock, quantities of hideous Victorian furniture, mirrors with prices whitewashed on, washstand complete with jug and basin right on the pavement – very dusty, religious pictures and bedside mottoes'.

The notes highlight the importance of visual touches; in one instance, regarding 'Connie's pot plant', the comment counsels: 'I think we should go through the script and find about three or four places where Connie could do some little thing to her plants. What there is already is not quite enough.' In another example, the notes propose using the cat to demonstrate the difficulties presented by the new border fencing between England and Burgundy:

> I don't see how a cat would get imprisoned in the wire. But I think that if the
> constable and Shirley were talking near the gate through the wire there might be a
> saucer of milk on the English side and a cat on the Burgundian side. The constable
> could open the gate, pick up the cat and bring it through to the saucer of milk and
> shut the gate, leaving the cat drinking the milk.

Extra visual and comedic touches are proffered: for instance, when the Burgundians are under siege and only saved from starvation by food being thrown over the border fence, the notes detail that 'somebody is throwing over circular French rolls; Cowan is catching them hoop-la fashion – on a walking stick', while 'Two old housewives are holding out a sheet and catching a load of the stuff which is flying over; as firemen catch people who jump from a burning building.'

The need to enhance the comedy and satire in the story is highlighted, with a proposal that the script emphasise the problem in feeding the cats and dogs, also victims of the siege:

> A carrier pigeon arrives, with a note. Wix unrolls the note. It reads:
> 'Dog biscuits arriving tomorrow STOP signed Mayor of Barking!'

The importance of satire is often stressed, with one note reading 'I would also still like to retain some posters (either home-made Burgundian posters satirising well-known English ones or

English ones adapted for Burgundian home conditions)', and in another instance, 'Try and keep the satire on No.10 with people outside and the cat being left out.'

The detailed script notes collate and compare the treatment and drafts of the screenplay, pointing out if a previous version is better. They are particularly valuable in helping to understand better Ealing Studios' approach to the screenplay development process.

The Lavender Hill Mob

The idea for the film began when Balcon asked Clarke to develop a crime story about the theft of gold bullion on the River Thames, to be called *Pool of London*. Clarke changed the story's focus completely, transforming it into a comedy, having been inspired by the idea of stolen gold being moulded into models of the Eiffel Tower, shipped to France and sold to tourists. This line of thought evolved into a plot involving the central character becoming a Bank of England employee who decides to steal the gold.

Clarke presented the story as a 500-word outline to Balcon, who 'exploded' as he was expecting to read a treatment for *Pool of London*.[4] But, as Clarke explains, a few hours later Balcon called him back,

> 'I've been reading this outline of yours', he said as though we were meeting for the first time that day. 'You know I believe we have a promising idea for a comedy here. Go away and get on with it.' (1974: 166)

Clarke's account of the research and how he adapted the story to his findings at the bullion department of the Bank of England is fascinating.[5]

The Lavender Hill Mob collection includes a short story outline of eight pages, a treatment of nineteen pages (Item 2.a) and two drafts of the screenplay, a fourth draft, dated 18 August 1950 (2.b) and a shooting script dated 15 September1950 (2.c). The plot in the short outline is very similar to that in the fourth draft script, apart from the way in which Holland, a bank employee, meets Pendlebury. In the outline, Pendlebury is a client at the bank, whereas in the script he is a new arrival at the boarding house. Certain details about the robbery are changed; in the outline, Holland attempts to embezzle £10,000 to pay Pendlebury for his business of making models of the Eiffel Tower, but the plan fails when 'there is a surprise inspection of the books and he has to return the money'. Pendlebury is annoyed and Holland agrees to take him on as a partner in his plan to steal the gold bullion. The screenplay's version of their initial meeting is more believable because it happens in their private lives, with a gradual transition to their becoming partners in crime.

Fourth draft – 18 August 1950

Clarke's fourth draft is an entertaining read; the writing is fluent, the description vivid and the situations and dialogue often very funny. The two central characters, Holland and Pendlebury, are ordinary men placed in an extraordinary situation and, while it is their 'greed' that precipitates their downfall, this 'fault' is made understandable because we witness the contrast between the wealth of the bank and their dull and frugal lifestyles.

The screenplay begins by cleverly introducing the protagonist, Holland, as a 'fish out of water', creating an element of mystery as to why he is paying a bill in a smart café in Rio de Janeiro:

The cashier looks across the room. All at once his guarded look gives way to a gleaming smile.

CASHIER
Ah!

He cashes the cheque without further ado, counting out a huge pile of notes on the plate. CAMERA TRACKS with the waiter as he carries the money to a table at which two Englishmen are seated side by side. The one in the dark suit, GREGORY is the burly, affable, pipe-smoking type. The other man, HOLLAND, looks even more out of place than his companion in these exotic surroundings; despite his white drill suit and his sophisticated manner, he has an appearance of suburban respectability more in keeping with the 8.15 to London Bridge. (D4: 1)

This intriguing, imaginative introduction to the character of Holland makes him seem an unlikely master criminal.

In the following extract, the two scenes contrast Holland's meagre weekly salary as a bank employee with the bank's vast wealth, and mitigate his motivation to carry out the heist:

EXT. ENTRANCE TO BULLION YARD. BANK OF ENGLAND. DAY

The iron gate leading into the Bullion Yard at the Bank of England is being opened to admit the van.

HOLLAND (voice)
Nobody could say that my precautions were not fully justified.
On many a Friday afternoon I entered the Bank of England with
bullion to the value of half a million pounds …

The van moves in.

EXT. MAIN ENTRANCE. BANK OF ENGLAND. DAY

Employees of the Bank are streaming out after the day's work. HOLLAND is among them. He is in the act of opening a pay envelope and taking out a few notes.

HOLLAND (voice)
… and nobody except me saw the irony of my exit an hour later with
a salary of eight pounds, fifteen shillings, less deductions. (ibid.: 7)

The script features many comic and ironic touches; for instance, when Holland reads an American crime novel to the old lady at the lodging house, this acts as a reminder of his own situation:

Holland's eyes return to the page.

HOLLAND (reading)
'I wanted that money bad. Right now there wasn't a guy in town
with a better use for that ten thousand shekels …'

Again his eyes wander from the book as he goes into a brief reverie. The bell rings
once more.

MRS CHALK (looking up impatiently)
Mr. Holland – you're not concentrating.

HOLLAND (returning to earth)
I'm sorry … (reading) 'Right now there wasn't a guy in town with
a better use for that ten thousand shekels …'

The front door knocker is rapped impatiently. HOLLAND puts down the book and
gets up.

HOLLAND
Miss Evesham must be upstairs.

He walks out of the room.

HOLLAND (voice)
Little did I realise that this was the opportunity knocking for me
at last … (ibid.: 9)

Besides the verbal association with Holland's want – the gold bullion – the scene neatly alerts
us to the fact that a new person is about to enter Holland's life. Pendlebury knocks at the door
and will become the enabler who facilitates Holland's achievement of his goal.

Economically told, the story cuts elegantly from one scene to the next; for instance, in the
transition from the boarding house to the factory, where Holland and Pendlebury begin to hatch
their plan, the way that they evolve from barely knowing each other to becoming partners in
crime is subtly portrayed, Pendlebury planting the idea that, if they do nothing, they will have
to live with their regrets:

Of all sad words of tongue or pen,
The saddest are these 'It might have been' (ibid.: 13)

The carefully handled release of information demonstrates both men to be in similar situations
and, with a superbly written series of scenes climaxing on their mutual realisation that they
really are considering a bank robbery:

HOLLAND
Say one had a means of melting the stuff down …

> PENDLEBURY
> Ah, but one wouldn't.

HOLLAND frowns, giving vent to his exasperation in an increase of leaf-plucking.

> HOLLAND
> Unless, of course, he took on a partner.

He resumes his pacing as PENDLEBURY turns at last from his work.

> PENDLEBURY
> Risky bringing other people in.

He puts down his mallet and chisel, gets up and stands looking out of the window.

> HOLLAND
> That would be essential in any case. No one man could rob our
> van unaided.

> PENDLEBURY
> He'd need accomplices?

> HOLLAND
> Precisely. A gang.

The scene ends with a description which builds up to the reveal that they are no longer just talking hypothetically:

> PENDLEBURY
> By Jove, Holland, it's a good thing we two are honest men!

HOLLAND echoes his laugh.

> HOLLAND
> It is indeed, Pendlebury!

There is a longer silence. Gradually, their eyes meet – and each knows the other isn't really joking. (ibid.: 17)

Learning that he is to be promoted within the week and thus will no longer travel in the van carrying the gold, Holland realises that he has no choice but to take action. This is the trigger point that forces him to make a decision.

An entertaining complication involves the two men's initially unsuccessful attempts to find crooks to help in the robbery. Only when they talk loudly on the underground about the contents of the safe in Pendlebury's office, mentioning the address, do they procure accomplices. They are overheard by three criminals who turn up at the factory and become their partners in crime.

Much of the humour and, later on, the pathos of the script derive from the dramatic irony in the screenplay. After Holland has planned the robbery, his boss at the bank, Turner, explains to the head cashier that there is no point in promoting Holland because:

> TURNER
> I'm afraid it wouldn't work, sir. His one and only virtue is his
> honesty. He has no initiative, sir, no imagination. (ibid.: 18)

A little later, after the robbery has been planned, Holland talks to Turner about holidaying in Paris before he takes up his promotion. The city is also where they intend to take the gold.

> TURNER
> Abercrombie tells me you're taking your fortnight's holiday before
> joining him.

> HOLLAND
> Yes, sir. I'm planning to go to Paris.

> TURNER (with a patronising smile)
> Paris, eh? You're stepping out, Holland? Wonderful, isn't it what
> a bit of extra money will do?

> HOLLAND
> Yes, sir. It's going to make a big difference to me. (ibid.: 34)

Holland's wry understatement enhances the dramatic irony.

The complications begin in earnest once the robbery goes into action; all seems to be going smoothly until Pendlebury accidentally picks up a painting and is accused of theft. This event leads to further complications, which finely balance the humour and tension, building up to the arrest of Pendlebury and the anxiety about whether this will foil their scheme. Further tension is created between the crooks and Holland as events escalate out of control, with the robbers being chased by the police. While much comedy derives from Holland being tied up by the crooks and having to act as though he has been roughly treated:

> HOLLAND tries in desperation to tear by himself the handful of shirt which SHORTY
> pulled out, but finds that his hands are too tightly secured for him to get a grip on it.
> He blunders around the room, groping for something to help him. He discovers a
> hook on the wall, manages to force the piece of shirt over it, then pushes against the
> wall with his foot. For a moment the material perversely holds out, then it gives way
> with a satisfactory tearing sound. Holland falls on his back, gets up quickly and
> gropes again for the hook. This time he forces a piece of his waistcoat over it,
> and again starts pushing himself away from the wall. (ibid.: 47)

NEW 53

C.100 INT. M.S. CHARGE ROOM. POLICE STATION. PENDLEBURY, CLAYTON,
STATION SERGEANT AND POLICEMAN. DAY (STUDIO)

The Charge Room at the local police station. A counter with
a flap in the middle runs along that side of the room which
gives out on to the street. At the back of the room is a
door leading to Inspector Farrow's office. In the middle
of the room is a statuesque group composed of PENDLEBURY,
who stands before a desk, looking downcast, but determined;
the STATION SERGEANT, seated at the desk, with the charge
book open before him; the POLICEMAN who caught PENDLEBURY
is beside him; CLAYTON sits on a chair behind the group.
There is no sound but the scratching of the Sergeant's pen
as he writes in the book. CLAYTON can bear the silence no
longer. He jumps up irritably and strides over to the desk.

                    CLAYTON
              Three pictures in a week I've missed from
              there...

                    STATION SERGEANT
              You can't accuse him of taking those
              others, too.

                    PENDLEBURY
              I should hope not! I'm no thief, officer.
              My character is an open book...

He breaks off, aghast, as the door opens.

C.101 INT. M.S. CHARGE ROOM. POLICE STATION. PENDLEBURY, CLAYTON,
STATION SERGEANT, POLICEMAN, HOLLAND, TALBOT AND ROSE.
DAY. (STUDIO)

Shooting towards the door. HOLLAND, dripping and dishevelled,
is coming into the police station with TALBOT and ROSE. He
has been thoroughly shaken by his experience and each of the
two POLICEMEN has a hand under his elbow to support him,
which makes it appear to PENDLEBURY that he has been brought
in under arrest. PAN as he is led through the flap in the
counter and behind the group at the charge desk. HOLLAND
looks at his partner with silent commiseration as he is
conducted through the room to the door of Farrow's office.

C.102 INT. C.S. CHARGE ROOM. POLICE STATION. PENDLEBURY. DAY
                                                    (STUDIO)

PENDLEBURY interprets Holland's quick look as a confirmation
of his suspicions. He stares in dismay towards the door.

                    STATION SERGEANT (off)
              Well?

C.103 INT. M.S. CHARGE ROOM. POLICE STATION. PENDLEBURY, CLAYTON,
SERGEANT, POLICEMAN. DAY (STUDIO)

CAMERA SHOOTING from the office door towards the group.
The SERGEANT is waiting for PENDLEBURY to continue his
statement. But in Pendlebury's mind a landslide has
developed. He sinks down on to a bench in the background.
His accusers are gathered ominously in foreground.
PENDLEBURY takes his head in his hands.

C.104 INT. M.C.S. CHARGE ROOM POLICE STATION. SERGEANT AND POLICEMAN.
DAY (STUDIO)

They wait for PENDLEBURY to speak. After a moment the
SERGEANT raises his head and looks over at him.

Misadventure in an extract from the screenplay
The Lavender Hill Mob (1951), written by T. E. B. Clarke

The end to this section is carefully crafted, with each thinking the other has been arrested: parallel events intersect, meaning that neither Holland nor Pendlebury is sure what has happened. In fact, both men are free and the charges against Pendlebury dropped, while the police have rescued Holland from the Thames. The last scene in the sequence reveals the truth and movingly reunites the two when Pendlebury returns to see if the police have raided their lodgings, believing Holland to be in custody:

INT. ENTRANCE HALL. BALMORAL. DAY

The front door opens quietly and Pendlebury puts his head furtively around it. Finding the coast clear, he comes in and tip-toes through the hall. Suddenly he stiffens and comes to a frightened stop at the sound of footsteps ascending the basement stairs. The next moment his face changes from alarm to incredulity, and then stupefied delight.

Cut to reverse angle. Holland stands at the top of the basement stairs gaping at Pendlebury with precisely the same expression. He has a bottle of beer in each hand, and he is wearing a pair of blue police trousers, several sizes too large for him, and a white singlet on which appear the words METROPOLITAN POLICE SPORTS CLUB.

For several seconds the two stand staring at each other with unbelieving eyes; then, moving by a simultaneous impulse powerful enough to submerge their racial instincts, they rush together and joyously embrace. (ibid.: 53)

The first half of the screenplay revolves around the question 'Will they commit the robbery?', while the second half asks 'Will they be found out?'. Holland is the sympathetic hero of the film and, once the robbery has been committed, we root for him to achieve his goal and keep the gold.

Holland and Pendlebury now have to go to Paris to collect the gold. The story no longer needs the crooks and, to allow the focus to fall fully on the two protagonists, ways are found to let them go: Lackery's wife won't let him go to Paris, and, perhaps even less likely, Shorty elects to stay and watch the test match (ibid.: 59–60). A more serious drama would have demanded stronger reasons for their decisions, and be bound by the conventions of realism, whereas a comedy can break these conventions more readily.

By the time of their departure, Holland and Pendlebury have gone through a transformation and taken on new names and identities:

HOLLAND
Good-night, Miss Evesham. Good-night, Pendlebury.

A thought occurs to him. It is sufficiently important for him to leave his door and come back to Pendlebury.

HOLLAND
Or may I call you Alfred?

Pendlebury looks quite moved.

> PENDLEBURY
> Call me Al … . And I will call you – Henry, isn't it?

> HOLLAND
> A name I never cared for. Call me Dutch.

> PENDLEBURY (nodding gravely)
> Good-night, Dutch.

> HOLLAND
> Good-night – Al.

They shake hands solemnly. (ibid.: 62)

The scene also solidifies the partnership between the men and their removal from the life they have previously led, into a new world – the criminal one.

The sequence ends on a literal high note: on arrival in Paris all seems well; Holland and Pendlebury stand at the top of the Eiffel Tower; and everything has fallen into place:

TOP OF EIFFEL TOWER. DAY

Shooting down on to the platform of the tower. The lift doors open. Holland and Pendlebury are the only ones to emerge. They walk towards the balustrade, and as they do so, a great panorama of Paris comes into view. They stand alone, looking out and down. The whole world seems to lie below them. (ibid.: 63)

The sequence is elegantly and carefully plotted, as their high point is disrupted by the noisy arrival of a group of schoolgirls, which is also when their downfall begins. The plan goes disastrously wrong once they realise the schoolgirls are carrying gold Eiffel Tower ornaments from the souvenir shop, which were supposed to be in storage. The chase down the steps tragically sets up the duo's fall from grace:

EXT. SPIRAL STAIRCASE. EIFFEL TOWER. DAY

A fast-moving sequence covering the wild descent of the two panic-stricken men. Round bend after bend they come, panting, stumbling, staggering, sliding, all the time getting giddier and giddier. In the course of the above this dialogue:

> PENDLEBURY
> Who's going to know they're gold?

> HOLLAND
> We can't afford to take chances!

EXT. FOOT OF EIFFEL TOWER. DAY

Holland and Pendlebury come tottering down the last section of the spiral staircase
and reel drunkenly out to the street, where the last two girls of the party are in the act
of entering a couple of taxis. Pendlebury makes for the one taxi, his mouth opening
and closing convulsively as he tries to find his voice between gasps. The effort is too
much. He performs a final spin, loses his balance and subsides helplessly on the
pavement. Meanwhile, Holland has managed to stagger up to the second taxi,
almost equally breathless. He stands waving his arms and swaying.

HOLLAND
Wait! Wait! (ibid.: 65)

The downturn in the men's fortunes continues as they chase the girls to the quayside at
Calais. The rest of the sequence involves further thwarted attempts to reach the girls before they
board the boat for England. The sequence finishes on the two men watching the schoolgirls
from the quay, and serves to remind the reader there are six paperweights to retrieve, 'The
schoolgirls are spread along the rails waving good-bye to France. Six of them are flourishing
Eiffel Tower paper-weights' (ibid.: 69).

At this stage Clarke introduces a tenet of the classically written screenplay, 'What is the
worst possible thing that could happen to the central character(s)?' The script imaginatively
develops elements of humour and pathos as we see their dreams fall apart. The final sequence
shows the police closing in, first by finding the gang's getaway van, and then more literally
when Holland and Pendlebury take a wrong turn into a police training school. The tragicomic
events in this section show the situation becoming more and more hopeless, creating anxiety in
the reader as to whether the two will escape. The characters are in the worst possible place they
could be – a police crime convention – and this is compounded by there being a demonstration
of a working case, 'the big gold robbery', with Detective Farrow, the investigator, in attendance.
The coincidence may be huge but the plotting plunges the characters into increasingly desperate
circumstances, with the audience wondering if they can get out of them.

In the denouement and the ensuing chase through the police training school, the directions
in the screenplay are very explicit and followed almost to the word in the film. The whole of the
chase sequence is quite entertaining to read but, as in the film, slightly overlong. The finale
though, when Holland and Pendlebury are eventually trapped, elegantly brings together a
number of strands. The audience is led to think that the two men have evaded capture so that
the tension relaxes while the radio in the police car they have stolen plays 'Old Macdonald Had
a Farm', broadcast from the Scotland Yard switchboard. The tension is heightened again when,
suddenly, a policeman stops the car:

CITY POLICEMAN
Would you mind giving me a lift to the box, sir? They're flashing
for me.

He points along the street to where a light is flashing imperiously above a police box,
and steps onto the running board of the car. It moves on.

> CITY POLICEMAN (genially)
> Nice to have a bit of music while you're driving.

He sings in harmony with the choir from the loudspeaker.

> CITY POLICEMAN
> Yee-hi – yee-hi – o … we do that thing in our station choir … .
> All right sir – thank you.

The car has reached the police box. Pendlebury pulls up. The city policeman is just stepping down when the one thing that Holland and Pendlebury have been dreading occurs. The singing ends abruptly and is replaced by the voice of the Chief Wireless Operator at Scotland Yard.

> CHIEF WIRELESS OPERATOR (from loudspeaker):
> Hullo all cars from M2GW … Stolen police car is now known to
> be Q3 not Q4 …

Holland realises the game is up as the city policeman spins round.

> HOLLAND
> Quick, Al – out!

He opens the door on his side and scrambles out. The city policeman, still reacting to the message, sees the microphone that Holland abandoned and the metal plate with 'Q3' on it. He makes a dive at Pendlebury, who realises at the same moment that Holland in his panic has left his suitcase in the car. He snatches it up as the city policeman reaches him.

> PENDLEBURY
> Dutch! Dutch!

He flings the case out of the farther door. Holland catches it and flashes him a fleeting smile of gratitude as he starts running. The city policeman shouts to the passing public, holding firmly on to Pendlebury.

> CITY POLICEMAN
> Stop that man!

Holland disappears round the corner of an alley running alongside the Bank of England.

EXT. ALLEY. BANK OF ENGLAND. DAY

Holland comes dashing along the alley towards CAMERA. A second policeman, blowing his whistle, has started in pursuit.

EXT. MAIN ENTRANCE. BANK OF ENGLAND. DAY

Employees of the Bank are streaming out after the day's work. Holland, almost
out of breath, sees his big chance. He pulls up to a walk and mixes in with them.
His pursuer appears from the alley. A third city policeman dashes up. The two
policemen frantically scrutinise the crowd. Almost every other man is dressed
like Holland, and is carrying a small case. The policemen stand helplessly, baffled
while Holland, in the middle of the crowd, walks calmly into the entrance of the
Bank Underground Station and disappears from view down the steps.

HOLLAND'S VOICE
And instead of changing as usual at Charing Cross …

DISSOLVE:

INT. CAFE. RIO DE JANEIRO. DAY
(ibid.: 89–90)

The rhythm of the scene, the ramping up and easing of the tension is convincing; we
believe the two men are free, until the policeman asks for a lift. Luckily, he does not know the
car is stolen but, just as we think the two are free again he hears the Scotland Yard alert. There
appears to be no escape until Pendlebury offers some hope by throwing the suitcase to
Holland, who makes his bid for freedom. The focus is then on Holland and whether he will
be caught, the clever end to the scene allowing him to revert to his previous identity as an
anonymous bank clerk, disappearing into the crowd of men in suits.

The narrative narrows the options of the two men, as elements of cruel farce and coincidence
in the plot deliver them to the detective training school in Hendon and the potential end of
their dreams, in which only Holland escapes. The final twist, at the end of the last scene,
shows Holland handcuffed to a detective: he has to pay a price for his year of pleasure.

The book ending to the script reveals that, while Holland has been in Rio he has adopted a
new lifestyle, mixing with the elite. As he leaves, the British ambassador thanks him for his par-
ties, which have boosted British prestige. While the narrative may not suggest that crime pays,
Holland explains the price he will pay was worth it, as the proceeds from the robbery were:

HOLLAND (with a satisfied smile)
Enough to keep me for one year in the style to which I was
unaccustomed. (ibid.: 90)

The theme of changing identity is a central part of the narrative, creating a fantasy gangster world which becomes reality. Elegant descriptions and sophisticated plot, combined with
complex and believable characters and excellent dialogue, create drama and tension. The likeable protagonists attract the empathy of the reader/viewer, who root for them to succeed in
their quest, adding up to an engaging and effective screenplay.

The collection also holds a short article by Clarke, 'The Cinema' (Item 2.d) in which he
discusses the changes between the shooting script and the finished film. Clarke was told that

the shooting script was too long at 105 pages and needed to be cut back to ninety pages, a more suitable length for a comedy. Clarke notes this is when he had to, at least partly, lose control of the script:

> This was the stage – an all-too-familiar stage in scripting – when a conflict had to take place between my own personal desires and the more detached, more rational viewpoint of the director on the script as a whole. (Item 2.d)

The director and producer had to prioritise what should stay and this could mean sacrificing good scenes that did not move the story on in favour of scenes which 'might be inferior, but which were essential to the development of the plot'.

The notes demonstrate the continual process of refinement which occurs in script development, even once filming has begun. Clarke mentions as an example the police chase scene where a sand pit, found at the location, is introduced to enhance the comedy. 'As often happens when a screenwriter eventually sees what an accomplished director has made of his script, I watched the "rushes" of this scene wishing profoundly that I had thought of something like that during the writing of it' (ibid.: 3–4). Clarke also welcomed input from the actors; for instance, Alec Guinness worked on dialogue and character when reading the script and made 'suggestions that would never have occurred to us' (1974: 167).

Clarke recalls that the writing process for *The Lavender Hill Mob* was demanding, requiring many rewrites before everyone was happy with the script:

> it was not an easy script to write. One scene … had to be written and rewritten eleven times before it satisfied all concerned; and a really good climax eluded me through four or five versions of the screenplay. As with much of my work, the solution when it came was based on an actual happening … . As soon as I made Alec and Stanley steal a police car our final sequence promptly clicked. (ibid.)

He points out the need to stand back from a script and read it through in its entirety. Reading a draft of the *The Lavender Hill Mob*, he realised the tone lent an unintended menace to the central characters by aligning them with the 'real' criminals, leading him to alter this aspect.

Clarke's next comedy *The Titfield Thunderbolt* (1953) was a box-office failure, possibly because it didn't fit into the wish-fulfilment mould of his earlier films. His last Ealing script, *Barnacle Bill* (1957) was similarly unsuccessful and, by the mid-1950s, Ealing's and Clarke's storylines in particular had fallen out of line with a rapidly changing Britain. Clarke and Balcon had lost touch with the audience who had connected with so many of their most popular films and thus the interest of the mainly lower middle classes at whom Ealing's repertoire had been aimed.

When Ealing moved to the MGM studios at Borehamwood, Clarke was no longer a paid employee but instead contracted to write three original screenplays over a three-year period, which meant he could take on other commissions for better pay. The ratio of scripts developed to those made was much lower at MGM; at Ealing, Clarke could have expected one in three to be made but the ratio at MGM became one in six (ibid.: 185). The Ealing production system had allowed writers and directors to work closely together, nurturing projects to fruition.

Clarke wielded substantial influence at Ealing, writing some of their most popular films but his later scripts were symptomatic of an Ealing that was outdated and unable to look forward. As Barr notes, Ealing had become a '"little old" institution, determined to keep going as before' (1974: 119).

CONCLUSION

The importance that Ealing accorded its scenario department and the freedom afforded the regular writers were, and still are, unusual. The emphasis on teamwork and the encouragement when developing story ideas meant that for many years Ealing Studios produced films which were imaginative, original and yet appealed to a mass audience. The demise of the studios meant the loss of a style of British film that was story-centred, and a production process that acknowledged the vital importance of the writer.

Ealing may indeed have been a modern-day Camelot with Balcon its King Arthur, surrounded by his team of knights (Brown 1984: 32); his most loyal writers, MacPhail, Dighton and Clarke, helped Balcon to produce films that, at their best, were witty, warm and optimistic about life in British society, while the mild anarchy of the comedies was never really threatening. The collaboration of writer and director especially, engendered creative partnerships, which were benignly overseen by Balcon, who developed a method of working with no direct comparison in the British film industry.

Ealing was not a studio that welcomed women, as Diana Morgan has noted, though some women did manage to make inroads as writers; Muriel Box, the writer discussed in the next chapter, was also an accomplished script editor and director. Working with husband, producer Sydney Box, their relationship enabled them to manage a prolific output, especially when Sydney was head of Gainsborough Studios and Muriel ran the scenario department. Muriel wrote and directed with some aplomb, Sydney's support facilitating a career that few women could aspire to in that period.

NOTES

1. See the chart in Barr (1998: 209–16), which provides a revealing breakdown of the numbers of writers and the films they are credited with working on at the studios.
2. See Screenonline, http://www.screenonline.org.uk/people/id/447569/index.html.
3. Barr argues that the films scripted by Clarke are very different to those directed by Robert Hamer and Alexander Mackendrick (1974: 113). He suggests that Crichton was the director who was on the most similar wavelength to Clarke.
4. The screenplay for *Pool of London* was eventually credited to writers John Eldridge and Jack Whittingham.
5. See Clarke (1974: 164–6), for details on the gestation of the idea for *The Lavender Hill Mob*.

04
MURIEL BOX
A LIFETIME OF COLLABORATING WITH SYDNEY

> Usually one hears people refer to a Hitchcock film or a David Lean film or a Billy Wilder picture and so on. But in reality a film is not made by one person but is the co-operative effort of a considerable number of technicians all bringing their talents, expertise and skills to its creation. (Muriel Box, Ernest Lindgren Memorial Lecture)[1]

Muriel Box's output of theatre plays and screenplays was prolific, many penned in collaboration with her husband, Sydney Box. She made a notable contribution to British cinema in the 1940s and 1950s, credited as the author of twenty-two films, *The Seventh Veil* winning an Oscar in 1946 for Best Original Screenplay. Muriel is better known as one of the few successful women directors in British cinema, helming fourteen feature films between 1952 and 1964. Research has mostly focused on her directing rather than her screenwriting yet Sue Harper describes her as 'the most important female screenwriter in post-war British cinema', and surmises that she did the lion's share of the writing in the spousal partnership (2000: 179). Muriel also co-wrote and script-edited a number of films not credited to her, especially while head of the scenario department at Gainsborough Studios, and influenced the subject matter of many films produced in that period. Caroline Merz notes that she was a 'wry, witty commentator', particularly concerning gender issues (1994: 125) and observes that her films 'clearly reflect her concern with feminism in a way that must have been, at some level, read positively by women audiences of the time' (ibid.: 126). Although critics were not always kind about Muriel's films, she was without doubt a great talent adept at making films that audiences, especially women, liked.

Muriel Violet Baker was born in Surrey in 1905, leaving school at sixteen to train as a shorthand typist. She moved to Welwyn Garden City, Hertfordshire and found poorly paid and unrewarding work in a corset factory, but life became more tolerable once she joined a local amateur dramatics society, where she became involved in acting and producing. Amateur dramatics inspired Muriel to write a three-act play about marital problems, based on the characters in a hit comedy play, *The Fanatics*. She contacted its author, Miles Malleson, whose helpful and positive advice had, she comments, 'a remarkably encouraging effect on my spirits' (Box 1974: 98).

Muriel's career in film began when a contact in amateur dramatics found her a job as a typist in the scenario department at British Instructional Films (BIF), based in Welwyn Garden City.[2] She was taken on in 1929, a time of great upheaval in the film industry when the studios were converting to sound and the scenarists learning to write film dialogue for the first time. Typing out screenplays at BIF helped Muriel gain a clearer picture of the structure and narrative aspects of a story and she began to suggest improvements to the dialogue. These were often adopted, as she explains: 'the actors found themselves saddled with some execrable lines, quite unaware of the fact that they were enabling me to learn the craft of scriptwriting. A privilege I was not slow to realise and appreciate' (ibid.: 99).

While at BIF Muriel also worked in continuity and enjoyed the atmosphere on set, learning a great deal about how films are made. When BIF was taken over by British International Pictures (BIP), she was determined to remain in continuity but was only at BIP for a short time before being made redundant. Muriel was freelance for more than a year until in 1931 she was taken on by Westminster Films, run by Jerome Jackson and Michael Powell, based in Wardour Street. She gained valuable experience while there, acting as secretary and continuity girl as well as typing screenplays and dialogue sheets and was given the opportunity to read scripts, submit reports and assess their suitability as film material.

Despite her apparent success, Muriel was unhappy in her personal life and missed acting. She applied for a scholarship to the Royal Academy for Dramatic Arts (RADA) but froze in the audition, and realised she could never be a professional actress. The experience renewed her interest in the theatre, prompting her to begin writing again, although she had little confidence in her abilities.

MURIEL'S PARTNERSHIP WITH SYDNEY

Muriel first met Sydney Box in 1932, at a performance of his play *Murder Trial*, which had won the Best New Play and the Welwyn Theatre Cup, awarded as part of the Welwyn Drama Festival.[3] An experienced writer, Sydney was employed as a journalist, but the play impressed Muriel enough for her to recommend him to her employers at Westminster Films, who had asked her to look out for new talent. Unfortunately, Jackson did not rate the play, judging it an unsuitable project.

The following year Jackson and Powell were in financial difficulties after a series of films did poorly at the box office. They struck a deal with Gaumont-British Studios, which included Muriel moving with them as a permanent member of staff, with her own office and enough free time to write the first drafts of two plays (ibid.: 127).

Muriel and Sydney corresponded for over a year about plays and playwriting before they met again and their relationship blossomed, so much so that in autumn 1933 they moved in together, despite Sydney still being married. Muriel considered the arrangement very convenient as it also enabled them to work on their joint projects:

> It was then we began to collaborate in earnest. Every evening I sat down and worked on the first draft of a play we had roughed out over our meals or in bed at night. As soon as each draft left my pen it passed to Sydney to polish and amend in any way he thought would improve it. Our collaboration worked smoothly and happily and in 1934 our first joint effort, *Ladies Only*, was published. (ibid.: 139)

The play was well received, garnering them substantial royalties and they went on to write a number of one-act plays together, which were in demand by the amateur dramatics societies, finding particular success with plays for all-women casts. A second volume of six short plays for women, *Petticoat Plays*, was published in 1935. Their only screenplay produced in that period was a comedy, *Alibi Inn* (1935), directed by Walter Tennyson, which did not do well. By 1939, they had published more than fifty plays though the onset of World War II saw many dramatic societies disband, and the demand for new plays disappear.

The next stage in Muriel's life began when Ralph Smart, who she knew from BIF, asked if she could suggest anyone able to write advertising shorts for his new company, Publicity Films. Muriel recommended Sydney, who stayed there until 1939 but, as war loomed, confidence in advertising and documentary films fell and he was made redundant. During the first years of the war, they both penned plays and stories for feature films but none were bought, so that they only survived by selling the copyright of their stage plays to Samuel French publishers.

Sydney's short time at Publicity Films had furnished him with the experience needed to set up on his own and he founded Verity Films with Jay Gardner Lewis in 1940, to specialise in documentary shorts. Lewis left the following year after serious differences of opinion about the running of the company but Verity quickly built up its reputation, allowing Muriel to direct her first film, *The English Inn* (1941) for the British Council. She was set to direct the next film she wrote, *Road Safety for Children* (c. 1942), when the head of the Films Division at the Ministry of Information, Arthur Elton, decided the subject matter was not suitable for a female and handed it over to a male director. Despite this prejudice, Verity was very successful, employing a number of people, including Sydney's sister Betty Box. Muriel notes their punishing work schedule in her 1943 diary: 'I have been busy adapting three of our one hour plays to script form' while 'Sydney worked like a Trojan all week-end scripting' (Box 7.15, 14 March).

The Boxes' writing relationship in this period was prolific and creative They valued each others' opinions, tackling projects together and separately and giving each other feedback at frequent intervals. Muriel explains their approach:

> I used to do the over-all plot, then Sydney would start on it and 'diddy it up' wherever he could. Then I'd have another go at the script, then he'd do a further one; it would usually go through five or six drafts. (McFarlane 1997: 89)

Muriel's diary entry praises Sydney's rewriting skills on a draft of her play *The Heart Has Wings*, 'All his suggested alterations so far have been excellent, and I feel strengthen the first act considerably, and as the weakest of the three am very grateful'(14 March 1943). But the stresses of writing and the need to come up with filmable ideas are also evident, Muriel remarking, 'At the moment I am sitting back, collecting my wits in preparation for my next literary feat, but just can't make up my mind what it is to be ...', concluding, 'I suppose I shall settle down to something eventually – I hate a "mental vacuum stage"' (30 June 1943).

Sydney produced his first feature film, *On Approval*, in 1944 and was then approached by Two Cities Films to make three films as a contract producer, *English without Tears* (1944), *The Flemish Farm* (1944) and *Don't Take It to Heart* (1944). Muriel's experience in feature-film production was invaluable and she was able to give Sydney advice on the technical side. But he enjoyed little creative freedom at Two Cities so that he and Muriel decided to move into feature films as a writing, producing and directing team, enabling them to control all aspects of the production process. They took a long lease on Riverside Studios to make their first film there, *29 Acacia Avenue* (1945). The screenplay was adapted from a popular play by Mabel and Denis Constanduros, about what the teenage children in a family get up to when the parents go on holiday. In fact, Muriel acted as advisor rather than co-writer, her experience as script editor proving invaluable:

I didn't do much on *Acacia Avenue*. It wasn't necessary, she'd (Mabel Constanduros) got the script there and it was all set. The main thing from the very beginning was that I was able to advise on the way scripts were done and constructed. I knew that. I'd worked on them for several years at Elstree. (Muriel Box BECTU tapes)

The theme of teenage and female sexuality, in particular, was to feature in many of Muriel's films, but the narrative of *Acacia Avenue* caused Arthur Rank some consternation. He refused to back the film, offering the Boxes £40,000 not to distribute it, an offer they rejected. Rank's concern though made it difficult to secure anyone else's backing for the film, as Sydney explains:

Rank's rejection of this 'dirty picture' meant that other distributors were very wary of taking it on and it was turned down by several companies, before Alfred Shipman interceded with Joe Friedman, the London Head of Columbia Pictures, which added the film to its 'package'. (Box and Spicer 2005: 73–4)

Shipman, founder of Shipman and King Cinemas Ltd, with S. S. King, invested £20,000 in the film and went on to act as a producer financier on *The Seventh Veil*.

While waiting to produce *Acacia Avenue*, the Boxes began a new project, *Close-Up*. With its title changed to *The Seventh Veil*, this became the international success that was to make their name in the film business. The film was, in many ways, the pinnacle of their achievement, as Muriel points out:

Although Sydney and I were subsequently responsible for a number of original films as writer-collaborators, producer and director respectively, none of them could hope to achieve the success of *The Seventh Veil*, despite the fact that each received the same care and attention that was lavished on the former. (1974: 184)

A further two of the Boxes' screenplays were filmed at Riverside Studios, *The Years Between* (1946), an adaptation of a Daphne du Maurier novel about an MP leaving England to become a resistance fighter during World War II. He returns to find that his wife has supplanted him as an MP, after he had been reported dead. Muriel wanted to make a film with a feminist and political message (Aspinall and Murphy 1983: 65), and this powerful story demonstrates that a woman is capable of succeeding in a profession generally considered the province of men. The film is a sensitive portrayal of the difficulties that both men and women faced in adjusting to the wartime and post-war world, in which women expected a greater degree of freedom and equality and men had to learn to cope with these new expectations. Andrew Spicer thinks it one of the best of the Boxes' screenplays (2006: 61).

While the comedy, *A Girl in a Million* (1946), from an original screenplay by the Boxes, was less well received because, as Spicer comments, the story 'betrays Box's tendency to think of a script as a one act play rather than a multi-minute feature'(ibid.: 64). The film seems a peculiar choice of subject for Muriel: the central character having divorced his wife because she talks too much, falls in love with a woman who has lost her voice after a severe shock, only to realise that he would like to be able to talk to her. Another shock restores her ability to speak but she becomes more and more like his ex-wife, talking incessantly. They separate, reuniting after he finds out she has given birth to a son. To keep her husband happy, she pretends not to be able to talk. The message seems to be that it is better to lie to your husband than tell the truth. It is difficult to believe that the script was written by the author of *The Years Between*.

The success of *The Seventh Veil*, combined with the fact that it only cost £92,000, led Arthur Rank to offer Sydney the job of head of production at Gainsborough Studios, taking over from Maurice Ostrer when he resigned in 1946. Muriel became scenario editor, in charge of developing scripts. The new post was extremely demanding, with Sydney contracted to make ten to twelve pictures a year, which left no time for either to write their own scripts. Extra staff were taken on to help Muriel, including a secretary, a trainee writer and reader. Peter Rogers, later to produce the *Carry On* films, was employed as assistant editor. In Sydney's report on 'Production and Future Planning for 1947/8', he refers to the problem of making quality films with so little time for script development:

> Difficulty in obtaining 12 first class scripts each year. We have now used some 24 different writers, with mixed results, but we have been forced to work on the majority of the scripts ourselves in order to obtain the standard we require. A reduction of four pictures in the year would enable us to give 50 percent more time to each script. (Box 4, 12.1)

The studio faced a shortage of good stories and experienced writers who were not already contracted elsewhere. The Boxes could not afford to employ prestigious names like Terence Rattigan, who was paid £10,000 for a script. Muriel explains:

> in 1949 I had forty-two scripts in various stages of preparation which, though it sounds a lot, was only just enough to keep the studio wheels revolving smoothly and the numerous stages regularly filled. For every one that went into production, three others were generally standing by in readiness for a switch of programme due to a change in circumstances. (1974: 186)[4]

The quantity of output required had repercussions, as Robert Murphy notes, 'Predictably quality was sacrificed to the pressure of time and money' (1998: 150). This was the major reason behind the poor performance of many of their films: they needed to be more selective in their choice of projects and to devote more time to development.

The first films written by the Boxes for Gainsborough were adaptations. Graham Greene's novel, *The Man Within* (1947) a period story of smugglers and revenge, received poor reviews; as Murphy comments, 'there was a lack of consonance between Muriel Box's script and Bernard Knowles's direction, and the film is shapeless and unsatisfactory' (ibid.: 150). *The Brothers* (1947) was an adaptation of an L. A. G. Strong novel, about two feuding Scottish families, while *Dear Murderer* (1947), the story of a man who plans to kill his wife's lover only to find out she has more than one, was adapted from a play by the Boxes. A writing credit also goes to Peter Rogers, Muriel's assistant editor in the scenario department.

Murphy suggests that 'a sort of drabness shrouds the Box films' (ibid.) and argues that, 'though they acted with the best of intentions, the Boxes wrecked Gainsborough's lucrative tradition of costume melodrama' (ibid.). Indeed most of the subsequent films Muriel is credited on are more grounded in everyday life, and often centred on the family. *When the Bough Breaks* (1947) and *Holiday Camp* (1947) are early examples of this more realistic approach, the former an issue-based drama following what happens when a young mother's baby goes to foster parents and the latter a follow-on from *29 Acacia Avenue*, again featuring the Huggett family.

In 1948 Muriel is credited with co-writing six films, none of which are original stories: another Huggett film, *Here Come the Huggetts*, *Easy Money*, adapted from a play by Arnold Ripley, about a family who think they have won the football pools until they find the coupon wasn't posted; *Portrait from Life*, based on an original story by David Evans, about an army officer who goes to Germany after becoming obsessed by the portrait of a German woman with amnesia, a film with elements of *The Seventh Veil*; while *Good Time Girl*, loosely based on a novel by Arthur La Bern, is about a teenager, Gwen, who becomes involved with a criminal underworld and is sent to an approved school. The film is credited as written by Muriel, Sydney and Ted Willis, as Muriel explains: 'I worked very hard on the script, and went round homes for delinquent girls to make it realistic. After it was filmed the censor got his hands on it and he was an absolute bastard!' (McFarlane 1997: 90).

The in-depth research lends the writing a degree of realism that makes the scenario and the characters believable. Spicer called it 'an accomplished thriller', yet the film is more than that, depicting a harsh system of social justice for teenagers, often shown to be at the mercy of predatory adults (2006: 116). Harper points out that Muriel has shifted the focus from that in the novel, noting that the film script 'carefully locates social deprivation as the source of Gwen's problems' (2000: 180)

Muriel's last credit at Gainsborough was for *Christopher Columbus* (1949), a film that the couple reluctantly inherited and that Rank insisted they must make because so much money had already been spent on development. A new and carefully researched script did not translate into good box office, although Murphy declares the film redeemable even though 'long and slow with few action sequences – resembling the history films made by Roberto Rossellini in the 1960s … it is by no means a bad film!'(1992: 130).

AFTER GAINSBOROUGH

When film production transferred to Pinewood Studios in 1948, Muriel decided to leave Gainsborough to give herself more freedom to write, though her 1949 diary entry suggests her schedule remained hectic. Despite the fact that she was freelance and Sydney was on the board of directors at Pinewood, they were both busy writing and developing scripts, often dividing the projects between them and completing work Muriel had begun at Pinewood. The following entry in Muriel's diary lists the screenplays they were involved in, with notes as to their stage of development:

Work completed in 1949:
Tonight at 8.30 – shooting script of 3 plays N. Coward by MVB
Boys in Brown – revise shooting script by SB Dialogue MVB
Sanatorium – 2 drafts script by MB and SB
Mantilla – 1st draft shooting script by MVB
Lost People – re-write of film by SB Directed by MVB
So Long at Fair – 3rd and 4th shooting scripts MVB and SB
Heaven is Here – Original Story MVB and SB
A Novel Affair – as above
The Verger – 1st draft shooting script MVB. (Box 7, 16)

An extract from Muriel Box's diary that she co-wrote with Sydney. This shows the number of screenplays they had worked on in one year, 1949

The Lost People, adapted from a play by Bridget Boland, included scenes rewritten by Sydney and Muriel, who then went on to shoot new scenes when the original director was not available. This was to be Muriel's first feature-film credit as director.

In 1950, Sydney decided to take a year-long sabbatical, ostensibly due to ill health, but in reality because he was unhappy at Pinewood because all their screenplays had been turned down by the National Film Finance Corporation. He and Muriel toured the US, working on many projects while travelling.

On their return Sydney decided to resign from Pinewood and set up London Independent Producers, with Muriel and William MacQuitty as partners, in 1951. This would afford them the freedom to develop their own projects again and allow Muriel to prove herself as a director. But they were still finding it difficult to get films into production, Muriel complaining, in their diary of 1952, 'Sydney and I have both been very down in the mouth today, feeling that we were never getting anywhere with films after months of waiting, negotiating and slogging at script after script' (26 January 1952). Later in the year she again refers to the fact that few films made it into production, 'we will have completed 8 screenplays and only 'The Happy Family' has been made' (31 March 1952). They still remained optimistic, Muriel mentioning, 'We seem to have so many ideas for plays and films and are beginning to wonder which one we should tackle first' (17 March 1952). Reflecting on the unpredictable nature of the industry, Muriel comments, 'our

The Happy Family (1952), co-written and directed by Muriel Box, about a family who refuse to leave their home when the government decides it should be demolished

sense of complete frustration with the film business continues to lower our spirits. The only way to get above this is to plunge into more work' (5 April 1952).

Apart from the tremendous acclaim for *The Seventh Veil*, the period between 1952 and 1960 could be considered Muriel's most creatively productive, in which she wrote and directed five feature-length films; the first of these was *The Happy Family* (1952), co-written with Sydney, with the intention of proving that she could direct the film 'on a reasonably low budget with a measure of success' (Box 1974: 212). An adaptation of a play by Michael Clayton Hutton, the story concerns a family who barricade themselves into their grocery shop when it is marked for demolition to make way for the Festival Hall. *The Happy Family* performed well at home and was also popular in the US, receiving many positive reviews. Its lively story, about the people versus the state, presents the family's plight with sympathy and humour. The subject matter tapped into Muriel's interest in social issues, since the compulsory removal of housing on the Festival of Britain site on the South Bank had attracted considerable criticism.

The next project, *Street Corner* (1953), an original screenplay, was credited to both of the Boxes, and marked Muriel's second feature film as director and one of their most popular films. The story was close to Muriel's heart, about female officers in the Metropolitan Police, complementing her desire to explore women's issues. The film had a difficult gestation, involving many draft scripts while Muriel frequently disagreed with Scotland Yard about its content. The screenplay's interesting structure is composed of different sequences, each telling a story about the role of women in the police force. The film boasts lively dialogue, believable characters and some moving scenes. Again, the research undertaken contributed to the realism, as Muriel explains: 'My research for the policewoman film gave me an insight into the force and its work which I should otherwise never have obtained' (ibid.: 214).

Muriel's next film as co-writer and director was the entertaining and witty *The Passionate Stranger/A Novel Affair* (1957). A first draft in 1949, is described by Muriel as 'a mild satire on romance as opposed to reality and the unhappy consequences of confusing the two' (ibid.: 221). Muriel was keen to experiment with narrative form, explaining that the plot had something different to say about the relationship between men and women:

Muriel Box's *Street Corner* (1953) is a carefully researched and entertaining film

Intended to debunk the sentimental novel, it concerned an author who creates a story around the members of her own household, thinly disguised, and the odd and embarrassing results when one of them recognises himself on reading the manuscript and proceeds to try and make everything come true. The film was unfolded in colour, the real life sections in black and white … . (ibid.)

This light, but imaginative, narrative reveals elements of conflict between the husband, Roger, and wife, Judith; he asking her to withdraw the book from the publishers because of its embarrassing content:

JUDITH

And if I don't agree to withdraw it?

ROGER

Then you'll have to choose between me and the book.

(Box 2, 3: 192)

In the end Judith does not have to make this choice and a happy ending and compromise are reached, but the tension between the couple is vividly true to life.

Muriel explains that the following film, *The Truth about Women* (1957), was the most personal film that she wrote and directed, in which she wanted to:

support the cause of equality between the sexes. Thus my approach to this subject was perhaps more enthusiastic and dedicated than to any other theme previously attempted. Unable to chain myself to the railings, I could at least rattle the film chains! (1974: 222)

The film's subject matter prevented it achieving the publicity and strong theatrical opening that it deserved. Possibly, as Muriel suggests, the film was not the type of comedy that the distributors expected, being lighthearted rather than broad comedy, and was not accorded a West End run, thus limiting its exhibition. The critics though, when they did eventually get to see the film, were much more positive, Leonard Mosely of the *Daily Express* declaring it 'deliciously sly and funny' (ibid.: 224), but the film suffered from poor box-office receipts. (See pp. 101–6 for further discussion of the screenplay.)

The last film written and directed by Muriel was *Too Young To Love* (1960), an adaptation of an American play, *Pick-Up Girl*, by Elsha Shelley, set in New York in the late 1940s. Muriel was in contact with Shelley while writing the script, gaining feedback on the drafts and the meaning of American expressions and slang.[5] The subject matter, concerning a teenage girl from a poor background who contracts syphilis, proved controversial. Muriel approached the new censor at the BBFC, John Trevelyan, in the hope that he would sanction a film of the play. Even though the play had already been shown on television, Trevelyan professed himself only willing to pass the script if Muriel edited out any mention of abortion or syphilis. Muriel refused and Trevelyan 'finally agreed that the film might possibly act as a warning to them (young people) instead of an encouragement to moral laxity but all that would depend on the good taste exercised by me in interpreting the script' (ibid.: 226). The film was eventually passed without any cuts by the British Board of Film Censors and Trevelyan praised Muriel for the final outcome.

After a cerebral haemorrhage in 1960, Sydney took a break from filming. Muriel directed two more films, *The Piper's Tune* (1962) and *Rattle of a Simple Man* (1964), but thereafter failed to secure support for any other film or television projects, so focused her creative energy on prose. The result was the novel *The Big Switch* (1964), about a future in which women run the world, with men relegated to a subservient role. Muriel remembers how Sydney helped in revising the drafts when her professional life was at a low point:

> His help, for which I shall always be grateful, came at a time when I had lost confidence in everything
> I had written during the last three years. A play, several film and television scripts, besides short
> stories, had failed to come to fruition and I felt marooned in the literary doldrums .... (ibid.: 233)

While Muriel's interest in politics and women's issues evolved, her marriage to Sydney began to founder when she found out he was having an affair. She continued to work, directing one of their co-written stage plays in London, ironically called *Stranger in My Bed*. The couple's separation left Muriel devastated and unwilling to take on any new film projects. She decided instead to direct her creative energy into setting up Femina Books, a feminist press especially innovative for its time. Muriel filled her time reading submissions to Femina and became increasingly involved in fighting for sexual equality. She and Sydney were divorced in May 1969 after thirty-six years of marriage. Muriel continued her political activities, marrying Lord Gardiner in 1970, after meeting him while petitioning for divorce law reform.

THE MURIEL AND SYDNEY BOX COLLECTION
This section discusses the changes between the draft screenplays for *The Seventh Veil* and *The Truth about Women*.

The Seventh Veil
The Seventh Veil, originally titled *Close-Up*, cost only £92,000 to make. Initially, the Boxes funded the film themselves until Rank agreed to a distribution contract after viewing some of the reels. The story idea developed from a short documentary film made by Sydney in 1943, about shell-shocked soldiers being rehabilitated, *The Psychiatric Treatment of Battle Casualties*. This demonstrated that some soldiers had been successfully treated by hypnosis and truth-revealing drugs. Muriel was fascinated by the subject matter, recognising the dramatic potential in transferring the treatment to an artist or dancer. She wrote an outline of the story and scripted a 'skeletal' first draft in just a few weeks; then she and Sydney began to rewrite:

> discarding the violinist idea in preference to a pianist, since Paganini had already been announced for
> production in the near future. Sydney and I mulled over what I had written, embroidering the plot
> and characterisation. As soon as it assumed a more definite outline shape he decided to write a fresh
> outline incorporating all our new ideas. (ibid.: 170)

The new outline was based on a female pianist interviewed by Sydney when he worked in Fleet Street. The central character was written with actress Ann Todd in mind, who both Boxes thought would be ideal for the role. The first draft no longer exists but Todd remembers it being radical and experimental, explaining 'the girl was the only person who appeared on the screen. The other characters were to be filmed in shadow voices-off and reflections in the piano or mirrors' (Spicer 2006: 52). Spicer suggests that this stylistic decision was influenced by Sydney Box's expressionist theatre plays, though when Ann Todd thought the ideas too avant-garde, they switched to a more conventional treatment (ibid.).

Once the script was complete, the quest for finance commenced: Columbia Pictures turned it down so Sydney asked Arthur Rank for funding. The board of directors gave it a mixed reception but Arthur Rank and his wife saw its potential:

> I gave this script to my wife to read and she said how much she liked it. So I read it myself and I agree with her. It's original, a jolly good story and I propose to go ahead with it – and that's final! (Box 1974: 171)

The screenplay went through many changes, even once production was underway. James Mason, a major star at the time, was only taken on to play Nicholas, the male lead, after production had begun. He was attracted by the quality of the script but demanded revisions to enlarge his role. Mason's wife, Pamela Kellino, also suggested changes which the Boxes accepted, rendering Mason's character more 'complex, enigmatic and much more romantic' (Spicer 2006: 53).

The ending was not finalised until well after filming had begun, as Muriel elucidates:

Muriel Box (third from left) and Sydney Box (standing to the right) with James Mason below and next to his wife, Pamela Kellino

There was a great deal of rivalry between the four males in it as to which one Ann went to in the final shot, so we spent many a night working on three alternative endings which were kept secret till the last day of shooting, for diplomatic reasons. Even then, none of the four was quite certain who was going to get the girl! (1974: 174)

Two different drafts of *The Seventh Veil* are held in the collection; a third draft (Box 1.1, 81 pages) and a final draft screenplay (Box 1, 1.2, 102 pages). Both scripts feature a similar storyline about an orphan, Francesca going to live with her guardian, Nicholas. She proves to be a brilliant pianist but is dominated by her controlling guardian and mentor. She finally rebels, leaving him for another man (Peter) but Nicholas, desperate to get her back, threatens to hit her hands with his walking stick as she plays the piano. After a car accident, Francesca suffers a neurotic reaction, convincing herself she can no longer play the piano, becoming suicidal and refusing to talk. The central thrust of the film is Dr Larsen's quest to discover the cause of the neurosis and enable Francesca to play again.

Although both drafts begin in a very similar way, once the story passes the initial setup, numerous changes can be detected, the most radical being the ending. The third draft (D3) shows Peter coming back into Francesca's life with Francesca finally spurning Nicholas, whereas the final draft (FD) holds back on the revelation as to which of the four men will gain Francesca until virtually the last page.

The first few pages of both drafts show Francesca lying in bed, then running away and throwing herself into the river in a suicide attempt. She is rescued and recovers but refuses to talk, going into a trancelike state. Larsen is certain her problem is a mental one due to some trauma which he must try to reveal or unveil. As the story progresses, the differences between each draft increase, the final draft (FD) adding more detail and clarification, as in the following example, when the addition of an extra sentence (shown in italics) gives a greater sense of visual and dimensional space to the scene when Dr Larsen is about to hypnotise Francesca:

> He motions with his hand to the nurse, who has appeared alongside Francesca. The nurse pulls up the sleeve of Francesca's dressing gown, dabs her arm with a piece of cotton wool and gives her the injection. When the needle enters the skin, Francesca's eyes give the merest flicker. Otherwise she is un-moved. Larsen never stops talking in his caressing voice. *The nurse switches off the light and seats herself across the room.* (FD: 7)

The two drafts use powerful, often Freudian symbolism in the imagery: the emphasis on Nicholas's cane, his limp and his hands are referenced in the third draft but more developed in the final draft. There are major changes to the final draft in the scene when Francesca first meets Nicholas. The third draft begins with the same dialogue, revealing that Nicholas is suffering Francesca's presence:

NICHOLAS
It means I don't like women about the place. When I came to live in this place I promised myself that no woman should ever enter it. So far, none ever has. You're the first.

FRANCESCA
I see.

NICHOLAS (Sharply)
What do you see?

FRANCESCA
That I must do my best not to intrude on your privacy more than
I can possibly help.

NICHOLAS
Humph! Ring the bell – over there. By the fireplace. (D3: 16)

In the final draft a cat is added to the setting and dialogue included around this. When Francesca enters the room, Nicholas is seated with a cat curled up on his lap:

She crosses to the fireplace and rings the bell. When she does so, she remains
standing by the fireplace. Her eyes steal around to glance at the cat on Nicholas's lap
– and then glance away again, hurriedly:

NICHOLAS
Would you like to stroke him?

FRANCESCA
No.

NICHOLAS
Why not?

FRANCESCA
I hate cats. They frighten me.

NICHOLAS
Oh, well. You'll soon get used to them in this house. (FD: 16–17)

Imagery is strengthened and the sexually repressed relationship between Francesca and Nicholas emphasised.

Further background about the characters augments the final draft: for instance, Francesca finds out from a servant that Nicholas's mother, whose portrait hangs above the fireplace, ran away with a singer; and that Nicholas had to give evidence at the divorce hearing when he was only twelve. This extra scene helps to explain why Nicholas is so disturbed by women and possibly why he wants to control them. Parker tells Francesca that Nicholas 'doesn't like the subject to be discussed. Her name is never mentioned in this house' (ibid.: 18).

A key turning point in the plot, when Nicholas finds out that Francesca can play the piano, is handled differently in the final draft. The third draft establishes the fact that Nicholas hates the sound of music but, when he overhears Francesca playing the piano hidden in the attic, elects to become her teacher.

The final draft simplifies this revelation to Nicholas finding Francesca's school report, which he reads aloud:

> NICHOLAS
> Mmm. What else does the encyclopaedic Miss Donkin say of
> her fledgling?
>
> (reads) 'She has studied French, German, Elementary
> mathematics, history' – And so on. Ah, 'Francesca has an
> extraordinary talent for music. She plays the piano extremely well
> and has an appreciation for music far in advance of her years.'
> (ibid.: 24)

The new scene informs us of Francesca's skills as a pianist as well as furnishing more background to her character.

In both drafts, when Francesca says she wants to marry Peter, Nicholas plans to take her away to Paris. The final draft is more emphatic, stressing her guardian's control over Francesca's life, as she tells us, 'From that moment on Nicholas never let me out of his sight':

> FRANCESCA'S VOICE (O.S.)
> Nicholas was always at my elbow. He never left me for a day. I
> don't suppose anyone ever led such a sheltered life as I did with
> Nicholas … . (ibid.: 44)

In the final draft, when Francesca finally makes a break to go and find Peter, Nicholas watches her leave after her concert. His inaction is moving because we recognise the fact that this time he has opted to let her go without trying to intervene: 'Francesca comes down the ramp from the platform to where Nicholas is waiting. Without a word, she walks straight past him and out of the building' (ibid.: 58).

In the third draft, when Francesca locates Peter, he is married. She breaks down when talking to Larsen about this. The final draft is more cryptic, cutting away before Peter's marriage is revealed and returning to Larsen, who asks Francesca:

> LARSEN
> Well? What happened then?
>
> FRANCESCA
> I'd rather not talk about it. (ibid.: 60)

This places the audience in the same position as the doctor – we want to know more but are left in suspense as to what happened, with a question to be answered later in the script.

At this stage the two drafts develop very different narrative strands: in the third draft Larsen suggests a break, saying that, 'She has suffered enough' (D3: 48), while the final draft uses Larsen to push the story forward, facilitating Francesca's next relationship with 'Max'. Larsen rethinks his strategy in a series of cleverly linked scenes:

FRANCESCA (Very agitated)
I don't want to talk about it.

LARSEN
All right …

(Consults notes)
Tell me about Max.

FRANCESCA
Max.

LARSEN
Yes. You remember Max? Max Leyden?

FRANCESCA
Yes.

LARSEN
Tell me about him.

FRANCESCA
I was outside the door, listening … (FD: 61)

The script then cuts back in time to Francesca overhearing Nicholas and Max talking.

The relationship between Francesca and Nicholas is more complex in the final draft. In the third draft, Francesca is very vague about why she stays with Nicholas:

MAX
You're frightened of Nicholas, aren't you?

FRANCESCA
Yes.

MAX
Then why do you stay with him?

FRANCESCA
I don't know. I don't think I can help myself. Please don't let's
talk about it.

MAX
But –

FRANCESCA
I'd really rather not discuss it. It's an unpleasant subject. (D3: 57)

The final draft expands Francesca's reply, explaining the powerful dynamic between herself and Nicholas:

MAX
You're frightened of Nicholas, aren't you?

FRANCESCA
Yes.

MAX
Why?

FRANCESCA
He has some extraordinary power over me. You'll think this
absurd, but he knows what I'm going to do almost before I
know it myself. And he's quite determined I shan't do anything
which interferes with his plans.

MAX (Puts arm round her)
Then why do you stay with him?

FRANCESCA
I don't know. I don't think I can help myself. Don't let's talk about
it. (FD: 72)

The additional lines serve to highlight Nicholas's hold over Francesca and his apparent ability to read her thoughts, planting the idea in the audience's mind that he truly understands her. This makes the ending, when she chooses Nicholas in preference to Max and Peter, more credible.

In both drafts, when Francesca tells Nicholas of her plan to go to Italy with Max, his reaction is even more extreme than when she told him of her intention to marry Peter, earlier in the script. The final draft acknowledges Nicholas's neurotic dependence on Francesca and wins him some audience sympathy: 'You didn't love that boy, and you don't love Leyden – And I'll tell you why. You belong to me. We must always be together. You know that, don't you? Promise me you'll stay with me – always. Promise! (ibid.: 77)

The doctors, particularly in the third draft, are presented in an almost godlike way, and as being as controlling as Nicholas. The final draft focuses more on Larsen as central to Francesca's cure, as the investigator seeking to unravel the causes of her trauma. The other two doctors, Kendal and Irving, remain shadowy figures rather than rounded characters, with the final draft further reducing their role. In the third draft it is Dr Kendal who stops Larsen treating Francesca when she collapses, whereas in the final draft Max Leyden, Francesca's fiancé fulfils this function.

The latter stages of both drafts feature Larsen asking Nicholas to play the music that had upset Francesca, in the hope that this will reveal the roots of her trauma. The third draft presents Nicholas's emotions differently: after throwing the record on the floor in anger, Nicholas orders Larsen to leave. The scene finishes on Nicholas: we know he is devastated, but the precise meaning of the scene is ambiguous:

Larsen turns and goes without a word. Nicholas flings himself into his armchair in front of the fire. He looks up and we see that he is looking at Max's portrait of Francesca which is hanging over the fireplace. The camera goes back to Nicholas. He has tears rolling down his cheeks. (D3: 74)

In the final draft it is Larsen who informs the audience how Nicholas feels about Francesca, after he has exploded in anger:

> LARSEN
> Allow me to thank you. You have helped me, after all. I always
> knew the power you had over Miss Cunningham, but now I
> know why. I realise what she means to you. He turns and walks
> out of the room, leaving Nicholas leaning against the radiogram.
> (FD: 90)

The less visually explicit revelation allows Larsen, as the commentator, to explain the couple's complex relationship to the reader; in this case, words are more powerful than images.

The final scene in both drafts revolves around Dr Larsen playing the problem music to Francesca to help heal her neurosis but, as the screenplay reaches its denouement, the differences between the drafts multiply. The third draft is twenty pages shorter with less depth, especially in the last act. At the end of the third draft, Larsen meets Peter and asks him to bring a record of the waltz he and Francesca danced to when they first met. Larsen sits Francesca at the piano and Peter plays; then, encouraged by the doctor, she begins to play the waltz, finally turning to Peter and kissing him:

INT. NURSING HOME OFFICE. DAY

Larsen and Peter come in. Francesca is seated at the piano and Irving and the nurse are in the room. Larsen guides Peter to the chair besides Francesca. He sits down and starts to play. Larsen places Francesca's hands on the keys of the piano and begins to talk to her.

> LARSEN
> This is your special waltz – Remember? You can play it, too,
> if you like. Wouldn't you like to play it?

In a moment Francesca begins to play. Peter stops playing and watches her. She goes on to the end of the tune and then, apparently quite normal, turns to Peter, says: 'Peter'! and kisses him. (D3: 78–9)

In the final scene Larsen invites Max to the nursing home to see Francesca's progress, warning him that all may not be well and she may have changed. He uses the analogy of the seven veils, referred to at the beginning of the film, as a metaphor for the mind of a woman: 'with you perhaps she may drop five, or even six. But never the seventh' (ibid.: 80). Larsen then pulls aside a curtain to reveal Francesca and a divorced Peter, talking intimately. The scene and the screenplay end with the following description: 'During these last four speeches they have been getting closer and closer together and now as Peter says "never", he is actually kissing Francesca. She returns his embrace and … . FADE OUT' (ibid.: 81).

Although the ending is quite sweet, the absence of suspense renders it contrived and flat. The final draft develops the suspense more successfully, delaying the revelation as to Francesca's fate and whether she will be cured, as well as setting up the question as to which man she will choose. A scene added to the final draft shows Nicholas going to see Francesca after Larsen has visited him and played the music that upset Francesca:

> NICHOLAS
>
> Francesca! So you're still angry with me! I'm not forgiven, eh? It's of no consequence. I'm not stupid enough to expect forgiveness of anyone, except myself, and I'd never forgive myself if I allowed you to go on like this. (FD: 91)

The dialogue creates some sympathy for Nicholas because he is seen to put Francesca's needs before his own and evidently regrets his past actions.

At first Francesca is reluctant to try Larsen's techniques again but the scene turns to finish on her agreeing to do so, its classic construction showing an arc of change from one viewpoint to the acceptance of the opposite:

> NICHOLAS
>
> You know there's nothing the matter with you, don't you? You know you can be cured quite easily and play again, if you want to? (ibid.: 91)

Nicholas is still anxious to control and dominate Francesca, asking her later in the scene, 'Don't you want to be the real Francesca Cunningham?', suggesting he knows who this is and she does not. When Francesca avows, 'I have no future', Nicholas replies, 'Larsen can give it back to you.' It is the male characters who control her and who can give her back her life, with Nicholas playing the intimidating father figure, even asking Francesca:

> NICHOLAS
>
> Frightened of me? Am I such a frightening person?
>
> FRANCESCA
>
> Yes.
>
> NICHOLAS
>
> You're not frightened of me now. You're smiling. (ibid.: 93)

The atmosphere lightens slightly, as Francesca reacts with a smile, but the outcome remains uncertain until Nicholas says, 'I tell you there's nothing to be frightened of ever again' and she repeats his words as if in a hypnotic trance. The scene concludes with Francesca agreeing to see Larsen.

The portrayal of Nicholas in the final draft, possibly at James Mason's insistence, is stronger and more sympathetic. The ending plays with the audience, withholding which of the men

Francesca will choose until the last minute when she finally runs to Nicholas. The closing scenes see Max and Peter at Nicholas's house where Larsen tries to cure Francesca by playing the music that she and Peter had listened to together. The scene is set like the ending of a crime drama as the three suitors await the revelation. Larsen comes to join them and explains:

> LARSEN
>
> I think I can promise you a complete cure. But you will have to
> prepare yourselves for a new Francesca – a new and very
> different person. (ibid.: 101)

Larsen surmises as to the changes that might occur in Francesca and the type of man she may prefer, until the music stops playing and she comes down the stairs:

> For a moment, it looks as though she might be running to Max – or Peter – or Larsen
> – but she passes all of them, runs to the doors of the drawing room, opens them and
> goes inside. Through the half-open doors, WE CAN SEE her fling her arms around
> Nicholas's neck and embrace him. (ibid.: 102)

The last section of the final draft concentrates on maintaining the mystery right until the end, while planting clues that Nicholas is the right choice for Francesca.

The two drafts yield a fascinating insight into the development of the Boxes' most important film, and demonstrate how the third draft developed from a much shorter and skeletal script with many interesting ideas, into a compelling melodrama with strong characters and a suspenseful climax. As Spicer notes, the Boxes demonstrated 'their accomplishment as playwrights, particularly in the crisp exchanges between Nicholas and Francesca' (2006: 56). The film was extraordinarily successful and the screenplay highly thought of, gaining the ultimate accolade when awarded the Academy Award for Best Original Screenplay in 1946.

The Truth about Women

Muriel notes in her autobiography that

> the film personally significant to me above all others was *The Truth about Women* since the original
> screenplay (again written by Sydney and myself) was a comedy with serious undertones concerning
> the status of women in various societies from the turn of the century until today. (1974: 222)

The story is light, often amusing, with the 'serious undertones' becoming more explicit in the second draft. The drafts exhibit slight variations at the beginning and end but concern a young man, Anthony, who falls in love with a feminist and tells Sir Humphrey that he wants to marry her. In the first draft, Sir Humphrey is the uncle; in the second he is the father-in-law. Sir Humphrey relates, in flashback, how, as a young man, he also became involved with a feminist, Ambrosine. His family opposed the marriage, tricking him into taking a job in the Foreign Office. The bulk of the story then describes Sir Humphrey's love affairs in the different countries he travelled to and the narrow escapes that he sometimes had. In both drafts the script finishes with a return to the present when we realise the twist: Ambrosine is now Sir Humphrey's wife.

THE TRUTH ABOUT WOMEN

1.   EXTERIOR. COUNTRY LANE. DAY

Eight o'clock of a summer's evening.

A country lane, silent except for the birds and bees.

In the distance a church steeple and the roofs of a village.
Away to our left the imposing pile of a country house. In the
meadow,   a few sheep calmly feeding.

The scene breathes peace and contentment - but only for a
moment.

Then the silence is shattered by the roar and crackle of a
sports car engine.

Away at the far end of the lane the car appears.   It tears
at break-neck speed down the lane, turns in at the
ornamental wrought iron gates of the house with a protesting
squeal of brakes and gears and roars angrily up the drive.

The sheep scatter across the meadow.

The car pulls up at the front door of the house.

2.   EXTERIOR. TAVISTOCK HOUSE. DAY

If the car sounded angry, its occupant is obviously angrier.
He pulls up with a gravel-scattering jerk alongside the small
decorous family saloon which is already standing outside the
house, slams his way out of the car and rings the front door
bell.

As he waits for his ring to be answered we have time to notice
that, close to, the house is old and that its occupants have
given up the unequal battle against the forces of dilapidation.
It still has the graciousness and charm its designer gave it,
but it is the sort of property which is usually to be found
in estate agents' advertisements described as "Suitable for
Prep. School, Nursing Home or Institution".

The angry young man now tapping an impatient foot on the door-
step is ANTHONY DAVENPORT. He is thirtyish, handsome, well-
dressed in country clothes - and, as we shall discover, very
much a man's man.

As he turns to ring the bell again the door is opened by
APPLETON, an aged manservant who is in much the same condition
as the house. ANTHONY steps inside.

3.   INTERIOR. HALL OF TAVISTOCK HOUSE. DAY

As ANTHONY steps inside and APPLETON closes the door behind him.

                    ANTHONY: Ha!   Thought you were never
                                 coming! I want to see my
                                 wife.

                    APPLETON: Miss Diana's not at home, sir.

This extract is from the beginning of *The Truth about
Women* (1957), written and directed by Muriel Box

Two drafts are held in the collection; a first draft (Box 2, 5.1, 8 June 1956) and a second draft (Box 2, 5.2, 14 January 1957). The most noticeable differences between them occur at the beginning and end of the story, when the second draft highlights the feminist viewpoint, against the first draft's much milder tone. In the earlier draft Anthony announced his intention to marry:

HUMPHREY
Sure you love her?

ANTHONY
Yes.

HUMPHREY
Had any experience of women before?

ANTHONY
No.

HUMPHREY
Then how can you tell?

ANTHONY

I just know. If there's one thing I'm absolutely certain about it's Daphne.

HUMPHREY

Listen, my boy. I've lived a long time and known a great many women – you'd be surprised how many – and the one thing you can be certain of about a woman is that you can never be certain. How do you know she isn't after your mother's money? (D1: 5)

The relationship advice and patronising view of women does not suggest a feminist viewpoint, whereas the second draft begins very differently, with a married Anthony complaining to his father-in-law, Sir Humphrey, about his wife Diana's feminism:

ANTHONY

You're right you know … man can't be master in his own house – not if she's in it.

HUMPHREY
Then why marry her?

ANTHONY

Well, I didn't know she was going to turn out a ruddy feminist, did I?

> HUMPHREY
> I could have told you.

> ANTHONY
> Pity you didn't.

> HUMPHREY
> Are you still in love with her?

> ANTHONY
> I suppose so. But it's all this modern women stuff. Sex equality.
> My job's just as important as yours. I want a wife who'll settle
> down and make me a home. (D2: 4)

In both drafts, Humphrey recollects his own involvement with a feminist who reminds him of Diana, by the name of Ambrosine. He tells Anthony how they met and her terms for agreeing to marry him, which included living together for a year:

> AMBROSINE
> After that, if we're still happy together, I'll marry you – but only in
> a Registry Office. No 'love, honour and obey' – no 'so long as
> you both shall live' – just a legal partnership. And one more
> thing. If for any reason it doesn't work out, then you must
> promise that we'll part amicably – swiftly – cleanly … (D1: 15)

But Humphrey's Foreign Office posting in the Middle East allows him to see how women are treated in other cultures. For instance, when he asks after the young woman, Saida, who has been serving them, he is told: 'The slave market. People like these can't afford to keep their daughters – and wouldn't want to anyway if they could make a few dinars out of them' (D2: 26). At the market the beautiful Saida is bought for the Sultan's harem and Humphrey's attempts to rescue her from this terrible fate end with his capture by the Sultan. The Sultan asks Humphrey if he has studied his country's religion and laws and advises:

> SULTAN
> Then perhaps you should. In our religion Mr. Tavistock, it is
> written 'For a woman there is no God on Earth other than her
> man'. And again it is written 'It is a law of nature that women
> shall be kept under the control of men and not be allowed any
> will of their own'.

> HUMPHREY
> I do not accept that. It's barbaric. (ibid.: 36)

The Sultan does though give a witty reply:

> SULTAN
> To us it is barbaric to expect. One woman to be wife, playmate,
> mother, housekeeper, business partner and slave. Here, each
> of these things is a different woman – and I think if women in
> England had a trade union they too, would insist on one woman,
> one job … (ibid.: 36)

Humphrey is then transferred to Paris, lucky to escape with his life. While there he takes a lover, only to be confused that married people in France are expected to have affairs:

> COMTESSE
> I can see you do not understand. In France when we speak of
> love and marriage it is not always the same thing. Marriage is
> important to a woman. (ibid.: 47)

The majority of the narrative content in both drafts seems more concerned with the customs and mores in other cultures than any argument for feminism, although the screenplay is book-ended by the disagreement between Anthony and Diana, while Humphrey and Ambrosine act as the older parallel.

The first draft ending features no feminist discussion but focuses on Sir Humphrey's gift to Anthony of a book titled *The Truth about Women*. Daphne reads aloud the witty conceit written in the final pages:

> DAPHNE
> 'During a long and not uneventful life I have known intimately a
> great many women – modesty forbids me to say how many.
> From each of them I have learned something – and I pride
> myself that my understanding of women is probably greater than
> that of any other man in the world. Here, preserved for the use
> of posterity is a distillation of my experience. The first and
> essential truth about women is –' (D1: 116–17)

She flicks through the book but every page is blank (ibid.: 117). The clever ending plays into the cliché of the unfathomable and unknowable female and tritely emphasises the difference between the two sexes.

The second draft focuses more directly on a 'battle of the sexes' and the case for equality. Anthony explains to Humphrey that he wants his wife back but only on his terms: 'I want her to settle down and make a home for me. I want to come back at night and find my slippers by the fire and dinner on the table and Diana there to welcome me' (D2: 106).

Anthony continues to voice his desire for a wife with traditional values, one who doesn't want to be a man, but Ambrosine retorts that women don't want to be like men, they just want to be equal:

> ANTHONY
> I want a wife who's a wife. The truth about women to-day is they
> don't want to be women – they want to be men.

> AMBROSINE
>
> Oh no, you're quite wrong! They want to be women all right.
> They just have a different definition of what the word means.
> To a man it generally means unpaid cook – housekeeper –
> nursemaid – mistress. To a woman it means a <u>person</u>, an
> equal partner in the business of life, free to do what's right
> and best for herself.
>
> ANTHONY
> Then why get married at all?
>
> AMBROSINE
> Because nobody's invented anything better to take its place.
> (ibid.: 107)

The last two lines provide a 'down-to-earth' but banal end to the argument, especially after Ambrosine's impassioned speech. Although this is undercut by the script ending on the couple arguing and Diana declaring that she will only return to Anthony on her terms.

That Muriel thought this one of her most significant films may seem surprising, because the feminism aspect of the story is minimal and dealt with very lightly. While wanting to make films which addressed women's issues, she also accepted reality:

> We were not under contract with Rank to make films with overt statements on social problems or those with strong propaganda themes … we were not engaged to indulge our own political or social views, however much we would have found satisfaction in doing so. (Aspinall and Murphy 1983: 65)

Muriel may have been a feminist but she was also a pragmatist, recognising that her brief was to make films which were popular and profitable yet certain films were able to fulfil these requirements and also tackle social concerns or focus on women in a thoughtful way, *Good Time Girl*, *Street Corner* and *Too Young to Love* being prime examples.

CONCLUSION

Of her prodigious output, Muriel Box's most successful screenplay was undoubtedly *The Seventh Veil*, yet she co-wrote and script-edited many other well-received films. Most of these were the more 'homely', British-centred stories such as *Here Come the Huggetts* and *The Happy Family* or were linked to social issues such as *Street Corner*, *Good Time Girl* and *Too Young to Love*. Muriel's experience as script developer and editor was crucial to many of the Boxes' films, especially when Sydney was busy in his role as producer. Muriel's significance as a writer might have been more widely recognised were it not for the pressure to develop screenplays in quantity in order to keep the studios turning over. With no time to author original stories, Muriel often had to resort to adaptations of plays and novels, with the consequence that the Boxes were never able to match the quality of writing and dramatic intensity of *The Seventh Veil*.

The Boxes' partnership lasted for more than three decades. Muriel's career would not have been possible without Sydney; not only did they complement each other as a writing team but Sydney's abilities as a producer facilitated their control of the whole of the production process, especially important in allowing Muriel to direct films.

The next chapter discusses screenwriter Janet Green who, like Muriel, demonstrated a will to highlight social issues, particularly in her later films, though Green was no supporter of feminism and women's rights. She also enjoyed an enduring writing partnership with husband John McCormick, who collaborated on many of the screenplays, though without credit until *Victim*. Unlike Muriel, Green had no interest in directing but spent much of her writing career ensconced in European hotels, where she penned such challenging and innovative films as *Sapphire*, *Victim* and *Life for Ruth*.

NOTES

1. The quote is taken from a talk by Muriel Box about her time in the film business (Muriel and Sydney Box Collection, Box 4, 12.2).
2. BIF began in 1910 making documentaries before switching to feature films in the late 1920s with 'quota quickies', attracting directors like Anthony Asquith. BIF was taken over by British International Pictures in 1931.
3. In 1939 three of Sydney's plays were entered in the festival, each acted by a different theatre group. See http://cashewnut.me.uk/WGCbooks/web-WGC-books-1939-1.php for images of the 1939 programme.
4. Muriel's diary entry of 14 March 1948 refers to the pressure to use studio sets whenever possible and the shortage of ready screenplays:

   They want to use a set that is now free for filming and need to get the script right. … the snag is that the plot isn't right yet and although I've been puzzling over it for two days. I still can't hit on the right plot angle. It will be a pity to waste those sets.

5. See the letters held in Box 3, 8.3 of the Muriel and Sydney Box Collection, BFI.

05

JANET GREEN

COLLABORATION, CONTROL AND
THE SOCIAL ISSUE FILM

Janet Green and her husband John McCormick were highly regarded writers, both in the UK
and Hollywood, as producer Bernard Smith notes, when recommending them to director John
Ford: 'I told Jack that the only people in the world capable of that extraordinary gamut of style
are the McCormicks, capable of deep and honest emotion on the one hand and pure bitchiness
on the other' (JG 48/1: 14/5/63).

It is surprising that Green's career has attracted so little attention. Her screenplays were nominated for many awards and often praised by film critics, but contemporary focus on the director
and producer has meant her contribution to the success of films like *Victim* (1961) has been largely
forgotten.[1] Sue Harper draws attention to her in *Women in British Cinema*, but describes her work
as 'solid', while *Eyewitness* (1956), one of Green's early screenplays, is deemed merely 'a modest
little thriller'(2000: 195). Harper argues that Green appealed to the studios because 'Rank's hench-
men valued her reliability, and her scripts for *Lost* (1956) and *Sapphire* (1959) were socially liberal
but conservative on the gender front' (ibid.: 183). Alan Burton and Tim O'Sullivan do acknowl-
edge the importance of Green's screenplays to the success of the films produced by Michael Relph
and directed by Basil Dearden, citing Paul Dehn's review of *Victim* for the *Daily Mail*, in which
he comments, 'it was Janet Green who deserved the plaudits, for her humane, observant and often
very moving plea for tolerance towards the homosexual' (2009: 238).

Green tackled a variety of different genres, through detective stories to bodice rippers and
the three social issue films for which she is best known: *Sapphire*, about the hunt for the murderer of a mixed race woman; *Victim*, about the blackmailing of homosexuals; and *Life for Ruth*
(1962), the story of a couple whose daughter dies because of their religious beliefs. All three
films were for Michael Relph and Basil Dearden.

GREEN AS SCREENWRITER

Janet Green's prolific career spanned three decades, from the 1940s to the 1970s. Born Ethel
Victoria Green, in 1908 in Hitchin, Hertfordshire, she loved writing from an early age and had
short stories published before she was sixteen.[2] Becoming an actress, from 1931, she had leading parts in West End productions before going on to stage productions for the armed forces
until the end of World War II. Green began to write professionally, mostly for theatre and film
and occasionally for TV and radio. By 1946, she had met theatre director John McCormick and they
collaborated on numerous plays, achieving early success with *Lighten Our Darkness*, performed in

the West End and touring the country between 1945–7, and *Love Is My Reason*, performed at the New Lindsay Theatre in the same period.[3]

Green's potential had been spotted by Muriel Box, whose assistant contacted Green's agent in 1949, commenting on a screenplay submitted by Green:

> Mrs Box has asked me to return the script of 'Many Happy Returns' and to say a little more than the usual bare 'Thank You', because they have a high regard for Janet's work and would like to encourage her, and they think she is developing with everything she writes ... her power of visualization is excellent, her construction improved and it is only because the subject is so airy that we return it. (JG 48/1: 16/3/1949)[4]

Later that same year, Sydney Box rejected a treatment Green had submitted, *Lady in Hock*, approving the idea but observing that the dialogue might upset the British Board of Film Censors, 'It's great fun – but not more than one line in three would pass the film censor. So I'm afraid it's destined to be a play or a novel' (JG 33/13: 10/11/1949).

Seven years later, Green and McCormick were in such demand that between 1956 and 1959 they were under contract to Rank to deliver two original screenplays a year. Although the two did not share credits until after *Sapphire*, they developed the screenplays together, with McCormick acting as critic and sounding board and Green as author, as she explains:

> The basic ideas seem to be equally distributed between us ... it is then a question of discussions, reading, and research until we are ready to create the 'whole'. At this point, the entire writing is undertaken by me, but my husband remains closely in the picture. (JG 11/5: 28/2/62 – Letter from JG to Diane Carter)[5]

Sapphire and *Victim* were Green's most critically acclaimed films, yet she scripted other hit movies, before and after. *The Clouded Yellow* (1950) was Green's first original screenplay to be produced, for which she was paid £1,000. It is a lively and suspenseful script, with enjoyable plot complications, in which a former secret agent takes a job cataloguing butterflies and ends up trying to solve a murder mystery. The suspect, a disturbed young girl, Sophie, has a difficult relationship with her Aunt Jess. When Hicks, the lascivious country poacher, is murdered, Sophie is accused of the crime. The story is plot-driven with little in the way of character-isation but the twists and turns make it an exciting read, despite the overlong chase sequences, while the description is particularly effective.

Although not credited for her contribution, Green's next project was an adaptation of a Somerset Maugham play, *Trio* (1950). The film is divided into three segments, Green providing a full treatment for the 'Sanatorium' section in

Janet Green reading a screenplay with Michael Relph (left) and Basil Dearden

1948.[6] Her next film, *The Good Beginning* (1953) credits Green with the story and screenplay, though this is shared with director Gilbert Gunn and producer Robert Hall, but the story is not as credible as *The Clouded Yellow*. The thin and clichéd narrative concerns a newly married couple, Johnny and Kit, and how matrimony changes their relationship. Kit turns into a brittle, unpleasant character whose demands lead her husband to murder in the first draft and steal money from his employer in the second: that Johnny would murder for money to buy Kit a fur coat is not believable, nor that Kit would stand by him. The second draft lightens the storyline and features a less hysterical Kit, but a conservative view of women's place in society dominates the film, as Johnny tells her: 'You know Kit, I don't think pants suit a woman. I do wish you wouldn't try to wear them' (JG 3/3:16). Yet it is Kit's prompt action that saves Johnny's theft from being discovered when she realises he is in trouble and sells the fur coat to pay back the money he has taken.

Eyewitness is a hospital thriller, in which a girl who witnesses a murder lies in a coma. The murderer wants to kill her so she cannot identify him but, even though the premise holds promise, the story is static, theatrical and plot-bound and the characters unconvincing. The director Muriel Box apparently 'skewed Green's script to give more narrative attention to the female characters' (Harper 2000: 195). Despite some amusing moments, the tension fails to ignite in a film hampered by a clunky and predicable plot that also suffers from a problem common to many of the Boxes' films; they seem more like one-act plays than feature-length film material.

Lost, an original story by Green, is a much more interesting and accomplished film, about the hunt to find an American couple's kidnapped baby. Although implying that the working mother is to blame for leaving her child with a nanny is typical of the negative portrayal of women in the film, it still struck a chord with the contemporary audience. As Harper notes, 'Small script touches make women seem fallible … . By contrast it is the men who are more fitted for motherhood' (2000: 76). The thirty-five-page story treatment is particularly emotionally engaging, presenting events from the parents' point of view, but the first draft screenplay is rather insipid and the ending clichéd (JG 5/2). The later draft (JG 5/3) adds more character development, although the ending remains melodramatic. Both drafts expand the role of the police, with Detective Whitehead, who leads the investigation, afforded more emphasis.

Green's ability to supply credible police/crime stories and engaging detective characters continued with *The Long Arm* (1956), adapted from a play by Robert Barr, with Barr and Green credited as screenwriters. Engrossing and often moving, this tale focuses on a Detective Superintendent's mission to catch a dangerous safebreaker. The sometimes conflicting demands of detective work and family life are perhaps clichéd but the characters are rich and the story well researched in the only film that Green wrote for Michael Balcon at Ealing Studios. Although not an original story, it did give Green valuable experience in writing about the world of the police and police procedure, which would prove useful in later films with Relph and Dearden.

Her next screenplay, *The Gypsy and the Gentleman* (1958), was also an adaptation, of the novel *Darkness I Leave You* (1956), by Nina Warner Hooke. Produced for Rank, and directed by Joseph Losey, this costume melodrama's triangular storyline concerns the downfall of the protagonist when he marries a gypsy, Belle, whose lover manipulates them. Belle's character is one-dimensional and, even though later drafts improve the story, the subject matter does not bring out the best in Green's style. Disliking the finished version, Green became distressed after seeing the rough cut (see p. 114 for more on this).

THE JANET GREEN COLLECTION

Fortunately, Green had the foresight to preserve her screenplays and correspondence, affording us the opportunity to more fully understand her contribution to British cinema. The collection allows access to a large archive of writing and correspondence produced over a period of three decades, from the late 1940s and Green's first screenplay, *The Clouded Yellow*, to her last produced work, *7 Women* (1965). Drafts of screenplays, outlines, notes and correspondence provide an important insight into a screenwriter's work for different directors and producers. Letters in the collection are especially revealing about Green's working relationship with producer Michael Relph and director Basil Dearden, on *Sapphire*, *Victim* and *Life for Ruth*.

These three screenplays, all original stories, are without doubt Green's most valuable contribution to British cinema. Produced by Michael Relph and directed by Basil Dearden, it is this collaboration which made the landmark films such a critical triumph. Relph knew Green as an accomplished writer of detective stories such as *Lost* and *The Long Arm*. The idea for *Sapphire* was inspired by the Notting Hill race riots in 1956 but Rank put up a great deal of resistance to the project because of its subject matter. It was only given the go-ahead once Relph offered to make the film for nothing, arguing that there would be redundancies if it did not proceed (Burton *et al.*, 1997: 247). The story concerns a young woman, Sapphire, whose body is found on Hampstead Heath and Detective Hazard's subsequent quest to find the murderer. Ingenious twists to the script include the revelation that Sapphire's father is black and in the finale we find out that the racially motivated murderer is her boyfriend's sister. Green's screenplay is much more dynamic and fine-tuned than most of her previous work, her experience in the genre invaluable, with issue-led drama proving her forte. Her characters boast light and shade, while the police are not presented as perfect. The dialogue is often very believable and the plotting and addition of red herrings imbue the tale with drama and tension.

The two drafts in the collection are quite different: the scene order is rearranged in the later draft to add more impact to the storyline and the dialogue is improved. The endings are also rearranged; the first draft concludes with the court scene after the admission of guilt whereas the later draft cuts this out, ending on the admission and the repercussions this has on the family. The second draft is more polished, with a stronger voice emerging to engage the emotions. The fine writing occasionally encompasses some stereotyped ideas, for instance, the revelation that mixed race Sapphire wore racy clothing underneath her smart clothes, the black beneath the white: 'Suddenly, unexpectedly Hazard lifts a

The murder scene in writer Janet Green's *Sapphire* (1959), attended by the victim's brother and Detective Superintendant Robert Hazard

flame-red chiffon petticoat, holds it high for a moment then lays it against the quiet tweeds' (JG 8/2: 3). But many aspects of the story are handled with sensitivity, as when Dr Robbins, Sapphire's brother, is sceptical of the police's commitment to finding her murderer because she is black:

DR. ROBBINS
Superintendant, I've been black for 38 years. I know. She may
have looked white, but Sapphire was coloured.

HAZARD
Sapphire was murdered. We'll find out who killed her.

DR. ROBBINS (wearily)
I'm sure that's your intention.

HAZARD
It's my job. (loses his temper) Don't be so damn sceptical.

Surprised at himself, he looks at Dr. Robbins.

The black man softens.

DR. ROBBINS
I'm sorry. (after a moment) When I was a child, another boy touched
me, then held out his hand, 'Look' he said, 'nothing's come off on
me!' (shrugs) Trouble is something came off on me. (JG 8/2: 3)

Some bold writing and clever cross-cutting is evident in the scenes of murder suspect Johnnie Guitar being questioned by Superintendant Hazard and Detective Learoyd. These effectively cut into scenes of David, Sapphire's boyfriend, being questioned by his mother, who thinks he might be the murderer.

Tim O'Sullivan and Alan Burton describe the film as 'a timely and brave initiative, given the backcloth of recurrent tension, conflict and associated press coverage that had resulted from the so-called "Notting Hill Riots", and which had commanded widespread public and political attention' (2009: 223). The film found some critical success in the UK and the US, where Green was often singled out for praise; Arthur Winton of the *New York Post* reports: 'there is a crispness of dialogue that makes you know it's a winner … . Perhaps the screenplay writer, one Janet Green, deserves her own special notice for a picture that is so special'.[7]

Relph, Dearden and Green were keen to collaborate again, with Green and McCormick proposing *Victim* as their next film. (See pp. 115–32 for an analysis of the development of the screenplay and comparison of drafts.)

Although their relationship had been tested by the writing of *Victim*, the four were enthusiastic about working together on another issue-based drama, *Life for Ruth*. Initially called *God the Father*, the plot concerns an injured young girl, Ruth, who needs a blood transfusion to survive, but her parents' religious beliefs prohibit this. Eventually, the mother relents but the transfusion comes too late and the child dies. Dr Brown, who treats Ruth, is appalled by the outcome and

A dramatic film poster for *Life for Ruth* (1962), written by Janet Green, though not as well received as her previous two films

brings manslaughter charges against the father, Harris. After an emotional court case appearance, Harris is found not guilty but, racked with guilt, tries to kill himself. Dr Brown saves him and is filled with doubt about his own actions.

The final screenplay is moving and well written despite numerous disagreements between Green and Relph during its development. The first shooting script in the collection (JG 11/1) is a little pedestrian, lacking the drama of the later scripts but the court scenes are exciting and the central characters sympathetic. The second shooting script (JG 11/2) is similar to the third draft (JG 11/3), although the ending is less powerful. Green and McCormick refused offers to work on other dramas while writing the screenplay, and explained they were 'deeply interested in the subject and believe in it wholeheartedly' (JG 11/5). They spent months researching, which included learning about medical and legal procedures. Earl St John, the executive producer at Rank, did not like the first draft, as Relph relates in a letter to Green and McCormick:

> Earl has some reservations about its appeal as popular entertainment in its present form. He feels that modern audiences are in general either irreligious or not interested in religious issues being mixed up with entertainment. He sees the value of the story as an emotional human drama. (ibid.: 24/8/1961)

Relph needed to appease St John if he was to procure funding from Rank so Green agreed to make the requested changes, but balked at writing a happy ending: 'We have done all that you asked for, but as you know, disagree profoundly with the end, and feel it drops the subject into nothing' (ibid.: 21/9/1961).

Letters go back and forth between Green and Relph, who agrees that the ending doesn't work and suggests they meet to discuss this. Green eventually bows to pressure: 'You both seem to want a happy ending ... . This we are going to write, but remain as positively of the opinion that the picture must not tail away to a sweet, sickly end ... (ibid.: 17/10/1961).

Green's argument proved persuasive and the filmed ending has great pathos and is certainly not sweet or sickly: Harris nearly kills himself by walking into the path of a bus but Dr Brown pulls him back. Harris then goes home, on his own, in a very downbeat finale, but with the hint that he may get back with his wife. The conclusion seems fitting for such a complex subject in which both father and doctor have been forced to examine their beliefs. Whether the subject matter has audience appeal is debatable but the argument, the characters and the scenario are sensitively written and the emotional issues handled with dexterity.

The writing of *Life for Ruth* seems to have been an unhappy experience for Green, who was so disappointed with the final script that she worried the film would empty cinemas, telling St John:

> A strong dramatic story has disappeared and a dull religious tract has been put in its place. I am really so distressed Earl, I haven't felt like this since I saw the rough cut for 'The Gypsy and the Gentleman'. (JG 11/5: 1/1/1962)

Burton and O'Sullivan praise the tenor of the film and the power of the conclusion, noting that *Life for Ruth* is, in fact, 'admirably open-ended and intentionally provides space for a thoughtful audience to work through the complex ethical issues at stake' (2009: 274).

Brian McFarlane appreciates the quality of the film and its focus on a serious concern, calling it:

> A finely crafted and undeservedly neglected film, which, like so much Dearden–Relph work, particularly from the post-Ealing days, has had scant critical notice. It offers not only an absorbing entertainment, but also an honest attempt to consider a serious ethical issue. (McFarlane 1997: 20)

Robert Murphy observes that the film was able 'to penetrate to a deeper level of realism than mere surface reflection' (1992: 42). Critical reception at the time though was mixed, and often polarised, considering the film either 'outstanding' or 'offensive' and it was not a box-office success (Burton and O'Sullivan 2009: 273).

After *Life for Ruth*, Green was approached by director John Ford to write the screenplay for *7 Women*. She and McCormick went to Hollywood for what was to be their last produced script. Green continued to work on a number of projects in the UK and US and later, unproduced, screenplays are held in the collection, including *The Big Fric Frac* dated around 1969. By the mid-1970s, Green had ceased writing professionally.

Victim

Background to the development

The correspondence in the collection relating to *Victim* reveals much about the writer and pro-
ducer/director/writer relationship as well as the role of others in the development process: the
British Board of Film Censors (BBFC), Green's husband, John McCormick, the film's star,
Dirk Bogarde (who instigated dialogue changes in the later stages of development) as well as
the executive producer, Earl St John, who financed the production with the support of John
Davis, managing director of the J. Arthur Rank Organisation.

Although Green and McCormick wrote at least four drafts of *Victim*, the basic plot outline
changed little with each rewrite, the story centring on a blackmailing ring which preys on homosexuals. Melvyn Carr is a successful barrister and seemingly happily married until his life is
turned upside down when a young man, Barrett, to whom he is sexually attracted, commits suicide. Carr had stopped seeing him, realising things were getting out of control, but did not
know that Barrett had become the victim of blackmailers and, in the hope of protecting Carr,
stolen money to pay them off. Carr is so shocked by the suicide that he resolves to find the
blackmailers, helping the police to trap them. Once they are caught, Carr agrees to be a witness,
aware that this will end his career. Carr's wife, Laura (Loretta in earlier drafts), is devastated by
the revelations but stands by her husband.

Victim was written at a time when practising homosexuality was still a criminal offence in
Britain. However, there was increasing pressure for reform of this law in the more liberal post-
war era. The Wolfenden Report of 1957 recommended legalisation of homosexuality but the
government balked at such a drastic move, arguing that the public were not yet ready for such
a radical change.[8] The report resonated with Green and McCormick, who 'felt impelled to write
an original screenplay which would reflect the plight and life of the homosexual in London' (JG
10/6: 12/9/61). They interviewed homosexuals, doctors, social workers and the police to help
them create convincing characters, but they insisted on the need for a strong plot, 'so that the
sociological side-kick would be part of the story and not stick out like a sore thumb' (ibid.).
Relph and Dearden were enthusiastic about collaborating with Green and McCormick again
after *Sapphire*.

From the outset, *Victim* was seen as groundbreaking due to its exploration of a subject
never openly portrayed on the screen in the UK. Green, Relph and Dearden were aware that the
development process would be particularly sensitive and John Trevelyan of the BBFC was
closely involved, especially in the early stages. Trevelyan, in a letter to Green, advises 'it would
be wise to treat the subject (of homosexuality) with the greatest discretion', and emphasised the
need to consider his suggestions carefully: 'in this revision you will take serious account of the
comments that I have made in this letter' (JG 10/6: 1/7/60).

The drafts and letters relating to *Victim*

The four drafts of *Victim* in the collection span a seven-month period: an early draft dated June
1960; a second draft dated August 1960; and a third draft dated October 1960, of which there are
two versions – one annotated, one not. There are also two versions of the final shooting script,
dated January 1961, one with notes from the star, Dirk Bogarde, outlining Carr's emotional
journey and suggested dialogue changes. Also in the archive are detailed letters between, not
only Green and Relph and Dearden, but also from John Trevelyan, as well as personal letters
from Green's agent, Curtis Brown.

The correspondence tells a fascinating story of the screenplay and film development process. Matching the letters to each of the drafts enables us to see when and where problems, disagreements and changes arose and judge to what extent the screenplay development process is a mix of collaboration, negotiation and struggle for control, with each participant pursuing their own agenda.[9]

Resisting and defending – Green and the rewriting process

By 1960, Green's status as a writer allowed her to exert an unusual degree of authorial control over the screenplay when negotiating her contract with Rank. A letter from the J. Arthur Rank Organisation to the agent, Curtis Brown, confirms that Green and McCormick were to be paid £10,000 and 5 per cent of the profits, a considerable sum of money at that time. The agreement also restricted the changes allowed once the screenplay was complete, Rank conceding:

> as regards the script acceptance we are prepared, so long as it is not considered a precedent to agree that after final approval by the Company and the Producer and Director no changes of a major nature will be made. (JG 10/6: 20/5/60)

This agreement put Green in a powerful position, as the screenwriter often has to concede many changes in a screenplay because of the ease with which a writer can be 'hired and fired'. This contract meant Green could veto changes that she did not agree with, having the equivalent power of 'final cut', typically only accorded to prestigious directors.

The letters from Green to Relph and Dearden cover a nine-month period, from May 1960 to January 1961, and impart a sense of their working relationship during script development. Generally polite, the letters feature many robust exchanges. Some of Green's letters have a critical subtext, appearing more openly defensive and at times emotionally charged. Understandably 'protective' of the story idea and the screenplay, Green argues that many of the suggested changes will not improve the script. Yet she is often co-operative, first rejecting an idea but then implementing it at a later stage. For instance, when discussing the structure of *Victim*, Green is concerned that the screenplay not use *Sapphire* as a model, even though Dearden is very keen to do so. Green argues 'your clear indication at Pinewood that you want the two policemen to be the opposite sides of the coin worried me considerably as it seemed Hazard and Learoyd all over again' (ibid.: 8/7/60). The same point crops up again, in a later letter by Green, though this time she backs down, complaining 'we are still unhappy about the two policemen being so clearly, one each side of the fence' but, as the police have less screen time than those in *Sapphire*, 'perhaps it has worked out satisfactorily' (ibid.: 29/7/60).

At other times, Green is less willing to compromise and her intransigence appears justified. Regarding the revelation about Barrett's sexuality, which Relph would like to postpone until later in the screenplay, Green argues 'if the parts are played with any honesty at all, the secret will be out long before this scene' (ibid.). She is right to insist – in the film the actors need do little for us to understand their sexuality and clues early in the screenplay make this clear. Green also intimates how the characters she has created would behave; for instance, Relph proposes a passionate scene between Carr and his wife after she learns of his relationship with Barrett, to 'blot out the memory of the boy' (ibid.: 8/7/60). Green was set against this and any negative change to Laura's character, pointing out:

We must not make her a bitch in this new reflection of her character. After all, Mel (Carr) had the strength to put the boy out of the car when he felt himself going and that in itself should earn her respect. (ibid.)

Green's sensibility is correct; Laura's role is particularly powerful because she is portrayed as a tragic and dignified figure.[10]

There are many signs of strain in Green's relationship with Relph and Dearden and, even though she ends most letters affectionately 'with love to you both as always', she becomes increasingly impatient with their methods, especially when it comes to experimenting with ideas. She is reluctant to make the requested changes and eager to move on to her next project, *Ashenden*, an adaptation of Somerset Maugham's collection of short stories.[11] Green, exasperated, remarks, 'since we have agreed to do what you want there is no more time for experimenting' (ibid.: 6/7/60). In her next letter she complains bitterly, indicating the tension that has built up during the rewriting, 'our experience with you on this project has been to destroy, experiment, destroy again. You have now done this for the third time' (ibid.: 29/8/60). The relationship seems to be at breaking point, Green arguing that producer and director are now contradicting previous notes and making clichéd suggestions. She concludes though, on a more positive note, that she and McCormick will continue to work on the script, remembering their track record of collaboration:

Dear Basil and Michael, I really feel very distressed and hardly know how I have brought myself to be so blunt. But we have had much success together and can have it again. We will pitch in as always for the 3 weeks left, but you must be as fair with us as we have tried to be with you. And that takes time. Quiet time. (ibid.)

Relph and Dearden's proposals do force Green to examine the screenplay more deeply and to justify her writing decisions. For instance, she explains that certain changes requested by Relph will not work, but would adversely affect the logic of the story and render the characters less believable. She insists that Carr and Laura's brother, Scott, both wealthy men, would employ housekeepers, and that Laura would drive an Alfa Romeo rather than a Consul. Green's understanding of Laura's character is that she would display little emotion and certainly not weep when her husband shows her the blackmailers' telegram: 'This woman is a woman of character, and would not dissolve in tears when she knows her husband is facing the greatest decision of his life. If she did weep it would be when she was alone' (ibid.: 13/12/60).

Green opposes Relph's idea to give Miss Benham (one of the blackmailers) a scene similar to the dramatic outburst by Mildred, the murderess in *Sapphire* because, unlike Mildred, Miss Benham is a minor character. Green's points are made with such conviction and insight into the characters' lives and social background that Relph and Dearden were persuaded and the characters remained true to Green's intentions.

Green's frustration with the development process increases with each draft; she worries the script is becoming stale and looks forward to a change of subject matter. In September 1960, a letter to producer Robert Arthur declares how much she is looking forward to finishing *Victim* and working on *Ashenden*:

the whole thing has been something to hold onto during the final desperate stages of Boy Barrett … . I cannot tell you how wonderful it is to have Ashenden ahead. It could not possibly have a sociological effect on a flea. (JG 23/3: 28/9/60)

Later, talking about the December 1960 draft, Green pleads for the screenplay to be left as it is, insisting that any further changes could 'make the screenplay laboured, and perilously near a tract or lecture' (JG 10/6: 13/12/60). She ends the letter with a reference to the executive producer and head of production at Pinewood, Earl St John: 'We think that Earl should see this letter and would like you to show it to him since it expresses what we feel at this time' (ibid.). Green's trump card is to warn Relph and Dearden that she is seeking support from St John.

Even though often annoyed by Relph and Dearden's comments, Green is aware they are a development team with a common aim – to produce the best possible film while pacifying the censor. In July 1960, Green writes: 'We have tried to follow all your requirements and desires, and also satisfy the censor' (ibid.: 29/7/1960). Green understood the powerful role of the censor. John Trevelyan wrote to her after reading the first draft of the script, on 1 July 1960, explaining what would and would not be acceptable to the BBFC. In her letters to Relph and Dearden, she frequently mentions the need to bear the censor in mind, proposing substantial changes to some scenes. She refers to the scene where Henry the hairdresser describes how he would be treated in prison as a homosexual:

This scene is now greatly changed since we believe that the Censor will always object to an account of Henry's tribulations in and out of prison. We think the scene is now probably even more effective and makes Henry more understandable and a clear reflection of what the law, as it stands now, does to some of the more tragic inverts. (ibid.: 8/7/60)

In the same letter, Green mentions Dearden's request for more camp humour and suggests this will 'be asking for trouble as far as the censor is concerned' (ibid.).

Green does incorporate some of Relph and Dearden's ideas into the screenplay. In a placatory letter, referring to the October 1960 draft, she notes that the script is very different, with changes on almost every page. The tone of the letter is much less defensive, Green commenting,

it has been a great stint and we do hope that you and Basil will be pleased with the result. Please don't attempt to read it until it is typed again straight through since there is scarcely a page left of the last draft. (ibid.: 4/10/60)

She clarifies further, 'we have tried very hard to give you both what you want and keep what we ourselves believe in' (ibid.). Green's language is much more diplomatic than that of the earlier letter of 29 August 1960 and, à propos of Dearden's request for more dramatic scene endings, she responds, 'may we diffidently say … "punch endings" for their own sake might cheapen scenes and not enhance them' (ibid.).

Despite the often difficult development process, Green still felt passionate about her work, even though frustrated by the BBFC interventions. She refers to feedback the screenplay received from Pinewood Studios:

The reception at Pinewood is great and I am told that the powers-that-be consider it 'completely compelling'. Since it was written with the shadow of the Censor's axe right across the paper we are pleased at any rate with that reaction. But, oh! What more could have been done had we been left alone. (ibid.: 25/10/60)

The letter imparts a sense of the limitations imposed by the censor and indicates how personal the project was to Green. She really did want to go much further with the subject matter, further maybe than her responses to Relph and Dearden's requests in the correspondence indicate.

Pushing and persuading – the role of Relph and Dearden

Producer Michael Relph and director Basil Dearden had developed an interest in 'social issue films'. Relph believed that 'the Cinema is a genuinely mass medium and that it has social and educative responsibilities as well as artistic ones' (Relph 1961: 24). His task as producer of *Victim*, besides acting as script developer, was to oversee the project, ensure funding and continued support from the financial backers, Rank, while completing the film to the deadline and within budget. He reminds Green of the problems facing the film, including the fact that the subject matter posed difficulties in securing finance as 'Every American major has turned it down because of its homosexual theme, which means, in effect, little or no U.S. revenues, and … you will understand with no American potential, the difficulties of raising the finance' (JG 10/6: 7/9/60).[12]

Both Relph and Dearden were experienced in developing screenplays and appreciated the need to work closely with the writer or writers. Relph explains his approach: 'we used to see every draft of a script, and give notes, and send the writers away to rewrite, and very often we would bring in other writers' (Burton *et al.* 1997: 247). This practice may be a reason why Green was so keen that her contract allow her to keep control of the script. Relph's aim was to improve the script with each draft and his notes cajole and encourage Green, reminding her of the importance of the topic and the responsibility they bear as the creators of the film. Both he and Dearden gave detailed notes; for instance, Relph's comments on the second draft were accompanied by four pages of comments from Dearden. In the same letter, Relph tactfully praises Green for 'an excellent second draft', calling it a great improvement. He then tries to push her further, positing that, if the film were purely a blackmail story, the script would be nearly complete but 'it is likely to be the first wholly adult and serious approach to homosexuality that the British cinema has made. This imposes great responsibilities and obligations upon us, we feel' (JG 10/6: 22/8/60).

Relph focuses on two aspects in the rewriting process: first, the emotional tone of the story; and second, the development and believability of the characters. He repeatedly asks Green to present the homosexual characters more sympathetically, reminding her of the social purpose of the film: 'What I think we are trying to say is that the homosexual … is a human being subject to all the other emotions of other human beings, and is deserving of our understanding' (ibid.). Relph encourages Green to dig deeper into their problems and emotions rather than working on plot, outlining in detail how he sees the key characters: 'Mel (Carr) is a man on the rack. He feels love for the boy…. Our hearts should go out to him' (ibid.). Relph urges Green to look at the script again and 'see where you feel that the emotional values and characterization could be deepened and extended' (ibid.). He points out that well-rounded, believable characters are essential:

To make our audience shed its long and accumulated prejudice against these people we must show
our characters in such depth that the audience will not only pity them ... but understand them and
identify themselves to some extent with their problems and emotions. (ibid.)

Dearden's four pages of notes relating to the August 1960 draft are more directly critical,
emphasising the need for greater character development, less theatricality and more powerful
scene endings:

I want to know more about these people, and because of this understanding I will pity or condemn.
... the homosexuals seem to me to be types rather than human beings, human beings, let's face it,
different in only one respect from heterosexuals. (ibid.)

He also suggests that Carr's relationship with his wife needs rethinking and is particularly caustic
about one scene: 'I think this dialogue rather more suitable to a stage drawing room play than a
realistic modern problem film. Indeed the whole family relationship seems more rooted in the
theatre than in life' (ibid.).
Dearden calls for more drama and emotion, as well as stronger scene endings, observing of
one scene:

The end of the scene lacks bite. Could Harris, as Eddy get to the door in effect accusing him say:
'Blackmail's a serious thing, Mr Stone.' And Eddy says: 'So's death – Find out who murdered Jack'
and goes. I just feel a lot of the scenes lack punch endings. (ibid.)

Perhaps anticipating an unhappy reaction from Green and McCormick, Dearden finishes with
a backhanded compliment, explaining that 'it is only after careful reading, re-reading and reading again that one discovers the potential wealth of the script that lies beneath the surface'
(ibid.).
Dearden stresses that his criticism is meant to be constructive rather than destructive and
that a degree of trial and error is necessary when working on a screenplay, pointing out that
there has not been enough experimentation because of Green's other writing commitments:

You accuse us of experimentation. This is an experimental subject if there ever was one and, in
our opinion there has not been *enough* experiment, mainly because of your other heavy, prior
commitments elsewhere ... its very nature demands extra time, care and caution .... The right script
could be a triumph, we should set our sights on nothing less. (ibid.: 7/9/60)

The interests of each party are seen at play in these letters, all motivated by different objec-
tives: Relph and Dearden continually drive Green to reflect on and improve her writing, first as
regards plot and then character and believability. Relph, with input from Dearden, often acts as
'bad cop' because he is also overseeing the whole project, including funding the film and ensuring that the screenplay is fine-tuned to keep the BBFC happy. Dearden, on the other hand, while
he has a common interest with Relph in procuring finance, is more concerned with the overall
story, the characters and how specific scenes are developed and made ready to be 'acted' at
shooting stage.

The star – Dirk Bogarde

Victim propelled Dirk from matinee idol to respected international star. However, Bogarde was not the first choice for the role of Melvyn Carr. Letters between Relph and Green show that it was originally hoped that Jack Hawkins would take the part. Hawkins was initially interested but lost confidence in the script, probably because of the subject matter: 'He was not very explicit about what he felt was wrong but just didn't feel it was right yet' (ibid.: 8/11/60). A letter from Relph to Green on 2 January 1961 informs her that, after James Mason had declined and Stewart Granger had been rejected, 'Earl (St John) suggested Dirk Bogarde to us. ... We sent him the script, and in spite of the obvious dangers for him, he jumped at it' (ibid.: 2/1/61). Relph was delighted to get someone of Bogarde's fame and calibre and the actor was allowed to make changes to the shooting script, especially to the dialogue in the climactic scene with Laura (played by Sylvia Syms). Bogarde and Syms apparently improvised some of their scenes, Syms commenting that her part was somewhat underwritten (Bourne 1996: 159). Bogarde, in his autobiography, points out that every actress turned the part of the wife down, apart from Syms, 'who accepted readily and with warm comprehension' (1979: 241). Although Bogarde did not feel the screenplay was a literary classic, he did realise the film's importance:

> Janet Green's modest, tight, little thriller, for that is all it was fundamentally, might not have been Shaw, Ibsen or Strindberg, but it did at least probe and explore a hitherto forbidden Social Problem, simply, clearly, and with great impact for the first time in an English speaking film. It was refused a Seal Of Approval in America for being too explicit and it was many years before Hollywood even dared to tread the same path with any truth or honour. Some critics complained that it was only a thriller with a message tacked on rather loosely; but the best way to persuade a patient to take his medicine is by sugaring the pill – and this was the only possible way the film could have been approached in those early days. (ibid.: 241–2)

The money men – John Davis and Earl St John

Relph and Dearden were part of the film-making consortium, Allied Film Makers, whose funding agreement with Rank allowed them access to 70 per cent of the finance without consulting the Rank Organisation, and thus a degree of financial independence (Relph 1961: 37). Support from the Rank executives was still essential because they had a stranglehold on exhibition and controlled the cinema chains. In addition, because of the film's subject matter, Relph notes:

> We felt compelled to ask John Davis to read the script and it would have been possible for him in his capacity as Exhibitor to deny the film a showing. Not only did Davis endorse our distribution guarantee but he offered to put up the end-money. (ibid.: 37).

Relph praises the contribution of the executive producer and head of production at Pinewood Studios, Earl St John, describing him as 'enlightened' (ibid.).[13] St John has been accused of being a 'yes' man (Harper and Porter 2003) to Rank managing director, John Davis, but he was involved enough in the development of the film to make regular comments about the script's content and appears to have read the letters between Relph and the BBFC.[14] Relph writes to Green, 'Earl feels that there are still too many queers in the picture and is particularly worried about the blind man and his companion' (JG 10/6: 8/11/60). It seems that Relph's relationship with St John and Davis was excellent and he mentions the support given by both when developing *Sapphire*, describing Davis as its 'staunch champion' (1961: 37). Whether Relph's words of praise are diplomatic or true, he certainly needed Davis's commitment to making *Victim* for the film to gain completion funding and, as importantly, distribution and exhibition.

The censor's axe

The British Board of Film Censors had a crucial role in the development of the screenplay, with Green lamenting that *Victim* was under the continual threat of 'the censor's axe' (JG 10/6: 25/10/60). John Trevelyan was especially concerned with the initial stages of the script, categorically stating his position on the depiction of homosexuality, making detailed requests for changes to the screenplay which, if ignored, would make certification difficult. He explains, 'Frankly we would not want this amount of emphasis on homosexual practices nor the somewhat frank dialogue about it that is in the present script' (ibid.). Relph apparently used his position as producer to 'soften up' Trevelyan, inviting him to lunch with the stars at Pinewood (Bourne 1996: 160).

The earliest letter in the collection from Trevelyan, relating to *Victim*, refers to a synopsis of the screenplay, which was originally titled 'Boy Barrett', outlining his concerns about the depiction of homosexuality and suggesting that 'a film-maker should approach the subject with caution' (JG 10/6: 18/5/60). Trevelyan asks for more balance in the script as 'the film may give an impression of a world peopled with no-one but "queers"'. In the same paragraph he requests that Relph 'keeps the homosexual relationships as far as possible in the background' (ibid.). Trevelyan worries about the public response and delineates clear guidelines as to what is considered acceptable in the storyline: 'I think it really important that a film on this subject should be one of serious purpose and should not include any material which might lead to sensationalism and would lessen its claim to seriousness' (ibid.: 1/7/60).

Trevelyan is specific as to what is acceptable, referring to theme, character and dialogue, pointing out 'We do not like such dialogue as is given to Sylvia (a minor character in the story) here – "Filthy un-natural things they are, all of 'em", "sticking up for Girlie", and "perhaps you're one yourself"' (ibid.). He makes further suggestions about how Carr's story should be developed, asking that 'The character is built up in a way that is credible and his essential courage and morality is clearly shown ... In fact I would like this film to be essentially a story of his tragedy' (ibid.).

Green, Relph and Dearden were aware that, to gain film certification, they would need to satisfy the censor and mostly followed Trevelyan's wishes, only quibbling over a point they felt was winnable. More often, they made adjustments to scenes to appease Trevelyan. For instance, of a pivotal scene when Carr discloses to Loretta (Laura) his relationship with Barrett, Relph suggests:

> This is one of the best scenes in the picture although it will have adjustments to suit the new Mel and Loretta story. We would be sorry to see too much modification here, but the specific line, 'I would touch him and be lost', could perhaps be softened. (ibid.: 6/7/60)

In fact, the lines are eventually withdrawn from the script. In the same letter, Relph asks Green if she 'can think of any suitable modification in detail to help the Censor's point, so much the better' (ibid.). Occasionally, Relph insists Green make changes to the screenplay. When discussing a scene strongly disapproved of by Trevelyan, in which the blackmailers attach a razor to the gate of Carr's house and his brother-in-law is hurt as a result, Relph dictates 'the razor scene must be cut' (ibid.).

Once the film had been shot, it was submitted to the BBFC on 12 May 1961 and was received positively with only relatively small changes requested (Robertson 1981: 124). One of the BBFC concerns was a dialogue in which Carr replies to his wife's question as to why he stopped seeing Barrett, 'Because I wanted him. Do you understand? Because I wanted him' (JG 10/5). Relph and Dearden fought to keep these words in the film and Bogarde was able to give them their full dramatic impact, as Andy Medhurst observes:

> simply writing these words cannot convey the strength of Dirk Bogarde's delivery of them …
> until we have some adequate account of film acting behind the loose and the impressionistic, it is
> impossible to pin down precisely how or why it is this exchange that shatters *Victim*'s carefully
> tolerant project. (1996: 128)

Yet it was the suggestive power of the words in Green's original screenplay, not solely Bogarde's acting, which concerned the censor.

The struggle for control

Victim was nominated for many awards on its release, including the Golden Lion at the Venice Film Festival and the BAFTA for Best British Screenplay.[15] Indeed *Victim* can be seen as a highly successful collaboration by the writer, director and producer in shaping a complex social issue into a convincing narrative. Why was the relationship so effective, especially with the letters revealing considerable disagreement during the development process? Green was at the pinnacle of her career: she could create plausible detective characters in central roles and had a track record on more emotive fiction too, in films such as *Lost*. Relph and Dearden, both very experienced film-makers, encouraged Green to make her scripts more naturalistic, by removing the staginess and theatricality of initial drafts. The fact that the three shared an interest in issue drama, along with their previous collaboration on *Sapphire*, made for a robust and productive working relationship. In all the correspondence, it appears that Green is very much the writer, with the other two accepting and respecting this, partly due perhaps, to the contract granting her final approval of major changes, but also because they knew she would eventually deliver the script they wanted. The producer and director provoked and encouraged Green to shape the screenplay, draft by draft, developing plot and character into what is one of the most powerful films on the subject of repressed homosexuality.

The development of *Victim* can be seen as two separate struggles for the control of ideas: first, that between writer and producer and director; and second, that between the writer/ producer/director team and the BBFC. Both struggles are resolved by a complex process of negotiation and collaboration in which ideas are tested out and accepted or rejected depending on their importance, appropriateness or relevance. Green and McCormick resist any changes they do not agree with, and Green passionately defends her case; but she does at times defer to Relph and Dearden, with their awareness of the 'bigger picture', reminding Green that the screenplay will only be funded and exhibited if it has the support of the BBFC and the executives at Rank. The heated arguments during the development of the screenplay produced a stronger script, making the final outcome more effective.

The letters also reveal the hierarchy of power in the development process. The BBFC could not be ignored because of its ability to refuse certification. John Davis and Earl St John of the Rank Organisation had to be appeased if the film was to attract completion funding and distribution. Relph and Dearden may have exerted pressure on Green to make script changes but she also held a certain amount of power as a successful and well-regarded writer who was in constant demand. Though Relph and Dearden made some alterations to the *Victim* shooting script, they clearly regarded Green as the writer and their role as that of developer.[16]

The *Victim* drafts

The four draft screenplays of *Victim* in the collection, dated between June 1960 and January 1961, allow a study of the changes made during development. By the fourth draft, the screenplay had been cut from 124 pages to ninety and tightened considerably, cutting and changing scenes to lend more focus and develop the characters. Green's skill as an author ensures that by the final draft the description is vivid, the dialogue flows and the characterisation is more logical.

The first draft, though plot heavy, is still an involving read and features some effective withholding and revealing of information. The scene when Mel is interviewed by the police officer about his friendship with Barrett, whom he assumes is held in the cells, ends with a dramatic revelation when Mel asks:

MEL

Has Barrett got a solicitor?

HARRIS

He won't need one, sir. Barrett hanged himself in his cell this afternoon. He's dead. (JG 10/1: 36)

The scenes between Mel and Laura/Loretta are powerfully honest; when Mel explains that Barrett was being blackmailed because of his homosexuality and that the extortionists have now turned to him, his wife's reaction is complex and reveals her disquiet:

LORETTA

I've always known what I would do if this happened. And now I don't know at all.

MEL

Nothing did happen.

LORETTA

Everything happened in your heart, Mel. And the heart by itself is such a lonely thing. (Pauses) I'm going to bed. I can't stand another minute. (ibid.: 79)

The first draft has an over-complicated plot which focuses too much on the police hunt for the blackmailers at the expense of characterisation, an aspect Relph asked Green to address:

By concentrating on structure, storyline and plot and largely because of shortage of time certain key scenes lack depth in the writing. I want to know and understand more about these people, and because of this understanding I will pity or condemn. … I feel that in straining to make the story work dramatically, character has been sacrificed to plot, whereas in the final analysis, plot must give way to the demands of character. (JG 10/6: 22/8/60)

Green took these comments on board and the second draft (JG 10/2) is cut back to 112 pages, and is more suspenseful with less theatrical dialogue; the scenes are tighter; and the character logic more convincing. Loretta is stitched more directly into the narrative and she becomes critical of Mel, accusing him of contributing to Barrett's death. Mel responds:

> MEL
> You've made up your mind that I'm a villain. What do you want
> to do?

> LORETTA
> I've always known what I would do if this happened. Behave
> nicely. Be helpful. Understanding. And now I don't know at all.

> MEL
> Nothing did happen.

> LORETTA
> Not to you. You walked to the edge. Stepped back and saved
> yourself. But the boy fell in and died. (ibid.: 69)

Her attack continues as she tells Mel that he will now be able to 'hound some other poor devil' (ibid.: 77/8). Overall, the second draft is more polished, although some of the dialogue is overlong and rhetorical rather than naturalistic. When Loretta and her brother Scott discuss the problems in her marriage, it is presented as a debate:

> SCOTT
> I'd like to know where tolerance ends and licence begins. And I'll
> tell you this, Loretta. Take a consensus of opinion amongst the
> ordinary man and you'll find that most agree with me. (ibid.: 90)

The scene itself is too long and adds little to the narrative other than to present Scott's opinion about their sham of a marriage and his concern for his sister. This is changed in the next draft.

The third draft (JG 10/3) is cut to 107 pages, the plot simplified and there is more focus on the characters. Some early scenes with Barrett are deleted because they are unnecessary to the plot. Mel and Loretta now boast clearer character arcs, Mel more ruthless and determined in his career, while Loretta is portrayed as loving Mel from early in the story. In this draft Mel, realising that he was wrong about Barrett, explains his own motivation to find the blackmailers, exclaiming, 'Do you think I could rest another minute if I let his death go unpunished?' (JG 10/3: 37). In the third draft, Detective Harris and Inspector Bridie are more believable, with

Harris painted as more enlightened early in the script, explaining his antipathy to the black-mailers, while his subordinate, Bridie appears less tolerant:

> HARRIS
> That boy's not a born thief, Bridie. He's more victim than criminal
> if my supposition is right.

> BRIDIE
> I'm always worried, sir. When I find myself allowing the motive to
> mitigate the crime.

> Amusedly, Harris cocks an eyebrow.

> HARRIS
> Yes. Our lives would be much easier if we just had to deal with
> Bill Sykes. (ibid.: 27)

Loretta's dialogue is emotional and more focused on her own sexuality in this draft. Her distress is evident in the scene when Mel discloses the reason behind the blackmail:

> MEL
> I told you. Nothing happened.

> LORETTA
> But you wanted it to. That's what destroys me.

> She goes to him.

> LORETTA (cont.)
> Look at me, Mel. I'm a woman. Wholly feminine. I love my
> husband. And I want to know what kind of man I love. (ibid.: 65)

In the third draft, Loretta's brother functions slightly differently, to present the choices facing Mel: to pretend nothing has happened and blackmail the blackmailers and still become a judge, or go to the police and take the consequences. Scott is protective of his sister and wants her to leave Mel:

> SCOTT
> ... I don't want you to be destroyed with him. You're young enough
> to start again. Clear off. Leave Mel to fight his own battles. (ibid.: 91)

The fourth draft (JG 10/5) is cut to ninety pages with the deletion of scenes not essential to the plot ensuring there is greater clarity and fluency to the story. The revelation that Barrett has hanged himself is made more poignant and Laura (Loretta in earlier drafts) is granted a bigger part in the narrative. The story becomes more focused around Mel and Laura, Mel displaying uncertainty about their relationship much earlier in the script when he asks her:

MEL
Do you love me?

His voice is curiously insistent.

LAURA
Yes. Yes, I do.

She is perplexed. Mel laughs and bends to kiss her.

MEL
A little reassurance helps. (JG 10/5: 16)

His question foreshadows what is to become a test of their love. In the fourth draft, the major midpoint scene between the couple is extended and ends on a note of uncertainty, as Laura asks whether Barrett loved Mel:

MEL (slowly)
Yes … for him I think it was love … the only sort of love he could
feel … He died for me. Died protecting my name.

They are both very drained now and very quiet. There is silence before Laura speaks.

LAURA
That thought will remain with you for the rest of your life.

She looks at the photograph in her hand.

LAURA
I don't think there's going to be room for me as well. (ibid.: 59–60)

The well-crafted scene ends on Laura's ominous words. The fourth draft gives a greater sense of this being Laura's story as well as Mel's and in the next scene, by the river, Laura confesses her pain: 'He's still in your heart, Mel. I can see that. I feel … I feel utterly destroyed' (ibid.: 66).

Green was able to write convincingly for a wide range of characters but the rewriting process was essential in honing the screenplay into shape. If we compare the third and fourth draft of Henry, the hairdresser's, speech, the changes can be seen to enhance the narrative trajectory. Henry is also being blackmailed for his homosexuality and Mel hopes to discover more about the blackmailers from him but Henry is very scared:

HENRY
Yes. I'm weak and I'm selfish. You're different. Strong. Not afraid.
I can see that. You ought to be able to state our case. Take the
lid off. Tell the public how we walk in fear and loneliness.

> Tell them there's no magic cure behind prison bars. I'm
> driftwood now. I've come to feel a criminal, an outlaw. Once with
> a bit of help I might have been able to lick this thing. D'you know
> what I think, Mr. Carr? (JG 10/3: 51)

The emphasis has altered by the fourth draft: the dialogue has been pruned, the speech ends on a stonger note, highlighting what Mel can do in his position as a barrister:

> HENRY
> Yes. I'm weak and selfish. You're different. You've got a big
> position – they'd listen to you, a lawyer – you ought to be able
> to state our case. Tell the public how we walk in fear and
> loneliness. Tell them there's no magic cure for how we are.
> Certainly not behind prison bars. I've come to feel a criminal,
> an outlaw. D'you know what I think, Mr. Carr? (ibid.: 49)

As well as reminding the audience that Henry is in a desperate situation because of his sexuality, the speech propels Carr into taking action that could jeopardise his career.

An emotionally wracked Dirk Bogarde in the last scene of *Victim* (1961), co-written by Janet Green

Comparing different drafts of the last scene

The resolution of the screenplay is particularly interesting to study. By the fourth draft, the narrative is more focused, the emotional resonance heightened and Mel and Laura's dialogue less expositional. In all four drafts, the end features Mel and Loretta/Laura discussing their future together, deciding that Loretta should go away while the scandal is ongoing and realising that Mel's high-level career is over.

The first draft (JG 10/1) ends with Mel meeting Loretta in the tea lounge at the Savoy, after he has helped the police arrest the blackmailers. Rather oddly, this intimate discussion about their future together occurs in a public place. When Loretta asks Mel why he went to the police and exposed the blackmailers, he stodgily replies: 'I came to the conclusion that an individual has no right to usurp the prerogative of administering justice' (JG 10/1: 122).

Mel explains that he can no longer hope to become a high court judge, as his homosexuality will be exposed and tells Loretta he has booked a holiday to keep her away from the scandal. She asks if he loves her and Mel replies: 'As much as I am capable of loving a woman, I love you and will go on loving you' (ibid.: 123).

Loretta, in a rather improbable exchange, declares her intention to stay with Mel, despite his sexuality: 'I'm not going to Florida. I've come to a conclusion, too. I believe there's a relationship beyond sex and I've found it with you' (ibid.). Even when Mel tells her 'Please go away', Loretta declares, 'The only place I'll go is home. That's where I want to be' (ibid.).

The final lines of the first draft are spoken by two women in the tea lounge who recognise Mel and comment:

FIRST SMART WOMAN
A handsome pair, aren't they?

SECOND SMART WOMAN
Very handsome.

Approvingly, admiringly, the two smart women watch as Mel holds the door for
Loretta to pass out of the lounge. (ibid.: 124)

The irony of these comments adds a poignancy to the ending, as we know they are far from an ideal couple, with Loretta condemned to an unfulfilled marriage, while Mel has sacrificed his career by revealing his homosexuality.

The second draft, JG 10/2, moves the couple to the study in their home and the dialogue is more detailed, though still theatrical. This time Mel's reason for going to the police is given as securing justice for Barrett's death, a more powerful motivation:

Couldn't stand the thought of his murderers going scot free.
I think of him splashing along in the mud that night. Cold.
Haunted. Then at the police station. Pulling the tie around his
neck. Glad to die. To still his tongue. (JG 10/2: 111)

Loretta still refuses to leave Mel, and her dialogue underlines her resolve that they should face the consequences of his actions together:

LORETTA

You need me, Mel. Before, you've always been the strong one.
Completely self-sufficient.

She circles his arm with her two hands.

LORETTA (cont.)

You said you'd weather it. We'll weather it together. (ibid.)

The ending changes in the second draft, becoming private and reflective as Loretta exits the room. Visually, the scene's emotional punch occurs when Mel takes out the incriminating photo of him with Barrett, as he 'crosses to the fire. Untidy, dishevelled with emotion, he takes the photograph from his pocket. Drops it into the fire. Now watches the flames consume his own and Barrett's face' (ibid.: 112).

The third draft (JG 10/3) cuts the final scene to three pages, and the language is more natural. Loretta asks Mel, 'When did you make up your mind to blow the lid off?' In this version Mel points out the case's consequences for their private lives, which is why he wants her to go away:

MEL

This is going to be a cause celebre. I shall be called abominable
names. In court and out of court. My friends will turn away their
faces, my enemies say they always guessed. … (JG 10/3: 106)

There is more emphasis on the price they would both pay by staying together. Loretta still insists that she loves Mel, despite his homosexuality, but the dialogue is more credible:

MEL

Loretta, I'm still the same man, with the same impulse. Twice in
my life I've felt it –

LORETTA

And controlled it.

MEL

But at what a cost.

He releases her hands.

LORETTA

Sex isn't the whole of a man, or a woman either. (ibid.: 107)

The fourth draft script, JG 10/5, cuts the last scene to two pages, making it much tighter and eschewing the expositional and theatrical dialogue of the earlier drafts.

The scene highlights the effect of Mel giving evidence, as Laura notes:

LAURA
You deliberately chose to plead a case for a minority in the court
of public opinion.

Mel explains his reasons for doing this, even though he will be sacrificing his career:

MEL (slowly)
I don't want to go into court as Mr. X. If I can appear as myself,
I believe I can draw attention to a weakness in the existing law.
Of course the young must be protected, but I've come to believe
that adult men, who by nature are different, have as much right to
find a partner in kind as the normal man or woman. (JG 10/5: 89)

Although somewhat rhetorical in tone, the penultimate page serves as a final reminder to the reader that this film directly addresses the unfairness of the law regarding homosexuality.

After this short speech the emotional timbre is heightened when Laura replies:

LAURA
Go into court and say that, Mel. And you're destroyed.

MEL (levelly)
I'm destroyed anyway. And I won't have you destroyed with me.
(JG 10/5: 89)

As in the third draft, Mel refers to the case being a cause célèbre, but the dialogue has been cut in favour of description to demonstrate Mel's anguish: 'Mel's voice is almost unrecognisable in its intensity, and he is untidy, dishevelled with emotion' (ibid.).

The fourth draft now ends on Mel's declaration of his love for Laura while reminding her of his sexuality:

MEL
I love you very deeply. But I'm still the same man with the same
impulse. Twice in my life I've felt it …

LAURA
And controlled it.

MEL
But at what a cost.

He releases her hands. She looks at him with compassion. Knows that he cannot
bear anymore. Goes quietly from the room. (ibid.: 90)

This quiet and downbeat ending raises the question about the cost of living a lie, personalising the dilemma involved in being homosexual at that time, but turning Laura into a martyr.

By the final draft the central characters are clearer and their fears and motivations lead the story. Green's powerful but logical plot features sympathetic and believable characters who are organic to the story, complying with Dearden's request to let the story emanate from the characters. Green has taken on board many of the comments from Relph and Dearden and produced a final screenplay that really does convey emotions on the rack, particularly between Mel and Laura, while at the same time tackling a 'social issue'.

The development of the *Victim* screenplay marked an extremely successful collaboration, which, despite some serious disagreement resulted in the common aim – to produce the best possible film about what all agreed was an important subject. The development process entailed some difficult negotiations with the BBFC, which proved immoveable on certain points, but did try to resolve issues and indicated a willingness to find alternative solutions.

Green's contribution to the film was pivotal and her courage and passion as a writer incontrovertible. Whether one considers the completed film, as Bogarde suggested 'a modest, tight, little thriller' (1979: 241) or rather more complex, it was certainly groundbreaking, and perhaps even more so in retrospect. As Richard Dyer professes, *Victim* had been 'the first film to defend homosexuality as a cause in a mainstream context, the first to deal with gayness explicitly … the first to have a major star playing a gay character' (1993: 71).

CONCLUSION

Green's contribution to British cinema of the 1950s and early 1960s deserves greater recognition. She enjoyed a long and successful screenwriting career, from her first approaches to the Boxes, and their encouragement of her skills, to her collaboration with Relph and Dearden on what would represent the zenith of her career: writing three of the finest films in British cinema. The studios appreciated Green's reliability, though she did not hesitate to challenge their judgment when it affected her scripts. Green's depictions of men were often at the expense of the less sympathetic female characters, but she was a committed, passionate writer who sought to highlight important social issues.

This collection of Green's work and correspondence is historically and culturally significant, documenting her career and writing process, allowing access to a wealth of texts rarely available for study.

In contrast, the next chapter on Mark Grantham examines another prolific writer whose output may not always have been of the highest quality but remains significant because of the conditions he worked in, constrained to complete a screenplay in two weeks to fulfil the demands of producers the Danziger brothers.

NOTES

1. See JG 10/7 for press cuttings and reviews of the films.
2. Green's birth certificate states she was born in 1908, although she was often vague about her exact age.
3. In an interview with the author, Janet Green's stepson Barry McCormick noted when the couple started writing together.
4. See the Janet Green collection JG 17 for two drafts and a part draft of the unrealised screenplay.
5. Barry McCormick confirms that the couple collaborated equally in the creation of a screenplay (interview with author, 11 November 2012).

6. As in so many cases with uncredited writers, it is possible that the treatment represented a separate project – but the Janet Green Collection notes 'Dialogue and additional scenes for 'W. Somerset Maugham/Pormanteau'.

7. For further reviews of *Sapphire*, see Burton and O'Sullivan (2009).

8. The Wolfenden Report was set up to investigate both homosexuality and prostitution. It recommended the legalisation of homosexuality between consenting adults over the age of twenty-one. The recommendations were rejected by the government and homosexuality was not legalised until 1967.

9. For discussion of the development of the screenplay and the screen idea, see MacDonald's article on the Screen Idea Work Group (2010: 45–58).

10. Reviews at the time referred to the quality and dignity of Sylvia Sym's performance as Laura. See JG 10/7 for press cuttings.

11. See JG 23/3 for more on *Ashenden*, a project that never came to fruition.

12. Relph explains, in response to an accusation from Green and McCormick, that when meeting with them to discuss the script he had been inattentive, this was because he was trying to get funding from John Davis, head of production at Rank, and 'Without reading a word … Davis advanced £10,000 to finance the script' (JG 10/6: 7/9/60).

13. For more on John Davis and Earl St John, see the chapter 'The Rank Organisation' in Harper and Porter's book *British Cinema of the 1950s* (2003) and the somewhat negative description of both men in *J. Arthur Rank and the British Film Industry* (Macnab 1993: 200, 222, 226, 238).

14. Ibid.

15. See press cuttings in JG 10/7.

16. In a letter dated 2 January 1961 Relph informs Green and McCormick that Dirk Bogarde has accepted the role of Carr, advising, 'Don't worry about the script alterations. They will only be minor ones which we can do and submit to you' (JG 10/6).

06

MARK GRANTHAM
WRITING A SCREENPLAY IN TWO WEEKS!

Mark Grantham became one of the kings of the British 'B' movie screenwriters, working for the Danziger brothers, producers who moved to the UK from the US in 1953.[1] Grantham, a fellow American, born in 1931, came to Britain as a GI in World War II, before moving to Ireland, where he created and co-wrote a long-running radio drama series, *The Kennedys of Castleross*, which became Ireland's top-rated radio soap opera. Grantham left for London to improve his career prospects.[2] Grantham's experience on the daily, fifteen-minute soap proved valuable preparation for the quick turnaround required by the Danzigers. Grantham wrote at least sixteen films and sixteen TV programmes for the producers between 1957 and 1963. In 1962 alone, he is credited with six films and two episodes of *Richard the Lionheart*. He also went by different pseudonyms, adopting his wife's maiden name, McCormack, for four films.

Grantham began writing 'B' movies at a time when they were enjoying a short-lived revival. The 'B' movie or second feature was a shorter and less expensively made film, shown in cinemas before the main feature. By the mid-1950s, film production numbers in the UK were in serious decline, with many films suffering large losses, provoking concern that the second feature would not survive. Pressure from the British Film Producers Association persuaded the Board of Trade to increase the Eady Levy[3] to support production and, as a result, in 1958 the Eady Levy was doubled to include financial support for second features. This gave a much needed boost to the 'B' movie and encouraged the Danzigers to produce more films.

The 'B' movies were often castigated by the press for poor character motivation and implausible plots. Frederick Woods in *Films and Filming* complains, 'These films – it's still safe to generalise – are inept, stupid, badly written and acted, ludicrous and worthless' (1959: 6). The cinemagoing public were also critical of the dubious quality of the 'B' films, as evidenced by their letters in *Films and Filming*. Peter Pitt takes issue with this criticism because, with such a glut of product, many were bound to fail:

> when assessing the quality of British second features of that period it must be admitted that the majority of them were pretty poor … they came in for so much criticism because so many of their films flooded cinemas in a comparatively short time. (1984: 16)

The Danziger brothers had become associated with poor-quality films and low production standards, with a tendency to rework stories from other films, borrowing ideas and adapting them for their own movies. As Steve Chibnall and Brian McFarlane observe, the name of Danziger, 'unfairly or not, has become virtually synonymous with bottom-of-the-barrel slipshoddiness in film production' (2009: 90). Their reputation was such that an anonymous film reviewer coined the term 'to danzigerise', to describe a film which gave him 'a dull pain between the eyes' (1964: 33).

The Danzigers employed Grantham when he sent in a sample of writing and they asked him to write an episode of their popular TV series, *Saber of London/The Vise* (1954–61), which they liked enough to buy. Grantham's short article 'Life on the Cheap with the Danzigers' is a revealing account of the period he spent working for the brothers at New Elstree Studios. On arrival at the studios, Eddie Danziger showed Grantham around, boasting: 'We make the cheapest TV series and films in the world … . Nobody makes 'em cheaper' (MMG34: 1–2).

Grantham is critical of the quality of the Danzigers' output and especially of *Saber of London*, arguing that screening the series for 'years on both sides of the Atlantic, proved that television stations everywhere would buy the tackiest of codswallop if the price was low' (ibid.: 1). While developing a screenplay adaptation of Edgar Allan Poe's short story *The Tell-tale Heart*, Grantham took out a scene which the Danzigers wanted to retain, showing Poe watch a woman undressing, protesting, 'The scene reduces Edgar Allan Poe, a great author, to a masturbating voyeur' (ibid.). The Danzigers were not impressed and assigned the project to another writer, Brian Clemens, who also scripted many of their films before going on to create *The Avengers* (1961–9). Grantham did write, under the pseudonym Norman Armstrong, *The Nude Prude/For Members Only* (1960), one of a flurry of naturalist films produced in the early 60s.[4] None of the crew, not even the Danzigers, wanted to be credited on the film but, as Grantham remarks, the brothers were quick to capitalise on any film subject if they thought it would make money: 'The smell of profit could send the Danzigers rooting for truffles at strange trees' (ibid.: 2).

The Danzigers' desire for historical accuracy was easily compromised; when Grantham was developing the TV series *Richard the Lionheart*, eventually writing the pilot and seven of the episodes, he was advised to 'do careful historical research' as 'There'll be professors and other experts watching every episode.' When Grantham unearthed rumours of Richard's homosexuality and adultery, Eddie Danziger changed his attitude, insisting: 'you don't have to be too finicky about the facts … . The series is aimed at kids' (ibid.: 6).

More recent assessment of the Danzigers' output, including Grantham's scripts, suggests that not all their films were poorly written; some were effective, despite being made in haste. Chibnall and McFarlane offer a more positive view of the 'B' movie in general, contending that the better ones, 'show what can be done under the most rigorous writing conditions: plots get underway swiftly, care is taken to fill out a sense of character and of relationship' (2009: 167).

The Danzigers were ruthless in keeping costs to the absolute minimum. The brothers bought New Elstree Studios in 1955 and the budget for each film was very low, between £15,000 and £17,500. Winston Wheeler Dixon contends that the Danzigers were involved in development and production at all levels, and that 'in some perverse, and not altogether fathomable manner, the brothers Danziger were proud of their films' (1998: 92). At New Elstree Studios a film was made every ten days, the short turnaround allowing little time for script development. The factory-like turnover put the emphasis on speed. Elstree managing director Eric Blakemore claimed that, despite this, they were still able to create a product with some artistic merit:

> At new Elstree we can compare our work with the lightning sketches of a good artist who, capable of creating masterpieces, can, with adjustments, bring his talent to the production of quick satisfactory work without shedding inspiration … . Artistic talent, yes, but we harness [this] to commercial deadlines. (Chibnall and McFarlane 2009: 93)

The Danzigers made a profit at a time when many production companies were struggling to survive. David Mann believes the brothers were pioneers:

> Like their compatriot Hannah Weinstein, the Danzigers were trailblazers, bringing American production methods to British cinema, acquiring a studio base and creating a factory system that was efficient and prolific … . More pertinently, they were pioneers in the making of TV/Film series. Revealingly, their industrial ethic translated itself into a recognizable aesthetic, not glamorous or stylish, but pragmatic, with interchangeable parts that could be swapped around according to the needs of the factory production line. (Mann 2009: 86)

Even though the hastily penned scripts were often underdeveloped, as Mann explains, writers at New Elstree Studios were generally considered

> more important than directors. But they had to accept the stringent conditions. They were paid a set salary and had to provide the script for one episode of a series per week or a supporting feature script every two weeks. (ibid.: 167–8)

Although Grantham and Clemens were the Danzigers' favoured writers, other regulars were also employed, including the very experienced John Gilling, A. R. Rawlinson and Brock Williams (Mann 2008: 82). Experienced Americans occupied many of the regular writing posts in the UK industry, working for instance on Hannah Weinstein's historical adventure series *The Adventures of Robin Hood* (1955–60).[5] The Danzigers' studio became a training ground for new British talent, providing valuable experience in writing quickly for TV as well as film. At least a handful of key writers began their career at New Elstree, including Norman Hudis, who later worked on *Danger Man* (1964–6), *The Saint* (1962–9) and *Gideon's Way* (1964), before moving on to the *Carry On* films; John Kruse contributed to *The Third Man* (1959), *Interpol Calling* (1959), *The Avengers* and Roger Marshall and Dennis Spooner worked with Clemens on *The Avengers*.[6]

GENRE AND WRITING STYLE

Grantham's writing spanned a wide range of genres, from detective mystery, to melodrama and comedy. Though often marred by unbelievable scenarios and clichéd, one-dimensional characters, his scripts remain entertaining to read and tautly composed, particularly considering the limited development time. The stories feature strong female characters, who are often central to the narrative. At times Grantham presented an unrealistic view of England, perhaps with the US market in mind, entailing country houses and titled characters, as in *Date at Midnight* (1960) and *Man Accused/ Whirlpool of Suspicion* (1959). The dialogue tends to flow, thanks partly to Grantham's nationality, as Robert Baker, a prolific director of 'B' movies, notes, 'American films will cut out dialogue if they possibly can, relying on the action. In England we tend to use six words when two will do' (McFarlane 1997: 47).

The prolific screenwriter was not averse to borrowing storylines from other films and Mann points out that *So Evil, So Young* (1961) was influenced by the American film *Reform School Girl* (1957), based on a popular pulp novel, tagline: 'a shameful path led her there – scarlet secrets kept her there'. The Danzigers' version, Mann contends, 'has all the stock characters associated with the sub-genre – Top Dog, Freak and Stooge prisoners as well as a sadistic warden … and, most important of all, plenty of fights between women …' (Mann 2009: 92) *So Evil, So Young* attracts praise from Chibnall and McFarlane for its 'unusual acknowledgement of female sexuality as an issue in drama' (2009: 161), although the lively story and strong characters prove more rewarding reading than the fleeting discussion of female sexuality. The scripts for *Feet of Clay* (1960), *Gang War* (1962) and *The Gentle Terror* (1962), they believe, were of better quality: 'As supporting features they are no worse than average, and have moments of invention that lift them intermittently above that level' (ibid.: 161). Chibnall and McFarlane are not so kind about other Grantham films, describing *Part Time Wife* (1960) as 'ludicrous' (ibid.: 94), *She Always Gets Their Man* (1962) as 'excruciating' and 'a witless spin on the provincial-girl-at-large-in-London theme' (ibid.: 96), and concluding that the Danzigers were unwise to move into comedy, a genre frequently tackled by Grantham.

Grantham left the Danzigers after *Richard the Lionheart* and his last credit for them was in 1963. He went on to write for other producers, but there is no further record of his work, although it is possible he continued under a pseudonym.

THE MARK GRANTHAM COLLECTION

The collection holds a screenplay of every film Grantham wrote for the Danzigers and scripts for some of the episodes of the TV series, *Saber of London* and *Richard the Lionheart*. Because there are only single draft screenplays, it is not possible to discuss the script development process, but we can look at Grantham's style and compare his work, while taking into account the intense time pressure he was under.

This section examines Grantham's writing and his developing of plot, story and character. Three screenplays are looked at in some detail: *Feet of Clay / Dead Angel* and *Night Train for Inverness* (1960) are examples of the best of Grantham's scripts, dramatic and fast-paced, while the comedy, *She Always Gets Their Man*, is much less effective, despite some amusing moments.

Grantham's screenplays make a fascinating study because of the circumstances surrounding their genesis, the short time frame and budget limitations imposed by the studio. Grantham injects his writing with an energy and pace which make most of his scripts highly readable, while the scene development, cross-cutting and story construction are very effective. The plots may often be incredible but the energetic writing helps the reader get over this hurdle. For instance, *Escort for Hire* (1960) is a light mystery about an actor who becomes a male escort when short of money. His first job is to escort a beautiful woman but the assignment turns sour when he arrives at the apartment to find her dead. The script reads well, the story is adequately developed and, although the revelation is contrived, the characters display some degree of complexity and we can empathise with the protagonist's predicament – he has been framed for murder.

Date at Midnight is the improbable tale of an American reporter sent to England to research an article about a famous barrister, Sir Edward Leyton. Although the script begins with some cumbersome character introductions of the reporter to Leyton and his family, it is an entertaining if clichéd mystery about a boy, Tommy, who accidentally killed his parents when he was very young and is then brought up by the Leytons, his aunt and uncle. When the boy's girlfriend is murdered, suspicion falls on him and a lively and suspenseful mystery ensues as to whether Tommy is the killer, though the final reveal at the end is absurd.

Man Accused / Whirlpool of Suspicion boasts an even more incredible plot about an American wrongly accused of stealing jewels from his fiancée, an English heiress. The many convenient plot contrivances combine with clichéd, one-dimensional characters, merely serving as ciphers for the story. When we first meet the heiress, Kathy, she is described by Grantham as 'a cheerful, pretty girl of 21, who isn't always successful in her attempts to be sophisticated. But she matures visibly as the story moves along' (MMG2: 1).

Kathy only reluctantly supports Bob, her fiancé, after much prompting by her father, but then goes on to help prove his innocence. There is some evocative description and the script flows but the contrived nature of the plot makes it difficult to engage with the characters on anything other than a superficial level. The screenplay becomes more interesting later, when seeds of doubt are sown as to Bob's guilt with an almost Hitchcockian feel to some parts of the story, for instance, when Kathy questions Bob about his past, trying to get to the truth:

> KATHY
> Am I the first girl you were ever engaged to?

> BOB (smiles)
> The first and only. Why?

> KATHY
> I was just wondering. I suppose it's because – well – you're such
> a good catch.

> BOB (laughs)
> Flattery will only get you another kiss.

> KATHY
> But, I'm sure you met a lot of nice girls when you were in South America.

> BOB
> Dozens! But none like you.

Kathy's questioning continues:

> KATHY
> Did you like living in those Latin American countries?

> BOB
> Loved it. Brazil and Mexico are great places.

> KATHY
> Then why did you leave?

> BOB (laughs)
> Hey, what is this? An inquisition? (ibid.: 26)

The scene concludes, 'Kathy smiles at Bob uneasily and they exit.' This uncertainty about who to trust is more or less successfully continued until the denouement and final revelation proving Bob's innocence.

Feet of Clay/Dead Angel

With a screenplay that sets up the plot clearly and economically, *Feet of Clay* is characterised by Chibnall and McFarlane as 'oddly compelling' (2009: 161), which it is, despite some overlong scenes. It begins as a straightforward detective murder mystery, when newly qualified lawyer, David, is assigned to defend a young man who has confessed to the murder of an 'angel of mercy'. David's investigation eventually unearths a home for the rehabilitation of young ex-criminals where, rather than the residents being reformed, they are coerced into acting as drug mules. Although the storyline is rather implausible and the characters simply drawn, both hold our interest; David is a likeable protagonist and his social worker girlfriend, Fay, who helps to trap the leaders of the drug ring, is depicted as bright and lively. The story is more developed than many of Grantham's other screenplays and the dramatic beginning has the right tone for a crime film set in the docklands area of London:

> EXT. BACK STREET. NIGHT
>
> A narrow street, even grubbier than the previous one. There is a small alley off it.
> Policeman is coming along street. As he passes the alley, he stops, as if he hears a
> noise, and flashes his torch into it. Then he moves cautiously into the alley.
>
> EXT. ALLEY. NIGHT
>
> Just a shallow spur off the man street – its three walls blank and unrelieved by
> doorways or windows. Policeman comes in with torch, flashing it around. Suddenly,
> with a shock effect, the beam picks out a middle-aged woman, Angela Richmond, at
> the end of the alley. She is leaning against the wall, deathly pale, and looking slightly
> dishevelled (although dressed in good clothes). Her eyes are wild, and she seems to
> be trying to speak.
>
> DOLLY IN QUICKLY as the policeman rushes up to her.
>
> > POLICEMAN
> > Here, Ma', – what's wrong?
>
> As if in reply Mrs Richmond pitches over into his arms – dead. (MMG7: 1)

The script sets up character expectations with some dexterity and then confounds these as it progresses. This particularly applies to the couple who run the home, Mrs Clarke and Sanders, who appear benevolent only to be revealed as villains, and to Jimmy, initially fingered as the murderer until David realises that he has been framed.

Some of the scenes are very long, especially in the earlier pages, possibly because of the need to fill picture time and make best use of the single sets and cheap studio locations. David questions Mrs Clarke, in a five-page scene early in the story, trying to find out more about Jimmy. An important scene because it confirms our impression of Jimmy as dangerous, and introduces the web of lies Mrs Clarke has constructed to make Jimmy seem capable of murder, judicious editing would have improved its impact.

The main dramatic obstacle in the first part of the film occurs when Jimmy refuses to see David, insisting on his own guilt, even when David is convinced of his innocence. The buildup is slowly paced at times, especially in these early stages, as David goes back and forth to Jimmy to try to get him to talk. Television detective-style question-and-answer dialogue is effective, as in the following extract when David questions Jimmy in prison, but Jimmy slips up:

> JIMMY
> Well, she kept looking at me and talking to me, and she wouldn't
> stop, and I lost my temper and stabbed her in the chest.

David reacts.

> DAVID
> In the chest?

> JIMMY
> I didn't mean to do it, but she wouldn't leave me alone.

> DAVID
> Mrs Richmond was stabbed in the back!

Jimmy reacts, but covers up quickly.

> JIMMY
> I meant in the back.

> DAVID (pressing hard now)
> But you said in the chest.

> JIMMY
> It was just a slip! My memory isn't so good. (ibid.: 27)

The above scene could have been substantially cut but ends on a dramatic and major turn – that Jimmy didn't kill Mrs Richmond:

> HOLD DAVID looking at JIMMY – realising that the entire case has suddenly
> changed. (ibid.: 28)

The revelation motivates David to investigate further and he questions people at the hostel who knew Jimmy. The story changes direction, from one of representing a murderer, to the much more dramatic need to prove someone's innocence. David's suspicion is aroused at the hotel where Mrs Clarke and Sanders behave strangely, with asides between the couple alerting the reader to their untrustworthiness. We are told 'Sanders exchanges another quick look with Mrs Clarke …'. These suspicions are confirmed when Mrs Clarke makes veiled threats to Diana, the girl who has agreed to act as Jimmy's character witness:

> MRS CLARKE
> I mean, when you get up in court, it wouldn't do to say anything
> foolish – now would it?

> DIANA (looks down)

> MRS CLARKE
> Good. I knew you'd see it my way. After all, as much as we all
> feel sorry for Jimmy, his guilt is his own affair. (pointedly) We
> wouldn't want to see him drag down anyone else with him.
> (ibid.: 35)

The story livens up once David realises that Diana is withholding information and tries to talk
to her on her own. The reader is privy to tantalising plot details ahead of the protagonist, hearing a friend of Diana's hint that the murdered woman, Mrs Richmond, was also in cahoots with
Mrs Clarke and Sanders to make some sort of illegal delivery.

More than halfway into the script David decides to take action as Mrs Clarke will not let him
talk to Diana. His girlfriend Fay acts as a decoy so that David can speak to Diana alone at the
hotel. Some effective cross-cutting of scenes builds tension when Fay arrives, pretending to be
compiling a report on the hotel for a welfare bureau. She lures Mrs Clarke away from David,
enabling him to question the reluctant Diana:

INT. LOUNGE. DAY

David and Diana. David rises, goes to the door, looks out, and closes it quietly.
Then he returns to Diana.

> DAVID
> Look, I've got to talk fast – before they come back.

> DIANA
> I don't understand.

> DAVID
> First of all – I want to know the truth.

> DIANA (reacts nervously)
> The truth?

> DAVID
> About you and Jimmy. I know you haven't told me the whole
> story.

> DIANA (protests)
> But I have!

>   DAVID
>   Diana, what are you afraid of?

>   DIANA
>   Nothing!

>   DAVID
>   But you do know Jimmy better than you've admitted?

>   DIANA
>   No, I'm telling you – I hardly knew him at all.

>   DAVID
>   And yet you sent him your personal regards – and when he
>   heard about it, he was upset.

DIANA reacts.

>   DAVID
>   And you're the only one who has offered to testify for him.

>   DIANA
>   It's what anyone would do.

>   DAVID
>   Not just anybody, Diana. You're the only one – here or
>   elsewhere. All right, I think I'd better lay my cards on the table
>   first. You see, I don't believe Jimmy murdered Mrs Richmond.

Diana reacts stunned.

INT. DIANA'S ROOM. DAY

Mrs Clarke is showing it to Fay.

>   MRS CLARKE
>   Now this is typical of the sort of room we provide for the girls.
>   (ibid.: 47–8)

The sequence cuts back and forth, the tension building up as Fay tries to distract the couple. We know David's time with Diana is limited and Sanders arrives just as she is about to reveal some vital information:

INT. LOUNGE. DAY

David and Diana. The latter has loosened up considerably in her anxiety to help.

> DAVID
> That's why I think Jimmy is holding something back.

> DIANA
> But I was so positive he did it.

> DAVID
> Why?

> DIANA
> Because – (impulsively) Mrs Richmond wasn't the person
> everyone thought she was.

David reacts.

> DAVID
> Wasn't she?

> DIANA
> No. And this place … it isn't …

DOOR OPENS suddenly and Sanders enters. At the sight of him, Diana clams up.
David reacts furious, but helpless.

> SANDERS
> I hope I'm not disturbing you, sir. I have to fix one of the window
> sashes in here. (ibid.: 50)

Tension mounts as infomation is dripfed to the reader and, while clichéd, this technique achieves its aim. Vital details are held back until the best possible moment; in this case just as Diana is about to tell more about Mrs Clarke, Sanders opens the door, the conversation ends and the reader is hooked in, wanting to know more. Further clues come to light, when Fay recognises Mrs Clarke as someone with links to drug dealing. The scenes link neatly together in furthering the revelation process and the final pieces fall into place in the next scene when David confronts Jimmy, who admits that the house is a front for running drugs, with young and vulnerable residents threatened if they refuse to do as they are told.

Although the plot is barely credible, the script is written with gusto and the dialogue flows easily and naturally. For instance, when Jimmy explains that he lied to protect Diana, David replies:

> DAVID
> There are enough mitigating circumstances to free her. Believe
> me, I know. You should have asked to see a lawyer before you
> said anything.

JIMMY
With my record? What chance did I stand? I figured they'd pin it
on me anyway. This way, at least Diana was protected.

DAVID (exasperated)
Protected? By who? A muscle-bound killer? A dope peddler?

JIMMY
I thought it would soon blow over and she'd be all right.

David gets up and starts moving towards the door.

DAVID
The next time you talk to the police, I want you to tell them
exactly what you just told me.

JIMMY
Where are you going?

DAVID
Scotland Yard. We're going to have to see about Diana quick.

Dissolve to

EXT. SCOTLAND YARD. DAY (ibid.: 60)

Ending the scene on the urgent need to do something injects pace and drives the story forward.
Even though the scene is more than four pages long, Grantham's writing propels the action from
line to line in a way that links the events together. As the scene cuts to Scotland Yard, we assume
something will be done to help Diana. In fact, the police there are reluctant to get involved and,
once they agree to bring Diana in for voluntary questioning, Mrs Clarke alleges that no one
knows where she is.

The denouement shows that Diana has been drugged by Mrs Clarke and Sanders. David
intends to rescue Diana but Fay, continuing in her active role, insists on going with him. By the
time David breaks into the house, Sanders and Mrs Clarke have resolved to murder Diana and
the story takes a darker turn. David attacks Sanders and, in a series of very short scenes, cutting
from the room, to the hotel corridor, to the outside, the script builds to a crescendo. David
knocks Sanders out and Fay arrives with a policeman, who catches Mrs Clarke. The dramatic
ending sees the villainous Sanders produce a gun:

INT. DIANA'S ROOM. NIGHT

Diana, dazed and sleepy, sits up and surprised in bed as David enters and locks the
door again quickly.

DIANA
Mr Kyle.

DAVID
Help me move some of the furniture against the door.

David starts to pull the dresser over in front of the door.

Diana lends a hand.

CUT TO

INT. HALLWAY. NIGHT.

Sanders who has just gotten up, blind with fury, moves to the door, and while Mrs. Clarke watches anxiously, tries to break it down with his shoulder.

CUT TO

INT. DIANA'S ROOM. NIGHT.

David keeps the dresser pressed against the door, as the door takes a terrific pounding from the outside. Diana watches terrified.

CUT TO

INT. HALLWAY. NIGHT

Sanders, unable to shoulder the door down, draws a gun.

MRS. CLARKE
No! They'll hear you all over the place!

But Sanders, fuming, pushes her away and shoots at the lock.

CUT TO

INT. DIANA'S ROOM. NIGHT.

As the shots are heard from the outside, David grabs Diana.

DAVID
Down!

They both dive away from the door.

CUT TO

EXT. PRIVATE HOTEL. NIGHT

Fay, waiting outside the hotel, reacts as she hears the shots. A policeman comes hurrying down the street. Fay stops him and says something anxiously, pointing to the hotel. They both move quickly towards the entrance. (ibid.: 68–9)

Tension is carefully built up to the catching of the crooks and the happy ending; Jimmy and Diana receive suspended sentences and go free.

Grantham's action scenes display verve and flair, making the screenplay dramatically engaging, despite the fact that the plot and story lack credibility. The film is remarkably true to the script, suggesting that the Danzigers expected it to be shot as written, unless there were compelling reasons to do otherwise.

Night Train for Inverness

This lively, seventy-seven page melodrama concerns a couple, Ann and Roy, who separate when Roy is imprisoned for a crime he did not commit, and what happens to their diabetic son, Tim. Ann's vindictive mother has turned her against Roy and will not let him visit their home or see his son. When released from prison, Roy resorts to kidnapping Tim to spend time with him, without knowing that the boy has recently been diagnosed as diabetic. Tim has to take insulin regularly and could fall into a coma and die if he eats the wrong food. The second half of the film revolves around the police hunt for the son, father and Roy's ex-girlfriend, Gloria before Tim lapses into a coma. Roy has enlisted Gloria's help and she hopes this will reignite their romance, before realising that Roy still loves Ann. Gloria leaves Roy and his son, but reveals their whereabouts so that Tim is found just in time, near to death. The film ends happily with Ann and Roy renewing their relationship, despite the mother-in-law.

The screenplay may be clichéd with few surprises but the suspense as to whether the boy will survive or not is often effective. Grantham successfully conveys the drama of the situation, with characters forced to overcome one obstacle after another. The most powerful aspect of the narrative concerns the mother's desperation to know her son's fate, but the dilemma of the girl-friend is also intriguing, with a careful handling of revelation.

Tim's diabetes is central to the spine of the story and set up clearly from the beginning. The reader is made aware that the boy must not eat sweets or miss an insulin injection, but his father remains ignorant. Almost four pages are dedicated to foreshadowing this point, highlighting the potential for tragedy. The dialogue may be 'on the nose' but is essential to the plot. Doctor Jackson reminds Ann (and explains to us):

Difficult choices in *Night Train for Inverness* (1960), written by Mark Grantham

JACKSON (nods)
As you know, Tim can't eat sweet things – ice cream,
chocolates, rich foods. For a diabetic, they can be deadly.

ANN
Yes, I know.

JACKSON
And it doesn't make them any the less deadly if someone
unknowingly gives a diabetic sweets out of kindness – especially
to a child who doesn't understand his condition and might not
refuse.

ANN
You mean a stranger …

The doctor's warning continues:

JACKSON
And I want to be brutally frank with you, Mrs Lewis, about the
grave responsibility you have with Tim. A diabetic cannot live very
long without insulin. If he misses so much as one injection …

ANN
It would never happen, Doctor. I love him too much. (MMG3: 4–5)

The mother-in-law functions as the catalyst for the drama, her actions having consequences
that drive the story. She hides Roy's letters and tells Roy his wife and son don't want to see him.
This is the trigger that makes Roy kidnap Tim. The mother-in-law's long and irrational tirade
against Roy, arouses our sympathy for him as a character as well as disclosing the unhappy backstory to their family life:

MRS WALL
I know more about men and their ways than you do! Your father
was the same way – lying, always lying about affairs I knew he
had! Only he was rich enough to afford his tarts! Roy wasn't!

ANN
But I feel so guilty! Never going to see him once since he's been
in prison! Never answering his letters!

MRS WALL
You were right to follow my advice! The man cheated on you
and lied to you! He's completely worthless!

> ANN
> But Tim misses him terribly. They were always so close! (ibid.: 9)

Roy's character is portrayed as being more complex than that of his wife, Ann, who does little other than cry and worry about her son. Our first introduction to him is crisp and informative:

> Pick up Roy as he gets off the train, carrying a single, cheap suitcase. Roy is about 30 – handsome, well-built, and, now, serious. He alights from the train with the air of a man who has been away for a long time and is glad to be back. (ibid.: 11)

The reader is placed in an interesting position: we know Tim is diabetic, while his father doesn't; we know what has happened to Tim; we know more than both the mother, the doctor and the detective, who do not know where Tim is. This powerful dramatic device endows the reader with omniscience, initiating more tension and anxiety, as we can see the events from all the characters' points of view yet remain unsure whether the boy will be found in time.

Some convincing dialogue between Roy and his ex-girlfriend, Gloria, when they meet again divulges their backstory in a subtle and believable way. They talk about their past in a long, seven-page scene and, although expositional, the reader is interested to learn why Roy stole money from where he worked; why he is not allowed to see Tim and how Gloria hopes to rekindle their relationship. When Roy asks Gloria to help with the kidnap, she replies:

> GLORIA
> Is that the only reason you're asking me? Because any old
> woman would do?

> ROY
> Gloria, you know how I feel about you.

> GLORIA
> Do I?

> ROY
> We've been friends for a long time.

> GLORIA
> We weren't always just friends, Roy.

> ROY
> Will you help me?

> GLORIA
> What about Ann?

> ROY
> I've just told you …

                                                                    64.
                                    ROY
                        Gloria, wait!

                                    GLORIA (bitterly)
                        For what!

              GLORIA slams out of the compartment. ROY looks at TIM sadly.

                                                    CUT TO:

90.   INT. TRAIN PASSAGE. NIGHT.

        GLORIA hurrying up it with her suitcase runs into the GUARD.

                                    GLORIA (still fuming)
                        When's the next station?

                                    GUARD
                        We make a twenty-one minute stop at
                        Perth at 4:54, Ma'm. Get to Inverness
                        at 8:59.

                                    GLORIA (pushing past him)
                        Who the hell wants to go to Inverness!

        GUARD looks after her slightly puzzled.

                                                    CUT TO:

91.   INT. COMPARTMENT. NIGHT.

        ROY is still holding the sleeping TIM. He suddenly leans over
        slightly and smells the boy's breath. He reacts slightly
        puzzled — more curiosity than concern. TIM's rate of
        breathing is worse than ever.

                                                    DISSOLVE TO:

92.   INT. COMMUNICATIONS ROOM. NIGHT.

        ANN is still tossing and moaning wide-eyed on the bench. She
        suddenly sits up with a start.

                                    ANN (vague)
                        Tim?

        JACKSON moves over to her quickly.

                                    JACKSON
                        It's all right, Mrs. Lewis.

                                    ANN (numb)
                        You haven't found him yet?

                                    JACKSON
                        We will soon. Don't worry.

        ANN suddenly breaks down and sobs uncontrollably.

                                    JACKSON
                        I'll get you a sedative. You'll feel
                        much better.

        PAN WITH JACKSON as he moves off to get his black bag on
        the other side of the room. KENT is already there. JACKSON
        looks at him questioningly. KENT shakes his head with
        futility.

                                    KENT (sotto)
                        How much more time do you think the boy
                        might have?

Cutting from scene to scene in the screenplay
Night Train for Inverness

GLORIA
You haven't told me how you feel about her now.

ROY
What difference does it make?

GLORIA
All the difference in the world to me! I don't have many more
years to waste! (ibid.: 21–2)

Grantham packs a great deal of practical and emotional detail into this scene. We learn of the
past relationship and that Gloria wishes to renew it; and that she needs to know whether Roy is
still in love with Ann. We are also reminded about what is at stake for Gloria, which provokes
our sympathy and helps us to understand her actions.

Showing time ticking onward is a stock dramatic device in films, in this case to increase the
suspense about whether Tim will be rescued in time. We are regularly reminded that time is of
the utmost importance: the first occasion is when Mrs Wall tells her daughter Roy called at the
house, after Tim has been kidnapped, Ann reacts furiously:

ANN
Oh, God, Mother, how could you have been so stupid!

Mrs Wall reacts hurt and martyred. Her daughter seldom talks to her like that.

MRS WALL
Well!

Ann hurries to the phone and dials 999.

ANN (into phone)
Give me the police! And, please hurry!

(to Mrs Wall) Mother, Roy, doesn't know that Tim's a diabetic!

TRACK IN to C.U. MANTEL CLOCK. It now read '6.20'. (ibid.: 30)

Many cuts to close-ups of watches and clocks underline the lapse of time as Tim slips into
unconsciousness, as in this sequence which refers back to the doctor's description of the symp-
toms of a diabetic coma:

INT. COMPARTMENT. NIGHT.

C.U. TIM

He is still licking dry lips. He is breathing just a bit more rapidly than usual, and making a slight hissing sound with his exhalations.

CUT TO:

M.S. COMPARTMENT

Roy runs his hand fondly over Tim's head. Gloria watches with ever-heightening annoyance. She is about to say something, but stops when she realises that Roy is only paying attention to the sleeping boy. She glances at her watch impatiently.

INSERT WOMAN'S WRISTWATCH. It reads: '1:55'.

FADE TO:

WOMAN'S WRISTWATCH. It now reads: '2:20'.

CUT TO:

C.U. TIM

He breathes just a shade more rapidly than before, and the hiss is that much more audible. His lips are drier than ever and his face a bit gaunt.

DISSOLVE TO:

INT. COMMUNICATIONS ROOM. NIGHT. (ibid.: 59)

The cutting back and forth between scenes to relay information is another device to develop tension and remind the reader about the situation in different locations; in this case from the police station, where the detective and the mother wait for news, to the train where Tim is descending into a coma. The drama is ratcheted up, first, by a false alarm as the police wrongly believe they have found father and son, and second, when a doctor (Higgins) joins them in the carriage. The reader's hopes are raised, expecting the doctor to diagnose Tim but, instead he tells Roy the boy is travel sick and proceeds to feed him sweets, the worst thing he could do:

HIGGINS

Ah, I know what'll make you feel better!

He produces a crumpled up little bag from inside his pocket.

HIGGINS (smiles to TIM)

Like a chocolate drop? (ibid.: 54)

As Tim's condition deteriorates, further information is disclosed: we find out that Roy still loves his ex-wife, Ann and that Gloria wants to marry Roy. Rather than seeming like exposition, these details come from Gloria, revealing her position in the triangle, putting pressure on Roy and reminding him of what she stands to lose:

> GLORIA
> I want to know if you're going to marry me! If you have any intention at all! I want to know now! I'm in a hurry! I've been on too many long train rides to Inverness! I don't want to die being somebody else's old Aunt Gloria! Are you going to marry me, or are you still thinking of Ann? (ibid.: 63)

The melodramatic scene evokes further sympathy for Gloria, who exclaims:

> GLORIA
> Then you still love Ann!

> ROY
> I haven't got a hope with Ann!

> GLORIA
> But you still love her! You won't ever forget her, will you? You won't even try! That's why you took the kid, isn't it? Because he's part of her! (ibid.: 63)

This realisation leads Gloria to leave Roy and we move into the final act of the script. Gloria gets off the train and the scene cuts back to Tim as his breathing deteriorates, then cuts to Ann sobbing, as she waits in the police station for news. Kent, the detective, asks the doctor:

> KENT (sotto)
> How much more time do you think the boy will have?

> JACKSON (glancing towards clock)
> An hour – maybe more, maybe less. (he shrugs)

> PAN UP TO WALL CLOCK. It reads: '5.15'. (ibid.: 65)

Once off the train, Gloria enters the station café and orders a coffee. The counterhand mentions the missing boy, having heard about it on the radio. He functions as a device to deliver the information that Tim is diabetic. She reacts, incredulous:

> GLORIA
> A what?

                              COUNTERHAND
            Diabetic. The kid can't live without insulin. His father took him
            away a couple of hours before he was due for another injection.

                                  GLORIA
                   You say he can't live without insulin?

                              COUNTERHAND
                               Not very long.

                                  GLORIA
                                 How long?

                              COUNTERHAND
            Well, my brother-in-law's a chemist. He says the kid may never
            see daylight unless he's treated before then.

     Gloria reacts, fights with herself, then visibly hardens.

                              COUNTERHAND
                               Tough isn't it?

                               GLORIA (snaps)
            I'm not interested in anybody else's troubles. I've got enough of
            my own. That kid and his father could drop dead for all I care!

     Counterhand reacts astonished. Hold Gloria still bitter, as she drinks coffee and eats
     the buns.

     PAN UP TO BUFFET CLOCK. It reads: '5:20'. (ibid.: 66)

There then follows a succession of quick cuts back and forth from the clock, to Gloria, to Tim
and back to Gloria, a tense atmosphere produced by the vivid description and sound direction:

     She starts to sip her coffee again.

     A PIERCING SHRIEK OF A TRAIN WHISTLE is heard. The sound should be
     electrifying like a sudden scream. It cuts off the sound of TIM'S breathing.

     GLORIA reacts.

     PULL BACK QUICKLY to include counterhand in frame.

                              COUNTERHAND
                    There's your London train, Miss. Right on time.

GLORIA rises as COUNTERHAND moves over to a small radio behind the counter
and turns it on.

COUNTERHAND
Just want to hear if there's anything more about that kid.

As Gloria leaves for the train the radio comes on with an emotional appeal for help for Tim
from his mother, Ann:

ANN'S VOICE
My little boy is very dear to me. But now he needs help, and I
can't give it to him. His life hinges on chance – the chance that a
stranger will see him and save his life. So, I beg you. Please – if
anyone knows anything about where my son is at the moment –
please! Please notify the police right away.

GLORIA stands fighting with herself.

LOUDER SOUND OF TRAIN PULLING INTO STATION is heard.

GLORIA suddenly wheels and hurries to the phone booth in the corner of the buffet.
THE COUNTERHAND, who has just turned off the radio, reacts surprised. (ibid.: 69–70)

The turn in the story is cleverly achieved: Gloria hears Ann's voice, the woman who Roy loves
and who is, in effect, her adversary. The scene is moving because we understand both women's
positions. Gloria informs the police that Tim is on the Inverness train and we see her look in the
mirror next to the phone booth:

C.U. MIRROR

Gloria is reflected in it. She is haggard and weary, and her face seems more lined
than ever. She slowly lifts her hand and sadly touches one of the lines under her eyes.
(ibid.: 70)

The whole sequence has a powerful momentum, from Tim's decline into a coma, to Gloria
finally electing to divulge the boy's whereabouts. The scene also has great pathos: Gloria's motivations are made understandable: she feels bitter and rejected and the gradual lead-up to her decision
to call the police, is sensitively handled, while our uncertainty about her character serves to build
suspense. The script focuses on Gloria's uncertainty, and the audience is similarly unsure as to what
she will do. The scene is poignant, as we know Gloria's relationship plans with Roy have been
thwarted and are aware that she feels her time as an attractive and eligible woman is running out.

The buildup to the dramatic finale is excellent and the emotional resonance is affecting.
When the train is halted, Roy tries to run into the train corridor, carrying his comatose son. He
knocks over a policeman, who is boarding the train, and is about to escape when a hospital
intern shouts out that Tim is seriously ill:

M.S. ROY

Angled from the other end of the passage, so that he is rushing into CAMERA, with others in b.g. Roy stops running and reacts.

INTERN

He's already missed an injection! He's dangerously ill. You must have smelt the acetone on his breath! Like nail polish! He's burning up inside!

Roy looks down horrified at Tim. (ibid.: 74)

Just in time Roy realises what is happening and Tim's life is saved.

Chibnall and McFarlane conclude this represents Grantham's most effective script for the Danzigers: 'There may be something mechanical about the way the strands of the plot are brought together in this suspenseful tale, but the writing catches the right social class ... the denouement has a quietly humane quality' (2009: 162). Despite some overlong scenes, the characters seem to act as real people, behaving in complex ways and making difficult decisions, particularly in the case of Gloria. The screenplay is carefully plotted and tension built up to the moving climax in which the emotionally wounded Gloria reveals where Tim and Roy are, saving the boy's life. In nearly all aspects the film remains true to the screenplay except for a slightly different ending, where the film heightens the emotion with a moving shot showing Roy carry his son to safety.

Despite severe budget restrictions and static sets, Grantham contrived a dynamic story, featuring moments of genuine drama and sympathetic characters while cleverly engaging cross-cutting, to add pace and drama as information is gradually disclosed.

To Hook a Man/She Always Gets Their Man

This screenplay follows an attractive young woman's move from the country to the city, to stay with her aunt, upsetting her aunt's friends when she attracts the attention of their boyfriends. The odd amusing moment cannot disguise the fact that the film is dramatically weak and the story and characters clichéd: the women are depicted as living in a world that revolves around finding and keeping a man, and are categorised as 'the mischief maker', 'the wronged woman' or 'the bitch'. Chibnall and McFarlane describe the film as 'a witless spin on the provincial-girl-at-large-in-London theme (ibid.: 96). This is a little unfair on the light comedy melodrama whose screenplay, despite the dubious politics, displays an energy which makes it readable and more enjoyable than the film, in which Godfrey Grayson's direction dissipates the low-key drama in the story. The two narrative strands, in the two locations, are artfully melded together: the office, where Betty, the protagonist, a very capable secretary, is in love with her boss, and the residential home for young ladies in Kensington where she rooms with her friends.

On the negative side, both male and female characters are stereotyped to the point of being unbelievable. The men appear silly and weak because they become obsessed by an attractive young woman, while the women are reduced to the single aim of hooking a man. Betty and her friend, Sylvia, are slightly more complex though, with Sylvia accorded some witty lines; for instance, when she complains to Betty about losing her boyfriend and the shortage of men:

SYLVIA
I've just lost a wrestling match with Arthur's Oedipus complex.

BETTY
Have you had a row?

SYLVIA (ironic)
Oh, no. Just a short argument with long knives. That line I just
pulled out marked the end of the most beautiful switchboard
romance of the century.

BETTY (sympathetic)
Oh Sylvia, I'm so sorry.

SYLVIA
That's all right. There's plenty of other fish in the sea. The
problem is getting them onto dry land. (MMG20: 5–6)

The character also drolly undercuts the gender clichés of the needy woman and displays a
cynicism in her desire for a man – it's not love that's she's looking for:

SYLVIA
Who said anything about love? Arthur just had two qualities
which appealed to me: he was a man and he was available.
(ibid.: 9)

Grantham neatly sets up the story problems: eligible men are difficult to find and Betty is in
love with her boss, who appears not to be interested in her. Sylvia is used to bring this up when
Betty tells her that her boyfriend wasn't 'worth loving', Sylvia retorts:

SYLVIA
It's easy enough for you to talk. You've got a man in Bob Conley.

BETTY (ironic)
All I've got is a man who is only just beginning to realise that
there's something missing in his life. He hasn't asked me to fill
the gap yet.

SYLVIA
Well, at least you've got a clear field.

BETTY
For the moment. The question is: how long can I keep it that
way? All I am is his secretary. (ibid.: 9–10)

She Always Gets Their Man (1962), a clichéd comedy written by Mark Grantham

Grantham introduces a dramatic question which needs to be answered and, in the next moment, Betty opens a letter informing her that her niece, Sally, is coming to London to stay for a while. When Sally arrives, the gangly young girl Betty remembers has been transformed into a 'man stealer'.

The initial setup satisfies the needs of the story; here is a world suffering from a shortage of men. Betty's boss proves increasingly difficult to catch as more hurdles crop up, in the form of a new competitor, Sally, who upsets all the women, including Betty, and generates further dramatic conflict. These conditions may be contrived but are required to produce the dynamics for the story: the women desperate to keep their men are put out when their boyfriends are more interested in the new girl in town.

To fit the logic of the narrative arc and to push the story to its limits, the central question becomes: what will Betty have to do to stop her niece taking their men, including her boss? The complications need to be compelling to maintain our interest. As the situation worsens, Betty hires a decoy, in the form of an actor, Waling, to pretend to be a millionaire, with the aim of seducing her niece. This action initiates lots more complications, with humorous consequences when it all goes wrong. Both Sally and Betty's boss, Bob, are completely taken in by Waling, a drunken Shakespearian actor. Bob asks Waling for financial advice, but the latter gets carried away with his role and begins to buy vast sums in stocks and shares:

> WALING
> Oh, here we are. United Potash is selling at only ten shillings.
> Must be worth at least twice that. We'll buy a million shares just
> to start off with.

> BOB
> But a million shares at ten shillings is five hundred thousand
> pounds!

> WALING
> Is that all? Better make it two million then.

> BOB
> Sir Basil, you don't understand. If you'd only look at the books
> first. I don't have that kind of money to invest.

> WALING
> How much money have you got?

>   BOB (calls)
>   Betty, how much money have we got?
>
>   BETTY (drily)
>   Including the post office savings account?
>
>   BOB
>   Yes.
>
>   BETTY
>   Three hundred and twelve pounds, fourteen and sixpence.
>   Of that we owe all but the fourteen and six.
>
>   BOB (to Waling)
>   See what I mean? Besides, what do I want with Synthetic Potash?
>
>   WALING (dramatically)
>   We'll build an empire on it!

Betty and Sylvia exchange worried looks. (ibid.: 75–6)

The story and dialogue are particularly entertaining in this section: as the situation becomes more extreme, Waling takes action, adding a dynamism to the story that the characters of Betty and Bob, although likeable, lack. The complications increase when Betty realises Waling might lose all of Bob's companies limited funds. In the final part of the script, Betty is pushed to the point where she has to do something and decides to reveal to Sally that Waling is a fake:

>   BETTY
>   It was silly of us to believe that he'd do some good just by a
>   fluke. He's going to spend every penny Bob has on worthless
>   shares and put him further into debt.
>
>   SYLVIA
>   So? What next?
>
>   BETTY
>   Sally's going to have to know the truth.
>
>   SYLVIA
>   Just call me when it's over. I'll be standing outside your door with
>   the first aid kit. (ibid.: 77)

Sally, however, refuses to believe that Waling is an imposter so that Betty is forced into doing the worst thing possible in order to convince her. She resolves to tell Bob, the man she loves, what she has done and risk losing him:

                              BETTY
No. (glumly). It's got to be like this. I know I'll probably lose Bob
when he finds out the truth, but it was my idea, so Waling and I
will have to drown together.

                              SYLVIA
You realise that with you gone, Sally's going to try to sink her
claws into Bob in revenge?

                              BETTY
                Yes, I know. But I can't help that.

                              SYLVIA
            Well, at least it'll do her good to be in on the kill.

                              BETTY
She won't be there. I told her that Bob was giving her the
afternoon off. So she won't be back after lunch.

                              SYLVIA
                            But why?

                              BETTY
I wouldn't get any satisfaction out of deliberately exposing
Waling in front of her just so that she would be humiliated.
No, it's better this way. (ibid.: 80)

As well as heralding the next plot development, Grantham here reminds us of Betty's intrinsic
good nature. We know she deserves Bob and this is therefore her lowest moment in the story,
emphasised by the spirit in which she refuses to humiliate Sally, even when she knows her niece
will probably take Bob from her.

    Grantham now resorts to a clever dramatic device: we are deliberately not told any more
about Betty's plans to expose Waling. The following scene in the screenplay, which differs from
the film version, shows Betty visiting a mystery man on a yacht and then the two at the office
together:

INT. YACHT. DAY

INSET of a bulkhead. (All this needs is a single porthole in it to establish that this is a
yacht interior.) Betty sits talking to an unidentified, distinguished looking middle-aged
MAN.

                              BETTY
                    And that's the whole story.

MAN (grimly)
This is a pretty serious affair. (ibid.: 81)

At the office the man is unveiled as the real Sir Basil Clayborn. The film version cuts this scene, possibly to save using another location, but misses out on the dramatic interest created.

The plot twists around when Sylvia enters the office, dragging a reluctant Sally with her. There is a further twist when Sally bursts into tears and Sir Basil, mesmerised by her beauty, asks her to 'go somewhere and have a good laugh over it'. Sally responds:

SALLY
You mean now?

CLAYTON
If you'll do me the honour.

SALLY (with wide-eyed innocence)
Oh, it's me who should be honoured, Sir Basil.

CLAYBORN
Then shall we go, Sally? You don't mind if I call you Sally? (ibid.: 83)

The scene end reminds us that Betty believes she has lost Bob:

SYLVIA (ironic)
Well trust Sally to fall right back on her gold-digging feet.

BOB (seriously)
Betty, I'd like to see you in my office.

Bob goes into his office. Betty looks glumly at Sylvia, then follows him in. (ibid.: 84)

Betty enters, expecting to be sacked, but the final scene confounds this expectation, providing a happy ending in which Bob tells her he would have done the same thing. There is a final humorous touch when Bob characterises Sally as 'so innocent', prompting Betty to explode with indignation.

The story, with some humour, depicts women as in desperate need of a man, and men as gullible and easily swayed by beauty. Sally represents the predatory female while the others, such as Betty and Sylvia, are shown as being at a disadvantage because of their niceness. The screenplay presents a pre-feminist perspective, where women have no hope of financial security or happiness unless they find a man, a rule applying as much to Sally as the others. Yet there are some contradictions: Betty is demonstrably the organiser in Bob's business, supremely capable, with an understanding of money, successfully keeping the accounts, and is, if anything, more talented than her boss.

The clichéd elements in the plot illustrate the extreme positions which drive the narrative. If the women were not desperate and in competition, there would be no dramatic motivation. Sally's arrival compounds the women's problems; her youth and attractiveness disrupt the status quo, which entails certain rules that are taken for granted, the primary one being that they do not steal each other's boyfriends.

Grantham's style displays a light touch and, while the characters are narrowly drawn, they are amusing and engaging. They may lack complexity but their problems are presented in a diverting way. Betty appears rather too saintly and devoted but she is an honourable and like-able character whose journey is interesting to follow. *She Always Gets Their Man* may stretch our credibility while presenting women in a hopelessly clichéd way, and be rather repetitive in the middle, but it is often imaginative and fun to read.

CONCLUSION

While Grantham's output was substantial, its quality varied, with the best screenplays, such as *Feet of Clay* and *Night Train for Inverness*, proving compelling reads that translated into watch-able films, but other scripts such as *The Battleaxe* (1962) are hampered by unbelievable plots and one-dimensional characters. Yet the range of Grantham's writing, from comedy, to thriller, to horror, is impressive. The screenplays often revolve around women and, even when concerned with the conventionally masculine world of the crime story, scripts like *Feet of Clay* boast female characters who are central to the narrative, such as the lawyer's social worker girlfriend and the drug ring mastermind, Mrs Clarke.

Grantham wrote with great speed and often with some skill, although constantly limited by the type of film required by the Danziger brothers: stories that could be written in two weeks and would be quick to film and cheap to make. Grantham's screenplays were often faithfully transferred to the screen because the Danzigers expected the director to film quickly and keep production costs low and any variation from the script would be expensive to implement. Ironically, this practice lent 'B' movie writers like Grantham more control, with their scripts not just considered the blueprint for the film.

When compared to the *Carry On* scribes discussed in the next chapter, Grantham enjoyed a degree of autonomy, whereas Peter Rogers, the producer of the *Carry On* films, and an experi-enced writer and script editor, kept a tighter rein on the content of his screenplays. Despite this, the two main writers, Norman Hudis and Talbot Rothwell, pressed their individual stamps on the popular series, whose scripts were similarly quickly written but to a particular comedy format that proved to be extremely popular in the 1960s and early 1970s.

NOTES

1. It was rumoured that the Danziger brothers left the US because of the McCarthy witch hunts but other gossip suggested they were fleeing substantial debts in the US film industry (MMG 1: 1).
2. Hugh Leonard, who replaced Grantham as the writer on *The Kennedys of Castleross*, explains; 'When Grantham got to the stage of dementia where even his milkman began to look and sound like Mrs Kennedy, he fled to London' (Leonard 1999).
3. The Eady Levy was set up in 1950 to help fund UK film-making. A levy was made on each cinema ticket sold and a portion of the proceeds donated to producers as funding. Money also went to the National Film Finance Corporation, the BFI and the Children's Film Fund. The levy was abolished in 1985 (McFarlane 2008: 13).

4. David Mann's article notes how Brian Clemens successfully survived the transition from film to TV series. See Mann (2008: 291–7).
5. The series, which ran from 1955–60, employed many blacklisted American writers, who had moved to Europe because of the witch hunts by the House Un-American Activities Committee (HUAC) (ibid.: 290)
6. Kate Barley was one of the few women writers taken on by the Danzigers, penning a number of episodes of *The Vise* (ibid.: 175).

07
NORMAN HUDIS AND TALBOT ROTHWELL
CARRY ON FROM INSTITUTION TO INNUENDO

The *Carry On* films played to cinema audiences for more than thirty years, beginning with the sprightly *Carry on Sergeant* in 1958 and ending in 1992 with the damp squib of *Carry on Columbus*, which reputedly bankrupted Peter Rogers, the series producer. The idea originated when Rogers adapted R. F. Delderfield's play about national conscription, *The Bull Boys*. With a title change to *Carry on Sergeant*, the film performed so well at the box office that Rogers decided to develop it into a series, following in 1959 with *Carry on Nurse* and *Carry on Teacher*. The combination of bawdy humour and entertaining, if clichéd, characters proved so popular that twenty-seven *Carry On* films were produced between 1958 and 1974, with *Carry on Nurse* running for over a year in one Los Angeles cinema.

The first six scripts were written by Norman Hudis, from *Carry on Sergeant* to *Carry on Cruising* in 1962. The hit films attracted the attention of the Hollywood studios and Hudis, tempted by lucrative offers of work in film and television, left for California. Talbot Rothwell took over, penning *Carry on Cabby* in 1963 and scripting eighteen further *Carry On* films until 1974 when, after *Carry on Dick*, he was forced to retire due to ill health. After Rothwell left, a number of different writers took over the mantle, resulting in ever diminishing standards: Dave Freeman, a well-regarded TV comedy writer, scripted two films, *Carry on Behind* (1975) and the last of the series, *Carry on Columbus*; David Pursall and Jack Seddon wrote *Carry on England* (1976); Anthony Church scripted *That's Carry On* (1978); and prolific New Zealand writer Lance Peters wrote *Carry on Emmanuelle* (1978).

Rogers began his career on five-minute shorts for Rank's religious film unit before joining the scenario department at Gainsborough Studios, taken on by Muriel Box as a new talent, and credited as writer on films such as *Holiday Camp* and *Here Come the Huggetts*. Rogers was to become a permanent member of the Box family, later marrying producer Betty Box, sister of Sydney.

Rogers was notorious for exerting absolute control over the production process and keeping costs to a minimum, although the writers were paid relatively well. There is little written evidence of Rogers's influence on the stories but some of the documents in the Gerald Thomas Collection suggest a close working relationship with the writers. The notes on *Carry on Sergeant* reveal that Hudis and Rogers exchanged ideas regularly in the preliminary stages of story development.[1] Rogers was an experienced screenwriter but his contribution to the *Carry On* films occurred at the rewriting stage. He explains that, once the script was finalised, there would be no further amendments:

> Now I'm lazy about it. I just rewrite. I don't think Norman Hudis or Talbot Rothwell resented that
> … once we've reached the shooting stage, though, there is never any further alteration to the
> screenplay, and no improvisation whatsoever. (Gow 1970: 71)

All of the films, from *Carry on Sergeant* to *Carry on Columbus*, were directed by Gerald Thomas. Rogers wanted to work with a partner director and he knew Thomas through his brother, Ralph, who had been a director at Gainsborough Studios. Rogers and Thomas set up their own production company, Insignia, making the horror *Cat Girl* and crime story *The Flying Scot* in 1957, then deciding to focus on comedy, working with Norman Hudis for the first time on *The Tommy Steele Story* (1957). They were looking for other ideas to develop when, fortuitously, *The Bull Boys* became available.

THE *CARRY ON* WRITERS

The first writer of the *Carry On* series, Norman Hudis, left school at sixteen to become a journalist, beginning his film career as a publicist after serving in the RAF, then becoming an apprentice screenwriter at Pinewood. His first film credit was as a floor publicist on *The Astonished Heart* in 1949 and his first screenwriting credit on *Face in the Night* in 1956. Hudis wrote a number of 'B' features including *The Flying Scot*, a film which Steve Chibnall and Brian McFarlane compare favourably to the French heist film *Rififi* (1955), pointing out 'the individuating touches which Bennett and his scriptwriter, Norman Hudis … have brought to bear on character and plot' (2009: 271). By the time Hudis wrote *Carry on Sergeant* he was already an established writer, with thirteen screenwriting credits, including *The Tommy Steele Story*, which had been a hit in the UK and US. Rogers was impressed enough to ask Hudis to script the next Tommy Steele vehicle, *The Duke Wore Jeans* (1958).

The early *Carry On* films were huge hits on both sides of the Atlantic, especially *Carry on Nurse*, and Hudis left for Hollywood after *Carry on Cruising*. Besides the *Carry On* films, Hudis also created and scripted the TV series *Our House* (1960–2) and wrote episodes of other TV series such as *The Saint*, *Danger Man*, *The Man from U.N.C.L.E.* (1964–8) and then *Hawaii Five-O* (1968–80), after his move to the US. Hudis was still working until fairly recently and is credited with additional material for *Midsummer Madness*, an Austrian film of 2007.

Talbot Rothwell took over, rewriting Hudis's screenplay for *Carry on Cabby* in 1963. Rothwell had less experience of feature-film writing than Hudis but had scripted successful stage plays, and was an accomplished radio and TV writer who had penned material for some of Britain's best-known comedians, including the Crazy Gang, Terry-Thomas and Arthur Askey. Rothwell was also adept in other genres, such as crime, in the popular TV series *No Hiding Place* (1959). Rothwell's first comedy was designed to entertain prisoners of war while captured in World War II and he injected the music hall tradition much more directly into the *Carry On* films, as an acknowledged master of the 'gag' and a great comic wordsmith. Rothwell's scripts generally lacked the story element of Hudis's plots, and he relied much more heavily on wordplay, puns and double entendres. But the best of his work demonstrated a richness of language that was comedic, bawdy and Shakespearian in quality, as Kenneth Easthaugh observes,

> Just as the *Carry On* scripts by Norman Hudis are distinguishable by their strands of pathos, so those
> of Talbot Rothwell … are the ones most responsible for this knockabout, mocking, sometimes
> brilliant trickery with words, plus situations of genuine satire. (1978: 42)

NARRATIVE CONTENT OF THE *CARRY ON* SCREENPLAYS

James Chapman identifies three periods in the narrative content of the series: the first period, from 1958–62 includes the Norman Hudis screenplays, which he describes as social realist comedy, in which the narrative restores order by the end of the film. The second period, from 1963–8, covers Talbot Rothwell's early screenplays, concentrating on parody and spoof, with more ribald and risqué language. The third phase, from 1968–78, Chapman suggests is unstable, with the series trying to adapt, not very successfully, to an increasingly permissive society (2012: 100–1).

Many *Carry On* stories were based on a similar premise featuring the same actors as part of either an institution or hierarchical group, with those at the top of the hierarchy set up for ridicule. Jeffrey Richards contends that each film repeats the same narrative pattern and is dependent on working-class seaside humour:

> The series deployed a talented cast of farceurs repeating in a variety of settings a familiar repertoire of sketches, jokes and characterisations derived from the saucy seaside postcard world of Donald McGill, a world of fat ladies, and overflowing bosoms, nervous honeymoon couples and randy jack-the-lads, chamber pots and bedpans. (1997: 165)

Andy Medhurst is also critical of the stereotypical characters and the meagre narrative content, commenting, 'I find it hard to suppress the observation that while they matter, they are often thin, limp and skimpy' (2007: 129). There is some truth in both observations but to allege all the films have the same formulae is to oversimplify their narratives. The *Carry On* films display major differences in style and storyline, especially between the earlier Norman Hudis films and those by Talbot Rothwell. Hudis's scripts were gentler and less obviously sexual, relying on innuendo. They were far less visually explicit than Rothwell's visually vulgar scripts, such as *Carry on Behind*, although that latter's funniest films, such as *Carry on up the Khyber* (1968), were satirical, poking fun at British colonialism and British values. Certain films in the series boasted better storylines, possibly because more time was spent on their development but, conversely, weak stories were sometimes developed when they should have been abandoned. As Robert Murphy points out, '*Carry on Cleo* [1964] had an energy and inventiveness which other films were never quite to recapture' (1992: 251) but he does concede that *Carry on Cowboy* (1966), *Follow That Camel* (1967) and *Don't Lose Your Head* (1967) also have solid storylines (ibid.).

Marion Davis believes that the narratives became more formulaic with time, the early *Carry Ons* featuring stronger storylines and characters with wants and desires that drive the story, citing *Carry on Sergeant* as an example in which, 'the main theme (the sentimental desire of an ostensibly hard-bitten sergeant to end his career in muted glory by training an all star squad of the intake) is seriously presented' (1983: 315).

Davis also questions whether the *Carry On* films need necessarily be viewed in a negative light, asking to what extent they are mocking, self-knowing, ironic and playful. As she points out: 'The films celebrate with fertile innuendo the ingenuity with which the common language, so subjected to bowdlerisation, nonetheless throws sexual connotations, and, in so doing, they celebrate the liveliness of sexual interest' (ibid.: 322).

The *Carry On* films depict a narrow range of characters, all with an element of the comic postcard about them. The busty young female, the nagging wife, the saucy older woman, the lecherous men, the gay clichéd characters are an essential part of the genre, but are further fleshed out because the same actors play more or less the same role in each film: we know that Charles Hawtrey will play the 'wimpy, effeminate man', Sidney James the lecherous hero, Hattie Jacques will be the dominant matron figure and so on. This affords the film a tremendous advantage in that the audience knows these characters and has expectations as to how they will behave.

The best of the *Carry On* screenplays tap into a vein of humour that is timeless, with the characters placed in awkward situations; for instance, Charles Hawtrey and Kenneth Williams appearing as keen new recruits in *Carry on Constable*, required to cross-dress as female store detectives. The acting is funny but the dialogue and the movement of the scene are constructed so as to maximise the humour.

Most of the early films are set in an institution or hierarchical group, from the army to the hospital to school, in which the characters have to prove themselves. They are subject to the different rules and regulations of each group, while the hierarchies are undermined and ridiculed by the comic characters, the police station inspector in *Carry on Constable*, for instance. Rothwell parodies other film genres, deriving much comedy from the class inversions which lend the scripts their anarchic quality. Rothwell's screenplays include the history cycle of *Carry on Cleo*, *Carry on Jack* (1963), *Carry on Henry* (1971) and *Carry on up the Khyber*, and the genre spoofs of *Carry on Spying* (1964), *Carry on Screaming* (1966) and *Carry on Cowboy*. As Nicholas J. Cull observes: '*Carry On* set out to invade the territory that had been dominated by the forces of high British culture and million-dollar Hollywood budgets, and reassert lowbrow British humour' (2002: 94).

The narratives of these films are generally stronger because there is a plot or story pattern to follow or subvert: *Carry on Cleo* echoed the narrative of the box-office disaster *Cleopatra* (1963), even using the same sets at Pinewood, while *Carry on Henry* lampooned Alexander Korda's *The Private Life of Henry VIII* (1933) and contemporary films such as *Anne of the Thousand Days* (1969).

At their best, the *Carry On* screenplays combine energy and gusto with sharp wit and clever innuendo, but many negative stereotypes are woven into the narrative, particularly of women. The unattractive and nagging wife is a frequent trope, as played by Joan Sims as Calpurnia in *Carry on Cleo* or Sims again as Joan Ruff-Diamond in *Carry on up the Khyber*. The scripts embrace many other subjects, such as refusing to grow up and disorder versus order, as well as exploring insecurities about male sexuality. The later films derive much comedy from an obsessive interest in bare breasts and bottoms, though one of the overriding themes is that of class.

Rothwell's original scripts often had a darker edge than the resulting films, particularly in the endings. Cull notes that in *Carry on Jack*'s first draft, the two main characters were press-ganged to serve on the Bounty under a Captain Bligh, while in the first draft of *Carry on Cleo*, Hengist becomes 'a cuckold raising another man's children' (2002: 100).

The relationship between Bakhtin's notion of carnival and the *Carry On* narratives is evident: the stories frequently ridicule pomp, ceremony, institutions and hierarchies and involve the reversal of hierarchies. The fact that Sid James plays Henry VIII in *Carry on Henry* or Mark Antony in *Carry on Cleo* is already a parody, with the working-class pretender substituted for these classic historical figures. As Bakhtin comments:

> Carnival laughter is the laughter of all people. Second it is universal in scope; it is directed at all and everyone, including the carnival's participants; the entire world is seen in its droll aspect, in its gay relativity. Third, this laughter is ambivalent; it is gay, triumphant, and at the same time mocking, deriding. It asserts and denies, it buries and revives. Such is the laughter of carnival. (Bakhtin 1984: 911–12)

Mikita Brottman suggests that through carnival, 'subcultures can access social or political conflicts by allowing the parent culture to seem ridiculous and therefore less "venerated" in Bakhtinian terms' (2005: 34). Indeed, *Carry On* humour is often subversive and the stories delivered by Hudis and Rothwell, while lacking finesse, at their best tap into a bawdy vein of comedy, fostering a mocking attitude towards institutions, well-known historical figures and contemporary films.

THE GERALD THOMAS COLLECTION

The collection, donated by the director, contains screenplays, general correspondence, notes and letters about censorship, production budgets and daily production progress reports for each *Carry On* film, apart from *Carry on Columbus*. This section focuses on two films, the first of the series, *Carry on Sergeant*, written by Norman Hudis and *Carry on up the Khyber*, written by Talbot Rothwell.

Carry on Sergeant

Carry on Sergeant had a complicated genesis. It is an adaptation of Delderfield's successful play *The Bull Boys*, about a newly married man conscripted to do National Service in the 1950s. Producer Sydney Box was originally attracted to the story and, as early as 1955, had asked Delderfield for a brief outline and a first draft to be delivered 'as soon as possible but not later than eight weeks from commencement' (29/8/55). Only a week later another letter changes tack and details that 'this National Service Story which Mr. Delderfield was preparing for Box has been abandoned' (8/9/55). By that time Delderfield had already supplied a short fourteen-page outline and a developed treatment. The project was revived again two years later, in 1957, when letters between Sydney Box and Delderfield's agent discuss terms and conditions.

Later in 1957 the project changed hands from Box to Rogers. Unfortunately, there is no explanation for this, but it is likely that Rogers recognised the comic potential of the story in light of a new hit TV series *The Army Game* (1957–61), also about men undertaking National Service. Rogers was married to Betty, Box's sister and they probably frequently talked about each other's projects. Rogers then employed an experienced comedy writer, John Antrobus, to produce a new outline.[2] Antrobus was to be paid a fairly small sum for his work: £250 if the script was commissioned, £250 on completion of the screenplay and £150 on the first day of shooting (10/9/57).

Both Delderfield and Antrobus were working on the script at the same time but little of

William Hartnell and Kenneth Connor in *Carry on Sergeant* (1958), written by Norman Hudis

either version survived into later drafts, as Rogers points out to Antrobus's agent in March 1958, querying the 2 per cent profit percentage agreed: 'Quite frankly there is not a great deal of Antrobus in the script because what he wrote was really a radio script …' (31/3/58).

Norman Hudis was brought in to furnish a new draft because Rogers felt that Antrobus's script was not filmic enough. Hudis's work for other producers, including the Danziger brothers, had gained him a good reputation, although he had little experience of comedy.[3]

The collection holds two treatments for *Carry on Sergeant*: the first by R. F. Delderfield, adapted from his play; the second from Norman Hudis, including an outline story, story plan and character breakdown.[4]

R. F. Delderfield's treatment (GT 26/2)

Discussions with producer Sydney Box on 21 August, probably in 1957, led to the project being revived. Delderfield begins the fourteen-page treatment, noting:

> He is confident that this film can be amusing and extremely entertaining, and is ready to undertake the entire work himself, without collaboration. It is already agreed between Mr. Box and the author that – when the script reaches shooting stage, or possibly before the producer and director may, if they wish, add scenes of their own devising in consultation with the author.

Delderfield characterises the story as a mix of comedy and drama: 'The background will be, for the most part, amusing, but the thread quite serious. There will be undertones of pathos, near tragedy, and two romantic interludes, one heavy, one light, involving leading men.' The mix of styles is also mentioned: 'the film will be one-third documentary, one-third exciting incident building up to the climax … . In all the film will be laughter plus emotion, arising out of both character and situation.'

Delderfield emphasises the educational aspect of conscription, suggesting that the story 'underlines the theory that conscription today is less concerned with making soldiers than with making men equal to all emergencies'. He outlines the five key ideas in the story as follows:

1   That the great compensating factor for enforced discipline is the comradeship it engenders.
2   That a modern army training can be an important educational factor in the lives of underprivileged men.
3   That there is still room for intelligent and more civilising improvements in the big machine.
4   That the youth of Britain is not as effete as some foreign critics declare.
5   That Britain does not seek to use either conscription as an army or as a bully, or an international threat, but rather as an instrument of democracy. (GT 26/2)

The above list intimates that the film will constitute both entertainment and National Service propaganda. The focus of the treatment is on the characters as much as the narrative, as the 'aim of the film is to project the stories of a group of seven to nine National Service men, between the ages of 18 and 20' who are 'a group of socially-mixed men'. The central characters are portrayed as possessing desires and motivations and are supplied with problems to surmount, so that, by the end of the film, they have been changed by their experiences. Mike, the first character in the outline is described as bitter because his adolescence so far has been wasted. His father and grandfather, both doctors, bullied him into the profession. He is also sadly confused, for his fiancée is expecting a child and he can do little to protect her. He can't even marry her without both parents' consent. Fundamentally an intelligent and likeable fellow – and very much in love – he is at first surly and un-co-operative towards the army.

The treatment further explains how, with the help of his commanding officer, Mike becomes a happier person: due to 'the mediation of the C.O. Mike and Jenny are married, and from then on Mike's whole attitude changes'. Mike's character develops in a classical way: a problem is set up; he negotiates obstacles which are resolved by the end of the film, when his experience in the army changes from being negative to positive.

Delderfield characters hail from different classes and he fleshes out their home lives and their backgrounds. The contrasting roles encompass types such as 'the know-it-all', 'the dim but nice one' and 'the womaniser'. The seed of the 'camp' *Carry On* character is sown in our first meeting with Ellison, the antique dealer: 'Horrified by the conditions of the wash-basins, he prefers to clean himself with a toilet-set given by mother. He rubs his face with soft papers and cream.' Some conflict is set up between the men and particularly between the Corporal and the Sergeant, as Delderfield explains, 'There is a polite "war" between the Sgt. (who doesn't believe in National Service) and the Captain, an intelligent regular, who does.' Yet all of the characters are likeable, even the commanding officers, and there is no equivalent at this stage of Hudis's Sergeant Grimshawe from *Carry on Sergeant*.

In Delderfield's treatment the soldiers move from the army camp to the Welsh hills for further training. The men keep watch on a reservoir after heavy rain makes flooding likely. When the reservoir wall breaks, Tank, the illiterate recruit, has to compose a note requesting help, which a sheepdog carries back to the camp. The men are rescued and the reservoir made safe. The story ends happily, with all of the group awarded Lance Corporals' stripes for their efforts. The soldiers have matured through their experiences and we reflect on these changes when we witness the arrival of the new group of recruits who 'might be a flashback of this group, six months ago'.

The Delderfield treatment is initially set in a closed world, which opens up to allow complications to develop when the men travel to Wales and are posted to the reservoir. The focus shifts from the group to Tank's individual predicament; it thus becomes his story. Drama around the rescue falls into a classical narrative style rather than that of situation comedy. Indeed, there is very little broad comedy in Delderfield's version, despite some light-hearted moments such as Tank falling in love with a NAAFI girl, introduced thus: 'This is Edie, the plain girl-of-all-work, who somehow never gets a pleasant job. The TANK extracts a splinter from her hand and the romance begins.'

Norman Hudis's story basis, characters and screenplay plan (GT 26/3)
The Hudis story outline is very different to Delderfield's version and often little more than a rough sketch of ideas. It is divided into three sections:

1 Story Basis
2 Characters
3 Screenplay Plan.

The 'Story Basis' section establishes a change in the central protagonist from Tank, in Delderfield's version, to the Sergeant:

> This is the story of a Sergeant on the verge of retirement, determined to achieve his life's ambition by heading a Star Squad of National Servicemen. Fate sees to it that his last squad of preliminary-trainees includes six human obstacles to the realisation of this ambition: any one of them would be sabotage personified: taken together they present him with a Herculean task: they are the original men who, if laid end to end, it would be a good idea. The army invariably orders 'Carry On, Sergeant!' at moments of crisis. This film tells how one Sergeant doggedly obeyed this time-honoured order – and what a carry-on it turns out to be.

Section 2, 'Characters' supplies a pithy breakdown of the main cast, with some parallels to the Delderfield version, similarly using class and background to categorise the men: Lieutenant Potts is described as an 'Efficiency-mad Platoon Officer', army recruit Horace Strong is a 'Hypochondriac (former bookies clerk)', Jimmy Bailey a 'Rebel (former student)' and Miles Heywood as 'Dreamboat (independent means)'.

The six-page 'Screenplay Plan' reiterates the impossibility of the Sergeant's misssion, a productive area for drama and conflict in which the obstacles appear insurmountable. The plan emphasises the humour of the story and the characters have greater comic potential than those in the Delderfield version; even their names are changed to sound comic: Grimshawe, Potts, Strong and Golightly. The plot centres on Sergeant Grimshawe with the others reduced to ensemble roles. Some popular *Carry On* tropes are enlisted for the first time, the sexually aggressive, older and unattractive woman being a dominant one. For instance, we read: 'Middle-aged Norah works in the NAAFI and falls for Horace, pursuing him at every opportunity.'

The events now take place in a single location, the army camp. The plan is very much a 'work in progress', many of the scenes just existing as brief notes, in contrast to the greater detail of Delderfield's version. For instance, Hudis simply writes, 'Firing – range and grenade practice. Full comedy–value extracted' and 'Grimshawe meets squad at station. Discouraging start, probably involving Golightly locked in carriage (or elsewhere)'. The notes suggest that even at this stage there is still much uncertainty about the story and location.

Some of the plentiful visually comic ideas in the treatment do not make it into the film, as in the following:

> First drill session. Very discouraging. Bailey argumentative, Golightly bemused, Horace made of glass, Charlie preoccupied, Mills only with eyes for passing WRACS. DEAN, as the least stupid (apparently) invited to take over, try his hand at simple drill-orders. He does so: finds jazz-rhythms more readily springing to his tongue than march-rhythms. Squad ends up practically jiving.

The Hudis outline conveys a sense of how quickly ideas evolved in the draft, the emphasis changing from drama to situation comedy:

> NEW SUGGESTION: Initiative tests! Recruits sent out of camp in pairs, with sealed orders. This could legitimately open out the picture and be productive of enormous, fast-moving, fast-switching comedy effect … and with me bearing in mind No night sequences and No extravagant settings – can we see how this works out in the script? All ideas, of course, gratefully received!

The comments also demonstrate that Hudis is mindful of the need to keep the budget low and the locations simple, a point no doubt stressed by producer Rogers. Hudis's work for the Danziger brothers, also noted for their low-budget film-making, would have been useful experience in this aspect.[5]

Hudis has developed a narrative arc around Grimshawe's resolve to turn his men into the best new recruits as it becomes clearer all the time that they are doomed to fail. Hudis creates a chart to be displayed in the film as a means of demonstrating their failure, referring to it as a 'UNIFYING VISUAL DEVICE' to 'bridge time without a tremendous montage of training shots – the chart is there to show the inescapably downward trend of Grimshawe's men and Grimshawe's hopes'. The hopelessness of his mission becomes apparent as we follow downward trajectory.

The treatment ends in a double 'happy ending'. The romantic strand is fulfilled when Horace falls for Norah, 'in a romantic situation, by the moonlit pyrotechnics shed, a kiss is finally exchanged and HORACE falls in love …' while the central strand, Grimshawe's quest to head the star squad and retire with honour, is achieved when the recruits learn that he is about to go and decide to unite as a team:

> Same evening: HERBERT discovers the facts about Grimshawe's imminent retirement, rushes to inform squad. (HORACE has left NORAH weak but happy, by now, and is back in the hut). Squad unity belatedly established, decision to dare all for Grimshawe's sake – and squad's pride – taken.

> Pay-off and finale of parade and success of the squad.

Norman Hudis's first treatment and development ideas (GT 26/1)

The 'first treatment and development ideas' relate solely to the first section of the story, ending on the arrival of the new recruits at the training camp and the climax of Act 1.

The thirteen-page treatment establishes a strong comic tone and is light, witty and very readable, with a list of suggestions about character relationships rather than any clear narrative outline. Although dated four days earlier than the story outline, the treatment would probably have been drafted about the same time. Different versions of a treatment are often written during development, each presenting different aspects of the story and possibly intended for a variety of readers. This version sets up the situation and the characters. The first six scenes of the treatment do not feature in the screenplay but here show how the previous recruits had failed abysmally under Sergeant Grimshawe's training. The scenes provide a backstory to Grimshawe, the recruits' failure helping us to understand why it is so important for him to head a promising group of new recruits before he retires. The scenes show the new arrivals, and as in the outline, focus on Grimshawe's desperation to gain a star squad rating before he retires:

> Next time though, it's going to be different. His next, and final squad, due in this evening with a new intake, have just got to be the Star Squad to crown his Army career. His luck must change.

The treatment ends with Grimshawe facing up to the fact that these latest recruits are far from perfect, but he hopes that handling this unpromising group of men men with tact and diplomacy could elicit a positive outcome:

He has seen, at a glance, that this squad is the very end. In no time at all he could have a deserter in BAILEY, a lead-swinging hospitalisation in HORACE, and a new and confused and confusing element in STARKE. … To get anywhere with this squad – which is a cross between a psychiatric ward and a particularly obstructive trade-union shop – he dare not take any chances and come the old heavy. This could only result in half the squad being on parade and the other half in the glasshouse – and goodbye Star Squad rating.

The ending underlines what is at stake for Grimshawe: he stands to lose money, his Star Squad rating and his pride. The Sergeant in the screenplay is not a particularly sympathetic character, with little personality and only one aim: to win his bet and retire. The dramatic device of reminding the reader what is at stake acts as a hook and provides a clear linear narrative. We expect things will happen to make Grimshawe's want seem impossible to get. The characters are set up to serve as problems or obstacles for the Sergeant to surmount and the situations they are put in create humour and tension. Each scene makes us question whether Grimshawe will succeed or not. Hudis adds further tension by making Grimshawe bet on his men's ability to become the star squad.

The characters are developed in greater depth than in the previous treatment; for instance, Horace Strong is described as a hypochondriac who has:

almost hermetically sealed the compartment against draughts, and has turned the heating full-on. He's in the midst of a monologue to Charlie. He claims that his head has suffered from a splitting, agonising migraine since the very second his call up papers arrived … .

Grimshawe collects his new recruits as they arrive at the barracks but is missing one whom he finds at the camp gates, Miles Heywood, who is similar to the upper-class Mike in Delderfield's treatment. Grimshawe thinks he is an officer but, on finding out he is one of his recruits, 'Grimshawe isn't angry. Or, at least, his anger is perfunctory and surface. For Miles is a ray of hope to him. Grimshawe could kiss Miles.'

The treatment drives home the reality that the squad represents a hopeless cause and that Grimshawe knows this. Hudis concludes the treatment having set up the enormity of the task in store for the Sergeant: 'With Grimshawe on the threshold of the hut – and his fate – and Copping wondering if he's hearing aright – the situation and characters are fully set up – and battle can commence …'.

The six pages of development ideas demonstrate how Hudis continually asks questions when writing and this section often reads as a 'work in progress'. Hudis explains that the narrative core is Grimshawe's wish to win his bet, with the events all linking into this:

the film can naturally resolve itself into a series of comedy sequences – but because there is a central idea, each situation and character can be related, however lightly, to the basic story of Grimshawe, and the film cannot fall into the trap of being an unrelated play-off of Army-life sketches.

Hudis notes that the key characters should cause mayhem: 'our six characters can be trusted to create confusion whatever their numerical ratio to the squad as a whole'. He discusses the type of comedy they should begin the story with, offering an alternative beginning in which the comedy could be scaled down, less exaggerated if it's desired to save the picturing of <u>real</u> incompetence for the central section of the film when our boys get to work. On the other hand, a slap-up comedy opening has something to commend it.

Hudis talks about how the characters can generate comedy: 'The recruit with a guitar. If he's built into a full character, he can tip the balance of the squad 7–5 in favour of disaster.' Another recruit, Starke, is described as being absolutely hopeless, 'at home with a pen, he's at sea with a grenade', with suggestions as to how he could display other qualities to provoke humour: 'Starke could have either or both of the following qualities: mathematical genius and a photographic brain. A great deal of comedy effect could be gained from both of these factors.'

Hudis suggests that, if the treatment is acceptable, then they should retain only elements of the story in line with the theme of the film, 'it seems necessary to judge each sequence–idea for the film against this thematic material, and to reject, quite ruthlessly, any idea or angle which goes over the top'. Many aspects of Hudis's outline and treatment found their way into the screenplay and the final film. Delderfield's treatment was abandoned, the story completely changed and there is almost no reference to the characters he had originally envisaged.

Carry on up the Khyber

Robert Ross describes the film as 'Talbot Rothwell's most assured historical parody' (1996: 73). The screenplay is different in style to the more narrative-driven efforts of Norman Hudis and is noticeably bawdier; even the frontpage screenplay titles reinforce this, ' "The Handyman's Kama Sutra" otherwise known as "The British Position in India" ', yet the storyline does possess dramatic interest. Two drafts are held in the collection: a first draft (GT 30/1) D1, with no date and a final draft (GT 30/2) D2, dated January 1968.

The plot is not sophisticated – the Governor needs to stop an uprising prompted by the Rajah after he sees a photograph showing that the Highland Guard wear pants under their kilts. He realises the troops are not the fierce warriors they thought and his men need no longer fear them. The Governor's officers' attempts to recover the photographic evidence fail and the British compound is attacked. All seems lost until the Khasi's men find out what really is under the soldiers' kilts.

The screenplay is one of the most enjoyable of the *Carry Ons* to read, the combination of social satire and parody resulting in a script which is often very funny. The story is entertaining, despite featuring the same stock characters and innuendo-laden jokes as the rest of the series, with the predictable humour about what a Scotsman wears under his kilt. The loose narrative thread, based on the British occupation of India and an ensuing revolt, adds dramatic tension that is cleverly combined with comedy. The narrator describes the privileged situation of the British in India: 'Here the British rulers and their memsahibs enjoyed a life of luxury and ease matched only by that of the great Indian Rajahs. None more so than Her Majesty's Governor of the North-West Frontier Province, Sir Sidney Ruff-Diamond' (D2: 1).

The two central characters are working-class pretenders to the aristocracy, as the story relates, 'Sir Sidney and Lady Joan have come from somewhat humble beginnings. Although both have studiously cultivated "posh" accents for use on undomesticated occasions' (ibid.).

The screenplay pokes fun at British imperialism, satirising the doublespeak of diplomacy, for instance, when the Rajah, the Khasi of Kalabar, and his daughter, Jelhi, discuss Ruff-Diamond, he tells her, in some witty wordplay:

The witty finale of *Carry on up the Khyber* (1968), written by Talbot Rothwell, shows actors Sid James and
Peter Butterworth looking at the head of the Fakir served on a platter

KHASI

That, Light of my Darkness, is His Excellency Sir Sidney Ruff-
Diamond, the British Governor, without whose benevolent rule
and wise guidance we could well do.

JELHI

Then why do you smile so favourably?

KHASI

Because in these days of British military supremacy, it is
necessary for an Indian to be as a basket with two faces.

And he smiles and bows across the field again. (ibid.: 4)

The aristocracy, stiff upper lips and typical British failings and incompetence are constantly parodied, with reference to films depicting the British Empire, from *Gunga Din* (1939) and *The Four Feathers* (1939) to the contemporary *Zulu* (1964). Cull notes how the heroic soldier's death is neatly satirised: 'As Widdle cradles the dying Ginger in his arms, Ginger murmurs: "Am I going to be all right?" Widdle replies: "Course not, Ginge mate"' (2002: 98).

The script capitalises on the *Carry On* stalwarts' skills at sending up their country's colonial past, as the narrator explains:

NARRATOR

Fearless fighting men, aptly referred to by the natives as the
Devils in skirts, their reputation for invincibility had always proved
an effective deterrent to the warlike border tribes. A reputation
however, that was soon to be dramatically undermined by the
actions of one man … (D2: 6)

The depiction of the heroic action man is wittily undercut in the direct link to a description of Private Widdle:

Bang straight in to C.S. of one soldier in the line, a miserable-looking character
looking even more incongruous than the rest of them, surreptitiously stamping his
feet on the snowy ground. At the same time we hear Macnutt's voice bellow …

MACNUTT
Private Widdle. (ibid.)

Private Widdle is played by weakling Charles Hawtrey, the *Carry On* regular whom Rothwell would have planned the script around, in this subversion of the genre. The narrator sets up the fact that Private Widdle will do something that will have consequences in the rest of the screenplay. The inciting incident occurs when one of the Khasi's men finds out that Widdle wears underpants, which provokes the Khasi to incite a rebellion, helped by the fact that Joan, Ruff-Diamond's wife, has fallen in love with the Khasi and given him a photo of the soldiers also revealing their underpants.

The continual references to 'what's under the kilt', the innuendo and play on words with references to male genitalia are often very funny, despite their basis in seaside postcard humour. The writing around this suggests a masculine vulnerability and insecurity, often undermining male pomposity and British imperialism at the same time. When the Governor's righthand man, Keene, and the Sergeant reveal they are both wearing underpants, this compounds the humour:

KEENE (in excuse)
But they're not woollen ones, Sir. Honestly. I had them made
here. Indian silk.

SIDNEY
That makes it worse! Can you imagine what they'll say when it
gets out that the commander of the Devils in skirts wears silk
drawers? !!!

MACNUTT
I would like to say, your Excellency, that I am only wearing them
from a sense of duty.

SIDNEY
Duty.

MACNUTT
Aye sir. You see, they were hand-knitted for me by my mother.

SIDNEY
I don't care if they were hand-embroidered by your father.

MACNUTT
Well he did do the flowers, sir. (ibid.: 27)

The women in the script and in the *Carry On*s can generally be divided into two categories,
young, beautiful and desirable or old, unattractive and predatory. For instance the Governor's
wife, Joan, falls for the Khasi and bribes him to make love to her, but she is presented as being
so unattractive that he is anxious to avoid this union:

JOAN
Can't you guess? I just thought that if I did something nice for
you … you might do something nice for me.

KHASI
Ah, I understand. You scratch my back and I will scratch yours.

JOAN
Well that might be interesting for a start.

KHASI
If, dear madam, you were to allow me to have this, what would
you want in return? Rubies? Emeralds?

JOAN
Oh no! Well, afterwards perhaps …

KHASI
After what, dear madam?

JOAN (getting close)
Need I tell you? Can you not tell by the quickness of my
breathing? The heaving of my bosom? The hot flush in my
cheeks?

KHASI
Ah! You are requiring Indian herbal purgative! (ibid.)

Despite the clichéd scenario, the comedy setup and timing are immaculate in the above dialogue. The twist at the end of lines is a technique often applied to other scenes: when the Governor is told that his wife has left him for the Khasi, he responds with angst so that his deputy Keene advises him:

KEENE
You must try and keep a stiff upper lip, Sir!

SIDNEY
I know. I'm sorry, Captain, but the thought of them together …
her lying in his arms … slobbering all over him … I just can't help
feeling sorry for the poor devil. (ibid.: 36)

The buildup to the turn is clever – we assume Sidney is devastated to lose his wife, making the line funny and cruel at the same time. Joan is presented as a woman so unappealing that her husband even feels sorry for the man she has run away with.

This very noticeable streak of misogyny runs through the *Carry On* films: the leading men seem to feel at ease with young women whom they can easily control, while older women are seen as difficult, demanding and worrying. Perhaps this trope is a way of avoiding a mother fixation or a sign that younger women are seen as less threatening and sexually demanding.

The final sequence in the compound is an amusing parody of the Empire genre, combined with Buñuel-inspired surrealism, in which the British soldiers have to 'hold the fort' while it is under attack by the Khasi's men. The Governor is given a final ultimatum that they will have to surrender or die; he refuses and, when asked by Captain Keene what they should do, Sidney replies:

SIDNEY (surprised)
<u>Do</u>, Captain? We're British! We won't <u>do</u> anything.

SHORTHOUSE (realistically)
Until it's too late.

SIDNEY
Precisely! That's the first sensible thing you've said to-day,
Shorthouse. No, no, gentlemen, as always, we shall carry on as
if nothing was going to happen.

KEENE
But surely, sir … we must make some decisions!

SIDNEY
Oh, I intend to. Major Shorthouse, we will have dinner at seven
this evening.

                                    SHORTHOUSE
                                  Yes, your Excellency.

                                      SIDNEY
                  Kindly ask Captain Keene, the Princess Jelhi, and Brother
                  Belcher to join us.

                                    SHORTHOUSE
                                      Yes, sir.

                                      SIDNEY
                                  White tie of course!

                  And goes serenely to his room. (ibid.: 93)

The Governor, his wife and senior officers have dinner, pretending that nothing is happening
while the Khasi's men attack the compound. The only exception is the missionary, Belcher, a
parody of the missionary in *Zulu*, who is terrified and serves as a contrast to the formality of
the proceedings as the others eat and listen to the orchestra playing.

                  INT. DINING ROOM. DAY

                  The cannons thunder again outside, and we hear the steady exchange of rifle fire.
                  Belcher looks slightly worried. Sidney puts his soup spoon down and dabs at his lips.
                  Another loud boom and Belcher drops his soup spoon into his plate.

                                  SIDNEY (pleasantly)
                            You didn't enjoy your soup, Mr. Belcher?

                                      BELCHER
                      Eh? Oh yes, a, er, very unusual flavour. What was it?

                                       JOAN
                                        Pea.

                                      BELCHER
                                  I beg your pardon?

                                       JOAN
                                      Pea soup.

                                      BELCHER
                                  And very nice too.

                  The cannons roar again. Nobody takes any notice except Belcher who jumps.

BELCHER
Oh, that horrible noise!

SIDNEY
I agree. Not a first class orchestra but they're doing their best.
(ibid.: 96)

The inclusion of the joke about the pea soup contrasts tonally with the bombardment of the compound that continues as the group dine. They pretend everything is perfectly normal, apart from Belcher, who tries but fails to follow their example, while Joan laughs about the debris in her hair:

Another great crash and half the ceiling falls. C.S. Lady Joan as she delicately
removes a piece of plaster from her plate and puts it on her sideplate. There are bits
of plaster in her hair. She turns to Jelhi and giggles.

JOAN
Oh dear, I seem to have got a little plastered.

Everyone laughs politely. (ibid.: 102)

The orchestra are flattened as a wall is blown apart and Sidney applauds the end of their playing, as if they have merely retired for the night. Finally, the compound is broken into and, in a more serious and poignant moment, Sidney asks the Major for his revolver, so that they can shoot themselves if necessary, before turning to Joan:

SIDNEY
Thank you. Oh, you have yours, me dear? Just in case?

Joan brings out a little pistol from her bodice.

JOAN
Yes, dear.

SIDNEY
Good. Oh, and try and save the last bullet for Mr. Belcher. After
all, he is our guest. (ibid.: 104)

Comparing the two endings of the final draft
There are two versions of the last pages in the final draft, the typed version, which is crossed out and a handwritten version noted on the opposite page. Both return to the running joke about what Scotsmen wear under their kilts. The typed version describes Sidney confronting the Khasi's men as Captain Keene tells him all is lost. Sidney replies 'All is not lost':

C.S. Sidney. He has undone his jacket, and now releases his trouser tops and lets the trousers fall down. We do not see what is underneath of course, just the reaction of the BURPAS. There is a gasp and they appear terrified. Then, with cries of fear, they turn and start running, throwing away their arms as they flee.

KHASI
Come back, you fools! Come back!

But it is ineffectual. He turns and looks in Sidney's direction again. Now we see Sidney in toto. He stands there dignified, every inch a Governor, his trousers around his feet and showing a startling pair of brilliant red bloomers, rather baggy, the leg ends gathered just above the knees with cute white satin bows. It is too much for the Khasi even. He shudders, turns and runs for it. (ibid.: 106)

The bloomers, we are told later, belong to Joan but there is no explanation as to why Sidney is wearing them and whether the scene is meant to be funny or humiliating. With no foreshadowing of the event, the revelation is too sudden to make a very convincing finale.

The handwritten version, reproduced below, links in more neatly with the foreshadowed kilts worn by the regiment, returning to the same narrative point when Sidney enters the fray with scimitar in hand and Captain Keene orders the Highlanders to form a line:

Sidney raises his hand against the Burpas.

SIDNEY
Stop!

And surprisingly they stop. Khasi pushes through the mob.

KHASI
Go on! There are no devils in skirts to be frightened of now. Go on!

SIDNEY
Company. Kilts … . Grasp!

The line of Highlanders grasp the edge of their kilts in their hands.

SIDNEY
Company! Kilts … raise!

The troops raise their kilts. We do not see what is underneath, of course. (D2: 106)

On seeing what is under the kilts, the Burpas flee the compound; Sidney orders the troops to lower their kilts; and the new section cuts back to the same ending, with Joan suggesting coffee in the drawing room.

The revised ending is stronger in a number of ways: a pattern of expectation has been set up around the kilts, which has been developed throughout the story and the ending cleverly brings this pattern full circle. The first version with the bloomers finale does not fit into the narrative pattern – and we are given no reason why Sidney should wear his wife's bloomers, although it does play to the cross-dressing strand common to many of the *Carry On* films. The idea is visually funny but the ending is flat, whereas the new ending successfully ties in the narrative strands already established, producing a much neater ending. It is this version that appears in the film.

Comparison of drafts D1 and D2

The two drafts are very similar but there are minor differences, especially at the beginning of the script regarding the characters. In the first draft Lady Joan is presented as a working-class character pretending to be 'posh', as described on first introduction, 'As soon as she opens her mouth, we realise that she has married way above her station. But she's trying hard to live up to it.' The script continues as Lady Joan and her husband, Ponsonby, watch a polo match:

LADY JOAN
Oh I say, he did not half crack it one, did he not?

PONSONBY
Young Keene. A top-hole player.

LADY JOAN
Oh yes indeed. He's scrummy.

PONSONBY
My dear, one does not refer to a Captain in her Majesty's army
as 'scrummy'!

LADY JOAN
Oh, I'm sorry, Hughikins.

PONSONBY
And stop calling me Hughikins! Try and remember that you are
the wife of Her Majesty's Governor of the North-West Frontier
Province! (D1: 1)

The final draft implies that both characters are from the same background with the characters sporting the same first names as the actors – Joan and Sidney. When the couple arrive at the polo match, their working-class origins become evident when Joan attempts to gracefully leave the carriage, hissing at Sidney:

JOAN
A gentleman would 'ave 'elped a lady out first!

Sidney keeps a tight smile on his face and hisses right back.

SIDNEY
Some bleedin' lady!

All of which should demonstrate that both SIR SIDNEY and LADY JOAN have come
from somewhat humble beginnings. Although both have a studiously cultivated
'posh' accent for use on undomesticated occasions. (D2: 2–3)

The final draft further emphasises their class and the couple are placed in situations where they
can lampoon the behaviour of the upper classes, in an often hilarious manner.
     The two drafts exhibit interesting variations in the scene when one of the Khasi's men
reveals that Private Widdle is wearing underpants. The first draft description is more condensed
as Widdle passes out when confronted with a tribesman waving a scimitar:

It's too much for Widdle. His eyes goggle, He gives a low moan, and keels over in a
dead faint, flat on his back. Bungdit looks down at him, surprised. Then he shrugs
and offers up a quick prayer to Allah. Then he starts towards the gate, stops, and,
after a crafty look round, comes back to the prostrate Widdle, bends down, and
cautiously lifts his kilt up and peers below it. Then he starts to chuckle, drops the kilt,
stands up and laughs triumphantly up at the skies. (D1: 8)

The final draft scene is the same in structure but when Widdle faints, the additional dialogue
from Bungdit makes the scene more involving:

It is too much for Widdle. He gives a low moan, his eyes close, and he keels over in a
dead faint. Flat on his back. Bungdit looks down at him, surprised.

BUNGDIT
What did I do?

Then shrugs, starts towards the gate, stops, comes back to Widdle and, after a
crafty look around, cautiously puts the tip of his scimitar under the hem of Widdle's
kilt.

BUNGDIT
I wonder … ?

Then he lifts the kilt and peers below. He exclaims in wonder and surprise, then starts
to chuckle.

BUNGDIT
Now we know!! (D2: 10)

Rothwell's economically written screenplay has pace and humour though the middle section, when the soldiers go to rescue Joan, drags a little. The misunderstandings and language confusion are important but the visual aspect is equally so: dress is a focal point of humour, from Widdle in disguise as an Indian dancer to the soldiers in kilts. The screenplay features some inspired comedy and its scenes at times read better than when acted in the film, where Gerald Thomas's often sluggish direction fails to ensure the quick delivery required for some of the lines.

CONCLUSION

The *Carry On* screenplays, from Hudis's entertaining, institutionally based comedies to Rothwell's innuendo-laden world of smutty jokes and obsession with genitals, could be variable in quality, tending to repeat the same tired jokes. As Robert Ross points out 'the *Carry On* films were not particularly original, wallowing in a collection of tried and tested comic ideas and stereotypes' (1996: 10). Yet some of the scripts, such as *Carry on Constable*, *Carry on Teacher*, *Carry on Spying*, *Carry on Cleo* and *Carry on up the Khyber*, are sharp and witty, engaging parody to good effect. The best *Carry On* screenplays are worthy of a place in the history of British cinema. Hudis's stories display a developed structure and a clearer narrative drive with more literate dialogue, while Rothwell's pared-down dialogue at its best gives the humour the space to be effective, though too often the underdeveloped stories seem skimpy and reliant on repetitive innuendo and smutty jokes, frequently lacking the narrative sophistication of Hudis's writing.

In direct contrast to Peter Rogers's relaxed attitude to the screenplay development process, the next chapter discusses the highly acclaimed screenwriter Robert Bolt and his close working relationship with the punctilious director, David Lean, a partnership which produced Academy Award-winning screenplays like *Lawrence of Arabia* and *Doctor Zhivago*. Letters from Lean to Bolt discussing the development of their screenplays reveal Lean's quest for perfection as well as Bolt's ability to produce screenplays of a very high standard when pushed.

NOTES

1. See GT 26/13, GT 26/14, GT 26/15 and GT 26/1.
2. John Antrobus went on to write for TV series *The Army Game*.
3. Eric Sykes and Spike Milligan had both been asked to look at the script (Ross 1996: 10)
4. The collection also holds an early draft screenplay by John Antrobus and three draft screenplays by Norman Hudis, one dated 7 March 1958, the other two undated.
5. See Chibnall and McFarlane's *The British 'B' Film* (2009: 271) for details of Hudis's work for the Danzigers.

08
ROBERT BOLT
COMMUNICATOR AND CRAFTSMAN

Considering that Robert Bolt was a prolific writer, often occupied with two or three projects at a time, the number of screenplays he produced over a career span of forty years is not at first sight impressive; Bolt is credited as screenwriter on only eight feature films. But when one considers that these include two of David Lean's most famous films, *Lawrence of Arabia* (1962) and *Doctor Zhivago* (1965), alongside the less lauded *Ryan's Daughter* (1970), then Bolt's contribution to cinema starts to look more significant. In addition, the triumph of *A Man for All Seasons* (1966) ensured his reputation as a skilled wordsmith, making him continually in demand both in the UK and in Hollywood. The highest paid screenwriter in Hollywood (for *Doctor Zhivago*), after winning the Academy Award for Best Screenplay (based on another medium) for both *Zhivago* and *A Man for All Seasons*, Bolt was able to choose any project and more or less name his price.

Bolt began his career as a radio and theatre writer. His first radio play, *The Master*, was broadcast on BBC radio in 1953, followed by *A Man for All Seasons*, in 1954. Bolt was employed by the BBC on a freelance basis and by 1955, he was inundated with offers from the newly formed ITV channels but, although tempted by the large sums on offer, declined. *The Last of the Wine*, also broadcast in 1955, an allegorical story about the dangers of complacency, caught the attention of Margaret Ramsay, a new agent looking for promising writers. Ramsay encouraged Bolt to write for the theatre but his first play, *The Critic and the Heart*, shown at the Oxford Playhouse in 1956, received mixed reviews. His next stage venture proved much more successful. *Flowering Cherry*, starring Ralph Richardson and Celia Johnson, was so popular that the play transferred to Broadway for a short run.

After *A Man for All Seasons* was transmitted on television in 1957, Ramsay suggested that Bolt write a stage version, and cast Paul Scofield in the role of Thomas More. This was so well received that a Broadway version followed, also garnering critical acclaim and performing well at the box office. At the same time, another of Bolt's plays was showing in the West End, *The Tiger and the Horse*, about nuclear disarmament, starring Michael Redgrave and his daughter, Vanessa. The play attracted the notice of film producers Sydney and Muriel Box, who were interested in adapting the play into a film. Bolt was keen to do the adaptation, as Ramsay commented, 'The prospect of a film thrilled Bolt, for it was the answer to his concern with naturalism. In the cinema anything was possible …' (Turner 1998: 174). This and a number of other film offers failed to materialise but in 1960 producer Sam Spiegel asked Bolt to replace Michael Wilson as writer on the screenplay for *The Seven Pillars of Wisdom*, which became *Lawrence of Arabia*. Lean was unhappy with Wilson's script and Bolt was hired to do a substantial rewrite.[1] A dispute erupted after the film's release when Bolt was given the sole credit as screenwriter.

Bolt argued that Wilson was merely following a story taken from the *The Seven Pillars of Wisdom*, while Wilson insisted that some of his scenes survived in the screenplay (ibid.: 208). Lean, though, was extremely happy with Bolt's script and impressed with his skill as a writer.

Lawrence of Arabia was a huge hit, making Lean eager to work with Bolt again. He thought highly of Bolt's work, singling out his understanding of narrative and use of dialogue, explaining, 'Most so-called script writers are adapters and "added dialogue" writers. The movies don't possess a dramatist. For that reason this film of ours has knocked the top film-makers sideways' (ibid.: 215). Even though Lean held Bolt in high regard, he still contended that Bolt had to adapt his writing to suit film, thinking visually rather than verbally:

> 'Do you realise, Robert, when he says that line, I can give you a big close-up shot of his reaction that will convey things even better than his line?' And I thought, 'Heavens, he's right.' But I tumbled to it very quickly once it was put to me. (Demby 1973: 29)

Lean speaks of their remarkable working relationship and how he would like to recapture that dynamic:

> This film has put me into a fantastic position and a team consisting of you and I would be backed up to the hilt – bigger than anyone in this so-called industry … . The more I see the reactions to *Lawrence* the more I realise we have something *very* out of the ordinary as a joint team. I won't say why. I know it's so. I'm just mad keen to work with you again. (Turner 1998: 215)

The stars and production team on *Lawrence of Arabia* (1962): (l to r) Anthony Quayle, Peter O'Toole, producer Sam Spiegel, director David Lean and screenwriter Robert Bolt, though later credit was also awarded to Michael Wilson

Bolt was similarly keen to collaborate with Lean because his latest play, *Gentle Jack*, had received poor reviews, only lasting for seventy-five performances. The failure of the play was probably the deciding factor in galvanising Bolt to move from theatre to film.

Lean thought that Boris Pasternak's *Doctor Zhivago* had the potential to become a film on an epic scale and suggested this as a joint project. Bolt acknowledged the book's possibilities: 'I am perfectly mesmerised by the idea of Zhivago. I love the book and it would be an honour to work on it with you.' Bolt had some doubts about whether the producer, Carlo Ponti, would accept him as the writer, but is full of enthusiasm and comments in some detail about how he visualises the film:

> I'm sure we could do a good thing on Zhivago. If the whole film could be made atmospheric in
> substance but clean and athletic in story. Snow – beautiful in landscapes, downright dreary
> sometimes around the house, settling affectionately or like death's fingertips on a man's clothing …
> (ibid.: 227)

Initially Bolt's focus was the depiction of the Russian Revolution while Lean's interest was in the love story. Lean considered that a great artist would also be a great lover, finally persuading Bolt of this, declaring: 'The love story is more powerful than anything else. If the love story isn't powerful then the film isn't powerful …' (ibid.: 231).

Finding the novel difficult to adapt due to the time changes and numerous connecting stories, Bolt likened the task to 'straightening cobwebs' (ibid.: 232). For a film narrative, he had to select a single strand of the story and thus lose much of the eloquence of the novel. Lean and Bolt eventually decided to use a narrator to meld the story together. The treatment was finally completed in 1964 and Bolt then began working on the script for long hours at home, while conducting his own historical research.

At this stage, many letters discussing the adaptation went back and forth. Lean was concerned that the portrayal of the women diverged from how they were originally envisioned and worried that Bolt's own marital problems were affecting his writing. Believing that the heroine was being depicted as a slut, Lean sent an eleven-page letter to Bolt explaining his fears (ibid.: 234). Bolt was generally in agreement with Lean's points and humble in his reply, 'Jesus, what a mess … . I'm getting really scared by this. I thought I'd done her marvellously, you know. I thought I'd written a mature woman stirred by grief and love to the very depths' (ibid.).

When Bolt had completed the first draft of the screenplay he went to Madrid to collaborate with Lean more closely. They would work on the script all day, then after dinner write long memos to each other, on occasion running to thirty-six pages (ibid.: 237). Days were spent going over a single page of script with Lean questioning Bolt about every detail.

The script was finished in September 1964 and the film released in 1965 to enthusiastic reviews from the popular press, though the film critics were less positive. *Doctor Zhivago* was an international success and MGM's biggest hit film since *Gone with the Wind* (1939).

After the broadcasting of the radio, stage and TV versions of *A Man for All Seasons*, a film seemed inevitable and Bolt began the screenplay in 1965 with Fred Zinnemann down to direct. Bolt was paid $100,000 for the screen rights and $50,000 for the script. The play proved hard to adapt due to its many Brechtian and non-naturalistic elements. Zinnemann respected Bolt's concerns: 'I knew Bob was the real creator of the story. I was an interpreter, not a conductor' (ibid.: 251), and they worked well together, Bolt happy to make changes after feedback from the director.

Bolt continued to develop ideas for film projects, spending some time in 1966 and 1967 on a screenplay about Mahatma Gandhi, with Lean attached. Lean pulled out but his interest renewed when Bolt presented him with a completed script. Turner intimates that the venture failed because of disagreements about financing and details over payments and royalties (ibid.: 288–9).

When Bolt proposed an adaptation of Flaubert's *Madame Bovary*, Lean's reaction was positive. They met in Italy to discuss the project further, refining ideas around the theme of a young woman leaving her older husband. They transferred the story from nineteenth-century France to Ireland in 1916, when the IRA were fighting against British rule (Brownlow 1996: 302). The script was completed in October 1968 and eventually titled *Ryan's Daughter*. MGM felt the ending should be more upbeat, requesting that the fate of Major Doryan, Rosy's lover and shell-shocked war hero, be changed from suicide to death in a struggle with the IRA, but the suicide remained in the final cut. In 1970 *Ryan's Daughter* opened to terrible reviews, which so upset Lean that he went into semi-retirement. Bolt was more sanguine, believing the film featured some excellent scenes and had been unfairly criticised.

Bolt then began to write projects as star vehicles for his wife, Sarah Miles. While filming in Ireland, he completed the play *Vivat, Vivat, Regina*, about Queen Elizabeth 1 and Mary Queen of Scots, with Sarah Miles down to play Mary. The play was well received but Miles was not happy in the part and was replaced by another actress. Bolt began a new screenplay for Miles,

Screenwriter Robert Bolt with muse and wife, Sarah Miles

Lady Caroline Lamb (1970), which he was also to direct. It tells the story of Caroline Lamb's relationship with Lord Byron, and William Lamb's decision to stand by his wife once the affair was made public. The producer, Fernando Ghia, thought the script beautifully written but the males 'too clean cut, too black and white' (Turner 1998: 322).

After writing *The Plumed Serpent*, an adaptation of a D. H. Lawrence novel, again for Miles to star in, Bolt resumed work on the screenplay *Gandhi* (1982) for a nominal fee of £1. Richard Attenborough had taken over the project but Bolt's screenplay failed to impress producer Joseph E. Levine or Attenborough himself, who opined that, 'Robert wrote an extremely efficient screenplay which veered unquestionably towards the academic. If you wanted to make a docu-drama for university library shelves, you would have made Bob's script' (ibid.: 357). Levine pulled out and Attenborough sought funding elsewhere. By the time this was in place, in the late 1970s, Bolt was with Lean in Bora Bora, concentrating on the Bounty films.

As a result of their collaboration on *Lady Caroline Lamb*, Bolt and Fernando Ghia set up a film production company, Filmit Productions, based in Hollywood in 1975. Paramount offered them a three-year deal and funded a $100,000 treatment for *The Mission* (1986), so Bolt and Ghia went to South America to research the story. Bolt eventually wrote a draft in four months, in 1976, which Paramount deemed 'distinguished, moving and thought provoking' but he turned down the money to produce a second draft, realising that, if Paramount extended its option to make the film, they couldn't take the project elsewhere. Ghia explains, 'It was a European film with the framework of a Hollywood movie' (ibid.: 373).

After this, Bolt returned to the theatre and wrote *State of Revolution*, about the 1917 Russian Revolution, for the National Theatre on London's South Bank. The play was first performed in Birmingham in 1977 to mixed reviews and, while addressing problems in the play, Lean contacted Bolt again to interest him in a new film about the mutiny on the Bounty.

Bolt was eventually employed to draft two screenplays about the saga: *The Lawbreakers* and *The Long Arm*. The second part of this chapter deals with the complex development process, which resulted in great acrimony between Lean and Bolt and the producer, Dino de Laurentiis. Lean was taken off the project, while Bolt was still under contract to produce the screenplays (see p. 195). The strain of the production coupled with Bolt's unhealthy lifestyle were probably to blame when he wound up needing major heart surgery, after which a serious stroke left him partly paralysed. Bolt had to learn to talk, write and walk again. His drive to write though was unstoppable and, with the help of an assistant-cum-editor, he began taking on assignments again. Producer David Puttnam asked him to compose a script for *The October Circle* in 1981 but this was shelved when the backers lost confidence (see Chapter 11 for further details on the development of the film). Then, in 1982, the Bounty surfaced again, still with Dino de Laurentiis as producer. Bolt was asked to amalgamate the two stories, while cutting the pages back to 100 in total, a task he found almost impossible. After toiling on the script for some time, he decided enough was enough and that he had fallen out of love with the story. Another writer, Ian Mune, who is not credited, was taken on to finish the screenplay (ibid.: 414).[2] *The Bounty* was completed in 1984 with Bolt credited as screenwriter.

By this time Bolt was back to his workaholic self and busy with numerous projects, most of which did not come to fruition; these included a film adaptation of *Twelfth Night*, and screen-plays about Leonardo Da Vinci, Thomas Jefferson and the IRA (ibid.: 433). Others followed in the mid-1980s: an adaptation of Gore Vidal's novel *Burr* and then a script about Michael Collins, founder of the IRA. But none of Bolt's scripts was produced until Puttnam took an interest in

The Mission and asked him to work on it again. The film was awarded the Palme d'Or at Cannes and Bolt won the Golden Globe and Evening Standard Awards for Best Screenplay. The script is powerful and beautifully written but the film received mixed reviews and the box office failed to recoup the costs of producing on location.[3]

In 1987 Lean got back in touch with Bolt and proposed that he produce a script for *Nostromo*. Lean had not liked the first draft supplied by Christopher Hampton so requested Bolt take over. Bolt spent two years on the script but the film was never made because Lean's health deteriorated (see the David Lean Collection for more on the development).

Bolt then went back to write for Puttnam on a TV film, *Without Warning: The James Brady Story* (1991). At the same time he drafted a screenplay for Bertolucci, *The Buddha*, supplied a script for David Frost about Nixon in 1992 titled *Trickie Dickie*, and took on the writing of a miniseries for the BBC of the book *Wild Swans*. Despite being ill, Bolt continued to work until his death at home in February 1995.

THE DAVID LEAN COLLECTION
The mutiny on the Bounty story

The second part of this chapter discusses Bolt's writing relationship with David Lean and the development process for the screenplays *The Lawbreakers* and *The Long Arm*, about the mutiny on the Bounty. The letters and script notes in the David Lean Collection offer a revealing account of the collaboration. Many of the letters are in chronological order, allowing us to construct a detailed picture of the development process.

When working on the screenplays Bolt and Lean kept to a regular routine, involving Bolt sending pages to Lean and the latter sending back pages of notes in response. There appears to have been very little producer involvement at the ideas and writing stage. Lean liked to oversee the script development process and contributed a great deal. A father/son relationship evolved, Lean chivvying and encouraging Bolt, often complaining, while occasionally granting praise. Bolt appears to mostly agree with Lean's suggestions, although the later stages of writing show evidence of friction.

Preparation and research

Lean approached Bolt about the film after he had moved to the Tahitian island of Bora Bora. Lean had been impressed by Richard Hough's 1972 book, *Captain Bligh and Mr Christian*, which shed new light on the events of the mutiny and the relationship between the two men. Lean first of all employed Eddie Fowlie, who had originally given him Hough's book, to work on the idea, but Lean had already discussed the possibility of a film on the subject with Bolt in 1973 while the latter was writing the play, *State of Revolution* (Brownlow 1996: 600).

When Lean contacted Bolt again in May 1977, Bolt replied that he had just finished *State of Revolution*, and was free to work with Lean even though he was also trying to complete a script about the artist, Augustus John. Bolt enthusiastically notes, 'here you present me with a project which I have to write … and that regarding the Augustus John project, I have no bloody director to satisfy; just myself'. He continues: 'The measure of my confidence is this, that I hereby commit myself to be with you in Los Angeles during the last week in July' (DL/12/47: 14 May 1977).

Bolt believes the subject to be perfect for him and for his style yet shows some modesty about his talents:

If you go and get another writer now you'll just waste time and money and then call me in anyway.
No, I don't think I'm the best writer in the world, I do think I'm a good writer for this particular film.
The background, the themes, the characters are right up my alley. (ibid.)

Bolt informs Lean of his disinclination to write for big films any longer because

I hate the ambience more and more. But I'm instantaneously in love with this one. Probably only or
mainly because of the team and your leadership. If I don't get to do it, it will be your fault not mine
and I'll be pissed off. (ibid.)

He discusses story ideas and the freedom they would have to be creative, suggesting how the
Polynesians might be conveyed:

There really is in this one the opportunity for what we've always wanted – a strong narrative plus a
bit of free-wheeling magic. For instance I think it would be marvellous if we never saw the natives
distinctly but always as unknown and unknowable presences like Sherif Ali in the mirage … . No
San Francisco half-caste Malaysians saying 'Me Tuapa, you Bligh' if you see what I mean. (ibid.)

   Bolt's enthusiasm for the subject is evident and his research meticulous, as shown in his
notes about the type of ship they should use and how it should be built:

I've always wanted to do a film about the sea and square-riggers. And they always get it wrong. The
reason is this: It's very expensive to get it right. And even when they've got the money they spend it
wrongly. They build a replica of a square-rigger. (ibid.)

He goes on to suggest that they buy an old Baltic schooner and explains how it should be con-
verted, enthusing, 'I've never seen a film which comes anywhere near doing justice to the glory
of those big square-riggers. Have you ever seen one under sail – ? – One of the most beautiful
sights on earth' (ibid.).
   In his next letter, Bolt emphasises the need to make the film authentic as well as poetic. He is
ambitious about the type of film they should make, and sees it as being the real version of what
happened on the Bounty, insisting that it will be different from the 'childish account of it previously
offered' while, 'As well as making something more poetic and beautiful than anything before let's
make something more credible and recognisable and therefore more moving' (ibid.: 24 May 1977).
   Bolt had already carried out a great deal of background research, particularly on the conditions the sailors worked in and the period detail. He mentions the need to learn about the
everyday life of the South Sea Islanders, as these facts may come in useful later: 'I don't suppose
any of this will be immediately relevant but sometimes an actual fact will trigger the imagination in a way that the imagination on its own would never manage' (ibid.).
   Bolt describes the islanders, the British sailors and how they would appear to each other. His
ideas about them have changed from his first letter and he now proposes that the script view the
islanders as the sailors would have done, commenting, 'we shall do well to steer clear of anthro-
pology and see the Polynesians as the sailors saw them, desirable and enviable, dangerous
(occasionally squalid?). But alien, other, not really intelligible' (ibid.). He also suggests that they
invert this at some stage to show how the British might appear to the Polynesians (ibid.).

Bolt's enthusiasm is infectious and he often addresses Lean directly:

> It's a little floating Europe dumped in Paradise that 'Bounty' don't you think? Bligh working it all
> out from first principles, by the book and getting it all wrong. Christian frightened and a bit
> hysterical … A wife at home, and yet … moonlight, frangipani, grass skirts. (ibid.)

In his letters Bolt seems to talk aloud, playing with ideas, presenting his thoughts in a very
open way, detailing various possible approaches to the narrative. He acknowledges the greed
and bloodlust that the British and other colonial nations inflicted on Polynesia and other parts
of the Pacific while he vividly recounts the terrible conditions the British sailors had to endure.
Bolt discusses Captain Bligh's character, how the men obeyed him at sea and not on land, trying
to fathom why this was, seeking to understand the thinking behind the characters in that period,
using the research to build a picture of the men on the ship and the need for strict discipline:

> And then the mutiny, such a mess. Nobody quite knowing what's happening. The more violent
> dominant at the moment of action, pushing the others further than they want to go. But it can't be
> red revolution, even for them, because only the officers can sail the ship. No possibility of going
> home now, they're dead men already. But even to get to the island, they need their officers. Need
> discipline too. Can't work a ship in a storm by committee. (ibid.)

Bolt points out how too much revelation can work against characterisation and that an enigma
is always more interesting, 'I don't think everything's explicable. We didn't explain and spell out
Lawrence, and it was what we didn't attempt to explain that made him credible – yes?' (ibid.). Bolt
remarks that he wants to keep everything fluid and does not want to argue because it will become
'too cut-and-dried and conscious. I want to dream it under your direction' (ibid.). His words remind
us of his respect for Lean as a director, and intimate that Lean is something of a father figure.

In what is probably the last letter before Bolt leaves to meet Lean, he alludes to the director's genius and their ability to produce a certain 'magic' in a film, which is intangible, 'very
wilful and explosive, like petrol vapour. I think the camera is very good at this and you with the
camera a genius when you leave it (your genius) alone' (ibid.: 17 June 1977). Bolt suggests they
let the narrative possibilities remain open until he arrives on Bora Bora:

> I'd like ideally to have the material at my finger-tips when I come out, and lots of possible
> 'approaches' and 'explanations' and then wander round the place with you and muse and chatter and
> let it come together on its own, more or less. (ibid.)

Bolt agrees with Lean that the audience should not feel muddled by the narrative but clarifies
thus: 'there's a difference between leaving them muddled and leaving them (and us, and us) a
bit of space for speculation' (ibid.).

Bolt refers to the representation of Bligh and Christian in earlier films, resolving that theirs
will be different, as 'we're onto something much more interesting than anything Gable showed
us'. He recommends that the homosexual element be hinted at but not as developed as in
Lawrence of Arabia, 'something to bear in mind but not dwell on, as we did in the case of
Lawrence' (ibid.).[4] Bolt considers the difficulties entailed in fleshing out the central characters,
especially Christian, and the need to prioritise historical accuracy:

Truth first, then the poetry. For instance, about Christian. I haven't got him in my sights at all. And he can't have been that, or merely that; he may have had – obviously must have had – a streak of weakness, but he'd been the first mate of a trading ship by the time he was 24, in which capacity a weakling wouldn't last. (ibid.)

Bolt ends the letter full of anticipation: 'I haven't in years looked forward so eagerly to anything as I do to seeing you both at Papeete airport' (ibid.).

Once in Bora Bora the writing of the drafts was to begin in earnest.

Writing the drafts

Warner Bros., the original financial backers of the film, initially contracted Bolt to write one screenplay. His contract stipulated advance payments of $50,000 on 1 August 1977, $125,000 when writing commenced, $125,000 'on delivery of first draft screenplay incorporating all suggestions required by Mr. Lean', then four further payments of $50,000 to include a second and third revision and polishes requested by Lean, making a total of $550,000. At this stage of Bolt's career, he was able to command huge sums for his work. The contract underlines the fact that Bolt's screenplay is subject to Lean's demands for changes in all of the drafts.

The genesis of the film would prove extremely complicated. Warner Bros. had pledged to finance a single film of the Bounty story but, early in the development process, both Lean and Bolt considered one film would not do the story justice, with Lean proposing Warner fund two films, *The Lawbreakers* and *The Long Arm*. Warner Bros. eventually agreed to this and producer Phil Kellogg informed Lean on 15 September 1977 that they 'have given us a blank cheque' (DL/12/47), although they wanted to see at least part of *The Lawbreakers* script before final approval, a request Kellogg thought reasonable.[5]

This decision was never finalised as Warner Bros. prevaricated, unwilling to confirm finance for the two-picture deal. Whether one or two films were to be made affected the screenplay development process radically. On 24 October 1977 Bolt contacted Kellogg, pointing out that a prompt decision was essential to prevent him wasting time on two screenplays if only one were to be made. Bolt was under the impression that Warner Bros. had already offered him $100,000 to write the script for the second film. If Warner Bros. opted for just one film, he argued that 'the work I am doing now will be largely wasted and through no fault of mine'. He ends the letter asking for a decision by early December 1977. In October 1977, Kellogg suggests that, if they can show Warner Bros. at least part of the first script, they would be more likely to fund both films (DL/12/47).

Warner Bros. eventually pulled out as production costs began to escalate. Lean and Kellogg tried to secure funding from a variety of sources and in early 1978 producer Dino De Laurentiis came on board, but restricted the total cost of both films to no more than $40 million, stipulating that Bolt was to write both scripts.

While the production funding problems were reaching a crisis point, Bolt and Lean's working relationship was deteriorating. Lean, clearly a hard taskmaster, expressed concern about the quality of Bolt's writing and his overall commitment to the project. In a letter to Kellogg on 26 October 1977, Lean discussed Bolt in a highly critical manner, describing his huge appetite with distaste and mentioning that he had eaten 'a steak in four gulps' (DL/12/47). Lean was under a great deal of pressure over financing at the time and possibly looking for a scapegoat. Lean complains that Bolt, rather than working, was playing with his son, flirting with his son's tutor,

Julie and regularly delaying or changing meetings. Lean opined that Bolt was not focusing enough on the script and that the standard of his output was poor:

> After three days Robert said he was ready for me to read his first bit of writing. It was quite a good idea as we had planned it – but the written scene was quite dreadful. I read it and had to go through that dreadful business of telling him so … . The scene he had written was so bad that I decided in future it was no good not going into things a lot deeper before he started writing – and I think he wanted to get rid of me that first day in order to take Tom (Robert's son) swimming – as he had no doubt promised … . We went back to the scene and it was so bad I lost all taste for the idea – like heating up yesterday's meat. As a result of this I decided upon a new method of work. For a solid week I sat down with him and made a complete synopsis and an exact scene continuity of the first 30 or so pages of the script. (DL 12/47: 26 October 1977)

The above extract gives a sense of how the collaboration operated, with Lean developing strategies and methods to extract the most from the writer. Lean devotes one week to going over and over a sequence. We can glean some idea of the precision he requires at this stage of the script and how he has to badger Bolt into acceding to his exacting requirements. Lean went through the draft, page by page, in minute detail, describing the first twenty-five pages:

> overlong, corny – and again he had missed the point of the flow. I was so fed up that good stuff was so mauled I told him so very directly. My adrenalin was going so fast I was able to reconstruct his own scenes for him off the cuff … . He's now back on page one and as humble as he can ever be. (DL/12/47: 26 October 1977)

In the same letter Lean derides Bolt's visual sense, a skill Lean would have developed first as a film editor and later as a director:

> it took me over two hours to explain how he had gone wrong in the first four pages. I slowly realised – for the first time in our partnership – that he has very little visual sense and no sense whatever of cutting from one picture to another. I had got hold of – I think – a quite original idea of putting pictures and scenes together … It ended with him saying he hadn't any visual sense and, 'will you please draw what you see'. (ibid.)

Lean believes that Bolt is not yet showing true commitment to the script but his previous experience with him means that he knows how to handle the situation:

> This has happened before with Robert – exactly the same on Zhivago when he made Lara a lying bitch and told me she was attractive – and I had to get him back from London where he was working at home – as he would like to be doing now.

Lean refers to Bolt envisioning himself as a 'second Shakespeare', and that he needs a shake-up to make him focus, 'I may have to give Robert quite a fright before I get him on board – because I think he does need a fright to get him out of his complacency.' Lean asks for Kellogg's help in doing this:

There are other writers. A word in Peggy's ear (Bolt's agent) to this effect might prove a nice finger
tip of mustard – English. You can be very worried about Robert's work being so affected and would
he like to withdraw? (ibid.).

Although worried about Bolt's ability to focus, Leans's tactics are designed to get Bolt back
on track rather than seriously contemplating bringing in another writer. Lean informs Kellogg
that Bolt is effectively blackmailing him by saying he can't work because of financial worries,
insisting, 'He's bluffing and I would like you to call it. If he goes he goes. We have a fine subject
and I'm at the top of my form …' (ibid.: 26 October 1977).

Bolt is very aware of Lean's concerns and writes to Lean six weeks later, voicing thanks
for his support: 'I have tried and failed to find words adequate to your kindness and trust in
standing surety for my good behaviour, or proper performance or whatever it is. It reduces itself
to a simple "Thank – you"' (ibid.: 12 December 1977). It seems likely that Lean had delivered
some sort of warning or ultimatum. Bolt refers to Lean having spoken to Julie, his son's tutor,
and

that you have once or twice expressed anxiety about my state of mind. Please don't be anxious; it's
nice to know of your concern but there is no real occasion for it. And in any event the work comes
first, last and all the time.

The tone is contrite, the letter ending by stressing Lean's dominance, with Bolt acting as the
prodigal son: 'It's a wonderful thing for me to know as I write that whatever is good on the
paper will be better on the screen' (ibid.).

Later letters, though, suggest that Bolt wasn't finding Lean at all easy to work with and he
complains to Julie in April 1978: 'His egoism is so extreme and takes such finnicking forms that
I get into a locked posture of rejection; and then he takes me off guard with some little act of
thoughtfulness and generosity like that' (Brownlow 1996: 614). Although Bolt considers the
script good, Lean's demands are taking their toll on him, 'everyone thinks it a masterpiece which
it damn well isn't. Oh why has everything to be larger than life? It's so exhausting and always
leads to tears' (ibid.).

Despite Bolt's criticisms, Lean was happier with his output; in a further letter to Julie, Lean
tells her:

Robert is in pretty good shape. Much longer hair than when you were here. Hardly goes anywhere
without his 'sarong' – which raises eyebrows in the super market – so I am told – but don't tell him
… We drive each other fairly mad from time to time but on the whole it's a good combination.
(DL/12/47: May 1978)

The first draft of *The Lawbreakers* was completed by the end of May 1978, earlier than
expected and one assumes to Lean's satisfaction. Bolt immediately began the second script, *The
Long Arm*, but Lean was finding him difficult again, and refers to Bolt's lack of dedication in a
letter to Phil Kellogg, 'he had dined and wined too well and told me that after such a good lunch
he wasn't quite in the right mood to concentrate' (ibid.: 28 July 1978). Lean continued to refine
the script while Bolt was resting. In the same letter Lean mentions being unable to find Bolt to
pass on notes on how to begin *The Long Arm*. Bolt appears to have gone into hiding to avoid

Lean, who protests: 'I can't contact Robert. I sometimes get really mad at him as you know. Can't do a damned thing for himself and is about as selfish as they come' (ibid.). Lean is also critical of Bolt's arrogance, 'The awful thing is that when he has any sort of success – as in the last few weeks – he immediately lapses back into pompous, talking down, self-satisfaction' (ibid.).

The Bounty project was beset with financial problems and, by the end of summer 1978, De Laurentiis was in difficulties after sinking his money into a hotel on Bora Bora and going $10 million over budget on the film *Hurricane* (1979), also being filmed on the island (Brownlow 1996: 622). In September 1978, De Laurentiis pulled out of the project. Bolt was only kept on because he had already been paid a substantial amount of money for the screenplays. This meant that De Laurentiis retained ownership of the two scripts, which were not far from completion. Understandably, Lean was angry about the situation and Bolt's loyalties were questioned. Bolt still asked for Lean's feedback on the new script for *The Long Arm*, despite the fact that he was no longer the director. Bolt responds to Lean on 16 October 1978:

> I fully take your point that at this moment I am working for Dino and that you have neither the desire nor the authority to influence my writing on this second script. That is very proper and correct. Meanwhile, however you remain my friend I trust, and I want your comments on what I've done so far, as I would on any script I was working on. I hope you will be willing to do that for me, simply as a friend. I think it would be pedantically unscrupulous for you to refuse. (ibid.: 627)

Considering Lean's position, Bolt's request seems insensitive and elicits the reply: 'I have scarcely known you more enthusiastic and am therefore the more put out' (ibid.). He metes out a very negative appraisal of the submitted pages:

> the script and letter are written as if from two different people. The letter is a highly intelligent appreciation concerning the aims and pitfalls of writing this second script as a dramatic scenario. An appreciation which the writer of the script has failed to read. ... I am going to have to go into battle against the intellectual who will defend the script with some pretty good verbal acrobatics. (ibid.: 627)

Lean thought *The Long Arm* script read like a documentary and its pacing was much too slow, unlike the first script, which is full of drama and excitement. Lean is critical of Captain Edwards, describing his character with distaste, ' I find him not only way over the top but an inexplicable and disgusting pervert ...' (ibid.).

By early November the finances around the film had completely fallen apart and, in a letter of 1 November 1978, Bolt warns Lean to be careful and confesses himself to be in a very difficult position which is

> clear and unpleasant. I am working for Dino and being paid by him. So long as he honours his side of our contract I must honour mine. I must press on with the second script and what is more on Dec 19th unless someone has bought him out, the first script, and whatever I have by then of the second, and when it is done the whole of the second will be Dino's absolutely to do what he wants with, and he need not consult either you or me. (DL/12/47)

Not surprisingly, the uncertainty around the project made it difficult to write and, probably exacerbated by these stresses, Bolt had a first heart attack in November 1978, going to hospital in Los Angeles. He returned to Tahiti in late November where he and Lean's relationship became increasingly strained. Bolt says of Lean, 'Demanding and forceful he is: fertile and fortifying he isn't. He has that blinkered quality which characterises all great achievers – apart from the very greatest …' (Brownlow 1996: 628).[6] Bolt had a second and more serious heart attack in April 1979, necessitating a triple-heart bypass, the next day suffering a major stroke which stopped him writing for over a year. Melvyn Bragg was taken on to complete *The Long Arm* but the partnership did not gel and Lean, despite many attempts, could not secure financial backing for the films.

This is a fascinating study of the complexities of the film production development process. The writer and director are highly vulnerable to the vagaries of the moneymen, especially when this involved the huge sums required by a director like Lean. The terrible irony for Lean was that he lost everything, his project and his writer: Bolt was contracted to write both screenplays for De Laurentiis and he could not renege on this.

Although Lean did eventually buy back the rights, he could not find a financier so the rights reverted to De Laurentiis, who eventually made the film as *The Bounty* in 1984. The script was rewritten by Bolt, incorporating some of the original material into a condensed version of *The Lawbreakers* and *The Long Arm*.

Suggestions for cuts and alterations to *The Lawbreakers* (DL/12/6)

Lean sent fifteen pages of densely typed notes to Bolt in November 1978, headed 'Suggestions for cuts and alterations to "The Lawbreakers"'. Lean appears to refer to the screenplay dated 23 July 1978 (DL/12/3), although there are some minor page differences. Lean's feedback paints a revealing picture of the pair's collaboration during the revision process. Lean is relentless, detailing how his suggested changes should work. Some notes request minor changes while others propose quite major amendments or cutting pages. Lean's comments often focus on the visual as he tries to make Bolt see the story as he does. Lean's early training as a film editor is apparent in his transitions and cuts from scene to scene, or shot to shot that improve the quality of the script.

The notes often refer to the pace of the story, its tone and the subtleties of character. Lean asks Bolt to tighten the script and focus more on the central characters, observing of Bligh, 'we take almost 2½ pages to get him into the scene with Captain Edwards. I think we should be able to do it in a page. Don't forget they have met before.' He later pleads: 'Can't we speed things up, just a little' and 'Take him below decks quicker.' Lean then suggests changes and cuts to the sequence on the Bounty's departure as it is too long:

> I know we are very much feeling our way but it amounts to very nearly 12 pages. (Mostly my fault because I got locked into the chapter heading, 'The Departure and the first night at Sea'.) It contains some really smashing stuff.

Lean calls for dramatic cuts between pages 28–40, feeling that there is too much background detail and 'there's quite a bit of leisurely stuff which we can't afford under the circumstances'. This would allow them to shorten the scenes, 'In other words make these 12 pages more like 6 pages using (Captain) Edwards for the jump cuts.' Lean wants events to proceed more quickly, advocating cuts as the Bounty crosses the meridian line on the Equator, despite the excellent writing:

I'm very much in two minds about crossing the line. It's almost 2 pages and it doesn't advance the story. It's exciting and it gives a very vivid picture of the roughness of the crew and 'the life of the times'. – On balance I don't think we can afford it.

Towards the end of the film, when Bligh has been cast adrift with his men by Christian, Lean tries to think of ways to link the two figures together in different locations that will help cut down the number of pages. He describes Bligh's plight as 'the 18th Century equivalent of being lost in space. Once I'd tumbled to that rather obvious fact pictures started to slide into place.' He offers an alternative scene:

> CLOSE UP BLIGH. He looks at them for a moment. Then lifts his eyes to scan the horizon. MUSIC (Space theme) begins softly.
>
> DISSOLVE
>
> MEDIUM SHOT. The reflection of a nearly full moon with its mountains and craters undulating gently on the surface of an almost flat sea. On sound, mixed with the music, the gentle electronic pulse, 'peep … peep … peep'.
>
> And then the approaching creek and splash of oars. Then the Bow of the Launch enters picture.
>
> CLOSE UP. BLIGH sits looking ahead. As the oars enter the Water little pinpoints of reflected light burst across his face. He looks down at:
>
> A BIG CLOSE UP of the compass on his lap: the moon and stars mirrored in its glass.
>
> CLOSE UP BLIGH. He looks up from the compass towards the rowers.
>
> > BLIGH (Hoarsely)
> > Alright men relax for five minutes.
>
> A murmured response and the sound of oars being rested.
>
> LONG SHOT, looking down on the surface of the sea.

Lean ends the scene with:

> CLOSE UP BLIGH. His face is dirty and disfigured …
>
> And we are at the top of page 154 and the beginning of the nightmare sequence preceding the Barrier Reef …

Lean's tighter version ensures 'a saving of two pages'. This effective visual change illustrates how closely Lean was involved in the writing process, at times devising his own lines.

Concerned about a clash of styles in the move from experimental and innovative to a more traditional approach, Lean points out:

> We started off the film with quite a daring technique; the rocket, the burning ship, the 18th Century young man, a jump to the mutiny ... Now Robert, we obviously had to slow it down and have a scene – and we did it with Edwards in his cabin with Bligh ... Then the first big scene, Hood.
> Then a chaos of thundering canvas – and we're off!! Really most exciting. But then we suddenly changed gear and went back into the old and usual method of telling a film story.

He advocates further development of the central characters:

> I don't know what happened to us. Perhaps we were daunted by the mass of new characters and the geography of the ship. We did well with the ship and not so well by the characters with Heywood looming rather larger than he should.

Lean favours ending the sequence with 'an exchange of looks between Bligh and Christian? The two friends over their first hurdle together. CUT.'

Lean's tone in the notes varies, from dictatorial to discursive; as in this instance, when thinking through ways of cutting a scene, 'We shall have to talk but I'm almost certain that CUT'S going to be to Edward's. Perhaps a knock on the door and Heywood coming in ... I don't know but it's that line of country.'

Lean is critical of some of Bolt's description: for instance, when Captain Edwards, whose task it is to find the mutineers, is first introduced, we are told 'his forehead is beaded with perspiration'. Lean remarks: 'It's a useful nudge for poor or unimaginative readers but I fear it's over the top in practice and that a good actor won't need it.' Lean is similarly dubious about Captain Edwards's line, 'Now let's have a look at the rest of these vermin', favouring a more interesting and subtle portrayal:

> In line with my thoughts about the perspiration I find the word, vermin, rather over the top.
> As things stand we have put Edwards over in one. Hitchcock would probably cast an actor of considerable charm and appeal and then, very gradually he would start insinuating doubts in the audience's mind.

Lean discusses the revelation regarding Captain Edwards's psychological disorder:

> I don't think it would be half bad if we arrived at the conclusion that he was very peculiar more or less at the same time as Bligh ... We should feel, as an audience, that we are in a secret which is certainly not known to the Admiralty or Hood.

Lean recommends a major rewrite of the scene when the audience first view the relationship between Bligh and Christian, with notes about how the characters should be perceived:

> The solitary Bligh, proud and touched that such an attractive young chap as Christian should disprove his and others' doubts about himself. Christian proud and touched that he alone has been able to pierce the emotional armour-plating of such an impressive personality.

Lean often comments on the transitions in the screenplay and, of the cut from the cabin of the Bounty to Admiral Hood's office, protests, 'It's *alright* – but it doesn't contain the elegant pleasures of cinematic sleight of hand. Hood and the breadfruit come on like the next slide at a lantern lecture …'. Lean's visual sense as a director and early training as an editor are evident in his improvements to the script.

Credibility and story logic are, understandably, seen as important by Lean, who questions aspects of Bolt's script. For instance, after the ice storm and battle around Cape Horn, Lean takes issue with Bligh immediately sitting down to write to his wife:

> I need a little help for the scene of Bligh writing to his wife, 'God knows when or by what means you will receive this letter.' We have just had a harrowing scene on deck with the hail and the ice. Bligh tells Christian to assemble the men – but instead of addressing the men he sits down and writes a letter to his wife.
>
> I don't believe it. I would believe it if the men had to be de-iced, warmed and given some rum – something like that in order to make it an hour or so later.

In the same vein, when Christian and his men are cast adrift and starving, Lean notices a lack of logic: 'When Bligh says "Make sure every person gets a piece of pork Mr Lamb" I think, "Pork!" Where the hell did they get pork? I thought they were at death's door."'

Lean supplies over two pages of notes on the Bounty's arrival in Tahiti, concentrating on the men's initial impressions of the island. He contends:

> Although no one has commented on it I think we have failed to exploit a wonderful situation. We have failed, in my opinion, because we have told the Tahiti story in the same style as the rest of the picture. We have made it too factual and we haven't been bold enough. I'll try to explain.

Lean then delineates his Gauguin-inspired vision of Tahiti:

> We sail half way round the world and find a beautiful Pandora's box. The crew open it and are almost immediately drugged by its magic contents. It's the stuff of Greek legends isn't it? Sirens and sailors, dreams and potions. When they leave Christian seriously thinks of going overboard; it's not just Mauatua, it's a spell.
>
> I would like to blow cocaine up everyone's nostrils. Yours, the Designer's and the actors. If we could create a kind of Gauguin-like atmosphere, exotic and heavily perfumed I think we could put the film into another class.

Comparing the story to *Ryan's Daughter*, he believes that the script needs to do more than hint at the danger in what appears to be paradise:

> If we are going to do this we mustn't make the same mistake we made on 'Ryan's Daughter'. We should have spelt out loud and clear, 'Ladies and Gentlemen, we are showing two young people caught up in the throes of physical passion.' … It's not as difficult as 'Ryan's Daughter' because the atmosphere is not so obviously pretty; it's heavier, more sensual and darker.

Lean's comments demonstrate the intensity of his imaginative approach, yet exhibit occasional moments of humour, for instance, when he teases Bolt about his use of the word 'mush':

> 'tonight I want as much hot mush as every man can eat'. You don't half like obscure words! … Can't he just say, '… as much hot food as every man can eat'? It's touching. When I hear 'mush' I think, 'What's mush? It must be an old fashioned word for food.' And by the time I've had that thought I'm no longer touched because it's an interruption.

Also, at the end, when Bligh and his men arrive half-dead in the Dutch colony, Lean intimates that the cost of the scene of Dutch Baroque houses in the harbour 'will scare … the daylights out of the budget chaps', pleading, 'Give them a little comfort please.'

The comprehensive notes imply that Lean expects Bolt to do his bidding. Lean vividly recounts scenes and images to enthuse him and offers creative solutions to the pacing of the film. Occasionally Lean praises Bolt's writing, noting that the screenplay 'contains some really smashing stuff' and ends his notes with the understated approval of 'Otherwise you did quite a good job. See you soon. D.L.'

Bolt's response to Lean (12/6)

Bolt replied on 27 November 1978 that he had made a number of cuts to the script and managed to lose seventeen pages, roughly 11 per cent of the script. He affirms that the pace has been sharpened by some major cuts, to the introduction of four and a half pages, three and a half pages from the overlong sequence on beginning the journey and four and a half pages from the Bounty crossing the meridian. Of the relationship between Bligh and Christian, he points out the dangers of trying to depict Bligh in a more positive light:

> we were feeling our way with the characters when I wrote those two incidents; I'm now convinced that, with competent actors we have enough to show that FRYER is a nuisance and CHRISTIAN a reliable friend without these two incidents. I think we were at this stage so keen to show BLIGH as a credible man instead of a monster that we went here from the sublime to the other thing.

Bolt raises four further points about the relationship which he thinks need adjusting to clarify its status and lend it a more masculine aspect, befitting that between naval officers:

1   The scene between BLIGH and CHRISTIAN is coy. For instance, BLIGH should either tell him where they are going or else not tell him. Here he teases him.
2   I don't see Christian as a practical seaman; they're more like a headmaster and his favoured pupil than a skipper and his mate. It's good when they are separated, CHRISTIAN aloft and BLIGH below, bad when they talk.
3   I (as an audience) identify with BLIGH, alone and expert, assessing his vessel, CHRISTIAN seems to pester him. I'd like CHRISTIAN to share the mood.
4   The main purpose of the scene was to show them as friends, so as to prepare for BLIGH'S over-reaction on Tahiti when he thought that CHRISTIAN let him down. It would therefore be good if we see that BLIGH *needs* or feels the need of Christian. This, coupled with a bit more dignity and manliness in CHRISTIAN, is in fact all that is needed.

Bolt appears to have embraced most of Lean's suggestions, often writing the revisions to scenes in script form in his reply and within the revised draft, including changing 'mush' to 'food'! Lean's feedback notes are the type expected from an excellent script editor.

Bolt's screenplay *The Lawbreakers*

Although Lean evidently had a great deal of input, the screenplay development for *The Lawbreakers* was the hand of Bolt, and he was much more than a cipher for Lean's ideas. The resulting screenplay was highly regarded. The following quotes indicate the impact of Bolt's writing. In a telex to Lean, producer De Laurentiis exclaims:

> It is the best material I have ever read, the construction is excellent, it has rhythm, it is always interesting, wit, suspense and beautiful dialogue and all the characters from Bligh to the very last sailor are superbly built. Bolt is without unique. Together you have done a truly excellent job and I am sure it will be the best script ever written (DL/12/47: 16 February 1978)

Kevin Brownlow, in his biography of Lean, enthuses,

> Despite Bolt's modesty, the script of the film – *The Lawbreakers* – reads most impressively … the interplay between the mutiny, the court martial and even the play of *The Pirates* is quite dazzling. Characters are introduced in original ways … . (1996: 614–15)

Bolt is known for his taut poetic description, flowing, masculine dialogue and craftsmanship. *The Lawbreakers* is a compelling read, from the first to the last page. The exchange in the following extract from the beginning of the first draft screenplay, written in 1977, artfully reveals much about Bligh's exacting character and the esteem he is held in by Admiral Hood, as well as telling us that he is expecting bad weather. Bligh learns of his mission to transport bread plants to Tahiti, before Hood asks if there is anything else he wants to discuss:

BLIGH
… I think I should have been promoted.

HOOD
So do I. Anything else?

BLIGH
She carries too much sail.

HOOD
Do you know how much we have taken off?

BLIGH
Yes sir and it's still too much. This is how I'd like her …

HOOD studies the copperplate writing and figures which BLIGH puts before him.

> HOOD (murmuring)
> Foretop forty-eight foot ten. Cross-jack thirty-one feet nine and a half-nine and a <u>half</u> Mr Bligh?

> BLIGH
> Yes sir.

> HOOD
> You're a devil of a man for getting things exact, aren't you?

Bligh knows he is being teased but it is not for him a teasing matter.

> BLIGH (quietly)
> Yes sir, I am.

Hood peruses the figures a little longer saying:

> HOOD
> All right, we'll trim her down again.

> (looks at Bligh very shrewdly)

> Expectin' a lot of heavy weather Mr Bligh?

> BLIGH
> Yes sir.

> HOOD
> Well you should know … (DL/12/3: 26–7)

There is great economy to the writing, Bolt's crisp style helping the dialogue flow naturally from Bligh to Hood. The scene is carefully constructed to leave a question at the end about the destination and reveal Bligh's ambition to circumnavigate the world.

The screenplay description and dialogue help to build an atmosphere of great tension on board the ship. In the middle of a terrible storm, as they are rounding the Cape, Fryer, the ship's sailing master, criticises Bligh's judgment. This is a pivotal scene in which Fryer is replaced by Christian; it is tense yet has a grim humour:

> FRYER
> In my opinion we should put about.

> BLIGH
> Thank you. In my opinion we should not.

He moves towards the ladder but:

                    FRYER
        I should like my opinion put in the log, Sir.

           BLIGH (ascending the ladder, unresponsive)
                    Very well.

CLOSE UP FRYER looking up at him:

                    FRYER
              The ship can't stand it.

CLOSE on BLIGH. He turns at the top of the ladder before pulling back the hatch.

                    BLIGH
        The <u>ship</u> can stand it very well Mr Fryer.

CLOSE on FRYER. We hear the sound of the hatch being slid back and daylight
brightens his face.

                    FRYER
      How long do you think the men can stand it?

POV FRYER. BLIGH steps onto the deck above, and turns:

               BLIGH (furious and loud)
                As long as the officers!

– and slams back the hatch. (ibid.: 53–4)

A hallmark of Bolt's writing is his vivid description of nature and the elements. In the scene after the argument with Fryer, Bligh comes up on deck to witness the terrible conditions the men are forced to endure:

CLOSE SHOT. The figurehead already somewhat travel-worn wears a crown of hard,
grey ice.

CLOSE SHOT. The man at the wheel, unshaven and red-eyed, is blue and white with
cold and fatigue. He watches dully:

His POV. BLIGH approaching. He takes his stance on the quarterdeck, the same
intransigent stance as before; legs straddled, hands clasped, chin up, cautiously
measuring the situation.

LONG SHOT angled up. High up in the rigging three MEN on an ice-caked yard are
feebly trying to release a reefed up sail.

CLOSE UP. BLIGH looking up at them.

CLOSE SHOT. They look like corpses and their fingers, like blue claws, can get no purchase on the frozen lashings. Above them:

CLOSE. Two black Frigate birds gliding effortlessly on the wind.

CLOSE. CHRISTIAN on the deck below, also looking up.

MEDIUM SHOT. His POV. The MEN somehow get the canvas clear; it drops like sheet metal to its place, releasing a shower of frozen sleet which clatters to the deck below.

BLIGH, on the quarterdeck, watches almost guiltily as:

LONG SHOT. The CREWMEN climb painfully towards the shrouds.

CLOSE SHOT BLIGH. On SOUND the wind whines louder and is suddenly filled with a rattling metallic uproar. BLIGH looks up at:

His POV. The vessel obscured in a fusillade of hail-stones.
(ibid.: 55–6)

The reader is taken shot by shot through the grim situation as it worsens, until Bligh has to admit defeat.

Lean's evocative picture of Tahiti, in his earlier notes, has made Bolt rethink the way he introduces the island. The new draft also shows some structural changes, including an engaging cut from Bligh and the Bounty's arrival in Tahiti to the English courtroom, where Bligh is facing court martial. Bligh's voiceover links the two locations:

BLIGH (V.O.)
I have seen many places in the world, but believe that Tahiti is preferable to them all. Perhaps our sensibility to what we now observed was magnified by what we had so recently endured. We had crossed twenty-seven thousand miles of salt sea water for ten long months, imposing and accepting all the harsh necessities of discipline at sea.

We walk with BLIGH through an enchanted garden, and through him we see as Gauguin saw. Pink sand and lilac branches splashed with gold and silver light; fruits of smouldering red and yellow hanging by the hundredweight; cascades of pure water flickering in violet shadows; pandanus roofs the colour of ripe corn beneath which golden children play in purple gloom; cats and dogs and rosy pigs and heraldic cockerels; convoluted trees whose baroque buttresses are sinuously streaked with

sunlight. The people whom they pass give silent greeting raising their arms like
people in a dream, smiling shyly out of melancholy eyes.

BLIGH (V.O.)
Here Nature herself appeared to be lenient, and if human
happiness results from natural abundance it is in Tahiti that we
may expect to find –

On SOUND a sharp English voice breaks in:

VOICE (S.O.)
Lieutenant Bligh –

CLOSE UP BLIGH. He starts from his reverié:

BLIGH
Yes sir?

He is in the Great Cabin of HOOD'S flagship … (ibid.: 73)

Bligh's voiceover and Bolt's visualisation of Tahiti is very involving, so the surprise cut jolts the
reader from the sensual paradise back to the reality of the court martial.

Bolt's description, the one aspect of the script that is not transferred to film, is more akin to
poetry, with metaphor and simile often enlisted to enhance the draft. The reference to different
types of sound adds a note of reality, as in this extract soon after the Bounty's arrival in Tahiti:

The stranded BOUNTY, like some prehistoric beast, has been hauled on to her side
and secured by ropes attached to trees, rocks and buried anchors. The beach is
swarming with industry of a sort that has never been seen before. A forge is blazing,
hammer on anvil banging unharmoniously. Another fire is heating pitch in a big
cauldron. Smoke drifts across the lovely coastline; the din and clatter echoing back
from the hills. In the foreground miles of rope are laid out in neat lines, bales and
barrels, cannon and shot. (ibid.: 94–5)

The final section of the screenplay follows the dangerous journey Bligh makes with his
men, from Tahiti to the Dutch East Indies. In the following dramatic scene, they try to find food
and habitation, upon reaching an island they believe to be safe:

CLOSE SHOT. NELSON and OTHERS looking up eagerly at:

LONG SHOT. The headland passing by.

CLOSE SHOT. BLIGH sitting upright, looking ahead.

LONG SHOT. The beach and the dwelling approaching.

CLOSE UP. BLIGH looks back at both headlands; returns to the beach.

CLOSE SHOT. LEBOGUE, the sternmost oarsman and nearest to BLIGH,
looks over his shoulder as he ends his stroke, checks and:

> LEBOGUE
> Sir … under these bushes.

CLOSE SHOT. BLIGH twists around and stares hard at:

MEDIUM LONG SHOT. At the foot of the nearest headland; low overhanging
branches with black shadows. Nothing stirring.

CLOSE UP. BLIGH sees something and turns quickly.

> BLIGH (softly)
> Helm down Mr Cole; backwater starboard, heave
> a port –

CLOSE UP. ELPHINSTONE suddenly alarmed:

> ELPHINSTONE
> Look out – !

LONG SHOT. A slender canoe propelled by the blue-black, muscular SAVAGES
bursts from the cover of the bushes, leaping through the water to cut off the retreat
of the labouring launch.

CLOSE SHOT. BLIGH AND COLE.

> BLIGH
> Give me the tiller Mr Cole –

He seizes it, looking ahead at:

LONG SHOT. The reef with pass to the open sea.

CLOSE SHOT. BLIGH directs the launch straight at the pass.

MEDIUM SHOT. LEBOGUE and the other OARSMEN almost standing, gasping.

CLOSE SHOT. BLIGH crouched forward like the cox of a racing-eight.

> BLIGH
> You're pulling for your lives lads!

CLOSE SHOT. LEBOGUE heaving forward for the stroke, flashes him a wry look.

> BLIGH (V.O.)
> Those men are cannibals.

> LEBOGUE (flashing a look over Bligh's shoulder)
> Sir –

CLOSE SHOT BLIGH, all his concentration on the MEN.

> BLIGH
> We're chops and liver to them lads – !

The scene is carefully shaped and crafted to maximise drama and tension to the chase through the water, which acts as a reminder of Bligh's skills as a leader and navigator. He steers the boat through the reef and away from the cannibals, Bolt injecting some black humour as the scene continues:

CLOSE SHOT BLIGH. He looks back to see:

MEDIUM SHOT. The canoe dreadfully close on the crest of a wave.

CLOSE SHOT. BLIGH turns and stares ahead.

MEDIUM SHOT. The launch approaches a towering wave. BLIGH deliberately straight at it, too near the reef for comfort.

The launch soars up – and over.

MEDIUM SHOT. The canoe shoots into the base of the wave – and is overwhelmed.

CLOSE SHOT. BLIGH shouting above the roaring surf:

> BLIGH
> Keep at it – !

He looks back and sees:

His POV. Nothing at first but the humpbacked waves. The passing of a roller reveals the overturned canoe. CREW struggling in the water.

CLOSE SHOT. BLIGH ecstatic, as though he had won the prize at an Admiral's Regatta.

> BLIGH
> Well done my lads – ! (ibid.)

Bligh is presented as a heroic navigator, likeable and brave, holding the men together on their incredible 4,000-mile journey to the Dutch East Indies. The script conveys vividly Bligh and his crew's suffering as they arrive in the port, more dead than alive:

> CLOSE SHOT. BLIGH is already well up the ramp, walking jerkily with the log-book jammed beneath his arm and in his other hand the now almost colourless ebony stick. His passage makes an eddy in the flow of people hurrying past him towards the launch. They turn their heads, some making a complete circle to look after him. His clothes are rags, his eyes are burning, he looks like someone who has escaped from burial. But the MUSIC is triumphant. BLIGH'S whole deportment is a weird caricature of the correct. He has no idea what he looks like; he is a naval officer coming ashore in a strange place with the reputation of his Service and his country to sustain. As he emerges from the shadow of the dark stone wall into the sunlight he actually gives a slight, curt nod and croaks:
>
>
>
> BLIGH
>
> Good morning. (DL/12/3: 137)
>
>

The screenplay is at its most convincing depicting Bligh on the Bounty, after Christian has set him adrift with his men. Our sympathies lie with Bligh and his men and how they survive the seemingly impossible, while Christian is a figure whom neither Bolt nor Lean ever quite manage to bring to life.

CONCLUSION

Some of those he knew best considered Bolt to be a craftsman and communicator rather than an artist. Roger Gard, Cambridge don and good friend expands:

> I used to tease him about his work which I didn't despise but put down as middlebrow. I said it wasn't real art. I said he was a craftsman and he liked that. Looking back, I think I was rather rough on him, though I did admire A Man For All Seasons .... Robert wrote about themes ... here's a problem and we are hoping to dramatise it. ... What I feel limited his work was the lack of unpredictability. You know that it's going to go that way, that there aren't going to be any surprises, that nothing is going to get out of hand. (Turner 1998: 355)

His brother, Sydney Bolt, comments, 'He had a communication theory of art rather than an aesthetic theory of art. ... I don't believe Bob was an artist, he was a communicator' (ibid.: 295). Bolt's agent, Margaret Ramsay, thought he was a better playwright than a screenwriter and had thrown away his talent in return for money and glamour.[7] There is certainly some truth in this observation – Bolt was attracted to the lifestyle of the film world and enjoyed his wealth. Yet his collaboration with Lean did produce some remarkable work. Bolt was able to draw on his playwriting skills while Lean developed Bolt's visual imagination; Lean was the creator of images and Bolt the creator of story, character and dialogue.

The two men had much in common: they were interested in grand themes of an epic nature, and seeing man pitted against moral quandaries. There are moments of outstanding writing in Bolt's scripts for Lean, as in the examples here from *The Lawbreakers*. Lean drove Bolt to write better scripts and their working relationship was fruitful but Bolt's screenplays never quite amounted to the sum of their parts. In contrast to Powell's relationship with Pressburger, for instance, whose work was more esoteric and often deliberately ambiguous, Bolt can be viewed as a bold and exciting writer whose work lacks the subtlety to make his screenplays truly memorable.

The screenplays Bolt wrote for Lean, both produced and unproduced, are usually considered the highlight of his career, yet his screenplay for *The Mission*, produced by David Puttnam, is of comparable status. When Lean died, Bolt found a home for his ideas with Puttnam, whose thematic interests echoed his and who admired his work. Puttnam's methods were less intense than Lean's and he was skilled at matching the right wordsmith with the right project. The next chapter discusses Puttnam's role as developer as well as the writers he worked with and the screenplays that resulted.

NOTES

1. Turner covers the dispute over the authorship of the screenplay in some detail (1998: 206–13).
2. See Turner (ibid.: 409–14) for further details on the development of *The Bounty*.
3. See article by John McInerney (1987), which discusses Bolt's screenplay for *The Mission*, comparing it to his other writing.
4. Bolt is referring to the earlier version of *Mutiny on the Bounty* (1935), starring Clark Gable as Christian and Charles Laughton as Captain Bligh.
5. Phil Kellogg had represented Lean at the William Morris Agency and Lean then employed him as his producer. He was to become a very influential figure in the development of the Bounty saga (Brownlow 1996: 604)
6. See Brownlow (ibid.: 628–33) for more detail on the deteriorating relationship between Bolt and Lean.
7. Bolt received many accolades as a scriptwriter and *The Mission* was presented with an award by the Writers Guild of America for excellence in the art of screenwriting on 8 November 1986, with the comment that 'Robert Bolt has consistently worked to illuminate that mixture of determination, free will and ambiguity that shapes our living rather than shapes our existence. We are all in some way or another in his debt' (Puttnam Collection, Box 4).

09
DAVID PUTTNAM
PUTTING THE RIGHT PEOPLE TOGETHER

David Puttnam developed a close working relationship with the scriptwriters on the films he produced, often initiating a film idea before selecting an author to bring it to life. He was noted for his ability to match people to projects, having an instinct for a good story, and was one of the most successful film producers of the 1970s and 1980s, respected for his ability to get films made in what is a notoriously difficult industry, while creating an environment in which the writer felt supported. Puttnam took an active part in the script development process, particularly on projects he instigated such as *Chariots of Fire* (1981), *Local Hero* (1983), *The October Circle* and *The Killing Fields* (1984), a process which is recorded in some detail in the screenplays and correspondence in the David Puttnam Collection.

Puttnam began his career in advertising, before building up a successful photographic agency, after which an interest in film led him to set up Good Time Productions, with partners Ross Cramer and Charles Saatchi. Puttnam later went into partnership with Sandy Lieberson, first producing *Melody* (1971) with Alan Parker as the screenwriter. After this moderate success, Puttnam and Lieberson went on to make several more films, including *That'll Be the Day* (1973), its sequel, *Stardust* (1974), *Mahler* (1974) and *Lisztomania* (1975), both directed by Ken Russell and *Bugsy Malone* (1976) directed by Alan Parker. The films were quite well received, but *The Duellists* (1977), Ridley Scott's first film as director, was a box-office flop and led to financial difficulties. Despite this disappointment, Puttnam's reputation was established because he had managed to secure funding for so many films. Puttnam took the job of Head of Casablanca Films in Los Angeles as this would exempt him from taxes for a while and allow him to develop *Agatha* (1979). But he found there were much greater limits on his autonomy in the US and left after only three films, *Midnight Express* (1980), written by Oliver Stone, *Agatha* and *Foxes* (1980), which bombed at the box office. Puttnam thought the failure of *Foxes* was partly because he had to rely on the experience of others in areas such as casting, and that his instincts about film content could be trusted in the UK but not in the US (Kipps 1989: 31).

Searching for new projects while in the US, Puttnam found inspiration while reading a book on the history of the Olympics. He learnt that in 1924 three British runners, including Harold Abrahams, a Jew and Eric Liddell, a Scot, had won medals. Liddell had refused to run in the 100 metres because the race was to be held on a Sunday, but went on to win the 400 metres the next day. This was the genesis of *Chariots of Fire*. Puttnam thought the story had enough potential to warrant employing a researcher and that it should concentrate on Abrahams and Liddell. Puttnam explains he was drawn to the project because:

There were elements of *Chariots of Fire* that were deliberately there to exorcise the type of life I feel I've led for the past ten years … . So it is a wishful film, trying to examine both sides of the coin of my personality. Eric Liddell, an evangelical Scot whose motivation on the track was entirely unselfish, is the kind of person I dream of being. Harold Abrahams, a somewhat aloof, unpopular figure who ran in order to satisfy his personal ambition, is more similar to the kind of person I find myself, a pragmatist, rather than an idealist. (Yule 1988: 173)

Alan Parker remembers not liking the idea when Puttnam pitched it, 'I thought it was a terrible idea … about a load of pompous English twits. I told him to forget it. That's how much I know!' (ibid.: 157). Puttnam envisaged a very different film though, characterising it as 'a film about the victory of the individual over the state' (Johnstone 1985: 102)

Puttnam asked Colin Welland to supply the screenplay. Welland had had some success as an actor and a writer in TV and film, beginning with Armchair Theatre in 1970 before penning many TV plays during the 1970s, and then the screenplay for *Yanks* (1979), a big-budget film about US soldiers in Britain during World War II, directed by John Schlesinger. Puttnam would certainly have held Welland in high regard but, even then, he insisted on the screenplay going through a rigorous rewriting process, as he explains:

'Colin did five drafts for Chariots', David recalls. 'A couple of times he was fed up and I'm sure he thought I was either pedantic or wrong, but we staggered through it. Some people aren't that lunatic. I suppose you could say I'm especially tenacious.' (Yule 1988: 169)

Puttnam liked to be in control of the development process from the initial stages, able to choose the writer, director and team for the project. He would oversee the collaboration while establishing, as Iain Smith, the location manager on *Chariots of Fire*, notes, 'a totally autocratic power base … . Where he will rule absolutely and there is no one to second-guess him. Particularly directors' (ibid.: 177). Despite this, Puttnam believes film-making to be a collaborative process, pointing out, 'The truth is it's Colin Welland's film, it's Hugh Hudson's film and it's my film, in just about equal parts' (ibid.: 181).

Chariots of Fire performed admirably at the box office but received mixed reviews, failing to impress US critics such as Andrew Sarris and Pauline Kael, yet it went on to win four Oscars, including Best Picture for David Puttnam and Best Screenplay for Colin Welland.

The success of *Chariots of Fire* helped Puttnam secure a deal with Warner Brothers, which paid for him to develop any number of screenplays, as long as they had first choice of subject. As Puttnam explains, 'It's good for them and good for me. My job is to deliver comparative bargains at a very keen price' (Walker 1974: 183) This put him in the enviable position of being able to select subjects he found interesting as long as they proved suitable material for a low-budget film.

THE DAVID PUTTNAM COLLECTION
Local Hero
One of Puttnam's first projects was *Local Hero*, written and directed by Bill Forsyth, whose first two films, *That Sinking Feeling* (1980) and *Gregory's Girl* (1981) had both won critical acclaim. Alexander Walker points out that Forsyth's background was very similar to Puttnam's, being, 'remarkable only for its unremarkableness' (1985: 186) yet 'Forsyth's characters are always

Bill Forsyth and David Puttnam on the set of
Local Hero (1983)

positioned at an angle to the more serious business of living. They are dreamers, forever
reversing our expectations of their reactions'
(ibid.).

Forsyth had first met Puttnam in the late
1970s and they had got on well. Puttnam was
impressed enough by *Gregory's Girl* to help
Forsyth get a distribution deal for the film. The
second time they met, Puttnam showed Forsyth
the Ealing comedy, *Whisky Galore*, depicting
events after Hebridean Island villagers find
cases of whisky washed ashore from a ship-
wreck. Puttnam had been thinking about
making a film set in Scotland with a similar storyline and discovered a newspaper clipping about
a Scottish island accountant who had successfully sued Exxon, after finding a clause that
guaranteed the corporation would not despoil
the environment. Puttnam at that time was
drawn to environmental issues[1] and further
developed the idea with Forsyth, hoping to:

repeat the organic growth that had brought forth Chariots and Forsyth wrote a 2 page treatment but
pointing the emphasis away from oil rigs and the hardware of the business, while still retaining the
concept of an American petrochemical giant being taken to the cleaners by the supposedly naïve
inhabitants of a small Scottish fishing village. (Yule 1988: 206)

Forsyth's contract clearly stipulated that the idea for the film belonged to Puttnam and that
Forsyth was the writer rather than the originator of the story (DP Item 49/2).[2] The first draft
script was completed in September 1981. Forsyth felt it needed to be funny but imposing
humour on the story didn't seem to work: 'after that I decided that it would be just as funny as
it wanted to be' (Yule 1988: 206). The length became an issue as it came to 150 pages, which
Puttnam considered too long. Forsyth resisted shortening it, believing they should shoot the
film and then cut it down if needs be; indeed, a second draft was almost the same length, but
Puttnam wanted to avoid shooting unnecessary scenes to save money (ibid.).

Puttnam was involved in the development stages and the writing of the screenplay but then
stayed away from the filming and post-production stage until the final cut, when he offered
input on certain aspects of the editing. He helped to improve the Houston scene of Happer,
played with great aplomb by Burt Lancaster, at the committee meeting. The scene lacked pace
but gained momentum when Puttnam suggested that Happer should be asleep and the manage-
ment talk in whispers around him. Forsyth wrote the part of Happer with Burt Lancaster in
mind, not really expecting to get him (ibid.).

Local Hero was a big hit, this time receiving positive reviews from Andrew Sarris and Pauline Kael, and almost quadrupling its production costs of £2.7 million. Worldwide sales reached £8.5 million by July 1983 yet the film failed to really take off in the US, where Puttnam had expected it would. The screenplay won numerous awards though, including the 1983 New York Film Critics Circle Award for Best Screenplay and the 1984 National Society of Film Critics Award for Best Screenplay.

The early two-page treatment in the Puttnam Collection (DP Box 1, Item 1), reproduced in full below, shows that the original idea had more to do with the men on the ground and less with the head of the company. Once Burt Lancaster expressed an interest, his role was expanded to include the important strand about the magnate's obsession with astronomy and the night sky. The treatment sets up the whimsy of the story, contrasting the big business of Gow Chemicals in the US with the faraway site it sought to acquire from the residents of the village of Ferness. The potential for conflict between the locals and the outsiders, both greedy to make money from their positions, is emphasised. Besides outlining the plot, the treatment sets up the characters, particularly MacIntyre, the Gow Chemicals representative involved in the venture and the village accountant Urquhart. The treatment immediately refers to a central theme of the story, greed:

This movie is about money. Monstrous amounts of money descending alien-like on an unsuspecting community. It's about what that money brings, and what it does to the lives that it touches.

To be accurate, the money doesn't descend on the place overnight. It has to be teased there. Money is generally very shy.

FERNESS BAY lies on the north east coast of Scotland. It lies and sleeps. It was quite prepared to sleep all through the oil book going on down the coast in Aberdeen. It was happy enough fleecing the tourists in the summertime. What Ferness doesn't know is that it is the only sheltered bay on the entire coast with a silt deposit level of less than two hundred feet.

On the whole of the sedimentary east coast it alone has bedrock. A geological freak.

Bare facts can sometimes take on very emotional overtones, And there are some oilmen who are becoming emotional about the Village of Ferness. These oilmen have a five hundred mile long pipeline making its way ashore from the wells in the wild North Sea. That pipe needs a place to make a landing, and where it lands will become the petro-chemical capital of the country. No less. Petro-chemical capital needs bedrock.

The headquarters of Gow Chemicals is in Dallas Texas. They have a big map of Scotland on the wall there, with a little flag indicating Ferness. On the map the projected pipeline hovers nervously offshore, still unsure of its landing place.

Gow Chemicals is homing in on Ferness. The computer has churned out decades of financial projections to arrive at a good buying price for the site. The chemical complex itself will cost one hundred million. The cost-effective maximum price for the land itself is fifteen million. That's what Gow will put on the table if it really has to.

Ferness doesn't yet know that it has turned into pure gold almost overnight. Mrs Fraser doesn't know yet that the piece of dirt that she calls a vegetable garden is now worth seventeen thousand, according to the Gow computer. But such figures are of course maximums. Gow Chemicals intends to 'negotiate'. Gow Chemicals would rather like to take Ferness to the cleaners. So the movie is really a game of cat and mouse. Is Dallas going to fleece Ferness, or will it be vice-versa?

Gow Chemicals reckon they have an ace up their sleeve. They intend to send over their very own 'Scotsman' as their Chief Negotiator. What they don't know is that MACINYTRE'S parents changed their name from something Hungarian and unpronounceable when they reached the States in 1934. MacIntyre is as Scottish as apfel strudel.

MacIntyre meets up with a local Gow man when he reaches Scotland. He is Danny Oldsen, a younger, cub reporter kind of guy. Neither of them are conmen at heart, but their task of saving money for Gow Chemicals hasn't yet begun to compromise them. It will, later.

Brian URQUHART is a man of standing in Ferness, one of the few people there who wears a suit every day. In a community of self-employers, like farmers and fishermen, the local accountant can take on the mantle of high priest or witch doctor. And despite his sober appearance Urquhart harbours a streak of wanton creativity when it comes to filling in tax forms for his clients. Urquhart is a quiet man. He might even be a match for Gow Chemical Industries.

It's only natural that Urquhart should take on the role of Chief Negotiator for Ferness, although the lobbying he has to cope with and rationalise becomes intense. Two men with fifteen million burning a hole in their pocket are bound to have an interesting and varying effect on the inhabitants of a small place like Ferness.

Urquhart of course has his sobering effect on things. All through the negotiations and the wheeling and blackmail and dealing and betraying that goes on, he continues to serve MacIntyre and Oldsen their breakfast and dinner every day, because the only Bed and Breakfast joint in the village is run by Urquhart's wife, and he has the position of head waiter. Urquhart plays these dual roles of Chief Negotiator and Table Hop throughout the intrigues that follow. And at the end of the day, without a flicker of emotion on his face he has them make out their cheque to 'Mary B. Urquhart', as he folds up his morning apron.

This is the setting for 'Local Hero'.

The treatment established the tone of the film, the scope for comedy and the conflict between two very different cultures, the islanders with their own way of doing things and the American outsiders, the oilmen. Rather than outlining the narrative, the background and the key characters are introduced, pointing the reader to areas where misunderstandings, tension and conflict will develop. The treatment does not describe the visual beauty of the locations or the magical quality of the story which is created in the screenplay drafts.

The later draft screenplays for *Local Hero* are engagingly written and at times the description verges on the poetic. Three drafts are held in the David Puttnam Collection; a partial draft of sixty-nine pages, dated July 1981, and two almost identical drafts dated November 1981 and March 1982, of 153 pages. The following analysis compares the drafts D1 and D3, identifying many differences in structure and story, including changes to scenes to add character detail, increase tension and comedy, or enhance the direction of the narrative.

The later draft has deleted some early scenes to speed up the pace, cutting from MacIntyre's arrival at Aberdeen Airport and going straight to the lab where plans are being hatched for the new oil refinery. The central characters are made fuller and more sympathetic, for instance, extra lines intimate that Urquhart, who has a greater stake in the story in D3, and his wife enjoy a passionate relationship. D1 ends the scene with the line 'Grace and Urquhart are sex maniacs', a rather cold assessment, whereas D3 replaces this with 'Urquhart and Stella are the most compatible married couple on the face of the earth. They are amazing' (D3: 7). The change makes the couple seem more likeable and charming.

Changes in D3 accentuate the dramatic tension: in the first draft MacIntyre and his helper, Oldsen, see the village from a helicopter. The scene is visually impressive and features some

lovely description (D1: 32) but it does little other than introduce us to Ferness from the air: in
D3 this scene is deleted.

In D1 the two men discuss their plan to 'buy off' the villagers before they have entered the
new world. Not only does this make for an emotionally flat scene with little tension but crucial
plot information is revealed too soon:

ABERDEEN

KNOX BUILDING. INTERIOR

Mac and Oldsen are in a corridor, beside a fast food machine identical to the one Mac
and Cal fed at in Houston.

The machine rumbles away in the background as they talk processing their order of
one hot chilli and the Irish stew.

OLDSEN
What's the plan when we get there?

MAC
We'll tackle them one by one … we have fifteen separate deals
to make … with forty million on the table, we've got lots to
bargain with … we'll keep things quiet. (ibid.: 35)

In D3 vital story information, their plan of action, is revealed much later, when they talk to
Urquhart, so the audience gain this information at the same time he does.

In both D1 and D3 Mac and Oldsen set off for the village but, get stuck in a heavy mist and
end up spending the night in the car. The layout of the sequence in both drafts is similar, but in
D3 they hit a rabbit, which they rescue and take with them on their journey. D3 evolves more
organically, with the two enveloped in a magical mist that transfers them to another world:

STILL ON THE ROAD TWILIGHT

The sun is low in the sky now, occasionally vanishing behind the peak of a far off
mountain, appearing again all of a sudden to assault Oldsen's eyes with its glare.

MAC is sleeping. And then suddenly he is awake.

Oldsen has skidded the car to a halt.

Mac comes fully awake very quickly and looks at Oldsen.

OLDSEN
I think we hit something … It got misty all a sudden and I think
we hit something …

The motor has stalled. There is silence. Sudden and total.

Oldsen looks at Mac, waiting for orders. Oldsen is in the habit of running out of ideas very quickly.

Mac gets out of the car, and Oldsen follows him. The mist is thickening around them, and dusk is settling quickly.

They inch towards the front of the car, afraid of what they might find there.

What they find as they come around either side of the engine bonnet is a rabbit, injured and stunned, but not dead.

The rabbit isn't twitching, but is sitting placidly, breathing rather heavily.

> OLDSEN
> A shit … I hate hitting things.

> MAC
> I think it's just kinda stunned.

They inch closer to it.

> OLDSEN
> Maybe a broken leg or something. Will we put it out of its
> misery?

> MAC
> What do you mean?

> OLDSEN
> Kill it … . Hit it with something hard …

> MAC
> You've already done that, with a two-ton automobile … put it in
> the car.

CAR INTERIOR DUSK

Oldsen has placed the rabbit in the back seat, on top of the car rug. The three of them sit in the ever-thickening mist.

> MAC
> Where are we?

OLDSEN
I don't know.

Mac looks at him, rabbit-murdering incompetent that he is.

OLDSEN
The last couple of road signs were in Gaelic … It's not one of my
languages … (D3: 31–2)

The entrance into the new world is dealt with in a classical way: the men get lost in the mist and
signposts are in a foreign language. The scene also establishes that both men are soft, likeable
characters as well as outsiders. This impression is reinforced in the next scene when, after spending the night in the car, Mac is shown obsessively doing his early morning exercises in the
middle of the road.

The introduction of the rabbit is important, adding a quirky, charming dimension and a narrative thread that continues until the rabbit is served up in a stew. The scene is quietly dramatic
and tells us much about the characters, especially Mac, who becomes an increasingly sympathetic character as he is transformed by his surroundings.

In D1 the scene ends with an old man telling them the way to the village in Gaelic. In D3
this is replaced with Mac surrounded by ancient landscape and commenting, 'Just a whole lot of
scenery. What do you do with it after you've looked at it?', as two jet fighters fly noisily over-
head, an ironic comment on his point of view.

In D3 the scene describing the duo's entrance to the village is quieter and less dramatic. It is
in a later scene at the beach that the beauty and magic of their environment are revealed to Mac
and Oldsen as they take a walk:

FERNESS BEACH. TWILIGHT

It is a long, glowing summer twilight. In this part of the world the sun hardly dips
below the horizon in high summer, so there is always colour in the sky. The beach is
in a long sweeping curve, firm sand and pebble. The light is horizontal from the low-
lying sun, and is full of colour and depth.

The sound of the sea-wash sets a rhythm to the scene, and the constant cries of the
wading seabirds, the plovers, the oystercatchers, the dabchicks, settles into the ears
gently. (D3: 43)

The two men are ironically set against the beauty of the landscape as they continue their stroll,
Oldsen pointing out how the beach will be desecrated if bought by Knox Oil, though by this
time Mac is not quite so enthusiastic about the proposal:

OLDSEN
That's where the jetty will be … and the storage tanks over here,
all the way up.

MAC
Yeh.

OLDSEN
And the pipeline terminal will just about join both sides of the
bay, far out there. (ibid.: 45)

Urquhart is the most important village character, 'the fixer', yet in D1 we do not learn this until nearly halfway through the script (p. 65), when Mac wrongly assumes the Reverend to be the first point of call for negotiations:

REV MAC
Well, you've got your facts about the church right ... I don't
know if I'm your ideal man though ... I think you should talk to
Mr Urquhart, in the village.

OLDSEN
Mr Urquhart at the hotel?

REV MAC
Yes ... he's the fixer around here, he's an accountant too,
handles lots of people's affairs ... he's kind of local High Priest.
(D1: 65)

This late revelation of Urquhart's crucial role does not help to build the story dramatically; D3's better solution is to develop the story more fully around his character, making him central at an earlier point. In D3 there is still a play on the many roles Urquhart has in Ferness society but the scenes are snappier and funnier; for instance, when Mac is being served by Urquhart at the hotel and asks to speak to the accountant about the proposal to buy the village, Urquhart teasingly replies:

URQUHART
Indeed yes ... he has an office right next door, to the left, on the first
floor. I know for a fact that he'll be in his office in about 15 minutes.

The scene then cuts to Mac and Oldsen entering Urquhart's office.

URQUHART
Hello again. I'm Gordon Urquhart. ... We tend to double up on
jobs ... I'm a taxi driver sometimes too ... sit down ... (D3: 39)

In D3 Mac gets more quickly to the point, explaining why they're there:

MAC
I won't be coy with you Gordon ... we want to buy the whole

place … we want to buy everything from the cliffs to the north side, and we want to go about a mile inland too … that's all.

Even cool Urquhart is taken aback. But he hides it well.

His mind is racing, but he keeps up his act well.

>   URQUHART
> That's a tall order … on the face of it I would say that it wasn't actually possible … You're talking about fifteen, maybe twenty properties, families, businesses, farms … You're talking about a lot of money … (ibid.: 40–1)

In D1 the approach to the land purchase is structured differently, with Mac and Oldsen planning to contact each villager individually. Their first target is a pig farmer, who asks Mac to hold one of his piglets. The scene is amusing and Mac mildly humiliated but the events do little to develop the story and we meet a character who does not appear again.

> Mac and Oldsen are still having a full-time job just breathing and remaining polite at the same time. Mr Burgess is inside one of the pig pens by now, trying to grab hold of one of the excited piglets. He gets it in his grasp.
>
>   MR BURGESS
> Could you hold this wee beggar for me? (D1: 50)

Mac ends up smelling of pig and we assume that Mr Burgess declines to sell the farm, as the scene cuts directly to the bathroom and Mac washing his clothes.

The third draft changes direction quite radically: Mac goes straight to Urquhart and asks him, as accountant and general fixer, to head the negotiations to buy the village. Although the humour is gentle and whimsical, it has a darker edge: the villagers are not idealised but portrayed as keen to make money from the oilmen. In D3, when we discover that Mac's rabbit has been served up for dinner, we feel sorry for Mac as he becomes more sympathetic.

> DINING ROOM. INTERIOR. NIGHT
>
> Mac and Oldsen are enjoying a hearty dinner, with Urquhart as usual acting out the role of perfect waiter-cum-host.
>
>   URQUHART
>   How is the lapin casserole?
>
>   MAC
>   Terrific!
>
> Urquhart leaves the room, smiling.

Oldsen's face has a concerned look. He is thinking.

OLDSEN
Lapin … that's rabbit …

MAC
Rabbit? (D3: 58–9)

The description and the dialogue in D3 is often sharp and witty: for instance, Urquhart is portrayed as a likeable villain, avaricious and ready to do almost anything for money:

URQUHART
Some people are concerned about your interest in the place … .
It's not just a matter of fixing the price … there are emotions to
be considered … people get attached to a place like this …

MAC
I can appreciate that.

URQUHART
I have to be able to offer them more than just money … .

MAC
How about more money? (ibid.: 76)

This kind of talk stimulates Urquhart.

D3 takes out excess dialogue and builds up atmosphere. When Mac sees the Northern Lights, while in a phone box talking to his boss, Happer, he tries to express how they look:

MAC
I'm watching the sky sir, and it's doing some amazing things … it
has everything … reds, greens … kind of shimmering … there's a
noise too, like a far away thunder except it's softer than that … I
wish you could see it. I wish I could describe it just like I'm seeing it.

HAPPER
Be specific MacIntyre … you're my eyes and ears there … give
the details … (ibid.: 103)

By the end of the film Mac has had a complete character reversal; he has fallen in love with Furness and also with Urquhart's wife, Stella, telling Urquhart: 'I want to swap with you … everything. I want to stay here and run the hotel' (ibid.: 150).

In D3 the story ends after Happer arrives and appreciates the spectacular location. He decides not to build an oil refinery but an observatory and a marine research station. Mac has to return to Houston and reluctantly leaves by helicopter, his sadness at exiting the magical world enhanced as they go higher and into the clouds:

> As the chopper gains more height we begin to see FERNESS through a neat hole in the surrounding clouds. The figures on the beach and on the jetty are by now just so many insignificant dots of movement.
>
> The bay is like a model now, an unreal place. The colours of the beach and the sea seem like toytown colours. then the hole in the clouds closes over, and the image is gone forever.
>
> As the vision of Ferness vanishes we are suddenly back in the real world with Mac. The static chatter of the air traffic in his headphones becomes the dominant sound. The chopper noise mixes with it. The magic is gone. Mac is simply an oil executive on the way to make a flight connection … (ibid.: 153)

The village is saved but the ending is rather downbeat with Mac returning to the US, although as a changed man. Back in Houston Mac looks out from the balcony of his apartment and we are reminded of the temporary nature of his experience in Scotland:

> The images of Houston from Mac's balcony, the lights and the endless traffic movement, are like a show, a kind of ballet of light with its own backdrop, dedicated to the Petrol-Chemical Age.
>
> There are no visible stars in the sky. The polaroid images of Ferness and Stella might last a year or two, in the harsh Texas light. (ibid.: 153)

Puttnam recollects that the backers, Warner Bros. thought the ending should be more 'feel-good,' posing him with something of a creative dilemma:

> The ending is not entirely happy. The American protagonist goes back to his apartment in Houston, having completed his task in Scotland. But he feels somehow hollow and unfulfilled. Warner Brothers offered us additional funding to reshoot the ending, so that the American, Mac, remained in Scotland, removing the lingering ambiguity. Were we to do so they felt, we would have a film more 'sympathetic' to the expectations of the audience. (Puttnam 1997: 335)

Puttnam and director Bill Forsyth declined the offer, feeling that if they did this they would have 'betrayed the spirit of the film' (ibid.).

In fact, Puttnam had received a great deal of audience feedback at different stages of post-production, testing the response to the film in Seattle, Toronto and London and, as a result, asked Forsyth to tighten up the pacing. He had also consulted with writer Jack Rosenthal, who recommended that 'we trim throughout whenever there is an opportunity to move the story along' (DP Box, Item 61: 18/10/82).

Puttnam sent Forsyth some final suggestions for improvements, advising that an early scene with Happer and his therapist be cut back:

And I'll never mention it again. I still believe that the first Happer/Moritz scene would work better in the way that I have been suggesting. It was quite clear from the audience reaction that the real value of their relationship is the cumulative one ending up with Moritz outside the window ... (ibid.: 8/11/82)

Melvyn Bragg praises the new version of the film in a letter; but expresses some concerns, 'I would be less of a friend, though, if I did not admit to one serious reservation. The ending' (ibid.: 3/12/82). He suggests that the film concludes with Mac getting into the helicopter rather than showing him return to his flat in Houston. Puttnam notes on a copy of the letter sent to Forsyth 'this is a reaction that we would be foolish to ignore!' (ibid.). But the film stays true to Forsyth's initial idea, retaining the downbeat ending, Puttnam supporting the writer/director's instincts.

According to Puttnam,

One of the reasons it all worked, still works, is because it was a very honest film. It didn't pretend the villagers didn't want to sell up. It has classic elements of absolute chaos ... . Although it was, yes, telling a story from its time, there were certain classic elements. The wise old man on the beach is a staple, down centuries.'[3]

The letters in the collection are a reminder that the rewriting process continues virtually to the day the film is screened: cutting, dialogue changes and tightening of the story in the post-production stages as a response to feedback are considered crucial. It is notable that Puttnam sided with the writer/director regarding changes to the screenplay. Forsyth certainly appreciated Puttnam's role as producer, commenting that this meant he had the

luxury, very rare in those days, of being paid. I got paid to write it. Because Puttnam had got involved, we knew that a) we had funding, and b) it was, come what may, going to be released. That was unusual. Very.[4]

The charm of *Local Hero* is at least partly down to Puttnam's championing of Forsyth and the fact that he enjoyed a great degree of autonomy with no financial pressure from the financiers, Warner Bros. This meant they could spend more time on the script development, the filming and 'indulge ourselves in the cutting room'.[5] Puttnam was able to override Warner Bros.' requests for changes and produce the film he and Forsyth wanted to make.

The October Circle

The October Circle, despite a prolonged development process, was destined *not* to go into production. The first screenplay draft was adapted from the 1975 novel of the same name by its author, Robert Littell in 1979. The last draft in the collection was penned by Robert Bolt in 1984. The screenplay had a long and difficult gestation with problems identified early in the script never really resolved, despite the input of a number of writers besides Bolt.

The David Puttnam Collection holds a particularly detailed series of correspondence outlining the screenplay development process, from the first letter in May 1979, when *The October Circle* was at an early draft stage, to the last letter in December 1983, when Puttnam is not sure if Bolt will be able to complete the script because he is recovering from a stroke.

At least five different writers were employed to work on the screenplay: first, the author of the novel, Robert Littell, then Mark Victor and Michael Grais, based in LA, then Littell again, then Jack Rosenthal, John Mortimer and last Robert Bolt. Trevor Griffiths and Tom Stoppard were also asked to comment on the screenplay, with the hope that they would agree to work on the script. Puttam thought the later drafts represented no improvement and favoured that by Victor and Grais (Puttnam 2012).

The novel is based on events in Bulgaria after the uprising in Czechoslovakia when a group of friends, highly regarded in Bulgarian society, resolve to express their concern and protest in public. The government reacts by punishing the protestors and the central character, a world record-beating cyclist, defects to the West but is sent back when he refuses to denounce the regime.

The problems in adapting a novel with an unconventional narrative and unusual characters are acknowledged by Puttnam in a letter to Eric Pleskow, head of US production company Orion Pictures, whom he had approached regarding funding:

> The following changes are being made to this draft of the screenplay in order to facilitate a strengthening of the film in its human terms. The screenplay has been adapted from an allegorical novel and this has resulted in an insufficient depth of character and motivation and a tendency for the script to read 'Felliniesque' in parts. This is not our intention, the film is intended to be essentially a human drama about a father and his son with all the political background and overtones to be considered as a bonus. (DP Item 4b: 16/5/79)

Puttnam breaks down the changes in some detail, emphasising the need to develop the characters, explaining that the girl is 'a cypher at present' and will 'become flesh and blood in the next draft'; that Yuri and his father, Lev, need 'history, depth and warmth': the relationship between the Minister, who has protected Lev and the group of friends, should be made clearer; and that the 'Felliniesque' elements referred to that create 'an air of surreality ... will be diluted or even if necessary, removed' (ibid.: 5/5/79).

Puttnam finishes by explaining the type of film he wants to make, comparing the theme of the film to that of Robert Bolt's *A Man for All Seasons*, a story he much admired:

> We want to make a strong, uncompromising film which leaves the audience with the same emotional commitment to the leading characters as 'A MAN FOR ALL SEASONS'. Yuri should represent the better 'contemporary' man that we all believe lies within us. This will not be a preachy film but a film about people set in the context of a modern political thriller. (ibid.: 5/5/79)

The October Circle was the third novel written by Littel, a specialist in Soviet-based spy novels. He had been taken on in the early stages of development to adapt his book. Dissatisfaction with his draft resulted in two much more experienced scriptwriters being called in, Mark Victor and Michael Grais, who collaborated on the TV series *Starsky and Hutch* (1975–9) and *Kojak* (1973–8), and later cowrote the films *Death Hunt* (1981) and *Poltergeist* (1993). Puttnam had been impressed by their writing and hoped that he could negotiate a package that would include Robert De Niro, an actor he admired (Puttnam 2012).

By June 1979 the screenplay has done the rewriting rounds, going back and forth between Littell, and Grais and Victor, then back to Littell, who was unhappy with its progress for two reasons: he is not credited as joint screenwriter and has concerns about the adaptation:

> I accidentally got my hands on a copy of the new revised screenplay (which is to say Littell's version rewritten by Grais and Victor, which has then been rewritten by Littell, which has then been rewritten by Grais and Victor). My general reaction is that it is moving further and further away from the things we all loved in the book. (DP item 4b: 9/6/79)

Littell is also critical of the approach in the new draft and the incorrect assumptions about the political regime in Bulgaria at the time of the film's setting. He explains that Bulgaria is not fascist but Communist and that, 'if they think it is a fascist country, they don't know what the word means. It is totally inaccurate.' Littell then worries that this version may even endanger friends of his in Bulgaria, ending the letter: 'I feel very strongly about this and couldn't live with this the way it is' (ibid.). In a later letter he continues to be concerned about the depiction of Bulgaria as a fascist state and suggests using Afghanistan rather than Czechoslovakia as the country under attack, pointing out that the invasion of Afghanistan by the USSR would be seen as reprehensible by many Russians as well as by those in the West (ibid.: 22/1/80).

A letter to the screenwriters Victor and Grais, from Frank Lowe Associates, demonstrates that Littell's concerns are very different to those of the production company, which is focused on making the script easier to understand. The following extract outlines particular areas that still needed addressing: 'Our concerns are a bit of a mixture of emotions but are basically embraced in the area of plausibility and comprehension' (ibid.: 6/7/79). The need for more realistic characters mentioned in the previous letter is not referred to but the ending of the film is viewed as a problem:

> What we would like you to do is feel fairly free to reconsider the ending, bearing in mind only one point. We believe it is necessary for Yuri to go back, otherwise the film will lose its credibility and be looked at as a rather simplistic piece of propaganda. (ibid.)

Yet the need for significant changes is reinforced by US producer, Jerome Hellman, who explained to Puttnam that, although he enjoyed the screenplay and considered it 'potentially marvellous material', 'I also understand why it has proven such a tough nut to crack.' He continues, 'I think it would be almost impossible for you to get this off without a major reworking' (ibid.: 27/11/79).

Despite the uncertainty about the script, by June 1980 production plans for the film were underway and actors and locations being considered. A Twentieth Century-Fox memo from producer Tim Hampton to David Field discusses the project and its financing. Even though the memo mentions the need to boost one of the characters the script is deemed ready to go into production and the director, Hugh Hudson, has a 'burning desire' to make the film, attesting to the fact that, 'A considerable amount of preparation work has been done already, and many of the locations have been found in the North of England' (ibid.: 12/6/80).

A few months later the script was still not finalised despite being looked at by some of the most respected writers in the UK. While this may be common practice, it signposts that Puttnam was experiencing problems. In December 1980 Puttnam received a letter on Thames Television paper from Trevor Griffiths, author of the screenplay for *Reds* (1981),[6] feeding back on aspects he had been asked to comment on. First, Griffiths suggests Yuri's superstardom could be demonstrated by showing him in a stadium full of people chanting his name. Second, when asked whether Christine, the love interest, could be substituted by an older sister, he posits that this should be a 'foreigner who could ask questions'. The third point refers to the ending of the film, which has been identified as problematic in previous correspondence. Griffiths notes the difference between fact and fiction:

> If the defector were some kind of national hero – and a world record holder to boot – he would be welcomed with open arms. No strings. However, dramatic truth need not always defer to the rigid demands of supposed documentary truth. Artistic licence wins the day. (ibid.: 10/12/80)

Griffiths then submits a page of alternative suggestions for the above scene. He declines Puttnam's invitation to work on the script, 'I'll stick to my day job for a while longer, in the meantime, thanks for letting me read the script, as I've already said to you, I think it's terrific … especially the ending' (ibid.).

The following week another highly respected author, Tom Stoppard, responds to a request from Puttnam to read the script, outlining why he feels it does not work. Again, Puttnam had contacted Stoppard in the hope that he would have some ideas as to how to fix the script and perhaps be interested in taking on the rewriting. Stoppard notes:

> I intended to write at some length about the 'October Circle' scripts but perhaps there is not so much to say. I can see why it was necessary to get beyond the density of R.L.'s own screenplay, and yet I preferred it on the whole to the second draft (which of course has the experience). I agree with you that – on the page – it lacks that 'inspiring' quality, but it has more than enough going for it to set loose an inspiring director, I would have thought. … But anyway … as for me there's nothing I can bring to it without starting again: And there is no reason why you *should* start again; and I don't have the zest for it. The script is so complete and detailed there is no way for a new writer to get into except on its own level, and you don't need that. Personally I think the screenplay explains too much, makes everything easy to understand: the book gives a strange oblique impression of its events – like a Fellini film, or maybe Altman – and the screenplay suggests a less original original. Sorry if I seem down on it – I don't mean to – I think I'm only being egocentric: it's a good job of work but I can't graft myself onto it. (ibid.: 17/12/80)

Stoppard makes it clear that he cannot do anything to improve the script without starting afresh. Puttnam responds a few days later, expressing his concerns about producing an expensive film based on an allegorical script:

> Your note re. 'The October Circle' threw me for a bit of a loop in that it reiterated my oldest concern with regard to the piece That I'm trying to craft an 'Accessible' film out of what is seen to be fairly dense allegorical material … I am unable to come to terms with risking 6 to 7 million dollars on an even slightly 'oblique' film, and I think that this attitude may be my *fundamental* error. Thanks for being kind, I'd pursue you if I thought it would come to anything. But I don't. (ibid.: 27/12/80)

This note infers that the whole project is at an end but only a few days earlier, on 23 December, Puttnam had written to Bob Sherman at Orion Pictures, Burbank, of Stoppard, 'Either accidentally or deliberately he has put us in a classic bind.' The letter continues:

It would appear that he is prepared to sit down and start again, but would wish to take the screenplay back towards the allegorical qualities of the original book. I have always been convinced that an allegorical version of this already complex story could not make a financially successful film (although we could probably win every international jury prize known to man. The very qualities he criticises in the screenplay are those which I am convinced give us a shot at a commercially viable picture – what to do! (ibid.: 23/12/80)

The need to solve the script problems in *The October Circle* and find a new writer continued and, in January 1981 Puttnam mentions another author to Sandy Lieberson, most likely John Mortimer,

You seem underwhelmed at the prospect of Mortimer, however it seems that Hugh and I could get him to do what we honestly think is lacking. In my view that wouldn't be the case with Tom even if he re-wrote the whole thing. Do you have any better ideas?' (ibid.: 8/1/81)

It appears that someone did have a better idea and by March, in a letter from Puttnam to Lieberson, we learn that Robert Bolt has been brought on board to make script changes and that 'most of what Mona (Moore) has to say conforms exactly with what Hugh and I have criticised and passed on to Robert Bolt' (ibid.: 17/3/81).

Puttnam further refers to 'various notes relating to the current script of *October Circle*', sent by Mona Moore, Jay Michaels and Mischka Herndon from the financial backers company, TWI. Puttnam mostly agrees with Mona and some of Jay's points but insists that they have 'missed the point. We are not trying to make an accurate film, but a personal story which is also an allegory. There is every chance that by the time the film appears Poland will have been invaded' (ibid.: 17/3/81).

Bolt's entry into the scenario did not dispel concerns about the script, a letter from Jay Michaels in June 1981, to Mona Moore, refers to the continuing problems. Michaels is quite critical of Bolt's draft and feels that two of the characters, Vinsky and Orkolf are caricatures. Michaels also points out that the central character, Yuri, is secondary to another character, Lev, for much too long (ibid.: 8/6/81).

In a memo to Moore the next day, Herndon agrees with these points and describes Vinsky and Orkolf as 'Cheech and Chong', continuing, 'I would say that they should be rather more subtle and nastier when they do appear.' He suggests that Christina, a foreign journalist and love interest should be more 'gutsy'. While critical in parts, he also acknowledges that some scenes are working well, noting, 'Great. More of it!' and that the scenes of 'Lev in lone museum listening to last words of Prague Radio are fabulous' (ibid.: 9/6/81).

Moore is much happier with the script by August 1981 and writes to Hugh Hudson:

I can hardly wait to have you know what wonderful progress I think you and Robert Bolt have made with the screenplay. I am beginning to *see* the movie and *feel* the tension. Furthermore, some of the scenes I thought were brilliant in the first pages have now been surpassed by others in this draft which are even more stunning. (ibid.: 25/8/81)

Moore still provides six pages of detailed notes, going through the script page by page, recommending that three areas need attention: first, the character of Christine, who Moore feels is clichéd as a photojournalist and could perhaps be an American athlete, perhaps a cyclist; second, more explanation of the Soviet invasion of Czechoslovakia is required as, 'it just isn't clear enough for general audiences …'; finally, she makes some suggestions regarding the boy who is given Yuri's bike at the end of the film, asking if this could be woven into the narrative more, perhaps Yuri and the boy could have already met.

Moore often asks for further clarification of Soviet history and events; for instance, why one character was named 'Octobrina':

> Yuri's line: 'The circle was named after her. She was named after the October rising in Russia.'
> Again, I suggest that for the average audience even this be more clearly spelled out. I don't think I'm being condescending when I say that I doubt whether the general audience will know the significance of the 'October rising'. (ibid.)

Moore is also concerned with some clichéd sexism in the description of Christine and proposes:

> Description of Christine; 'from the high heeled shoes to the flat tam O' Shanter'. Just as a joke why don't we reverse this to read, 'Christine glances appreciatively up and down Orkolf's obviously virile length, from the bulging groin to the rippling biceps.' I'm sure we've all outgrown seeing each other as sex objects, and while this might not be true for some of the audience, I don't think we should encourage the perpetuation of this anachronism. (ibid.)

The amendments made to this version still failed to produce a script that impressed Puttnam and, in a letter dated December 1981, he mentions that Jack Rosenthal had been asked to supply another draft. The letter notes Puttnam's preference was to continue with Rosenthal but Sandy Lieberson and Hugh Hudson had already met with Bolt, as Puttnam elucidates,

> I promised to write you a retyped version of Jack Rosenthal's amended screenplay. Unfortunately events have overtaken us, and Sandy and Hugh, during my absence, met with Bob Bolt and agreed to go ahead with him on a fully revised screenplay. (ibid.: 21/12/81)

There is some uncertainty about Bolt's ability to deliver a fully revised script due to his debilitating stroke in 1980. Puttnam writes that he went to dinner with Bolt and 'he certainly seemed in good spirits and very eager to get back into action, so I guess I am now a convert to that decision' (DP Item 5: 21/12/81).

Four months later, in April 1982, Moore is anxiously inquiring about the new draft Robert Bolt is writing and 'my prospects for co-financing are all asking me when it's due and what I think of it. I'd appreciate any update you could give me' (ibid.: 26/4/82). Puttnam responds,

> As for the Bolt situation, we are still waiting to get the final version of the draft that I read and liked – Robert was going to make a few minor amendments following a conversation that we had, but that was over a month ago and I haven't had the time to nudge him to find out what's happening. (ibid.: 12/5/82)

Puttnam is concerned about funding and asks for clarification as to whether TWI is still willing to supply a major portion of the finance. Puttnam's letter indicates that he has been so busy with other projects and principal photography on *Local Hero* that he has not been able to focus on *The October Circle* (ibid.).

Bolt eventually delivered a revised draft of *The October Circle* and in his note to Puttnam mentions, 'I know of course that it may need a few strokes here and there when it comes to shooting' (ibid.: 23/9/82). Puttnam replies, pointedly remarking,

> I spent a couple of days whilst I was away on holiday going through *October Circle* and making dozens of notes, it will be interesting to see how many of my own worries about the old draft you have managed to obviate in this latest version. (ibid.: 24/9/82)

By the end of September 1982 TWI have pulled out as backers and been replaced by the Ladd Company, formed by Alan Ladd Jr in 1979. Puttnam mentions to Bolt that he has 'notified the Ladd Company, of the fact that you have now handed in the last of your work' (ibid.).

The film was then put on hold. The next letter in the collection is dated a year later, 6 December 1983, and is Puttnam's response to an enquiry from Littell, the author and writer of the first draft of the screenplay, about the status of the project. Puttnam confirms that they have recently reignited their interest and that Bolt is attempting a 'cure' for the two major reservations regarding the script: the final meeting between Lev and Yuri and the scene with the Greek generals after Yuri has crossed the border. Puttnam states that if the script makes 'real progress, we would attempt to make the film in the autumn of 1984', for a September 1985 release (ibid.: 6/12/1983).

More importantly for the fate of the production, Puttnam reveals there is no definite financial backer, saying, 'Who exactly would finance the film is rather more complex but, in all probability, you could perm two out of three from Warner Brothers, The Ladd Company and Goldcrest' (ibid.). In a letter sent two days later to David Drury, the director of another film project, Puttnam refers to Bolt's stroke and expresses concern that he is not well enough to continue:

> The only question mark lies over the ability of Robert Bolt to still be able to pull out the stops. I will have a clearer idea of what kind of state he is in when he delivers the changes Hugh and I have asked for in the screenplay OCTOBER CIRCLE. I met with him last week and, without doubt, his speech has become 100% better during the past few months and, hopefully, that is indicative of an overall improvement in his health. I will let you know.' (ibid.: 8/12/83).

This is the last reference to *The October Circle* in the collection. The will to make the film seems to have fizzled out, partly through lack of funding but also because the script never made it to the stage where Puttnam was satisfied that it was ready to film. The gestation of the screenplay gives a sense of the difficulties in adapting a novel which is unconventional in its narrative and characterisation, but needs a relatively large budget, $5.5 million. Although Puttnam was very involved with the development process, none of the writers was able to get to grips with the difficult subject matter and produce a marketable screenplay that retained the integrity of the book. It is noticeable how many people were asked to comment on the screenplay: from the director, to the financiers, to colleagues and friends, suggesting that Puttnam saw feedback as important in the development of a screenplay.

The Killing Fields

The idea for *The Killing Fields* originated with Jake Eberts, the founder of Goldcrest, the production company which had helped finance *Chariots of Fire*.[7] Eberts had read a *Newsweek* article about journalist Sydney Schanberg's time in Cambodia, from 1970–5, until the Khmer Rouge took power. His colleague Dith Pran was captured by the Khmer Rouge, eventually escaping after brutal treatment. When Schanberg sold the story 'The Death and Life of Dith Pran' to the *New York Times*, it received a great deal of publicity and a bidding war for the film rights ensued, some production companies offering more money than Puttnam. But Schanberg decided to accept Puttnam's offer, possibly because of his interpretation of the subject, which could provide 'the broad canvas of the subject and the large theme he had long sought' (Yule 1988: 220).

By May 1982, Puttnam had obtained the £10 million funding to make the film, half to come from Warner Bros. and half from Goldcrest Films. Various writers and directors were considered, including Paddy Chayefsky, who wrote *Network* (1976), but Puttnam was clear about the type of writer he wanted and assigned the task to the younger and less experienced Bruce Robinson (ibid.: 220). Puttnam explains his reasoning in a letter to producer Jo Child, who favoured very different writers and directors:

> my enthusiasm for our project stems from the fact that the entire picture exists in my mind, and what I have to find is a writer with whom I can communicate and who can put down on paper the film as I see it. My job has only been worthwhile when I've had alongside of me contemporaries whose lives contain the same dreams, resonances and points of departure. (ibid.: 224)

Bruce Robinson, screenwriter of *The Killing Fields* (1984)

Robinson first met with Puttnam after he'd read *Withnail & I* (1987), which went on to become a cult movie. Although Puttnam did not like the script enough to want to produce it, he could see that Robinson was a talented writer and involved him in a number of projects such as *Treasure Island* and *The Silver Palace*. None of these scripts was made and Robinson was paid very little, but gained a tremendous amount of experience. Robinson points out that Puttnam knew what he was doing when offering him the script:

> he took a chance with me on a big-budget picture like *The Killing Fields* but he wasn't being the chairman of the Save the Children Fund. He wouldn't have asked me to do it if he hadn't thought I could do it. (ibid.: 222)

Robinson acknowledges Puttnam's ability to recognise talented individuals and potential collaborations, 'He has this amazing organic sense that if he puts *this* writer with *this* director he will get what he's after' (ibid.). The two enjoyed an extremely good working relationship, in which Puttnam openly expressed his faith in Robinson, a fact highlighted in a note to Iain Smith and director Roland Joffe in which Puttnam asks, 'Would you please ensure that *all* suggested script changes are discussed or shown to Bruce Robinson before incorporating into the screenplay in the form of agreed amendments' (DP Box 8, Item 43: 14/3/83)? This communication was also copied to Bruce Robinson because Puttnam was concerned that Joffe would change the screenplay without consultation, and valued Robinson's opinion as a writer enough to inform him of any changes to the script. Indeed in a recent interview, Puttnam recalls that he had to insist Robinson's drafts were not superseded by Joffe's and, at times, had to fight off the director, who was keen to use his own version of the script (Puttnam 2012).

Puttnam placed a great deal of importance on accuracy, ensuring that the Cambodian situation was carefully researched, and at times, information was unearthed that could present problems in the representation of historical and character detail. A researcher was employed and Robinson went to New York to interview Schanberg and then to Thailand, as they were not allowed to enter Cambodia. Puttnam was also involved, visiting Thailand and interviewing some of those who were part of the story of 'The Killing Fields', including the British Ambassador to Cambodia at the time of the withdrawal of the Embassy staff in March 1975. In addition, Puttnam spoke to other journalists who were in Cambodia such as photojournalist, Don McCullin, who provided valuable background, pointing out facts that would not be general knowledge such as 'The principal sound in Phnom Penh was insects, not traffic' and 'He remembers the people as being quite unlike the Vietnamese, not at all worldly, almost childlike' (DP Box 8, Item 42: 3/2/1983).

Robinson found the central character, Schanberg difficult to pin down and was uncertain about whether he could get to the bottom of his character, explaining this in a letter he drafted to Puttnam, which he elected not to send, but gave to Yule:

> I'm convinced Sydney needed to hang his dirty linen out. I'm also convinced the linen was a sacrifice of sorts, i.e., if we show them this much, nobody will ask to see more. Some of it is really dirty and I feel sorry for Schanberg. I'm sure he didn't expect this. I'm sure you thought it was going to be as simple as adapting his New York Times story. (Yule 1988: 222–3)

Robinson notes the problems his research has exposed and the dilemma he is in: 'What I want to write is not flattering. I found a lot out in the last two weeks. There's no way I can avoid the truth if I am to write this man properly, so what do I do?' (ibid.)

The letter expresses Robinson's doubts and how research can sometimes pose difficulties, especially when attempting to depict real-life events. When in Thailand, Robinson began to understand Schanberg's point of view more clearly. The sense of death seemed to be every-where, while some disturbing experiences made him realise that he had been seeing the situation from an outsider's perspective, and an admiration for Schanberg began to develop. Robinson explains that they had some hard thinking to do about how to represent Schanberg's relation-ship with Dith Pran and to take in Puttnam's notion that the real truth would not work:

> As a film-maker David was right in essence, that the *greater* truth can come from a few lies. If we'd made the film really truthful in the sense that Schanberg's relationship with Pran was pure Gunga Din ... I wonder if people would have been moved to tears by it. (ibid.: 223)

Puttnam says of the narrative for *The Killing Fields*:

> All you have to worry about initially is whether a particular idea has the right dramatic curve .... So long as you hold true to it you'll end up with something that works emotionally because it's the classic curve of every human being's life, hope passing through trouble and travail to some sort of resolution'. (ibid.: 229)

But many of the aspects of history touched upon in this true story were still highly sensi-tive and Puttnam had to tread carefully as to the depiction of the US's military and diplomatic role in Cambodia. Puttnam did not want to offend the US, but equally he wanted to present the story as truthfully as possible. The political angle taken in the screenplay implied that the US intervention and withdrawal in the region caused the 'killing fields'. A first meeting was held with US Ambassador Dean, who had read the script, and an Enigma Films representative on 9 March 1983. Ambassador Dean was concerned about the negative portrayal of the Embassy staff as drunkards and a number of incorrect facts in the script, observing:

> He does not drink and his people did not want to and were never allowed to behave in that fashion .... He felt that nothing is said about the fact that they evacuated Pran's family without question and a lot of others. (DP Box 8, Item 42: 9/3/83)

The Ambassador's concerns were not allayed though and, in a phone call to Puttnam, he com-plains that they had failed to take his criticisms on board. Puttnam wrote to director Joffe and production manager Iain Smith, outlining the situation:

> I explained that much of his concern lay in the descriptive inadequacies of the printed script, and the fact that the tonal alterations we have made as a result of our meetings with him are currently being incorporated into the film, but did not appear as printed pages.' (ibid.: 23/5/83)

The Ambassador's criticisms focused on two areas:

the point that he feels most strongly is the fact that, in response to a question regarding what would happen in the event of a Khmer Rouge take-over, his answer 'I believe there will be a "bloodbath"' was reported very fully in the international media … and was treated, to put it mildly, sceptically by the liberal press'. (ibid.)

The second point concerns the depiction of the Embassy staff as 'upmarket hooligans' and the failure to mention that they saved the life of a journalist-cum-adventurer called Rockoff, who had since been arrested on drugs charges in the US. Puttnam believed care was needed presenting his character 'warts and all' and 'it would become just too easy for the State Department and other critics to take the film apart, just on our portrayal of Rockoff's character' (ibid.) Puttnam's memo makes it clear how important it is to resolve these issues and to ensure the film cannot be criticised or ridiculed. A later memo from Puttnam to Joffe confirms that Robinson will rewrite the 'bloodbath' scene, putting it in its correct context (ibid.: 4/6/83).

In another memo on the same day, Puttnam informs Joffe about a call from Sydney Schanberg in which he refers to there being different versions of the truth, depending on the narrator. Schanberg argues that featuring Ambassador Dean's warning of a possible genocide

sounds more prescient than it really was, and the lack of attention paid to it by the best journalists consequently looks unforgivably complacent and ill-informed. His point being that now we know the measure and scale of what occurred, all the earlier bets are grotesquely highlighted, and thus Dean emerges with more credit than he really deserves. (ibid.)

Puttnam decides they should present both opinions and that 'Sydney's view must be given to either Sam (Sydney), or someone with, what he describes as "heft".' Puttnam considers this a crucial issue and: 'In many ways this debate does form the core of the film, in the same way that we agreed that scene 47 forms an emotional core. We have to get these two elements precisely right' (ibid.).

Puttnam's willingness to discuss the deficiencies of the script is an indication of his openness during the film production process. As with *The October Circle*, Puttnam consulted a range of people for opinions on the screenplay, from solicitor Frank Bloom (20/1/82) to newspaper editor Harold Evans, who comments in a letter to Joffe, 'Your new opening is infinitely better. The dog scene is terrible in the original' (17/11/82), before criticising the political bias of the film. Puttnam acknowledges that feedback suggests the script to be too long and too wordy, and that it needed to focus more on the characters and the relationship between Schanberg and his wife, in a letter to director Costa-Gavras:

I think in its present form it has the following defects:

(1) It is over-written, too dense, and too long.
(2) It concentrates too much on hardwear and violence when it should be concentrating on the inter-relationships – much of this will be automatically improved by a thorough editing job.
(3) In what I call the third act, i.e. after Schanberg's return to New York, there is an entire element missing. This is my fault because I have so far been unable to get Schanberg's wife to agree to being portrayed in the film, and therefore the break-up of his marriage (which is now a fact) is not dealt with in the strength that is required. …' (DP Box 8, Item 42: 24/5/82)

Debates about the length continued as it was still felt to be too long, even though the December 1982 draft of 126 pages had been cut to 121 pages in the February 1983 shooting script. A letter from Iain Smith, the production manager, emphasises the need to comply with the completion guarantors, who are concerned that the film finish on time and to budget:

> The original script was timed at 3 hours 32 minutes and it was immediately recommended that we cut 35–40 pages from the script. Our latest edition of the script has 18 pages less and has 76 scenes less than the original. This is not enough. (ibid.: 26/1/83)

Smith explains the implications if the script is not radically cut:

> It is my belief that we must reduce our latest version of the script substantially to avoid serious problems. On paper this reduction should be 56 minutes (39 pages) which I believe would seriously alter the film (which is in nobody's interest). I propose therefore that we look to i) reducing the page count by 27 pages (37 minutes) to 101 pages … . (ibid.)

These considerations were crucial to the film being made within budget and indicate how important screenplay timings are in ensuring this.

Puttnam informed the Enigma board, which consisted of Warner Bros. and Goldcrest, that the problems had been resolved.

> Roland Joffe and Bruce Robinson have succeeded in cutting the screenplay to a new page count of ninety-seven pages … . This represents an overall cut on the existing script of twenty-nine pages (43 1/2 minutes or approximately 25% overall). We are now confident that the film can be accomplished within our present overall schedule and budget. (ibid.: 4/2/83)

The Killing Fields was released in 1984, to great critical acclaim and was nominated for seven Academy Awards, including Best Picture for David Puttnam and Best Screenplay Adapted from Another Medium for Bruce Robinson.

CONCLUSION

The three films discussed in the chapter demonstrate above all Puttnam's ability to put the right people together to create a successful team and the importance he places on working closely with the writer. In the case of *Local Hero* and *The Killing Fields*, this resulted in two very impressive films while plans to produce *The October Circle* failed, partly because of the difficulty in adapting an allegorical narrative, but also because the number of writers involved caused the screenplay to lose momentum, with later drafts worsening rather than improving the story.

As Puttnam has acknowledged, 'All the best of my pictures are, one way or another, about men in moral crises' (Yule 1988: 229): this applies to Mac in *Local Hero* as much as to the more heavyweight subject matter of Pran and Schanberg in *The Killing Fields*. Puttnam was given a great deal of freedom after the success of *Chariots of Fire*, allowing him to make films about subjects that he felt passionately about, nurturing the writer through the complex development process. Puttnam notes that this freedom would be impossible in the contemporary climate and that throughout his career he has been a 'lucky bugger' (Puttnam 2012).

The writer considered in the next chapter, John McGrath, was also interested in stories with a political slant and examining men in personal and moral crises, such as the protagonists in *The Bofors Gun* and *The Reckoning*. But McGrath's background in theatre and TV lent him a different political viewpoint, a strong belief in socialism and a desire to make film and theatre that appealed to a working-class audience.

NOTES

1. Telephone interview with David Puttnam by the author, 13 August 2012.
2. A copy of Forsyth's contract is held in the Puttnam Collection and stipulates:

   The writer has agreed to render his services to the company upon the terms and conditions hereinafter contained in writing the material specified herein based upon an original idea by David Puttnam and a treatment by Bill Forsyth provisionally known as Local Hero (Item 49/2).

3. See http://www.guardian.co.uk/film/2008/sep/28/drama.
4. Ibid.
5. Interview with David Puttnam, 13 August 2012.
6. Trevor Griffiths was an influential film and television writer in the 1970s and 1980s, writing the miniseries *Sons and Lovers* in 1981 and the film *Fatherland* in 1986.
7. Puttnam was on the non-executive board of Goldcrest.

10

JOHN MCGRATH

IN THE PURSUIT OF TRUTH AND HONESTY –
FROM *Z CARS* TO *THE RECKONING*

McGrath was a respected writer and director in television and theatre but is less well known for his screenplays, despite being awarded a BAFTA Writers Guild Lifetime Achievement Award in 1993. The highlight of his scriptwriting career came during the 1960s, with two films in particular, *Billion Dollar Brain* (1967) and *The Reckoning* (1969), illustrating his writing range, from a surreal mock 'Bond' to a provocative critique of aspirational English society. Indeed Brian McFarlane argues, 'Narrative vigour and social conscience characterised McGrath's best work, as playwright and screenwriter' (2003: 419).

Born in 1935, McGrath came from a lower middle-class, Irish Catholic background in Liverpool. A bright grammar school boy, he completed two years' National Service, an experience serving as the basis for his play *Events while Guarding the Bofors Gun*, before studying at Oxford University in 1955. While there McGrath became involved in a university drama group where his writing skills were noticed and he was asked to write for the Royal Court Theatre. He stayed at the Royal Court until 1960, writing *The Tent* in 1958, which was well received. His next play, *Why the Chicken* (1960), however, was not. This failure, together with his belief that the Royal Court offerings were aimed at the bourgeois middle classes, encouraged him to move to television, which he thought a more populist medium. McGrath spent five years at the BBC, authoring, directing and producing a number of projects and collaborating with a new generation of talented writers and directors, most notably Troy Kennedy Martin, Ken Russell and Ken Loach. McGrath and Troy Kennedy Martin developed the idea for the groundbreaking TV series, *Z Cars* (1962–78). McGrath injected the series with storylines inspired by his left-wing political views about social issues, a preoccupation which continued throughout his life. He developed other dramas with Kennedy Martin at the BBC, in 1964, co-writing a series of six episodes of the drama *Diary of a Young Man*, three directed by Ken Loach. The series is described by Janet Moat as 'determinedly anti-naturalistic in its heady mix of theatrical stylisation, montage, song and documentary realism',[1] a mix that McGrath would employ in his work for the theatre and to some extent in his films.

McGrath's working relationship with director Ken Russell began at the BBC, first writing *Seven Lean Years* in 1964 for Russell, though this was not produced. His next project with Russell adapted George Grossmith's novel, *Diary of Nobody* in 1964, styled as a silent film comedy, which was positively received. McGrath then went on to write and direct the forty-minute drama *The Day of Ragnarok*, broadcast in 1965, with Nicol Williamson in the lead, an

actor he much admired and who was to star in two later films that he scripted. McGrath also wrote, directed and produced *Shotgun*, an adaptation of a story by Inoue Yasushi and co-written with Christopher Williams, which was broadcast in 1966.

McGrath's first film writing assignment was an adaptation of Malraux's *La Condition humaine*, but the project was abandoned after eight months' work on the screenplay. The same ending applied to *Man's Fate*, a major feature-film project that Fred Zinnemann was to direct, which was cancelled on the day filming was to begin. McGrath supplied a number of drafts before Graham Greene was brought in to do a rewrite, after which the film came to a standstill.

McGrath's early career as a screenwriter was condensed into the period 1966 to 1969. After this he transferred his passion to theatre, using the screenwriting proceeds from films such as *Man's Fate*, *Billion Dollar Brain*, *The Bofors Gun* (1968), *The Reckoning* and *The Virgin Soldiers* (1969) to start up his theatre company, 7:48, in Scotland in 1971. It was named 7:84 because 7 per cent of the country controlled 84 per cent of its wealth. As Michael Billington explains in his obituary for McGrath,

> The company's avowedly socialist aim was to take popular, political theatre to venues shunned by the established national and regional companies. Scotland was its prime hunting-ground and often its subject, and McGrath wrote much of his best work for the company.[2]

Indeed McGrath produced his most famous play *The Cheviot, the Stag and the Black, Black Oil* in 1973 for the company, an entertaining mix of standup comedy, music and drama, which was successfully adapted for television and broadcast by the BBC on Play for Today in 1974. By the 1980s the political environment was becoming less favourable to McGrath's socialist-inspired drama and funding for 7:84 was withdrawn from the Arts Council, England in 1984 and then in Scotland in 1988. After 7:84 disbanded he continued to write plays such as *Border Welfare* (1989) and *A Satire of the Four Estates* (1996), both critical of the government and the power of the media.

McGrath's socialist leanings made it difficult for him to fit in easily with a mainstream film industry predicated on the need for profit. He argued that a small number of powerful companies controlled distribution and exhibition and had no interest in producing films reflecting the interests of the population:

we need to get films that will come out into the cinemas. Rank and EMI subscribe to the same attitudes, the same ideology, as Wall Street, i.e. in spite of their commercial interest in popularising the merchandise, they are opposed to the interests of the people in Britain and we have never had a popular film culture in its real sense with Rank and EMI controlling distribution.' (McGrath 1978: 21)

He continued to be critical of the film industry and the narrow range of films produced throughout the 1980s, lamenting in the journal *City Limits* that, 'committed drama, like industrial militancy, is out of date' (McGrath 1986: 20).

As well as espousing socialism, McGrath was interested in experimenting with form and style, applying the same ideas to film and television that he had developed in the theatre. The theatre seemed more willing and able to accommodate his experimentation.

Yet, for a relatively short period of time, in the early 1960s at the BBC and when writing screenplays funded by the Hollywood studios, McGrath was given a great deal of freedom with very little interference from managers and with producers who were sympathetic to his views. McGrath expresses his concerns about the limitations of naturalism in drama, in an interview in 1977: 'In the naturalistic play, few characters are allowed to be articulate, they are more likely to emote incoherently. Every meaning is implicit, and ambivalent. Naturalism forces itself to present a world that is static, implied and ambivalent' (1977: 105).

When McGrath adapted his play, *Events while Guarding the Bofors Gun*, from the stage to film, it was largely unsuccessful because its theatrical devices made the characters seem non-naturalistic and stilted and the action static.[3] The screenplay, about a group of British soldiers on patrol in West Germany in 1954 ordered to protect the Bofors guns, does feature some witty dialogue, especially involving O'Rourke, who is in many ways a parallel character to Marler in *The Reckoning*. They are both tough, hard-talking Irishmen, driven, discontented with their lot and potentially dangerous. In *The Bofors Gun* O'Rourke reveals a death wish, absconds from duty, gets very drunk and refuses to go on guard. Evans, the Bombardier in charge, appears sympathetic at first because he declines to charge O'Rourke and tries to cover up the fact that he is drunk. We find out that Evans's reasons are not as altruistic as he pretends: he seeks promotion to Sergeant, which will be harder to achieve if there is trouble on his watch. The screenplay ends as Evans tries to hide the drunk and suicidal soldier from the duty Sergeant, but O'Rourke falls onto his bayonet and dies, leaving Evans unlikely to get promotion and facing charges of dereliction of duty. Despite some excellent dialogue and well-rounded characters, O'Rourke is overwrought and not naturalistic enough for the camera, and his lively nature makes him an unlikely suicide risk.

Although the BBC had given McGrath the freedom to develop new series such as *Z Cars* and allowed him to work with talented innovators like Russell and Kennedy Martin, it was the outposts of the American studios, which set up production bases in London in the 1960s to take advantage of the cachet of 'Swinging London', that enabled McGrath to adapt *The Bofors Gun* from his own stage play, to write *Billion Dollar Brain*, with Russell as director and write the script for *The Reckoning*. McGrath is also credited with outlining the adaptation of Leslie Thomas's novel *The Virgin Soldiers*, about a young National Service soldier who goes to Singapore in 1950, expecting to be office-based, but has to face the grim reality of war when the conflict escalates.[4]

It would not be until the arrival of Channel 4 in 1984 that such creative and experimental film-making would be possible on this scale again. The major Hollywood studios all had offices in London and US film investment in the UK was substantial, £31.3 million in 1968. This policy allowed for more freedom and experimentation by writers, directors and the producers who controlled the budgets and the films' subject matter, because, as Justin Smith points out, 'the paymasters remained conveniently distant' (2008: 57). David Robinson observes, 'Perhaps at no time in the remembered history of the British cinema have the money-men been so receptive to new people and new ideas. It was a brief utopia' (1968/9: 36). Indeed, when the Hollywood studios such as United Artists and Columbia closed down their London outposts, the opportunities for liberal and experimental film-making decreased and the funding for these films disappeared. Both *Billion Dollar Brain* and *The Bofors Gun* were financed by United Artists and *The Reckoning* by Columbia, films described by Robert Murphy as 'perversely anti-commercial' (1992: 273).

Despite his contribution to British cinema, McGrath thought it could only survive by focusing on the national audience, noting in his 1981 collection of essays: 'I don't think that British films will ever be any good, or even exist at all, unless or until they can be made with both eyes fixed on a British audience' (1981: 110).

McGrath is more positive about television's potential to reach large audiences, pointing out that this is an under-explored area. Indeed, the advent of Channel 4 in 1984 encouraged filmmaking which challenged and entertained the viewer and seemed a perfect fit for McGrath's dramatic interests. The three-part series *Blood Red Roses*, adapted from his play, was broadcast on the new channel in 1986. The drama covers a period of thirty-four years in the life of a single mother who rails against the political system in Scotland, at a time of working-class apathy, beginning with the Macmillan government and ending with the Falklands War, when Margaret Thatcher was in power.

The divide between TV and film narrowed when Channel 4 and BBC2 began to produce dramas that also had a cinematic release, a change which enabled McGrath to move back into film. His *The Long Roads* (1993), made for BBC Screen 2 by Freeway Films, is a moving tale about an elderly couple who visit their five children, each living in a different part of the UK. Janet Moat notes, 'the critics agreed, however, that the late flowering of the relationship between the parents was the emotional heart of the piece, and were moved by it'.[5] Although theatre was his real passion, McGrath went on to write the screenplay for Beryl Bainbridge's novel *The Dressmaker* (1988), co-write *Robin Hood* (1991) and produce *Carrington* (1995). He also continued to work on other film projects in this period, including Christopher Hampton's adaptation of his play *White Chameleon*, scheduled to be shot in 1998–9 and *Aberdeen*, a coproduction with Norway's Norsk Film to be shot in April 1999, though neither of these was filmed. Indeed, McGrath's involvement in all broadcast media continued and, as Michael Russell remarks:

> [his] prodigious talents found an outlet in other places too. He spent a period of time on the Board of Channel 4 Television, before which he had set up Freeway Films at the invitation of the Channel's first Director Jeremy Isaacs. Freeway contributed some important items to the Channel and to UK cinema over the years including *Carrington* and *Ma Vie en Rose* which won the 1996 Golden Globe for best foreign film.[6]

McGrath lived in Scotland for many years and in the 1990s was committed to developing a Scottish film industry, becoming increasingly concerned about the dominance of Hollywood cinema. He later set up Moonstone with the assistance of Robert Redford, modelling it on the

Sundance writer and director development programme in the US, particularly wanting to pursue an interdisciplinary approach, inviting theatre directors like Sam Mendes and Steven Daldry to the workshops (Brady and Capon 2005: xxi).

THE JOHN MCGRATH COLLECTION

The collection contains many scripts penned between 1960 and 1983 for television and unrealised and realised feature films. There are twelve scripts for the television series *Z Cars*; television plays such as *Diary of a Nobody*, co-written with and Ken Russell and directed by Russell; *Shotgun*, an episode of a TV series written, directed and produced by McGrath; scripts of television films produced by McGrath; and one BBC Play for Today, *The Adventures of Frank* (1980), authored and directed by McGrath.

Also in the collection are outlines and drafts of screenplays for *Billion Dollar Brain*, *The Bofors Gun* and *The Reckoning*. The following section looks at two outlines of *Billion Dollar Brain* and the changes to the draft screenplays of *The Reckoning*.

Billion Dollar Brain

Russell was asked to direct *Billion Dollar Brain* when the BBC documentary film he directed on Debussy (1965), as part of the acclaimed *Monitor* series, attracted the notice of Michael Caine. The actor had starred in the previous Harry Palmer films, *The Ipcress File* (1965) and *Funeral in Berlin* (1966) and recommended Russell to the Canadian producer Harry Saltzman, who was so impressed that he asked him to direct the film (Baxter 1973: 142). Russell did not like the screenplay as it stood, which was by Peter Bowes, and asked McGrath to help him rewrite it. Russell tells of the unexpected ease with which this came about:

> Both McGrath and I thought there would be some discussion about how the story should go and if McGrath should, in fact write it. Instead Harry simply said to McGrath: 'When can you start?' McGrath said something about 'soon' and Harry said 'like now' and that was that. (Baxter 1973: 142)

Russell remembers the difficulty they experienced adapting this Len Deighton novel because the narrative had no logical trajectory,

> John McGrath and I started to think about *Billion Dollar Brain*. The book was totally illogical. The reasons people did things, went places and said things had no rationality whatsoever … it was just a hotch-potch of ideas the author had strung together. (ibid.: 154–5).

Russell notes that McGrath tried to 'insert some logic into the events while at the same time we'd throw in something that tickled our fancy. For instance we both liked Eisenstein so we put in a modern "Battle on the Ice"' (ibid.).[7] Saltzman was very involved in developing the script and McGrath and Russell would regularly discuss progress with him, listen to his comments on the story and its lack of dramatic flow before he asked for another rewrite (ibid.: 155). Joseph Gomez believes that, 'the screenplay is even more successful than the book in establishing Palmer as a hero caught between insane conflicts' (1976: 79).

The story concerns Harry Palmer's quest to stop madman and Texan oil millionaire, Midwinter, invading Latvia and causing another World War. The screenplay is very different to the Len Deighton novel, changing many of the events in the narrative. Harry Palmer

Michael Caine, star of *Billion Dollar Brain* (1968), written by Len Deighton and adapted for the screen by John McGrath

becomes less an ex-grammar school boy and more working class, although this change is compounded by the casting of Michael Caine in the lead part. McGrath and Russell made the script increasingly anti-American and pro-Russian, Russell calling it the first anti-American spy film (ibid.). Gomez notes that, surprisingly, 'Universal liked the film, despite it doing badly at the box office and thought it should have received a much better critical reception. Perhaps in the US it was found to be too politically left wing' (ibid.: 78).

The section in the John McGrath Collection on *Billion Dollar Brain* holds two very different short outlines, dated 22 September 1966 and 8 November 1966.[8] The outlines reveal the extent to which the story altered in the early development stages and how the later outline has been refined and polished, changing the story considerably. The second outline is a stronger and more visual piece of writing, with the story flowing more easily stylistically, and a heightened atmosphere.

The first outline is characterised by an abrupt, shorthand style that suggests it was produced fairly rapidly and is less detailed and specific about events, with a sense that the ideas, plot and characters are still being worked through. The first outline (O1) begins less dramatically: we meet Palmer in his room talking to an unhappy customer, who refuses to pay his fees, and we learn that the detective is in dire financial straits. The atmosphere is slightly seedy but an element of mystery emerges as we are introduced to the 'Brain' itself.

> In his bed-sitting room in Fulham, Harry Palmer tells a disgruntled businessman the details of his wife's activities, which have been uneventful – she has no lover. The man is furious, tells Harry that he doesn't pay for that kind of testimony, and starts to leave. Harry says – what about my expenses? The man says sue me, and goes. Harry is even deeper in debt than ever. Then a strange, rather menacing figure appears in the doorway, asks Harry a few questions, and offers him £500 to do a job. Harry agrees. He has to. The man – Dr Pike – tells Harry he will get further instructions by ringing a certain number. He is now an employee of Facts for Freedom, and if he reveals anything he will be killed. The man goes. Harry dials the number. MUSIC. A strange voice, the voice of the Brain, speaks to Harry, telling him what he has to do. As the TITLES go up, we see the Brain in operation – weird, frightening. Harry's involved in Operation Free Latvia. Titles end. (Box 19.1: O1)

The second outline (O2) begins with Palmer's office door immediately informing us that he is 'Harry Palmer, Private Detective'. This opening follows the convention of the thriller or noir story and sets up a greater mystery as someone has broken into the office. It is instantly more dramatic than the first draft version, with Palmer interrupting the intruder, who we find out was his boss at MI5:

> Dusk on a rainy day in London. On a fretted glass door is written: 'Harry Palmer, Private Detective'. A figure whom we cannot identify tries several keys till he finds one that opens the door. In the dark room he finds only empty files, empty in-trays and signs of disuse. As he looks into the pantry cupboard, which is equally bare, a figure appears in the door, says: 'Stand quite still' and switches the light on. It is HARRY PALMER. The intruder turns to face him. It is MAJOR ROSS, of MI5, Harry's ex-employer, who has come to ask Harry to re-join the outfit.

> As Harry has only had one job in the last three months he is toying with the idea when a Special Delivery letter arrives full of £5 notes. Harry tells Ross that if he wants him back he'll have to send two men with a cosh and a straitjacket. Ross goes. Harry searches the envelope but can find no explanation of the money. The phone rings. The even, metallic voice of the BRAIN tells Harry that he has been employed to do a job for it, and gives him an address and code word. Harry asks: 'How did you pick on me?' (Box 19.2: O2)

Both versions refer to a large amount of money arriving unexpectedly after it has been established that business is not good, but the second version introduces Palmer's boss, Major Ross, much earlier. The second outline is more specific about the Brain, which now has an 'even, metallic voice'.

Some of the plot order is rearranged in the second outline, although in both drafts Palmer meets the mysterious Dr Pike before being instructed to deliver a parcel to a Dr Kaarna in Helsinki. Dr Kaarna is found dead, but the second draft is more specific about how he was killed: 'Harry checks up on Kaarna's real address, goes to it in the dusk, finds the body of Kaarna covered in snow in a window with a small puncture two inches to the right of the seventeenth vertebra' (ibid.: O2).

An important complication is added in the second outline when the Brain orders Harry's friend Leo (Harvey in the first draft) to kill his girlfriend Signe. He can't make himself carry out the order, but the fact that Harry witnesses this has repercussions for the story trajectory:

> Leo drives Harry out to the Facts for Freedom headquarters in a castle on an island in the Baltic. There Harry sees a whole convoy of warlike figures covered up waiting for action. He sees the computer link with headquarters in Texas and he is present when Leo receives an order to shoot a certain agent who will appear at a rendezvous. Harry is with Leo when he reluctantly sets about the assassination, explaining that he has to do it. When the victim appears it is Signe. Leo cannot carry through his instructions. (ibid.: O2)

Leo now has to get rid of Harry because he knows Leo was supposed to kill Signe. In the first outline the plot revolves around Leo/Harvey agreeing to help the detective because he'd saved his life. The second version is more complex: Leo and Harry have an unspoken agreement that Harry won't mention Leo not having killed Signe, and Leo won't mention Harry's suspicious meeting with Stok, the Russian Colonel:

> Back in Helsinki, Harry is very angry with Leo because he thinks Leo tried to have him killed. Leo denies this. A balance of power is established whereby Harry tacitly agrees not to discuss the fact that Leo failed to kill Signe and Leo will not discuss the fact that Harry was seen in the restaurant with Stok while an agent was arrested. (ibid.: O2)

The second outline fills in more background detail and lends the story greater context. For instance, although in both versions the events in Latvia are very similar, the second version outlines specific scenes. The first outline merely tells us that Colonel Stok visits Palmer at the Riga Hotel whereas the second describes the scene in more detail, 'Lying in his room that night, Harry is visited by Colonel Stok, his old sparring partner from the Russian Secret Service' (ibid.: O2).

In both outlines Palmer and Leo/Harvey go to Midwinter's Texan ranch but in the first outline Midwinter's fortune is in industrial chemicals; this is changed in the second draft to oil, presumably because it seems more apt for a US oil mogul to have an interest in invading Communist states.

The second outline simplifies the storyline around Leo/Harvey and the love triangle between Palmer, Leo and Signe becomes more bound up in the plot. In the first outline Leo/Harvey is working with his wife, Mercy, to extort funds from Midwinter, who employs her as his 'secretary-cum-nursemaid' but Mercy has also 'been blackmailing her own husband for years, ever since she found out about Signe' (ibid.: O1). The second outline dispenses with this aspect, Mercy no longer figuring in any significant way, except that Leo wants to leave her for Signe.

Midwinter is presented as a more sympathetic character in the first outline, partly because both Leo/Harvey and his wife are stealing from him, and he seems naive but dangerous rather than evil. The second outline still shows Harvey/Leo taking money, but Midwinter is depicted as verging on madness and, in a meeting with Palmer, he demonstrates his right-wing extremist views:

> Midwinter gives Harry the benefit of his philosophy while the dance goes on above. At the end of his extreme outburst of extreme anti-communism and aggression, he leads the dancers in a prayer which he makes beside a huge fire at the side of the dance floor. (ibid.: O2)

O2 focuses more on Harry and Signe's relationship while they are in Texas and the drama intensifies. When they kiss, Signe tries to kill Harry in the same way that Kaarna was killed, so linking her with the doctor's murder:

> Then he realises that standing beside him is Signe. She makes Harry take her away from the crowd while the dancing continues in the background. She kisses him and while they are kissing removes the long pin from her hair, counts Harry's vertebrae and is about to insert the pin in the same spot where Kaarna's wound had been. Just in time Harry stops her. (ibid.)

In both drafts Leo/Harvey enters the Brain, intending to erase its memory of him cheating Midwinter and then escapes. Midwinter refuses to heed Palmer's warnings that no real support exists for an invasion of Latvia and that Leo/Harvey has concocted the story to extort money from him. Midwinter arrives in Latvia with his troops, ready for invasion.

In the first draft Palmer finds Signe and Leo/Harvey, who expects Signe to go with him to Russia to escape Midwinter, except she refuses to go. Leo/Harvey then agrees to help Palmer find Midwinter and try to stop the invasion. In the second draft Palmer finds Leo and Signe in Helsinki but the couple then board a train to Russia. The plot in the second draft becomes more complicated, confusingly so, and the sequence concludes with Leo being taken off the train, getting in a car with Palmer, escaping to go with Signe, then falling back onto the railtrack while she continues to Leningrad.

The climactic ending in the first draft shows Palmer watching the invasion, but spring has begun and the ice melts as the troops fall into the sea:

> Meanwhile Signe is leaving Helsinki. She is going somewhere. The Russian investigator plane takes off. The invasion force goes on. Midwinter seriously thinks they are going to be met by a huge crowd of supporters and employees. He is clearly over the edge. Harry watches from a tiny island. Then he realises that there are snowdrops growing, and the snow under the trees is melting. Out on the ice, great cracks appear. Then, monstrously, little by little, with Midwinter still driving them on, the invasion force is tipped through the cracks in the ice into the icy cold water below. When the plane circles over the spot where the force is reported to have been, there is only a mass of broken ice floating on the water. Midwinter has been defeated by Spring. All over the world, the preparations are stopped – another false alarm. Then Harry remembers the eggs.
>
> Signe has them, of course, and she hands them to Stok, for whom she has been working all along. But when he opens them, they have hatched into chickens, it being that time of year. (Box 19.1: O1)

The second version forwards more detail about the Russian response to Midwinter's invasion, with Colonel Stok sending bombers to target the troops on the ice. The convoy sinks as the ice breaks but Palmer survives, escaping from his car just in time. The detail of Stok's plane landing on the ice adds a surreal note:

> Meanwhile the Russians have picked up the invasion force on the radar. Stok has prepared for this and has ordered a bomb to be set off to deal with it. When the bombs begin to fall on the ice Midwinter sets the Brain to automatically destroy itself in Texas. As the convoy sinks and the Brain explodes, Harry brakes hard and skids round and round on the ice nearer to the bomb craters. All the convoy sinks and the men slide off the lumps of ice into the water. Harry's car, with Leo's body still in it, stops with two wheels in the water, and the piece of ice on which it rests begins to crack. Harry jumps out and runs to safety just as the car and Leo go under. He is left, a solitary figure in the middle of the Baltic with nothing around for miles except a hole in the ice and a few bubbles. Out of the sky comes a small plane with skis. It lands and it is Stok. With Stok

is Signe who has been his agent in Finland all the time. Stok gives Harry the parcel of
eggs to take back to Major Ross. Harry goes back to Ross, and when Ross opens
the eggs that Stok has given him they have hatched into chickens. (Box 19.2: O2)

Palmer's life is at risk at the end of the first outline while in the second he watches the events
from a safe distance.

The first outline is impressionistic and sketchy while the second is more detailed, heighten-
ing the drama and moving closer to the screenplay drafts and the finished film. *Billion Dollar
Brain* can be seen as an anti-American right-wing film, using Midwinter's extremist viewpoint
to make playful digs at this mindset.

The Reckoning

McGrath was a talented wordsmith with the ability to adapt his style to suit different genres;
from the action spy thriller to this more downbeat drama about class, revenge and the being able
to 'get away with anything' morality of the film's anti-hero, Marler. McGrath developed the
screenplay for Ronnie Schedlo, an American producer with Columbia, and the film is directed
by Jack Gold. The screenplay is adapted from Patrick Hall's novel *The Harp That Once*, in
which the protagonist hails from an Irish family based in Birmingham. In the film, Marler is
from an Irish Liverpool background, an extremely ambitious salesman, who moves south, marries well but is deeply unhappy despite his success. McGrath cleverly adapts the free-flowing
nature of the dialogue and description in the novel, tapping into his interest in experimental narrative, especially in the early drafts. The screenplay follows the same plotline as the novel but
McGrath makes many elisions, cutting characters and events while altering the ending so that
Marler's wife, Elizabeth, returns to him at the instigation of his boss.

When Marler's father dies, after being beaten up by a young thug, he returns home to
avenge his death. After this turning point, Marler becomes increasingly unpleasant to where he
ends the film with the words 'I can get away with anything.' The narrative, Gold observes,
'anticipates Thatcherism by ten years because it is about a man who gets away with things – with
murder, with dishonesty at work, lying and cheating etc. – he's not punished but succeeds and
gets promotion' (Brady and Capon 2005: 195). Gold describes Marler as

> a man who has fought his way out of the tribal working class of Catholic Liverpool to become part
> of a different tribe, the rich middle-class English business class. Here in the South, he's a success. He
> has a posh marriage; he's climbed ruthlessly up the corporate ladder. He's cunning, violent, atavistic.
> (ibid.)

In both *The Bofors Gun* and *The Reckoning* the central characters, played by Nicol
Williamson, are articulate, clever and destructive, McGrath creating roles reflecting his own
background and experiences. They are ambitious, young and intelligent, with a different set of
values to the southern, middle-class Englishman.

The screenplay is a powerful and engrossing read; Robert Murphy dubs *The Reckoning*
'flashy' and full of 'raw energy that makes it as compelling to watch as a Tarantino film … *The
Reckoning* reflects a world where doors to the top could be opened if they were given a sufficiently
vigorous kick' (2008: 421).

Mick Marler: 20th Century Savage - or 20th Century Hero?

Rising young executive... product of the backstreets.
Respectable married man... ruthless exploiter of women.
Destined for the top-if he can get away with it.
HOW MANY MICK MARLERS DO YOU KNOW?

Columbia Pictures Presents
A Ronald Shedlo Production

starring

Nicol Williamson

in

The Reckoning x

co-starring

Rachel Roberts

also starring

Paul Rogers Zena Walker Ann Bell

Music by Malcolm Arnold Screenplay by John McGrath Based on the novel "The Harp That Once" by Patrick Hall Produced by Ronald Shedlo Directed by Jack Gold Technicolor

The Reckoning (1969), adapted by John McGrath, shows a disaffection with the class system

The rise of the ambitious, aspirational, working-class man in post-war Britain was a common theme in 1950s and 1960s cinema, from *Room at the Top* (1959) to *Saturday Night and Sunday Morning* (1960). But *The Reckoning* was different in that it showed a working- class man beating the smug middle classes at their own game, although the sense of loss in Marler's life is palpable and his success has come at a price – perhaps costing his soul.

The collection holds two similar first drafts; January 1968 (D1) titled *The Harp That Once* (Box 29.1) and March 1968 (D2) titled *Mick* (Box 29.2) and a second draft dated August 1968 (D3) and titled *The Harp That Once* (Box 29.3).

In all drafts the beginning is almost identical, describing the physical appearance and back-ground of the two central characters, Marler and his wife, Rosemary:

INT. CAR. NIGHT

At the wheel is Rosemary Marler. She is a sharp good looking, upper middle class English girl, with lots of drive, determination and aggression. She is dressed in all the angular finery of conventional evening dress, and her brittleness is accentuated by the diamond clasp and earrings which she wears without noticing how ugly they are. Beside her, slowly coming out of a drunken sleep is Marler, a big, extrovert bull-like man whom most women find irresistible and some unspeakable. He too is in evening dress, but he looks much worse for wear. He gazes around but before he can commit himself Rosemary cuts in.

> ROSEMARY (referring to the car)
> You can put it away.

She gets out of the car, slams the door and goes off towards the house. Marler looks after her amused at her aggression, pulls himself together and moves across to the driver's seat. (D3: 1)

Marler and Rosemary's backgrounds are contrasted from their first introduction. Marler's Irish, working-class upbringing is often mentioned and he is presented as a fish out of water, albeit a successful one, in a world of suburbanites. Food is used as an indicator of class: when the couple return from a party, we are told 'Marler appears in the door behind her, a half eaten bacon and egg sandwich in his hand' and in the same scene Marler complains about eating pheasant, while cooking himself bacon and eggs:

Marler cuts a slice of bread and as he dips it in the fat, says:

> MARLER
> You know that stinking rotten pheasant – Or partridge, or whatever Moyle gave us …?

> ROSEMARY
> Why pretend you don't know what it was?

> MARLER
> Do you know anybody who actually likes that muck? (ibid.: 2)

Rosemary frequently insults Marler's Irish heritage, sarcastically commenting when he thanks her for playing up to his boss:

> MARLER
> You did a magnificent job with old Moyle darling – great, great …

> ROSEMARY (glacially cool)
> That's what you married me for isn't it Paddywhack?

> MARLER
> Bitch. (ibid.: 3)

In a later scene, as they are about to go to bed, Rosemary insults him again and the viciousness of their relationship is revealed:

He opens her dressing-gown, looks at her, coldly, nods.

> MARLER
> That's what you married me for, isn't it?

> ROSEMARY (in a wild fury, belting him across the face)
> You stupid, drunken, Irish peasant!

She stops. He calmly hits her back. (ibid.: 5)

Loss of identity is a central theme of the screenplay, with Marler presented as an outsider in his new life in the south of England. There are many references to Marler's father having moved to an alien and unfriendly country and the inclusion of traditional Irish songs throughout the script reinforces the links to Marler's past life and his Irish heritage, for instance, when Marler and Rosemary make love roughly to a song, telling us about England's treachery (ibid.: 5–6).

> As Marler looks at her with a combination of lust and scorn, we bring in on the
> SOUND TRACK, the voice of an old Irish peasant, who is, in fact, John Jo Marler,
> Michael Marler's father, singing a wild beautiful romantic Irish song of fury and
> rebellion against the Anglo-Saxons. (ibid.: 6)

Marler's testosterone-fuelled nature is evident in every aspect of his life, from his relationships with women to his work. The sense of difference in physique, action and character between him and his colleagues is emphasised in the following extract; not only is Marler a man of action, he is charismatic and dangerous:

> We see him among other young men of his own status and age. Three or four of
> them. They are all the normal pattern of junior executives – mostly public school
> and/or army background, all bland and very Anglo-Saxon. Marler seems like Antony
> at Octavius's court as he prowls up and down amongst them. (ibid.: 10)

McGrath often employed the voiceover as a dramatic device and in earlier drafts it serves to let us know Marler's thoughts. This device can distance the reader from the naturalism of the film so Columbia insisted it be taken out. Voiceover can convey expositional detail about Marler so that the reader understands his view of the world, but it can also result in a flattening of the drama, as in the following example:

INT. CAR. DAY

> MARLER (voiceover)
> My name is Michael Larkin Marler. In the back streets of
> Liverpool I was nicer. The Jesuits of Liverpool, who dragged me
> out of the gutter, taught me a thing or two, and, entertaining high
> hopes of turning me into a Jesuit as well, called me Michael
> James. (ibid.: 8)

In the next example though, Marler is talking to his boss, while asides in voiceover apprise us of his cynical thoughts, lending humour to the scene:

INT. HAZLITT'S OFFICE. DAY

HAZLITT
Morning Michael, I hear it went very well last night.

MARLER
Fair to moderate.

MARLER (cont.) (voiceover)
How did he find out? Must have been creeping about the
shrubbery peering through the window.

HAZLITT
Very nice of old Moyle to have you young chaps around. Gather
he's taken quite a shine to your little woman.

MARLER
Oh really?

MARLER (cont.) (voiceover)
She'd eat him – kill him off within the week – (ibid.: 13–14)

Despite the voiceover's dramatic effectiveness, the next draft removes the aside and Marler talks
directly to Hazlitt, presumably at the request of the studio.

Marler's chutzpah and opportunism in the face of opposition make him attractive as a protagonist and are often alluded to in the screenplay. Marler does things that no one else would
dare; he is cheeky enough to get in the executive lift with the head of the company, an incident
that amuses his boss rather than annoys him. The script sets up the fact that Marler may be
brazen but also quick and clever, flawed but likeable; and he succeeds precisely because he is an
outsider. McGrath presents this scenario convincingly: we are appalled, fascinated and at times
sympathetic to his situation. When Marler goes to see his bedridden father, back home in
Liverpool, he finds that he has just died: 'No matter how long he has been away, his father's
death has really hit him very hard and below the belt. He closes his eyes and feels giddy and
steadies himself against the bed' (ibid.: 21). We are privy to his vulnerable side and his suffering renders him more sympathetic. The priest, Father Madden, lambasts Marler for his lack of
moral scruples:

MADDEN
He was worried about you, your father. About your obsession
with getting on in business. He felt that you lacked ideals, that
you'd turned into an opportunist.

MARLER
I don't need a debate right now, Father.

The priest continues:

MADDEN

Your father tells me you believe the human race to be a herd of
dumb beings to be preyed upon – a sort of predators and
victims arrangement.

MARLER

He's just died, father.

MADDEN

I'll pray for you, Mick. (ibid.: 22)

The priest reveals Marler's amorality, but we still feel sorry for him. The discovery that his
father's death was not accidental sends Marler on a journey of revenge and possible redemption
and, at first, we admire his desire to right a terrible wrong. The desire for vengeance is incited
when Cocky, his father's best friend, tells Marler he knows who beat his father up:

MARLER

That young fellow as good as murdered my old man, Cocky.

COCKY (Looking hard at Marler, and meaning every word he says)
If anything is to be done, Mick, it won't be the English police will
be doing it. Remember that.

He turns and goes out of the club, leaving Marler to the terrible realisation of what he
means. Marler gazes around him at the terrible crowd who are glued to their little
cards and to the steady patter of the COMPERE as he calls out the numbers. Marler
suddenly feels his sense of reality leaving him, and the beginnings of a nightmare
descend. (ibid.: 34)

Marler is propelled into a new world where he determines to avenge his father's death and
accepts that to do so will mean taking the law into his own hands. The direct cut from the above
scene to the wrestling match in the working men's club is a powerful reminder of what has
happened and what is to come:

An ugly BRUISER'S head is being bashed on the ground, distorted gruesomely by
the boot that is pushing it into the canvas. We pull back to see that it is, in fact, the
wrestling, which is now going on in the main part of the club … (ibid.)

Marler's taste for violence appears to increase after his father's death. When Hazlitt demurs at
the idea of using threats to further their careers, Marler responds: 'Why not? Don't be afraid to
put the boot in, Mr. Hazlitt. Because if you don't kick their heads in, they'll kick yours, and
Davidson won't bother to wipe his feet first …' (D3: 53). The metaphor of violence continues
as Marler plans an office coup, in the analogy of a hunter attacking his prey:

> HAZLITT
> What do you think we should do?

> MARLER
> Get Barnham in here after lunch. Ten minutes before the
> meeting, and leave it to me. You can come in for the kill.
> (ibid.: 53)

The description and dialogue become more unsettling as the screenplay builds up to Marler's explosion at the party that his wife, Rosemary, insists on holding just after his father has died. The script vividly accentuates Marler's isolation and difference from his colleagues: 'As Marler watches these complacent puddingy men, happily chewing their complacent puddingy lunch, we hear their conversation which is of central heating, oil, gas' (ibid.: 54).

The scene includes the sound of Marler's father singing Irish folk songs, which filter in and out of the conversation and then we hear the fight with his father, all overlaid in an impressionistic way:

> Over this we build a sound track which reflects Marler's frame of mind. We hear
> snatches of his father's songs, coming through loud and clear, their purity and beauty
> rendering these faces and these voices almost obscene, and the sounds of the fight
> in the pub, which Marler is constantly trying to recreate in his head – we hear scuffles,
> grunts thumps, and the sound of boots being applied to ribs. We hear the cries of his
> father as he tries to ward off the blows. (ibid.: 54)

The reader is reminded of what Marler is going through, gaining a sense of his state of mind, as he imagines his father's death and questions whether he should avenge it. Marler reveals his doubts to his secretary:

> MARLER
> There'll be no witnesses. It's like a bad joke about Sicilian
> gangsters.

> (He gets angry) For Christ's sake, it's way past the middle of the
> twentieth century, and here am I obliged to kill some yob I don't
> even know … (ibid.: 61)

The party sequence that follows Marler's return from Liverpool takes up ten pages but is pivotal to the story, leading up to a finale in which he creates havoc, insults everyone and punches his boss. The sequence racks up tension, as Marler gets more and more drunk. The motivation to hit out intensifies when Cocky phones to tell Marler that the inquest on his father has been a whitewash:

> MARLER
> What was the verdict?

COCKY
They didn't want to know: you could see it written all over their
faces. Mr. R. J. Bingham-Nutt, the standby Coroner, decided on
the advice of Creepy Carolan and the local bobbies, that your
father died of natural causes. (ibid.: 72)

This gives Marler's plans for vengeance more impetus and the links between his father's
killing and the party sequence, as it gets out of hand, are outstanding. His 'fish out of water',
Anglo-Saxon antipathy mounts until he, very drunkenly, begins to sing Irish protest songs:

CLOSE SHOT OF BISHTON, suffering in a jaundiced way, angry. He is not a man of
many words but he feels it is his job as Marler's employer and perhaps the most
eminent person present to administer a rebuke on behalf of all present. He strides
across to the piano and prods Marler in the guts.

BISHTON
Marler! I say, Marler!

MARLER
What?

He raises his blood shot eyes to stare at Bishton.

BISHTON
Never knew you were an Irishman.

Very slowly Marler draws back his fist, clenches it, and then plunges it into Bishton's
face. (ibid.: 76)

After this fracas the guests hurriedly leave, Marler is told he is suspended from work and he and
Rosemary decide to separate. On the trail of his father's killer, this chilling account sees Marler
chase and beat up Jones, the boy responsible. We see events through Marler's eyes as he realises
the murderer is in reality a pathetic teenager:

MARLER
I owe you this, Jones, for one old Irish peasant.

Jones looks at Marler, and runs. Backing on the car park are several gardens from
the council estate nearby. As Jones reaches the hedge from one of these and tries to
break through Marler swings at him, catches him a blow on the side of the head,
which knocks him into the hedge. He hangs there dazed. Marler raises the gear lever
again and he, and we, suddenly see Jones as an undernourished, underprivileged,
frightened schoolboy. He is shocked and appalled, and sickened at the boy's terror.
(ibid.: 97)

The event marks a key turning point in the story; Marler could have stopped, recognising his prey is a scared teenager, but he does not, and goes on to catch the boy and beat him up. Later we learn that the boy will probably die. We are not lured by McGrath into liking or accepting what Marler does but his actions are understandable.

The arc of the script turns again after Marler has achieved his revenge. He now seems able to do anything and get away with it. He is not caught by the police and, even though a murder suspect, manages to gain a promotion at work in an underhand way. His likeability, evident in the script until this point, now disappears. By the end of the screenplay, Marler is presented as a vicious manipulator. The company boss, Moyle, promotes Marler to head of sales after Marler has plotted and made false accusations against his predecessor. Moyle makes it clear that this promotion has certain conditions attached:

MOYLE
I've got great faith in you, Marler.

MARLER
Thank you, sir.

MOYLE
Pity about Rosemary running off like that.

MARLER
Mm. Don't think she's coming back though.

MOYLE (cunning, threatening)
Oh. I think you'll find she will.

(raises his glass) Here's to success in your new job.

MARLER
Cheers.

They raise their glasses. (ibid.: 111–12)

The script ends on Marler driving his Jaguar, Rosemary beside him, and we realise he has taken his boss's advice and reunited with his wife; for the sake of ambition he is prepared to endure an unhappy marriage. The couple have a lucky escape when their car narrowly avoids a collision and Marler comments in voiceover: 'If I can get away with that I can get away with anything' (ibid.: 113). We know that Marler is doomed and the priest was right – he has lost his soul and his conscience.

Comparative scene analysis – *The Reckoning*
The drafts and rewrites in the collection facilitate the study of the same scene at different stages of development. The three versions below are from the scene following the death of Marler's father. Marler's wife insists on holding a party to impress her friends and his boss. Marler

becomes drunk and offensive and is suspended from work. When he returns to the house, Rosemary tells him she is leaving him.

The first example is from D1 (March 1968) and includes the voiceover that McGrath was later asked to cut:

INT. MARLER'S HOUSE. DAY

A sad desolate scene.

The house is more or less back to normal. M. comes in, stops when he sees Rosemary grimly collecting a pile of objects and putting them together in the hall. She is sniffling as she does so: no matter how awful the marriage, they both feel unhappy that some part of their lives has come to an end.

M. watches her as she gets things; he slumps in a chair and lights a cigarette. We see her, and him. Neither speak. There is nothing to say.

> MARLER (voiceover)
> In spite of what kind of cow she'd turned into, I didn't want her to go. There was a time, not too long ago, when there was something. She'd been in the middle of a comfortable engagement to an E-type Jaguar with a small castle in Ayrshire, when she'd taken off with me: you could hardly call it running away, I suppose, at twenty-five. One orgiastic weekend in her girl-friend's country cottage was all we had to be truly nostalgic about – romance dissolved a week later in the Fulham Road Registry Office – but somehow, something was over. Gone. And. What's more, deep down, my pride had taken another boot in the teeth.

She goes out, after a long, bleak look at him. (D1: 78–9)

The scene is made more stylised by the use of voiceover and the fact that neither speak to each other. The voiceover reveals Marler's interior world and the fact that he doesn't want his wife to leave. This could possibly have been inferred by a look or brief physical connection or even a few words of dialogue, but the voiceover makes it explicit. It also provides expositional detail about their time together and how their relationship fell apart soon after they met. Marler's loss of pride is also directly referenced, a point not made clear in the script previously.

A second draft version of the scene, D2, dated August 1968, also exists. The scene has a similar beginning but has been severely edited, losing most of the voiceover, with Marler directly questioning Rosemary instead, before speaking in an aside. In this version Marler leaves quietly and there is less drama between him and Rosemary:

INT. MARLER'S HOUSE. DAY

A sad desolate scene.

The house is more or less back to normal. Marler comes in. Stops when he sees Rosemary grimly collecting a pile of objects and putting them together in the hall. She is sniffling as she does so; no matter how awful the marriage, they both feel unhappy that some part of their lives has come to an end.

Marler watches her, as she gets the things; Slumps in a chair and lights a cigarette. We see her, and him.

> MARLER (not expecting a reply)
> There never was much between us, was there?

(She ignores him) One weekend of pre-marital bliss in Philippa's country cottage is about all we've got to be nostalgic about (pause) and that bit of romance vanished six days later in the Fulham Road Registry Office.

She goes out, after a long, bleak look at him.

> MARLER (cont.)
> Another kick in the teeth.

CUT TO

EXT. BEACONSFIELD HOUSE. DAY

Marler comes to the door and watches Rosemary drive away. She does not look back.

Go into CLOSE UP: Marler hunched against the doorpost. (D2: 81)

This version is shorter and darker. The effect of the cuts to the scene is to shift the emphasis away from the couple's relationship. Their story has ceased to be the focus, as other aspects of the narrative gain greater prominence.

The rewrite pages, D3, dated September 1968, are very different. The voiceover and asides have gone, making the scene more naturalistic and it is extended and developed in a more complex way:

INT. MARLER'S HOUSE. DAY

MARLER comes in, knowing that she is in the house.

He storms through the place from room to room looking for her.

He stops abruptly in the doorway of the bedroom, where she is packing her stuff into a holdall. He gets the message at once, and leans against the doorpost.

It is a sad, rather desolate scene. No matter how awful the marriage, they both feel unhappy that some part of their lives might be coming to an end.

                              MARLER
                      I've had the sack.

                             ROSEMARY
              I'm surprised. Bishton wasn't all that popular.

                              MARLER
                I'm suspended till Moyle gets back.

                             ROSEMARY
         Hazlitt? (He nods) Most of the others would have promoted you.

Silence. She is trying to close the lid of the suitcase.

                              MARLER
                 I don't want you to go you know.

                             ROSEMARY
         We both managed to live very close to the borders of sanity,
         Michael. Last night you went right over. It frightened me. You
         didn't seem to know what you were doing, for the first time since
         I met you.

                              MARLER
              You think you really know me, don't you?

                             ROSEMARY
         You're getting more and more like Rasputin every day –
         an uncontrollable peasant, come to kill us all …

                              MARLER
         You know, with you, the class war becomes something very
         personal.

                             ROSEMARY
                Perhaps because we're both traitors in it.

                  MARLER (Getting more and more angry)
                               Ha!

                             ROSEMARY
         I think, given the choice, I'd rather be a traitor for love than for
         money.

> MARLER
>
> Love? Get out!
>
>
> ROSEMARY
>
> It was love Michael. Not the sort you write poems about – the
> sort you make. We made it and fought and stayed ourselves, we
> didn't get sludged up in the old matrimonial soup. So now we
> can both get out, intact.
>
> (Looks at him) I shall miss you.
>
>
> MARLER
>
> Stop being so bloody modern about it, and throw something,
> can't you?
>
> Marler looks at her very dangerously, and shifts his weight as if he might be about to
> attack her. She begins to giggle, half-hysterically, and seizes the nearest object to
> hand – a large pot of make-up. He smiles at this.
>
>
> ROSEMARY
>
> No more, Mister Marler …
>
> He starts to advance on her, smiling, thinking he has her back.
>
>
> ROSEMARY
>
> Here's to the old days …
>
> And she launches it straight at him. It catches him a glancing blow on the side of the
> head which really hurts. He bellows with rage, clutching his head. She runs out with
> her stuff, half-laughing, half-screaming. We hear this turn for a moment to strangled
> tears, then silence.
>
> Marler looks up, almost hopefully, thinking she is coming back.
>
> Then the car starts up, and we hear it drive away.
>
> Marler looks at the smashed vase, and as he draws his hand down from his head,
> at the blood on his fingers. (D3: 10/9/68)

The above version excises the exposition about Marler and Rosemary's past to focus on the couple as they are now and their feelings toward each other, showing them sparring together, bringing out differences in their class and their attitudes to love. It is longer than the earlier versions, quite dialogue-heavy and to some degree 'on the nose', as they express their feelings openly and rather theatrically. The direct confrontation is dramatically more interesting than voiceover. The scene also allows for the possibility of a reunion, Rosemary recalling that their marriage did involve a kind of love and Marler hoping she will come back. This scene is almost the same as in the film, suggesting the naturalistic version was preferred by the time the script had reached the latter stages of development.

CONCLUSION

McGrath was an accomplished and versatile writer who benefited from the freedom accorded to writers and directors in the 1960s, not only at the BBC, but also by the Hollywood studios with London production offices. His interest in politics and experimentation in narrative and style was encouraged in films like *Billion Dollar Brain*, *The Reckoning* and *The Bofors Gun*. In terms of output, his screenplay adaptation of *The Reckoning* is the most memorable and the most creatively successful, although *Billion Dollar Brain* has its entertaining moments.

McGrath's career was unusual: highly critical of Hollywood, he developed Moonstone to promote writers whose work eschewed Hollywood storylines and yet turned his hand to more mainstream screenplays like *Robin Hood* in later life. Gold elucidates:

> John gave his films a critical intelligence and a ruthless pursuit of truth and honesty. He had a profound understanding of people, a great ear for dialogue, from the scatological to the poetic; for humour; for music and for song. (Brady and Capon 2005: 194)

McGrath's work demonstrated great range and his description and dialogue were robust, fluent and readable. His film writing output may not have been large in comparison to his contribution to television and theatre but it was nonetheless significant.

McGrath worked with Ken Loach in his early years at the BBC, a director with whom Paul Laverty, discussed in the following chapter, also struck up a productive relationship. While McGrath wrote with Loach in the 1960s, Laverty has become Loach's regular writer in his later years, starting with *Carla's Song* in 1996. Both authors possess strong political convictions but, while McGrath's views were more clearly expressed in the media of theatre and television, Laverty's concerns about subjects as far-ranging as US intervention in countries like Nicaragua through the problems of mixed-race relationships in Glasgow, to the price paid for the Civil War in Ireland have proved suitable film material.

APPENDIX

Billion Dollar Brain – story outline 1, 22 September 1966 (Box 19.2)

In his bed-sitting room in Fulham, Harry Palmer tells a disgruntled businessman the details of his wife's activities, which have been uneventful – she has no lover. The man is furious, tells Harry that he doesn't pay for that kind of testimony, and starts to leave. Harry says – what about my expenses? The man says sue me, and goes. Harry is even deeper in debt than ever. Then a strange, rather menacing figure appears in the doorway, asks Harry a few questions, and offers him £500 to do a job. Harry agrees. He has to. The man – Dr Pike –tells Harry he will get further instructions by ringing a certain number. He is now an employee of Facts for Freedom, and if he reveals anything he will be killed. The man goes. Harry dials the number. MUSIC. A strange voice, the voice of the Brain, speaks to Harry, telling him what he has to do. As the TITLES go up, we see the Brain in operation – weird, frightening. Harry's involved in Operation Free Latvia. Titles end.

Harry picks up the parcel which has to be delivered from Pike in St James's Park. He is told that they are eggs, and have to go to a Dr Kaarna, in Helsinki.

Helsinki. Harry is very cold. He waits for his contact, who fails to appear. Instead he is picked up by a beautiful girl – Signe. She leads him back to an apartment, where he is held up, and the eggs taken from him. His attacker is an old friend of his – Harvey. Harvey says he is the Baltic area chief of FFF. Harry asks what it is. Harvey takes him to his control room and shows him Operation Free Latvia at work. Midwinter makes a telecast speech by satellite to all his operators, urging them to greater efforts. The day is at hand. Harry says this is crazy stuff – if he invades Latvia it will lead to World War Three. Harvey says – He will and it will. Harry – By the way, what happened to my contact? Harvey – He talked. He is dead.

London. Harry is picked up by Ross, and told that the man who died was their agent. Harry is to replace him in the hot seat. Ross blackmails Harry into accepting this. Ross – What are you carrying? They analyse the next batch of eggs. They are carrying virulent flu bacteria. They are swapped over. Ross – We need to know what is going on. Even the State Department is baffled. Harry – Don't ring me, I'll ring you. This lot has to be delivered to Latvia.

Finland, on the ice. Harry, and an expert, take off and are dropped into a snowdrift. Harry gets to the Riga hotel, where Stok visits him, and advises him to keep away from this lot. He will not protect him. But Harry goes out the next morning for his rendezvous with the Latvian Organisation. He finds they are pathetically inadequate. He plants the eggs as ordered in an ambushed Russian lorry, but they themselves are ambushed and captured by the Russian cavalry. He is knocked out cold, and wakes up under a pile of corpses, then is taken to Stok, who frames him by having the 'expert' arrested while he and Harry are eating together in the very restaurant where the arrest takes place, watched by Signe. Then he gives him his ticket to Helsinki, telling him to keep out.

Helsinki. The Control Room. Harvey is angry with Harry for what happened in Riga. But because Harry once saved his life, he will try to 'fix' the report to the Brain. Anyway, says Harvey, you've been accepted by the Brain for a regular job – I'd hate to ruin your chances of earning £500 a week, every week, so I'll keep quiet. You fly to Texas tomorrow. I'll join you there in a few days – I have to see my wife and children.

Texas. Harry arrives, is driven through the industrial-chemical empire which is the source of Midwinter's wealth, then taken out to his 'ranch' where, under cover of being cowboys, a small private army is training. Harry undergoes Basic Training. Then he and the Five Boys on the course with him are shown over the huge Computer Complex which is supposed to control the chemical output, and the merchandising of the Midwinter Empire. They are led through a door into the Central Operations Control Room, where the worldwide activities of the FFF are fed into the machine. The invasion will be very soon …

Harvey arrives, and takes Harry to a ball that Midwinter is having at his house – a real Texan affair. Because Harvey's wife is Midwinter's secretary-cum-nursemaid, Harry is allowed to meet Midwinter, who gives him some of his views on life. Harry begins to realise that Harvey is cheating Midwinter, and so is Mercy. At the Ball, while Midwinter makes a speech, Harvey slips away. Harry follows him. He is going to the Brain. Harry catches up with him, and accuses him of cheating the Brain, saying that he must be crazy, that his cheating may lead to a war in which millions of people will die. They arrive at the Brain. Harvey says he realises this, and is going to cover his tracks, and stop the operation, by performing a lobotomy on the Brain by erasing some if its memory patterns. Harry agrees to help him, but is taken prisoner by the automatic checking devices on the Brain, and led back, having been banged on the head again, to Midwinter, who is looking at photographs of Harry and Stok laughing together in Riga – the cause of his being held by the checking device. Midwinter accuses him of being in the pay of the Russians. Harry denies this. Midwinter, who is in his huge, fantastic living room with its own rifle range, has Harry tied up and placed as a target. Harry tells Midwinter that he can shoot him if he likes, but that he is making a mistake. The people who are really taking him for a ride are Harvey and Mercy. Mercy has been blackmailing her own husband for years, ever since she found out about Signe. To pay for her, Harvey has been cheating the organisation by taking wages for the Latvians – who do not exist. At that very moment, says Harry, Harvey is in the machine trying to erase the records of his embezzlement. Midwinter refuses to believe him, until the alarm hooter wails from the Brain, and a message comes that someone is inside the Brain trying to erase it.

Harvey is chased through the Brain, and somehow, by using his superior technical knowledge, he escapes. Midwinter is now more than ever determined to invade Latvia, and has the whole schedule brought forward. Harry tells him that he is basing all his deductions on false information. Midwinter doesn't believe him, and when Harry asks how he can convince him, he says – find Harvey.

London. Harry reports to Ross, and requests aid, as the situation is serious. Ross thinks the whole thing is another of Harry's fantasies, like the warehouse he has raided once, and doesn't believe him.

Finland. The invasion force arrives. Midwinter sets up HQ in an old castle. They intend to invade Latvia the classical way – across the ice.

Helsinki. Harry finds Signe, who takes him to Harvey. He is under the impression that Signe will go with him to Russia. Now that he has the first batch of eggs, he will be welcome, and he talks of the life they are going to have together. But Harry has to disillusion him. Signe won't go with him. Harvey is shattered at this, and agrees, as Harry thought he would, to go with Harry to tell Midwinter the truth, and stop the invasion. But when they get to the castle, the forces have moved off across the ice. They chase, catch up with, and join Midwinter. Harvey tries to convince him, but Midwinter is now out of his mind. Harvey tries to shoot him, but he and Harry are taken into the back of the vehicle and, although Harry escapes, Harvey is shot. The strange convoy journeys on. The Russian air force is alerted, and all over the world everything is prepared for all-out war.

Meanwhile Signe is leaving Helsinki. She is going somewhere. The Russian investigator plane takes off. The invasion force goes on. Midwinter seriously thinks they are going to be met by a huge crowd of supporters and employees. He is clearly over the edge. Harry watches from a tiny island. The he realises that there are snowdrops growing, and the snow under the trees is melting. Out on the ice, great cracks appear. Then, monstrously, little by little, with Midwinter still driving them on, the invasion force is tipped through the cracks in the ice into the icy cold water below. When the plane circles over the spot where the force is reported to have been, there is only a mass of broken ice floating on the water. Midwinter has been defeated by Spring. All over the world, the preparations are stopped – another false alarm. Then Harry remembers the eggs.

Signe has them, of course, and she hands them to Stok, for whom she has been working all along. But when he opens them, they have hatched into chickens, it being that time of year.

Back in London, Harry makes his report to Ross, who tells him that the Brain blew itself up that very morning. Ross has now finished with Harry's services, and Harry goes back to work, a free-lance agent, looking for work.

Billion Dollar Brain – story outline 2–8 November 1966

Dusk on a rainy day in London. On a fretted glass door is written: 'Harry Palmer, Private Detective'. A figure whom we cannot identify tries several keys till he finds one that opens the door. In the dark room he finds only empty files, empty in-trays and signs of disuse. As he looks into the pantry cupboard, which is equally bare, a figure appears in the door, says: 'Stand quite still' and switches the light on. It is HARRY PALMER. The intruder turns to face him. It is MAJOR ROSS, of MI5, Harry's ex-employer, who has come to ask Harry to re-join the outfit.

As Harry has only had one job in the last three months he is toying with the idea when a Special Delivery letter arrives full of £5 notes. Harry tells Ross that if he wants him back he'll have to send two men with a cosh and a straitjacket. Ross goes. Harry searches the envelope but can find no explanation of the money. The phone rings. The even, metallic voice of the BRAIN tells Harry that he has been employed to do a job for it, and gives him an address and code word. Harry asks: 'How did you pick on me?'

Under the TITLE we see a montage of the computer selecting Harry and gathering information about his past.

Harry goes to the rendezvous, very curious to know what is going on. The man he meets, Dr Pike, is suspicious of him and puts him off for a few days. When Harry goes out we see Pike telephoning the Brain to check up. Out in the street, Harry is being followed.

At the next rendezvous, Harry is given a parcel, a code word, and instructions to give the parcel to Dr Kaarna in Helsinki. Harry goes on the bus, an old lady points out to him that his pocket is ticking. He jumps off the bus and goes straight to an old friend in the MI5 laboratory, who tells him that the parcel contains eggs but cannot be opened without breaking the seal.

Helsinki. Harry arrives with the eggs, arranges a meeting by telephone with Dr Kaarna on a tram. But Dr Kaarna does not turn up. Instead, Harry is picked up by a young, blonde Finnish student called SIGNE, who says Dr Kaarna cannot come. She takes him back to a flat where, instead of Dr Kaarna, Harry finds an old friend, ex CIA man, LEO NEWBEGIN in the sauna. Out of friendship, Leo proposes, in the sauna bath, that Harry should join the organisation full time. He won't say what the organisation is. Harry agrees (then crossed out in ink to read 'does not agree'). They celebrate. Signe and Leo leave Harry at his hotel, very drunk. In a short, tight sequence Harry checks up on Kaarna's real address, goes to it in the dusk, finds the body of Kaarna covered in snow in a window with a small puncture two inches to the right of the seventeenth vertebra. As Harry steps towards the telephone he is banged on the head. At dawn the next morning Harry is led, in a straitjacket by two men inside a strange building outside Helsinki. In it is Ross ('in a car?' noted in ink). Harry protests, but Ross blackmails him into joining MI5, again, telling him that Kaarna was their man in the Facts for Freedom organisation and that Harry is his replacement. Harry is forced to agree to this (note in ink 'eggs').

Leo drives Harry out to the Facts for Freedom headquarters in a castle on an island in the Baltic. There Harry sees a whole convoy of warlike figures covered up waiting for action. He sees the computer link with headquarters in Texas and he is present when Leo receives an order to shoot a certain agent who will appear at a rendezvous. Harry is with Leo when he reluctantly sets about the assassination, explaining that he has to do it. When the victim appears it is Signe. Leo cannot carry through his instructions.

The next day Harry and Signe are ski-ing at the ski-jump outside Helsinki, when Leo appears and tells Harry that he has been accepted by the organisation to perform his next duty, which is to be dropped into Estonia that very night.

Inside the plane Harry is told to go to the Riga hotel. He drops out of the plane with a very scornful scientific expert, who is going to contact Signe in three days time with his first dose of information. They jump out and Harry makes his way to Riga and the Riga hotel, where he is met by a Latvian sub-agent, an Italian corset salesman called Frogolli who tells him where to go next.

Lying in his room that night, Harry is visited by Colonel STOK, his old sparring partner for the Russian Secret Service, who advises him not to go the next morning. However, Harry does go and discovers that the Latvian 'organisation' consists of one of Leo's cousins and some rather dreary petty criminals. They set off to ambush a Russian army lorry on a quiet road. Harry's mission is to place the parcel of eggs in the lorry so that they will be eaten by the Russian army (some words crossed out). The plan misfires. Harry runs away after Leo's cousin has tried to kill him and is caught by the Russian cavalry in the pine forests and banged on the head again.

He comes to underneath a pile of bodies and is led to Col. Stok's office, where Stok again warns him to get out of the organisation. They go for lunch to a restaurant in Riga and there, while Harry sits incriminatingly with Col. Stok, the scientific expert, who has turned up for his rendezvous with Signe, is arrested by the Russians. Stok has successfully framed Harry. He gives him his tickets back to Helsinki and laughs.

Back in Helsinki, Harry is very angry with Leo because he thinks Leo tried to have him killed. Leo denies this. A balance of power is established whereby Harry tacitly agrees not to discuss the fact that Leo failed to kill Signe and Leo will not discuss the fact that Harry was seen in the restaurant with Stok while an agent was arrested. Harry has orders to go to Texas.

At the airport in Texas, Leo is met by his wife and two children. Harry and the Facts for Freedom young men are driven off to headquarters, which is a ranch house belonging to General MIDWINTER, the millionaire who controls the organisation. On the way they pass the chemical complex from which Midwinter's ranch. All the Facts for Freedom employees are disguised as cowboys and Harry and the other four are told that their first public appearance will be when they are introduced to the others at an open-air hoe-down to be held that night.

The hoe-down. The dancing is interrupted while Harry and the other four run on to the platform to introduce themselves to the assembled people. On a closed-circuit television screen General Midwinter sees Harry and ask for him to be brought to him. Leo Newbegin makes a brief appearance with a speech, indicating that Latvia is in a state similar to that of Hungary before the 1956 uprising – which is obviously not true. Leo falters when he sees Frogolli amongst the dancers.

Harry is led away by a cowboy. The dancing begins again. Underneath the floor on which they are dancing we find General Midwinter in the Brain, a vast complex of computers of all kinds. He tells Harry that he needs confirmation that his matching is not wrong, because one of his chief scientists has discovered inconsistencies between Leo's report of the state of Latvia and the picture as seen from other sources. Harry supports Leo. Midwinter gives Harry the benefit of his philosophy while the dance goes on above. At the end of his outburst of extreme anti-communism and aggression, he leads the dancers in a prayer which he makes beside a huge fire at the side of the dance floor. While the prayer continues Harry notices that neither Leo nor Frogolli are to be seen. Then he realises that standing beside him is Signe. She makes Harry take her away from the crowd while the dancing continues in the background. She kisses him and while they are kissing removes the long pin from her hair, counts Harry's vertebrae and is about to insert the pin in the same spot where Kaarna's wound had been. Just in time Harry stops her.

She tells him that Leo is in the machine trying to erase the evidence of his cheating. Harry goes down into the Brain, finds Leo and tells him that Midwinter believes his report about the state of Latvia, Midwinter will try to support the uprising and could easily bring about a very dangerous situation. Leo says he doesn't care. Harry goes off to tell Midwinter but when he gets to the gates is arrested mechanically and banged on the head for the third time. When he comes to he is looking at a picture of himself and Stok in the restaurant projected onto Midwinter's living room wall. Midwinter has discovered his friendship with Stok and is going to kill Harry (some words crossed out). Harry tries to tell Midwinter that Leo is cheating the Brain, and that he is at that moment in the Brain. Midwinter doesn't believe him. Just when Harry is about to be shot the alarm sounds and Midwinter learns that someone is indeed in the Brain.

Leo is chased through the Brain and manages to escape. Midwinter still doesn't believe that Leo's report on Latvia is wrong and orders his chief scientist to programme the invasion of Latvia and the popular uprising on the computer so that there can be no mistakes like there were at the time of the Bay of Pigs invasion. Harry tries to convince him that Leo has misled the machine. Midwinter says there is only one way to prove it. That is to find Leo. And the invasion is planned to commence in six days time.

Back in London, Harry reports to Ross, who doesn't believe the story about the invasion.

But at the castle on the island in the Baltic, preparations are in full swing and Midwinter himself has arrived. Harry searches Helsinki for Leo, eventually tracking down Signe, who is saying goodbye to a handsome student outside the university. She is surprised to see Harry. Leo arrives to take her away. They are going to Leningrad and the train arrives in five minutes. They get on the train with another batch of eggs and it pulls away before Harry can get there.

At the castle, Midwinter briefs his troops before moving off.

On the Russian border the Leningrad train stops. Russian soldiers check passports. When they see Leo's they take him out of the train with his luggage and put him in a car on a road near the railway line. He is carrying the eggs. When he gets in the car, the driver is Harry Palmer. He leaps out the other end and runs back to the train which is just pulling out. Harry fires after him. Signe stands on the platform. Leo reaches out to her. She takes the egss but closes the door on Leo himself, who falls on the track and watches her disappear to Leningrad with his eggs. Harry sends one of his cars after the train. He and the wounded Leo drive off in another car to intercept Midwinter's invasion before the Russians get alarmed.

At the castle the invasion force moves off. Harry and Leo drive off at speed after it.

On the frontier Harry's second car is stopped and the train drives on. Harry and Leo arrive at the castle to find the invasion force already gone. They chase them across the ice. They catch them and drive alongside Midwinter's computer van. Leo leans out of the window shouting to Midwinter. Midwinter shoots Leo. Harry stops the car while Leo dies, then sets off himself after Midwinter.

Meanwhile the Russians have picked up the invasion force on the radar. Stok has prepared for this and has ordered a bomb to be set off to deal with it. When the bombs begin to fall on the ice Midwinter sets the Brain to automatically destroy itself in Texas. As the convoy sinks and the Brain explodes, Harry brakes hard and skids round and round on the ice nearer to the bomb craters. All the convoy sink and the men slide off the lumps of ice into the water. Harry's car, with Leo's body still in it, stops with two wheels in the water, and the piece of ice on which it rests begin to crack. Harry jumps out and runs to safety just as the car and Leo go under. He is left, a solitary figure in the middle of the Baltic with nothing around for miles except a hole in the ice and a few bubbles. Out of the sky comes a small plane with skis. It lands and it is Stok. With Stok is Signe who has been his agent in Finland all the time. Stok gives Harry the parcel of eggs to take back to Major Ross. Harry goes back to Ross, and when Ross opens the eggs that Stok has given him they have hatched into chickens.

NOTES

1. See http://www.screenonline.org.uk/people/id/472530/index.html.
2. In 1972 the company split into two to form 7:84 England and 7:84 Scotland. McGrath and his wife Elizabeth MacLennan remained in Scotland.
3. *Events while Guarding the Bofors Gun* was performed by the Finborough Theatre in summer 2012 to commemorate the tenth anniversary of John McGrath's death. It was so popular that an extra performance was added and it was awarded five stars by the *Guardian* critic.
4. The John McGrath Collection holds an outline of *The Virgin Soldiers* by McGrath and the screenplay by John Hopkins.
5. See http://www.screenonline.org.uk/tv/id/976152/index.html.
6. See http://www.scotsindependent.org/features/scots/john_mcgrath.htm.
7. The battle on ice is in Eisenstein's *Alexander Nevsky* (1938)
8. In addition there is 133-page treatment with detailed notes dated 18 August 1966, that refers to an earlier script. There are many versions of the fourth draft of the screenplay with differing dates and added rewrites and revisions, ranging from 8 December 1966 to March 1967, and a fifth undated draft with additional pages.

11

PAUL LAVERTY
CLASS, POLITICS AND COLLABORATING WITH KEN LOACH

Paul Laverty began screenwriting as a way of communicating his political concerns to a wider audience. Laverty wrote his first script for Ken Loach, *Carla's Song* in 1996, the collaboration proving to be so successful that he has since authored all of Loach's films, apart from *The Navigators* (2001), which was scripted by Rob Dawber. The writer/director partnership has produced engaging and often politically and socially significant stories, many reaping international acclaim, *Sweet Sixteen* (2002) winning the award for Best Screenplay at the Cannes Film Festival and *Ae Fond Kiss* (2004) one for Best Screenplay at the Venice Film Festival.

Laverty was born in India in 1957 to a Scottish father and an Irish mother. He trained as a lawyer in Glasgow but became disillusioned with the profession and went to Nicaragua for six months in 1984. He was impressed that the 1979 revolution had managed to transform society so that most of its people could read and write and diseases like polio had been wiped out. Laverty returned in 1986 to work for a Nicaraguan human rights organisation that monitored human rights abuses in the war zones, while the right-wing, American-backed Contras were trying to break up the country. Laverty's job was to report what was happening to foreign delegations but he felt powerless at his inability to change anything: 'I had a profound sense that we were still pissing in the wind against this huge blanket of information that crushed everything in its path' (1997: xii).[1] Laverty thought that making a film about the desperate situation there might raise awareness: 'I wanted to see if we could take just one character, and give human shape to just one of these thousands of statistics, by telling his or her story, set against the real backdrop of Nicaragua' (ibid.).

On his return to Glasgow Laverty sent out character profiles and a story synopsis to film production companies, receiving rejections from everyone but Ken Loach, who phoned Laverty to discuss the piece, and suggested he write a few scenes. They met up, got on well and Laverty prepared a story outline for the film, receiving funding from the Scottish Film Production Fund to complete the screenplay. The script took six years of development and included research trips to Nicaragua. The story begins when Glaswegian bus driver, George, meets a Nicaraguan refugee, Carla, after she gets on a bus without paying and is caught by the ticket inspector. George is beguiled by Carla but finds out she is haunted by her traumatic past. She plans to return to Nicaragua to see Antonio, the man she was in love with, who had been captured and tortured by the Contras. George accompanies her and, as a Westerner, is shocked by the terrible situation, but helps search for Antonio. Some plot contrivances and strangely placed

Screenwriter Paul Laverty on the set of *The Wind That Shakes the Barley* (2006), directed by Ken Loach

revelations make George appear very naive: for instance, the revelation that Carla has a child seems oddly placed and would have had more impact if disclosed earlier. But George's character is deftly written and his willingness to go to Nicaragua believable. The contrast between the two countries works well, although it is the Glasgow characters who really make the story come to life. George brings his own charm to Carla's world and there are some nice touches, such as when he demonstrates his knowledge of mechanics by using soap to stop a petrol leak in the car and also when he steals the local bus, in parallel to a similar event in Glasgow, at the beginning of the story.

On the last day of filming *Carla's Song*, Loach asked Laverty if he would be interested in writing a story set in Glasgow. Laverty was enthusiastic about the idea and wanted to focus on an older character

> who'd made lots of mistakes in their lives, who were in desperate need of love and attention, but were scared by their previous experiences, who were very lonely and had this great need to communicate and to make up for lost time. (Conroy Scott 2005: 277)

The film became *My Name Is Joe* (1998), centring on a middle-aged, unemployed man, the eponymous Joe, who has just taken the Alcoholics Anonymous pledge. Joe trains the local foot-ball team, a motley crue which includes Liam, who is trying to make a go of things with his part-ner, Sabine, and their young son. Joe meets health worker Sarah and, after a difficult beginning, they become lovers. Joe discovers that Liam is in trouble with the local drug dealer as Sabine has been taking heroin again and owes him lots of money. The drug dealer wants reparation and Liam's only way out of the debt is to have his legs broken. He tells Joe he can avoid this if Joe acts as a drugs courier. Joe agrees but when Sarah finds out, she breaks off their relationship. Joe refuses to do the drugs deal though he and Liam's lives are in danger. They hide when the dealer and his men come looking for them, but Liam sees no way out and hangs himself, while Joe survives. The ending is tragic but hints that Joe and Sarah will get back together. The screenplay is dramatic and moving and the dialogue, although broad dialect, becomes easy to read after the first few pages, while there is almost a poetry to the language. The male characters are more rounded and it would have added another layer to Sarah's character if we knew a little more about her background and her previous relationships.

The idea for Laverty's next screenplay, *Bread and Roses* (2001), came about during 1994 after he won a Fulbright Award to study screenwriting at USC in Los Angeles.[2] While living in a Latino section of LA, he noticed the number of Latina women who entered the office buildings early in the morning and left before the white-collar workers entered, realising how many workers were exploited and paid low wages. The screenplay follows May, an illegal immigrant from Mexico, who works with her sister as an office cleaner. She meets a union activist and they begin to fight for their rights and better working conditions. The story lacks the emotional impact of *My Name Is Joe*, despite some excellent scenes, especially at the beginning of the script and in the finale.

Sweet Sixteen grew out of Liam's character, from *My Name Is Joe*, and is again set in Glasgow. The narrative follows Liam as he becomes a drug dealer and his life has a similar rise-and-fall trajectory to the characters of many gangster films. Liam wants to help his mother get a home when she comes out of prison but is tempted by the lucrative amounts of money involved in drug dealing and descends further and further into this world, unable to escape.

Laverty's next feature-length script, *Ae Fond Kiss*, is the last of the Scottish trilogy and one of his most impressively crafted stories. This love story concerns a couple who come from very different backgrounds: Casim's family are Pakistani Muslim while Roisin's background is Irish Catholic. His parents expect him to marry a Pakistani bride and he is torn between his love for Roisin and his sense of duty to his family. The drama shows how the couple's relationship is tested by the demands of Casim's parents and his elder sister, who want him to follow a traditional way of life. Casim gradually separates from his family, valuing love over tradition while their out-of-wedlock relationship causes Roisin to lose her position as a music teacher at a Catholic school. Both have to make sacrifices and the screenplay succeeds in conveying the sense of the risks involved for them, though the story ends on an optimistic note for the future of mixed-race marriages in Scottish society.

The Wind That Shakes the Barley (2006) is Laverty's only historical film for Loach and a powerful script, discussed in more detail later in the chapter. After this, Laverty returned to contemporary drama: *It's a Free World* (2007) concerns the exploitation of immigrant workers. It centres on Angela, who, after being sacked, sets up her own employment agency with a friend and employs cheap migrant labour. Told from an unexpected perspective, it revolves around Angela and her exploitation of the workers. This technique does not quite work because Angela seems too likeable and needs to have more doubts about what she is doing to make her character believable. Her home background and her nice parents do not suggest a person who would so readily take advantage of others. The character logic might have worked better if Angela's parents had been depicted as having similar values to her. Angela's friend, Rose, acts as her conscience and eventually leaves the business. The portrayal of Angela's declining moral standards and resulting exploitation of the workers is quite shocking but lacks conviction.

In contrast, *Looking for Eric* (2009) is Laverty's first comedy and, despite moments of high drama and the presence of a vicious thug, who acts as Eric the postman's nemesis, there is a lightness of touch combined with a happy ending in which the thug gets his comeuppance and Eric reunites with his ex-wife. The story includes an element of whimsy in which Eric imagines he is followed around by footballer Eric Cantona, who dispenses advice on how Eric can be braver in his life and learn to say 'Non!' Eric and his friends decide to scare off the thugs who are causing mayhem and, as John Hill notes, the narrative, 'sets out to demonstrate the values of collective action' (2011: 197).

Laverty had also been toiling on another script for many years, which was to be directed by his partner, Iciar Bollin, and not, this time, Ken Loach. *Even the Rain* (2010) is part-historical drama about Columbus arriving in the Americas and mistreating their people and part-drama about making the film and the continued exploitation of the indigenous inhabitants. The historian Howard Zinn, who wrote *A People's History of the United States* (1980) and had been impressed by *Bread and Roses*, contacted Laverty about writing the film. The script went through many drafts because Laverty remained dissatisfied with the historical account but, when a colleague suggested the story mix past and present, it began to fit together. The film has been well received, Philip French of the *Guardian* describing it as 'gripping'.[3]

Route Irish, also released in 2010, is about a man who tries to find out what happened to his best friend who died in Iraq, while part of a private army. There are powerful moments as the widow of the best friend gets involved. The mystery thriller format helps to hold our interest as the protagonist unravels details about the murky world of mercenary armies.

Laverty's most recent work, *The Angel's Share* (2012), is entertaining despite its unbelievable plot, about four unemployed friends who are always in trouble and what happens when one of them takes an interest in whisky. The lead character, Robbie, has just become a father and decides he wants a decent life for his child. When the community service leader takes them to a whisky distillery, he discovers he has a special nose for the spirit and hatches a plan to steal some to sell on. Things more or less work out and the friends share the proceeds between them. Crime in this case does pay and Robbie is offered a job and a new life working for a whisky company. The story is slight and whimsical, with an almost fairy-tale ending, but for a question mark about the friends left behind who have to somehow make a living.

When discussing the writing process Laverty affirms that 'A great deal of writing for me is testing possibility, so in a strange way I don't mind testing a cul-de-sac, so I'll try it and feel it out ...' (Conroy Scott 2005: 287). It is this approach which accords Laverty's scripts the naturalism he seeks and allows him to view the screenplay as a fluid text. Laverty acknowledges the contribution of script editor Roger Smith to the screenplays, characterising him as 'just a troublesome bastard who always asks the really tough questions that you try not to ask yourself. He has great instincts' (ibid.: 285).

Hill suggests that, for Laverty and Loach, 'it is the shared experience of the working class that is the most important' (2011: 188). As James Mottram observes, 'In Laverty, Loach has found someone who sees the world in a similar way' (2004: 23). Indeed, Loach's style of working is better suited to some writers than others, as Hill points out, 'David Mercer and Trevor Griffiths, while displaying a similar socialist outlook, were writers of a different kind, less prepared for their work to be modified' and the partnership did not gel, whereas Jim Allen, Barry

Hines and Laverty were more amenable to his methods (2011: 264). Laverty is quite happy for the actors to play with the screenplay dialogue as he does not see the screenplay as a finite text but rather a tool to work with, which ties in with Loach's desire for the actors to be spontaneous and naturalistic (ibid.: 207). As Loach himself testifies of Laverty, 'He's a terrific writer and we see the world in the same way' (Fuller 1998: 109).

The Wind That Shakes the Barley

The following analysis of two drafts of *The Wind That Shakes the Barley* screenplay discusses the changes between these and how the focus shifts to a single protagonist and how narrative drive is prioritised over scenes with no obvious dramatic function. The drafts examined are an early one, dated April 2004 (D1) and the shooting script, dated April 2005 (D2).

Laverty and Loach were interested in making an historical film about Ireland around 1918, when the Irish were demonstrating increasing resistance to British rule. In 1921 a compromise was reached, in the formation of the Irish Free State, not including the six Protestant-dominated counties in the North which remained under British jurisdiction. Many Republicans felt this was a sell-out, and a bloody civil war began, which lasted until 1923. Laverty first wrote a forty-six-page treatment (2004a),[4] furnishing considerable detail about the historical background to the events and showing how the Republicans built support for their fight against the British occupation. The story focuses on two brothers: Damien, a newly qualified doctor about to leave for London, and Teddy, a hot-headed revolutionary, who wants Damien to stay and fight. After witnessing violence by British troops, Damien joins the Irish rebels, who prove themselves to be tough opponents.

Paul Laverty and Ken Loach strolling through the fields on location for *The Wind That Shakes the Barley*

A truce is called and the Irish Free State is formed; Teddy becomes an officer in the Free State Army while Damien stays with the rebels. When caught, Damien refuses to reveal where the rebels are hiding and Teddy decides he only has one option: he has Damien shot.

The overall story remains the same in both drafts, although there are many differences within each. The first draft, D1, is longer – ninety-nine pages of eighty-five scenes; while the shooting script, D2, is only eighty-nine pages with forty-eight scenes, although many of these have been combined. Some of the changes in D2 are major; the rewriting, editing and elisions resulting in a more focused shooting script with a stronger story spine, favouring a single narrative thread. The rewriting acts as a refining and filtering process, in which only the essential parts of the story are retained, while the structuring of the narrative through 'cause' then 'effect' ensures the linearity of the action.

One of the most noticeable changes between the drafts is the sidelining of the love interest in D2. Most of the earlier Damien and Sinead scenes in D1 are cut, with the development of their relationship left until much later, generating more forward impulsion and a clearer focus on the fight between the rebels and the British. The story changes from portraying Damien and Sinead's joint trajectory, and their battle with the British, to focusing directly on Damien as the central protagonist and his fight to free Ireland. The love interest highlighted in D1 diverts attention from the battle with the British. For instance, in the opening first scene the men are on their way home from a game of hurley, when Micheail (Sinead's brother) teases Damien about her, immediately drawing attention to the importance of her character:

> MICHEAIL
> Grandma wants to see you before you go … can you come up
> to the farm?

Damien hesitates.

> MICHEAIL (cont.)
> Sinead's coming too.

Damien's face changes in an instant. All the boys see it and laugh openly. Micheail catches Damien roughly by the ear.

> MICHEAIL
> That's different … . eh! (D1)

In D2 the above lines are replaced with dialogue linking to the next scene, the farm where Micheail is viciously murdered by British troops, so keeping our focus on more weighty matters:

> DAMIEN (to Micheail)
> I want to say goodbye to Peggy and your Mam …

> MICHEAIL
> Come on … they're up at the farm. (D2)

The elision of scenes from D1 helps to prioritise the flow of action: for instance, a scene in Damien's home following on from Micheail's killing is deleted because it is not crucial to the story, providing purely background detail about Damien's middle-class family, and it briefly halts the narrative flow. Again, the next DI scene, set outside Micheail's family farm, is cut from D2, which moves straight to the wake. This cut enables the story to focus on the consequences of the murder and maintains the emotional intensity.

D2 also cuts the scene after the wake; the first draft shows Sinead cycling through the town and countryside past the Black and Tans,[5] and offering to post their letters. It contains little important information and again slows the pacing of the narrative, digressing from the aim of the earlier pages to drive home the brutality of the British soldiers.

The next scene marks a major turning point in the story and so is retained in D2, showing Damien's resolve to stay and fight the British. In both drafts Damien goes to catch the train to London where he intends to work as a doctor but, in D1, the beginning centres on Damien and Sinead saying their goodbyes, and includes a great deal of expositional detail about the state of Ireland. In D1 the scene begins with Damien waiting at the station when Sinead arrives:

> A group of Tans, fully armed, board the train. The train driver leans out to stare at them.
>
> Sinead appears. They hurry towards each other and then hesitate as they come face to face. Tension and tenderness.
>
> DAMIEN
> Oh God … thought you weren't coming …
>
> SINEAD
> I tried not to.
>
> He holds out his hand to her cheek. She inclines towards it by a fraction.
>
> DAMIEN
> Will you come and visit me in London? (D1)

The beginning of the scene highlights the couple's emotions, suggesting some friction between them, but the tone changes as the action turns to the soldiers' brutal behaviour towards the railwaymen. D2 cuts the first two pages of the Damien and Sinead romance, getting straight to the central point of the scene, illustrating the Black and Tans' brutality and the railwayworkers' steadfast determination not to give in and transport British troops. Cutting Sinead allows the narrative to zoom in on the soldiers and the railwaymen. The juxtaposition of romance and aggression in the first draft is awkward and makes the scene overlong. In D2 we enter the scene as Damien hears the soldiers shouting and sees them:

> A group of soldiers surround a terrified station guard (older, frail and on the point of retirement) and stoker (young, fresh faced) on the platform. Other Tans are already in the carriage watching the dispute through a window.

                              SERGEANT
        This is the last fucking warning I'm going to give you … do you
        hear me!

The sergeant gets a nudge from a Tan beside him which stops him in his tracks.
Damien is amazed to see the engine driver stride toward them. Everything about him
is rough and rugged.

                               DRIVER
                      It's my duty to inform you.

                              SERGEANT
                   Who the fuck do you think you are?

                               DRIVER
        I'm instructed by my union not to transport British Army
        personnel. (D2)

The sergeant knocks the driver to the ground, then attacks the stoker and the old guard. It's a
powerful scene, made much more intense in D2 by the refocusing of the editing. In D1 the end
of the scene cuts back to Damien and Sinead:

                               SINEAD
        You know what this means Damien … or get back on the next
        train to London.

He studies her.

                              DAMIEN
                          Is that a threat?

                               SINEAD
        This time we are going to drive them out … Don't get in my way.

        There is something of Sorcha's [Sinead's mother] fierce
        stubbornness in her.

                              DAMIEN
              Could you do with someone to teach first aid?

A long moment.

                               SINEAD
                        I'll think about it.

> She walks towards him. She takes his cheeks in her hands and rubs her brow to his.
> After a moment they walk from the station hand in hand. (D1)

The romantic complications in D1 can be viewed as a distraction, diluting the portrayal of the more significant events. D2 presents the action solely from Damien's perspective, personalising the experience; we are with Damien as he reacts to the brutality of the soldiers and decides whether to get on the train or not:

> GUARD (to Damien)
> Close the doors for me …

> Damien closes the two train doors and then hesitates at the last one, opposite the guard. He stares down at the old man, badly shaken (bloodstains on his face) who looks up at Damien.

> GUARD
> Make up your mind son …

> Damien hesitates once more, and then, from the platform, slams the last door shut. The guard still sitting on the ground blows his whistle.

> Damien helps the guard over to a bench, and then, pondering, watches the train disappear into the distance as he feels the strongest emotions stir within him.

> He turns once more to stare down at the pale old man trying to catch his breath on the bench. The guard trembles even more.

> GUARD
> Ah Jesus … thought that was it … (D2)

D2 points up a contrast between Damien, who is planning to run away from the tyranny of British rule, and the old guard, who faces up to the bullying troops, the guard's words ending the scene. This draft is more visual with reduced dialogue. Damien's resolution to stay is conveyed by his expressions and his actions, closing the train door, whereas in D1 his offer of first aid skills is a much weaker proposition. Cutting the scene from over five pages to fewer than two pages lends the narrative greater focus and direction.

The subsequent scene in D1 shows Damien entering a church hall where a 'Baby Club' is being held. It is actually a front for women Republican supporters hiding arms and explosives. This is an entertaining scene, with an amusing contrast between the breastfeeding class and the revelation that the women are gun runners, carrying arms in their prams. Laverty's treatment suggests he wanted to show how important the women were to the war effort, which it does effectively but, because it does little to further the story, it is deleted from D2.

It is replaced by a scene which allows the narrative to follow the cause/effect pattern more directly. Damien, as a result of witnessing the solders' brutality at the station, is driven to swear allegiance to the Republicans in their struggle against the British. Importantly, this scene confirms Damien's loyalty and change of attitude. There is no longer any ambiguity or indecision about his commitment to the cause, and the swearing-in scene demonstrates this. D2 cuts from the trembling train guard at the station, saying: 'Ah Jesus … thought that was it' directly to:

BACK ROOM OF A PUB

The simplicity of a bare room has acquired the quiet stillness of a church.

Across a table Damien faces several volunteers. They all stand. FINBAR, around 30, is a born leader with easy confidence and natural gravitas. STEADY BOY (wiry, tough, thoughtful, with experience in the British Army) is always by his side. LEO and RORY, mid to late twenties, are both physically intimidating and solemn. (There is something dark and electric about Rory which makes him hard to ignore.) Teddy and Ned are there too.

FINBAR
You know what that means Damien?

Long moment between them. Damien nods.

Finbar hands Damien a little card as Damien lays his hand on the bible.

DAMIEN
I do solemnly swear that to the best of my ability I will support
and defend the Government of the Irish Republic … . (D2)

The scene ends with Teddy telling Damien, 'I knew you wouldn't get on that train.'

The narrative now establishes that these men are ready and willing to give up their lives and that Damien is unequivocally committed to the Republican cause. Damien's character trajectory is more ambiguous in D1; he is shown as undecided about his commitment to the Republicans and, when told he'll have to move from house to house to protect his safety in D1, replies:

DAMIEN
I'm not a soldier … .

(stunned silence)

I'm a doctor who volunteered to do first aid … . (D1)

However, D2 includes a second new scene showing the men learning how to shoot and preparing for battle at a training camp, another logical step in the cause/effect story direction, building the narrative, step by step, towards Damien joining the Irish forces.

A number of scenes from D1 are collapsed together and reordered in D2. There are also some additions: Sinead cycles, delivers letters and then at the end of the sequence gives Damien her murdered brother's (Micheail) St Christopher medallion. This is not in D1, and gains symbolic significance at the end of the film when Damien holds the St Christopher as he's shot, asking Teddy to return it to Sinead.

By what could be termed the end of the first act, D2 has set up the main thrust of the story and so a quiet moment between Damien and Sinead is not detrimental to its progress. The scene is not so much about their relationship but more about them acknowledging their sorrow at the loss of Sinead's brother, Micheail.

In D2 the story progression is much stronger and more directly designed around cause and effect. D1 has a very different sequence of scenes which are less consequential and more informational. The scenes cut from D1 result in a draft with a clearer trajectory and the sequence of scenes in the first twenty pages of D2 highlight Damien's dilemma over whether to go to London or stay and fight.

One of the other notable differences between the two drafts is the deletion of much of the exposition and rhetorical dialogue. In a film based on historical events, some context is needed and Laverty and Loach evidently[6] wanted to include some of the arguments for a socialist-inspired republic. The earlier draft contains much more exposition about this aspect than D2, which has either cut a substantial amount of the historical detail or found other ways to express it. D2 breaks up the dialogue, dividing it between different characters or replacing exposition with more emotive language. For instance, a scene in both drafts features the Republicans trying to persuade Damien to stay. Damien argues that their cause is hopeless because the British have all the arms and power. D1 uses Sinead to displace the tension, and Damien has more rhetorical dialogue:

> DAMIEN
> How many more will you lead to an early grave before you get a bullet yourself?

> SINEAD
> That's enough Damien.

> DAMIEN
> So you're all going to fight the British Empire … First Ireland!
>
> Then Egypt! India! … All the way round the pink globe till we're back here again.

> Teddy, controlled, doesn't shirk, he just watches.

> SINEAD
> This isn't the place Damien … come inside.

> DAMIEN
> It's the very place! A dozen rusty old German Mowzers [sic], a few shotguns … .

> (to Teddy)

> a pistol in your trench coat to make you feel like a big shot as
> the rest march to battle against the best trained army in history!
> Glorious self sacrifice Teddy? … Or just suicidal stupidity! (D1)

Most of this is scene is taken out of D2, which concentrates more directly on Damien, shifting
the attention from his brother, Teddy, and bringing in other characters. The dialogue in D2 is
broken into shorter sections, making the scene more naturalistic:

> DAMIEN
> How many more will you lead to an early grave before you get a
> bullet yourself?

> NED
> You are a fucking coward.

> DAMIEN
> And you're a fucking hero! Going to take on the British Empire
> with a hurley … stun the bastards. One by one.

> CONGO
> Damien, for Christ's sake … . What about Micheail?

> DAMIEN
> What about him? His young face crushed because he wouldn't
> answer in English!

> (to Teddy)

> Another one of your martyrs Teddy … eh?

> Sinead drifts in behind them.

> SINEAD
> So we all buy a one way ticket to London?

> Damien is stunned as he stares at her tearstained face.

> She holds his eye. (D2)

This scene in D2 brings Sinead into the story in a more subtle way, and she serves to drive home
an important point – that they can't all get out of the country like he can. There is also the suggestion that Damien is being cowardly by leaving Ireland.

D1 includes some rather unwieldy chunks of exposition, particularly when trying to convey
the state of the war and explain the complex and difficult political arguments that motivate the

different sides. For instance, when the rebels meet up to discuss the war, D1 introduces a new character, 'McGeever', to impart information:

> MCGEEVER
> It's a tribute to you all … internationally our support grows daily … fact finding missions have returned to England and the United States where detailed reports of British Army atrocities … especially the burning of Cork city centre, including the Town Hall and Carnegie library, have humiliated the British cabinet. … these reports have now been sent to Egypt, India and many other countries … (D1)

The speech continues in a similar vein for another nineteen lines and, because it is very talky and we do not know the character, is not especially interesting. In D2 McGeever is out, the exposition is pared down and shared out among the different characters we already know, making the dialogue more dynamic, less about specific details and more about what they are going to do. The dialogue becomes more personal and less rhetorical while the scene moves the story forward by ending on Teddy's change of fighting tactics:

> RORY
> And some big wig yanks are putting together a commission: Aim is to report what the English are doing to us …
>
> LEO
> Bishops! Congressmen! None of the small fry …
>
> FINBAR
> They're writing about us in Egypt and India!
>
> TEDDY (cutting through)
> But it's still not enough!

(silence)

> In London we're still gangsters and criminals … cowards who shoot them in the back …
>
> RORY
> Jaysus! That's the way they'll always paint us! No matter what we do!

Teddy is shaking his head.

> TEDDY
> Wrong. Not if we hit them in the field … (D2)

The scene changes from dispensing general information to revealing that the Republicans are perceived as cowards and ends with a plan for a direct attack on the British. D2 admits a small amount of expositional detail but also continues the story trajectory and the cause/effect changes, while creating a firm link to the next scene.

The difficulty entailed in conveying complex ideas without being expositional is particularly evident in this section; D2 goes only some way towards succeeding. The danger in cutting out too much exposition is that the audience will not have enough information about the background. The excision of a number of D1 scenes imparting contextual detail about the buildup to civil war does allow a greater focus on the emotions of the characters and developing story progression.

This comparison of the two screenplay drafts demonstrates how the rewriting process can edit and restructure scenes to produce a more powerfully driven narrative. The key points to emerge are that rewriting functions as a refining and filtering process, retaining the essential parts of the story; the story flow or narrative trajectory is developed and linearity emphasised with scenes reordered and juxtaposed to that effect; characters are refined and clarified; perhaps altering the focus to a single protagonist; and last, and no less important, exposition is replaced by emotion, thus prioritising the emotional arc of the story.

There are many smaller but significant points to note in the changes from D1 to D2; for instance, the ends of scenes are often rewritten to accentuate the poignancy, with sound sometimes enlisted to achieve this. In D2 the haunting lament at Micheail's wake is described in much more emotive language than in D1.

These changes have meant some losses to D2; the historical and factual exposition has mostly been eliminated, sacrificed it would seem, to the greater need for emotional engagement in the film. Some of the contextual detail about the politics of the period has also disappeared; D1 made some fascinating points about the role of the women's movement in Ireland during the war which are no longer in D2. In D1 the women represented a central force in the film; losing Sinead in the early part of the story in D2 leaves the script male-centred, and the war is presented as a mostly masculine battle.

Finally, some particularly fascinating questions have emerged, which are worthy of further consideration. Is it possible to determine what constitutes a 'good' screenplay by studying the changes in screenplay drafts? Further to this, one could ask to what extent the screenplay can be studied purely as text, and how important is it to understand the writer's intention in the redrafting process?

CONCLUSION

While Laverty has written other screenplays, it is his collaboration with Ken Loach that is most noteworthy and long lived. Laverty's view of the screenplay as non-finite allowed the men to work together and to produce some of the most thought-provoking contemporary films, boasting intelligence, rawness and believability, together with strong characters and a political and social agenda. It is interesting to note how a screenplay such as *The Wind That Shakes the Barley*, despite being politically driven, during the rewriting process reverted back to character and a classical narrative style for dramatic effect.

ACKNOWLEDGMENTS

This study has only been possible because of the generosity of screenwriter Paul Laverty, director Ken Loach and Sixteen Films, who donated the works referenced. In the past year Ken Loach has donated a great deal of his work to the BFI Special Collections and it is currently being catalogued (as of 2012/13).

NOTES

1. For a more detailed account of the political situation in Nicaragua at that time see the Introduction to *Carla's Song* (Laverty 1997: ix–xxvii).
2. The University of Southern California is a private university with a reputation for producing some of the top writers and directors in the US. Laverty recalls that he attended few classes and 'wasn't a good student really' but did enjoy Frank Daniels's classes (Conroy Scott 2005: 279).
3. See http://www.guardian.co.uk/film/2012/may/20/even-the-rain-review-source.
4. Laverty's treatment is very detailed and similar in storyline to the first and second draft. It includes dialogue, notes and research.
5. The Black and Tans were made up of World War I veterans employed as Special Constables by the British Prime Minister Winston Churchill to subdue the Irish Republican Army from 1920–1. They were noted for their ferocity and vicious reprisals, which probably worsened the conflict rather than dispelled it.
6. The treatment includes detailed research with reference to historians of the Irish Civil War, interviews with relatives of those who were involved in the fighting and some firsthand accounts from a few who were children at the time of the fighting, but could remember something of the atmosphere of those troubled times.

CONCLUSION

This book has discussed a group of very different writers, their equally different working practices and their screenplays: from Emeric Pressburger who enjoyed joint autonomy when writing films with Michael Powell, to Mark Grantham who was required to produce a filmable screenplay in two weeks for the Danziger brothers. Some of these working relationships produced exceptional results; Powell and Pressburger, T. E. B. Clarke and Michael Balcon, Janet Green and Michael Relph and Basil Dearden, David Lean and Robert Bolt, all delivered memorable screenplays after extremely rigorous and often difficult script development processes.

What is common to all the writers in this book is the degree of collaboration involved when finalising a screenplay, often revolving around the writer receiving and reacting to feedback from the producer or director: Muriel Box has acknowledged the help of husband Sydney Box in improving her scripts; David Lean's acerbic and painstaking letters cajoled Robert Bolt into writing with more engagement; and David Puttnam worked closely on at least five drafts of *Local Hero* with writer/director Bill Forsyth. Paul Laverty relates his sympathetic partnership with Ken Loach, also highlighting the valuable comments made by the script editor, Roger Smith. Where there is less direct evidence of input, as in Jeffrey Dell or Mark Grantham's writing, they had a close relationship with their producers. The Boulting Brothers appreciated Dell's expertise and all his scripts for them were co-authored with one of the brothers; and, although there was little producer involvement in Grantham's writing process, other than to ensure if there was enough salacious content, the Danzigers were involved at the initial development stage of a screenplay.

The screenwriter has a vital role in the production process, but even if the writer's stamp is so strong that he or she becomes an auteur, as Charles Barr argues is the case with T. E. B. Clarke's *Passport to Pimlico* (1998: 98), should we make critical and moral evaluations about their work, as in the 'great tradition' argued for by F. R. Leavis? Should there be a pantheon of screenwriters or screenplays which can be likened to Andrew Sarris's graded list of great directors? An auteur approach may help elevate the screenplay to a literary form but it is a very narrow way of looking at such a form. Indeed, once one accepts that the writing of a screenplay is to a great extent collaborative, then the need to identify a sole creator becomes less important.

Whether or not there are auteurs, the screenplay can still be deemed a literary text worthy of study. Some texts are, arguably, more interesting and can be grouped around highly regarded authors or collaborations. Many of the screenplays discussed in this monograph, including those by Pressburger in collaboration with Powell, those by Green with Relph and Dearden and those developed with Puttnam are outstanding examples of the form and equal to the best plays or prose; the screenplays for *A Canterbury Tale*, *The Lavender Hill Mob* and *The Reckoning* are, in their very different ways, able to move the reader and to engage, challenge and inspire.

Correspondence related to screenplays and drafts can be informative when considering what constitutes a 'good' screenplay. It is often possible to trace a pattern or trajectory to the changes made which almost always aim to clarify the narrative and to develop character, applying as much to *Victim*, when Relph and Dearden request more developed and believable characters, as to *The Wind That Shakes the Barley*, where the redrafting process entailed a new focus on the central character and a shift to a clear, linear narrative. Even in *A Canterbury Tale*, which appears to be loosely plotted, the story is structured in the format of the detective genre. At times these changes may not be agreeable to the writer; for instance, in John McGrath's case the experimental nature and voiceover in *The Reckoning* were altered at the request of the production company, which favoured a more naturalistic style.

Many of the chapters in this book have reflected on the literary quality of the screenplays in question, while other screenplays like Mark Grantham's *Night Train for Inverness*, though a reasonable read and tautly structured, could not be described as prime examples of the form. So how do we judge what constitutes a 'well-constructed screenplay'? If some screenplays are better than others, why is this? Robert McKee, the prominent screenwriting guru, argues that the central point of a good script is a good story and the better the storytelling, the more vivid 'the images, the sharper the dialogue. But lack of progression, false motivation, redundant characters, empty subtext, holes, and other such story problems are the result of a bland, boring text' (1997: 19). McKee believes that 'storytelling power' will procure work for those with less talent and that a writer's goal 'must be a good story *well told*' (ibid.: 21). His idea of a 'good' screenplay may be a Hollywood one but it is an aspect of the study of the form that would benefit from further debate and research.

Research on the screenplay development process highlights the many areas yet to explore regarding the different practices between writers, producers and studios. Ian Macdonald's outlining of the screen idea is important in trying to conceptualise this process; once the writer finishes a draft, he or she usually loses control of the project because of the hierarchical structure of the film development process and its collaborative nature (2010: 45). The correspondence and screenplay feedback from different sources held in the BFI archives is especially revealing on this aspect. The development of David Puttnam's *The October Circle* ilustrates how what should have been a 'good' screenplay, with experienced writers and a successful producer's backing fell apart after many drafts because no one could produce a screenplay 'good enough' to attract funding. In this case, the tone and style of the source novel proved too experimental to transfer to the screen and risk losing millions of dollars. Economic factors were the main consideration.

Social, cultural, historical, political and economic factors all affect the creation of a screenplay and are an ineluctable part in the film development process. A wealth of further research is needed on this aspect, with much to be gained from ensuring that notes and drafts of scripts are kept for posterity. This includes research based on studies of early screenwriters and screenplays, together with specific case studies of the development process as in Andrew Spicer's research on Michael Klinger, a British producer and the development of the script for *The Chilian Club* between 1972 and 1985 (2010), only possible thanks to access to the producer's archives. In this book, the chapters on Janet Green and Robert Bolt in particular show how outside factors can influence the outcome of a screenplay. In Green's case the intervention of the BBFC had an impact on the screenplay for *Victim* and Bolt's writing of the two Bounty films for Lean was thwarted by a dearth of production funds.

While a contextual approach is valuable in revealing the historical, social and political background and conditions of production that may affect screenplay content, the development for *Victim* being a case in point, close analysis of the screenplay itself is necessary if we are to understand the workings of the form in greater depth. There has, for instance, been very little analysis of the rewriting process, Steven Price's illuminating dissection of the three drafts of Alfred Hitchcock's *The Birds* (1963), by Evan Hunter (2010) is among the few exceptions. This book has often adopted a comparative approach to the study of screenplay drafts, but this approach has limitations: looking for differences and similarities can result in the distinction of the screenplay form itself not being addressed, though script changes are revealing about the preferences and choices made at certain stages of development. It is also important to examine the many unrealised screenplays still available, such as those for *The Lawbreakers*, *The Long Arm* and *Nostromo*, written by Robert Bolt for David Lean. Non-realised screenplays usually comprise a substantial part of any writer's output: most screenplays are not produced. T. E. B. Clarke noted that at Ealing Studios his scripts were made at a ratio of 1 to 3, which was high in comparison to other studios; when he moved to another studio, his average dropped to 1 in 6 (1976: 185).

Finally, this study is based on archival research only possible thanks to the availability of the BFI collections. There is still an urgent need to continue to preserve and archive screenplays and related letters. The screenplay has value not only as a record of a crucial part of the film production process but also as a literary text. Many early writers have left few traces of their work and more recent writing faces the same fate if the historical and cultural value, let alone the literary merit of the screenplay, is not appreciated.[1] Rightly, importance is placed on preserving film archives but the same value should be attached to the screenplay, as Ian Macdonald and Jacob U. U. Jacob note in their hunt for early British screenplays, 'A particular regret is that so little survives from the silent film period, to around 1930. The BFI has only around 75 British scripts from the approximately 8000 British fiction films of this period', whereas the French national Archive holds around 10,000 film scripts from 1907 to 1923 (2011: 164). Though the BFI screenplay collection is more substantial after 1930, holding over 30,000 screenplays, we still need to ensure important writing is archived and key collections are digitised.[2] A number of collections contain multiple screenplay drafts, such as the Margaret Herrick Library at the Academy of Motion Picture Arts and Sciences in the US, and of course the BFI Special Collections, while many production companies and screenwriters have preserved screenplay drafts deserving academic scrutiny. It is vital that screenplays are stored safely to enable research such as this.

There is still much to be learnt about the screenplay and the screenplay writing process. I hope this book will encourage further study of the screenwriter and the screenplay in British cinema, and contribute to the internationally growing body of work on this fascinating and underexplored subject area.

NOTES

1. See Brown (2008), which recalls the fate of many early screenplays stored in basements and neglected, only to be chewed to bits by rats.
2. For instance, the Ken Loach Collection was recently acquired by the BFI and is currently being catalogued.

BIBLIOGRAPHY

Aldgate, T., '"Obstinate Humanity": The Boultings, the Censors and Courting Controversy in the late-1960s', in A. Burton, T. O'Sullivan and P. Wells (eds), *The Family Way: The Boulting Brothers and British Film Culture* (Trowbridge: Flicks Books, 2000).

Anon, *Monthly Film Bulletin* vol. 27 no. 321, October 1960.

Anon, Review, *Films and Filming* vol. 10 no. 10, July 1964, p. 33.

Aspinall, S. and Murphy, R., *Gainsborough Melodrama Dossier* (London: BFI, 1983).

Bakhtin, M., *Rabelais and His World* (London: John Wiley and Sons, 1984).

Balcon, M., *The Producer*, BFI Summer School lecture, Bangor, 1945.

Balcon, M., *Michael Balcon Presents: A Lifetime of Films* (London: Hutchinson and Co. Ltd, 1969).

Barr, C., 'Projecting Britain and the British Character: Ealing Studios', *Screen* vol. 15, Spring 1974, pp. 87–121.

Barr, C. (ed.), *All Our Yesterdays: Ninety Years of British Cinema* (London: BFI, 1986).

Barr, C., *Ealing Studios* (London: Continuum, 1998).

Barr, C., *La Lettre de la maison Francais* no. 11, Autumn 1999, pp. 94–103.

Baxter, J., *An Appalling Talent: Ken Russell* (London: Michael Joseph, 1973).

Bogarde, D., *Snakes and Ladders* (St Albans: Triad/Panther Books, 1979).

Bordwell, D., *The Way Hollywood Tells It: Story and Style in Modern Pictures* (Los Angeles: University of California Press, 2006).

Bordwell, D., Staiger, J. and Thompson, K., *The Classical Hollywood Cinema* (London: Routledge, 1988).

Bourne, S., *Brief Encounters* (London: Cassell, 1996).

Box, M., *Odd Woman Out* (London: Leslie Frewin, 1974).

Box, M., BECTU Tapes, BFI, London.

Box, S. and Spicer, A. (eds), *The Lion That Lost Its Way* (Lanham, MD: Scarecrow Press, 2005).

Brady, D. and Capon, S. (eds), *Freedom's Pioneer* (Exeter: University of Exeter Press, 2005).

Brottman, M., *High Theory/Low Culture* (London: Palgrave Macmillan, 2005).

Brown, G., 'A Knight and His Castle', in J. Fleugel (ed.), *Michael Balcon: The Pursuit of British Cinema* (New York: Museum of Modern Art, 1984), pp. 32–40.

Brown, G., 'Life among the Rats', *Journal of British Cinema and Television* vol. 5 no. 2, 2008, pp. 242–61.

Brownlow, K., *David Lean* (London: St Martin's Press, 1996).

Brunel, A., *Filmcraft* (London: George Newnes, 1936).

Burton, A., 'From Adolescence into Maturity: The Film Comedy of the Boulting Brothers', in I. Q. Hunter and L. Porter, *British Comedy Cinema* (London: Routledge, 2012).

Burton, A. and O'Sullivan, T., *The Cinema of Basil Dearden and Michael Relph* (Edinburgh: Edinburgh University Press, 2009).

Burton, A., O'Sullivan, T. and Wells, P., *Liberal Directions: Basil Dearden and Post War British Film Culture* (Trowbridge: Flicks Books, 1997).

Burton, A., O'Sullivan, T. and Wells, P. (eds), *The Family Way: The Boulting Brothers and British Film Culture* (Trowbridge: Flicks Books, 2000).

Chapman, J., 'A Short History of the *Carry On* Films', in I. Q. Hunter and L. Porter (eds), *British Comedy Cinema* (London: Routledge, 2012).

Chibnall, S. and McFarlane, B., *The British 'B' Film* (London: BFI, 2009).

Christie, I., 'Alienation Effects: Emeric Pressburger and British Cinema', *Monthly Film Bulletin*, October 1984, pp. 318–20.

Christie, I. (ed.), *The Life and Death of Colonel Blimp* (London: Faber and Faber, 1994).

Christie, I., *A Matter of Life and Death* (London: BFI, 2000).

Christie, I., *Arrows of Desire: Films of Michael Powell and Emeric Pressburger* (London: Faber and Faber, 2002).

Clarke, T. E. B., *This Is Where I Came in* (London: Michael Joseph Ltd, 1974).

Conroy Scott, K., *Screenwriter's Masterclass* (London: Faber and Faber, 2005).

Cull, N. J., 'Camping on the Borders', in C. Monk and A. Sargeant (eds), *British Historical Cinema* (London: Routledge, 2002).

Danischewsky, M., *White Russian—Red Face* (London: Gollancz, 1966).

Davies, R., 'Don't Look Now: The Screenwork as Palimpsest', *Journal of Screenwriting* vol. 4 no. 2, 2012, pp. 163–77.

Davis, M., 'Carry on … Follow That Stereotype', in J. Curran and V. Porter (eds), *British Cinema History* (London: Weidenfeld and Nicolson, 1983).

Dell, J., *Nobody Ordered Wolves* (London: William Heinemann Ltd, 1939).

Dell, J., *The Hoffman Episode* (London: Jonathan Cape, 1954).

Demby, J., 'Interview with Robert Bolt', *Filmmakers Newsletter* vol. 6 no. 12, October 1973, pp. 28–33.

Deppman, J., Ferrer, D. and Groden, M., *Genetic Criticism: Texts and Avant-Textes* (Philadelphia: University of Pennsylvania Press, 2004).

Dixon, W. W., *The Transparency of Spectacle* (New York: State University of New York Press, 1998).

Drazin, C., *The Finest Years* (London: Andre Deutsch, 1998).

Durgnat, R., *A Mirror for England: British Movies from Austerity to Affluence* (London: Faber and Faber, 1970).

Durgnat, R., 'Two Social Problem Films', in A. Burton, T. O'Sullivan and P. Wells (eds), *Liberal Directions: Basil Dearden and Post War British Film Culture* (Trowbridge: Flicks Books, 1997).

Dyer, R., *The Matter of Images*, 2nd edn (London: Routledge, 1993).

Easthaugh, K., *The Carry On Book* (London: David and Charles Ltd, 1978).

Eberts, J. and Bott, T., *My Indecision Is Final: The Rise and Fall of Goldcrest Films* (London: Faber and Faber, 1992).

Ede, L., 'High Reason: The Boultings Meet the Ghost of Matthew Arnold', in A. Burton, T. O'Sullivan and P. Wells (eds), *The Family Way: The Boulting Brothers and British Film Culture* (Trowbridge: Flicks Books, 2000).

Ellis, J., 'Made in Ealing', *Screen* vol. 16, Spring 1975, pp. 78–127.

Ellis, J., 'At the Edge of Our World', *Vertigo*, Spring 1994, p. 23.

Fidelma, F., 'Ireland, the Past and British Cinema', in C. Monk and A. Sargeant (eds), *British Historical Cinema* (London: Routledge, 2002).

Fuller, G.,'Canterbury Tale', *Film Comment* vol. 31 no. 32, March/April 1995, pp. 33–6.

Fuller, G., *Loach on Loach* (London: Faber and Faber, 1998).

Ganz, A., 'Time, Space and Movement: Screenplay as Oral Narrative', *Journal of Screenwriting* vol. 1 no. 2, 2010, pp. 225–36.

Gelmur, J., *A Conversation with Robert Bolt*, Audio tape.

Gomez, J., *Ken Russell* (London: Frederick Muller, 1976).

Gough-Yates, K., 'Pressburger: England and Exile', *Sight & Sound*, December 1995, pp. 30–1.

Gough-Yates, K., 'Separating Powell from Pressburger', *Cineaste* vol. 23 no. 3, 1998, p. 61.

Gow, G., 'Carrying on Instinctively', *Films and Filming* vol. 16 no. 9, June 1970, pp. 70–3.

Grantham, M., 'Life on the Cheap with the Danzigers', BFI Collection, London.

Gulino, P., *Screenwriting: The Sequence Approach* (London: Continuum, 2004).

Harper, S., *Women in British Cinema* (London: Continuum, 2000).

Harper, S. and Porter, V., *British Cinema of the 1950s* (Oxford: Oxford University Press, 2003).

Hicks, Neill D., *Writing the Thriller Film: The Terror Within* (Los Angeles, CA: Michael Weise Productions, 2002).

Higson, A. (ed.), *Dissolving Views: Key Writings on British Cinema* (London: Cassell, 1996).

Hill, J., *Ken Loach* (London: BFI, 2011).

Hockenhull, S., *Neo-romantic Landscapes: An Aesthetic Approach to the Films of Powell and Pressburger* (Cambridge: Cambridge Scholars Publishing, 2008).

Houston, P., *Went the Day Well?* (London: BFI, 1992).

Johnstone, S., 'Charioteers and Ploughmen', in M. Auty and N. Roddick (eds), *British Cinema Now* (London: BFI, 1985).

Kipps, C., *Out of Focus: Power, Pride and Prejudice – David Puttnam in Hollywood* (New York: W. Morrow, 1989).

Koivumaki, M.-R., 'The Aesthetic Independence of the Screenplay', *Journal of Screenwriting* vol. 2 no. 1, 2010, pp. 25–40.

Laverty, Paul, *Carla's Song* (London: Faber and Faber, 1997).

Lazar, D., *Michael Powell: Interviews* (Mississippi: University of Mississippi Press, 2003).

Leach, J., *British Film*, (Cambridge: Cambridge University Press, 2004).

Leonard, H., *Irish Independent*, 9 October 1999.

Macdonald, I. W., '"… So It's Not Surprising I'm Neurotic": The Screenwriter and the Screen Idea Work Group', *Journal of Screenwriting* vol. 1 no. 1, 2010, pp. 45–58.

Macdonald, I. W. and Jacob, U. U. J., 'Lost and Gone for Ever? The Search for Early British Screenplays', *Journal of Screenwriting* vol. 2 no. 2, 2011, pp. 161–77.

Macdonald, K., *Emeric Pressburger: The Life and Death of a Screenwriter* (London: Faber and Faber, 1994).

McFarlane, B., *An Autobiography of British Cinema* (London: Methuen, 1997).

McFarlane, B., *The Encyclopedia of British Film* (London: Methuen, 2003).

McGrath, J., 'TV Drama: The Case against Naturalism', *Sight & Sound* vol. 46 no. 2, Spring 1977, pp. 100–5.

McGrath, J., 'Is a Popular Cinema Possible?', *AIP and CO*. no. 12, October 1978, pp. 20–5.

McGrath, J., *A Good Night Out* (London: Methuen, 1981).

McGrath, J., *City Limits*, 16 October 1986, p. 20.

McInerney, J., 'The Mission and Robert Bolt's Drama of Revolution', *Literature/Film Quarterly* vol. 15 no. 2, 1987, pp. 70–7.

McKee, R., *Story* (New York: HarperCollins, 1997).

Macnab, G., *J. Arthur Rank and the British Film Industry* (London: Routledge, 1993).

MacPhail, A., 'Film Writing', in A. Brunel (ed.), *Filmcraft* (London: George Newnes, 1936).

Mann, D., 'From Obscurity to Authority? The Changing Status of the Screenwriter during the Transition from 'B' Features to TV/Film Series (1946–64)', *Journal of British Cinema and Television* vol. 5 no. 2, 2008, pp. 280–99.

Mann, D., *Britain's First TV/Film Crime Series and the Industrialisation of Its Film Industry 1946–1964* (Lampeter: Edwin Mullen Press, 2009).

Maras, S., *Screenwriting: History, Theory, Practice* (London: Wallflower Press, 2009).

Medhurst, A., 'Victim: Text as Context', in A. Higson (ed.), *Dissolving Views: Key Writing on British Cinema* (London: Cassell, 1996).

Medhurst, A., *A National Joke: Popular Comedy and English Cultural Identities* (London: Routledge, 2007).

Merz, C., 'The Tension of Genre: Wendy Toye and Muriel Box', in W. Wheeler Dixon (ed.), *Re-viewing British Cinema 1980–1992: Essays and Interviews* (Albany: State University of New York Press, 1994).

Miles, S., *Bolt from the Blue* (London: Phoenix Publishing, 1996).

Morris, N., 'Unpublished Scripts in the BFI Special Collections: A Few Highlights', *Journal of Screenwriting* vol. 1 no. 1, 2010, pp. 197–202.

Mottram, J., 'Ae Fond Kiss', *Sight & Sound*, March 2004, pp. 22–3.

Murphy, R., 1992, *Realism and Tinsel* (London: Routledge, 1992).

Murphy, R., *Sixties British Cinema* (London: BFI, 1992).

Murphy, R., 'Gainsborough Producers', in P. Cook (ed.), *Gainsborough Pictures* (London: Continuum, 1998).

Murphy, R. (ed.), *The British Cinema Book* (London: BFI, 2008).

Nannicelli, T., 'The Early Screenwriting Practice of Ernest Lehman', *Journal of Screenwriting* vol. 1 no. 2, 2010, pp. 237–53.

O'Sullivan, T., 'Ealing Studios: 1947–1957', in I. Q. Hunter and L. Porter (eds), *British Comedy Cinema* (London: Routledge, 2012).

O'Thomas, M., 'Analysing the Screenplay: A Comparative Approach', in J. Nelmes (ed.), *Analysing the Screenplay* (London: Routledge, 2011).

Pitt, P., 'Elstree's Poverty Row', *Films and Filming*, September 1984, pp. 15–16.

Powell, M., *A Life in Movies* (London: Faber and Faber, 2000).

Pressburger, E., *Killing a Mouse on Sunday* (New York: Harcourt, Brace & World, 1961).

Pressburger, E., *Behold a Pale Horse* (London: Fontana/Collins, 1964).

Price, S., *The Screenplay, Authorship, Theory and Criticism* (Basingstoke: Palgrave Macmillan, 2010).

Prufer, S., *The Individual at the Crossroads* (Frankfurt: Peter Lang, 1998).

Puttnam, D., *The Undeclared War* (London: HarperCollins, 1997).

Puttnam, D., interview with author, 13 August 2012.

Relph, M., 'My Idea of Freedom', *Films and Filming*, September 1961, pp. 24–5, 37.

Richards, J., *Films and British National Identity* (Manchester: Manchester University Press, 1997).

Robertson, J. C., *The Hidden Cinema* (London: Routledge, 1981).

Robinson, D., 'Case Histories of the Next Renascence', *Sight & Sound*, Winter 1968/9, p. 36.

Ross, R., *The Carry On Companion* (London: B. T. Batsford Ltd, 1996).

Rossholm, A. S., 'Tracing the Voice of the Auteur: Persona and the Ingmar Bergman Archive',
  Journal of Screenwriting vol. 4 no. 2, 2012, pp. 135–48.

Sarris, A., *The American Cinema: Directors and Directions 1929–1968* (New York: E. P. Dutton, 1968).

Schoonmaker, T., email to the author, 12 May 2012.

Silver, A. and Ursini, J., *David Lean and His Films* (London: Leslie Frewin, 1974).

Smith, J. 'British Cult Cinema', in R. Murphy (ed.), *The British Cinema Book* (London: BFI, 2008).

Spicer, A., *Sydney Box* (Manchester: Manchester University Press, 2006).

Spicer, A., 'The Author as Author: Restoring the Screenwriter to British Film History',
  in J. Chapman, M. Glancy and S. Harper (eds), *The New Film History* (London: Palgrave
  Macmillan, 2007).

Spicer, A., 'An Impossible Task? Scripting *The Chilian Club*', in J. Nelmes (ed.), *Analysing the
  Screenplay* (London: Routledge, 2010).

Stollery, M., http://www.screenonline.org.uk/people/id/447569/index.html.

Turner, A., *Robert Bolt: Scenes from Two Lives* (London: Hutchinson, 1974).

Walker, A., *Hollywood, England: The British Film Industry in the Sixties* (London: Harrap, 1974).

Walker, A., *National Heroes: The British Film Industry in the Seventies and Eighties*
  (London: Orion, 2005).

Wells, P., 'Comments, Custard Pies and Comic Cuts: The Boulting Brothers at Play, 1955–65',
  in A. Burton, P. Wells, T. O'Sullivan (eds), *The Family Way: The Boulting Brothers and British
  Film Culture* (Trowbridge: Flicks Books, 2000).

Whitehead, T., http://www.screenonline.org.uk/film/id/444355/index.html.

Woods, F., 'Take That You Swine', *Films and Filming* vol. 5 no. 11, August 1959, p. 6.

Yule, A., *David Puttnam – The Story So Far* (London: Sphere, 1988).

WORKS REFERENCED FROM THE BFI SPECIAL COLLECTIONS

Michael Balcon Collection

Balcon 28/6/33.

Balcon 30/3/33.

Balcon 19/6/33.

Balcon 30/3/33.

Balcon 31/5/37.

Muriel and Sydney Box Collection

Box 1, 1.1 Box, Muriel and Sydney, *The Seventh Veil* (1945), third draft, no date.

Box 1, 1.2 Box, Muriel and Sydney, *The Seventh Veil* (1945), final draft, no date.

Box 2, 3 Box, Muriel and Sydney, *A Novel Affair* (*The Passionate Stranger*) (1956), second draft
  screenplay, 15 April 1955.

Box 2, 5.1 Box, Muriel and Sydney, *The Truth about Women* (1957), first draft screenplay, 8 June 1956.

Box 2, 5.2 Box, Muriel, *The Truth about Women* (1957), draft 14 January 1957.

Box 3, 8.3 Letters from Elsa Shelley to Muriel Box.

Box 4, 12.1 'Gainsborough Pictures', A Report by Sydney Box on Production and Future Planning.

Box 4, 12.2 Correspondence.

Box 7, 15 Muriel and Sydney Box diary, 1943–1947.

Box 7, 16 Muriel and Sydney Box diary, 1947–1954.

T. E. B. Clarke Collection

Item 1.a. Clarke, T. E. B., *Passport to Pimlico*, story outline, 97pp, 19 November 1947.
Clarke, T. E. B., *Passport to Pimlico*, treatment, 6pp, no date.
Item 1.b. unknown author, script pages and amendments.
Item 2.a Clarke, T. E. B., *The Lavender Hill Mob*, story outline and short treatment,
24 February 1956.
Item 2.b Clarke, T. E. B., *The Lavender Hill Mob*, fourth draft screenplay, 18 August 1950.
Item 2.c Clarke, T. E. B., *The Lavender Hill Mob*, shooting script, 15 September 1950.
Item 2.d Clarke, T. E. B., article, 'The Cinema'.

Jeffrey Dell Collection

JED/2 Jeffrey Dell, *Don't Take It to Heart* (1944), release script, no date.
JED/3 Jeffrey Dell, *It's Hard to Be Good* (1948), shooting script, 1948.
JED/4 Jeffrey Dell, *The Dark Man* (1950), no date.
JED/8 Jeffrey Dell, *Treasure of San Teresa* (1959), no date.
JED/9 Jeffrey Dell, *A French Mistress* (1960), 7 October 1959.
JED/27 Letter to Dell, 2 November 1956.

Mark Grantham Collection

MMG/2 Grantham, M., *Man Accused/Whirlpool of Suspicion*, screenplay draft, no date.
MMG/3 Grantham, M., *7.10 for Inverness*, screenplay draft, no date.
MMG/7 Grantham, M., *Feet of Clay/Dead Angel*, screenplay draft, no date.
MMG/20 Grantham, M., *She Always Gets Their Man/To Hook a Man*, screenplay draft, no date.
MMG/34 Grantham, M., 'Life on the Cheap with the Danzigers'.

Janet Green Collection

JG 3/1 Gunn, G., Green, J. and Hall, R., *The Good Beginning*, screenplay draft, April 1949.
JG 3/3 Gunn, G., Green, J. and Hall, R., *The Good Beginning*, shooting script, March 1953.
JG 5/1 Green, J., *Lost*, treatment, no date.
JG 5/2 Green, J., *Lost*, shooting script, January 1955.
JG 5/3 Green, J., *Lost*, shooting script, July 1955.
JG 8/1 Green, J. (additional dialogue Heller, L.), *Sapphire*, shooting script, 31 July 1958.
JG 8/2 Green, J. (additional dialogue Heller, L.), *Sapphire*, shooting script, October 1958.
JG 10/1 Green, J. and McCormick, J., *Victim*, screenplay draft, June 1960.
JG 10/2 Green, J. and McCormick, J., *Victim*, screenplay draft, August 1960.
JG 10/3 Green, J. and McCormick, J., *Victim*, screenplay draft, October 1960.
JG 10/5 Green, J. and McCormick, J., *Victim*, screenplay draft, January 1961.
JG 10/6 Correspondence.
JG 10/7 Press cuttings.
JG 11/1 Green, J. and McCormick, J., *Life for Ruth*, shooting script, 15 August 1961.
JG 11/2 Green, J. and McCormick, J., *Life for Ruth*, shooting script, September 1961.
JG 11/3 Green, J. and McCormick, J. *Life for Ruth*, shooting script, 29 December 1961.
JG 11/5 Correspondence.
JG 17 Green, J., *Many Happy Returns*, unrealised screenplay drafts, 1949.
JG 23/3 Correspondence.

JG 33/13 Correspondence.
JG 48/1 Correspondence.

David Lean Collection
DL/12/3 Bolt, R., *The Lawbreakers*, screenplay draft, dated 2 July 1978.
DL/12/6 Lean, D., Suggestions for cuts and alterations to *The Lawbreakers*, November 1978.
DL/12/6 Bolt, R., Reply to Lean's suggestions, 27 November 1978.
DL/12/47 Correspondence.

John McGrath Collection
Box 19.1 McGrath, J., *Billion Dollar Brain*, outline screenplay, 18 August 1966.
Box 19.2 McGrath, J., *Billion Dollar Brain*, story outline, 22 September 1966.
Box 29.1 McGrath, J., *The Reckoning* (titled *The Harp That Once*), first draft screenplay,
    January 1968.
Box 29.2 McGrath, J., *The Reckoning* (titled *Mick*), revised first draft screenplay, March 1968.
Box 29.3 McGrath, J., *The Reckoning* (titled *The Harp That Once*), second draft screenplay, August 1968.

Emeric Pressburger Collection
EPR 1/19/13.
EPR 1/19/6.
EPR 1/23/1 Letter, Powell to Pressburger.
EPR 1/23/3.
EPR 1/23/5 Pressburger, E., introduction to screening of *A Canterbury Tale*.
EPR 1/25/1 Pressburger, E., *A Matter of Life and Death*, handwritten early draft, 69pp, no date.
EPR 1/25/3.
EPR 1/28/1.
EPR 1/28/8 Review.
EPR 2/9/3.

David Puttnam Collection
Killing Fields
DP Box 8, Item 42.
DP Box 8, Item 43.

Local Hero
DP Box 1, Item 1 Forsyth, B., *Local Hero*, synopsis/treatment and script amendments.
DP Box 10, Item 46 Forysth, B., *Local Hero*, first draft screenplay, July 1981, 69pp.
DP Box 10, Item 47 Forysth, B., *Local Hero*, second draft screenplay, March 1982, 69pp.
DP Item 49/2 Bill Forsyth's contract for *Local Hero*.
DP Box 10, Item 61 Letters from David Puttnam.

October Circle
DP Item 4b Various correspondence.
DP Item 5 Correspondence.

Gerald Thomas Collection

GT 26/1 Hudis, N., *Carry on Sergeant*, first treatment and story ideas, 27 January 1958.
GT 26/2 Delderfield, R. F., *The Long and the Short and the Tall*, early treatment for what became *Carry on Sergeant*, no date.
GT 26/3 Hudis, N., *Carry on Sergeant*, story basis, characters and screenplay plan, 31 January 1958.
GT 26/13–26/15 Correspondence related to *Carry on Sergeant*.
GT 30/1 Rothwell, T., *Carry on up the Khyber*, first draft screenplay, no date.
GT 30/2 Rothwell, T., *Carry on up the Khyber*, final draft screenplay, no date.

SCREENPLAYS COLLECTION

S202 Clarke, T. E. B., *Passport to Pimlico* (1949), second shooting script, 9 July 1948.
S13976 Powell, M. and Pressburger, E., *A Canterbury Tale* (1944), no date.
S14828 Powell, M. and Pressburger, E., *A Matter of Life and Death* (1946), no date.

Paul Laverty

The following works were donated by Paul Laverty:

Laverty, P. (2004a) *The Wind That Shakes the Barley*, [treatment], London, Sixteen Films, 2004, 46pp.
Laverty, P. (2004b) *The Wind That Shakes the Barley*, [draft, April 2004], London, Sixteen Films, 99pp.
Laverty, P. (2005) *The Wind That Shakes the Barley*, [shooting script, April 2005], London, Sixteen Films, 89pp.

INDEX

Note: Page numbers in **bold** indicate detailed analysis; those in *italic* refer to illustrations; *n* = endnote.

LIST OF ILLUSTRATIONS

While considerable effort has been made to correctly indentify the copyright holders, this has not been possible in all cases. We apologise for any apparent negligence and any omissions or corrections brought to our attention will be remedied in any future editions.

Images courtesy of the BFI National Archive, except pp. 146, 157.

The Flemish Farm, Two Cities Films; *A French Mistress*, © Charter Film Productions; *The Red Shoes*, © Independent Producers; *A Canterbury Tale*, Archers Film Productions/Independent Producers; *The Happy Family*, © London Independent Producers; *Street Corner*, © London Independent Producers; *Sapphire*, Artna Films; *Life for Ruth*, Saracen Films/Allied Film Makers; *Victim*, © Parkway Films; *Night Train for Inverness*, Danziger Productions Ltd; *She Always Gets Their Man*, Ingram/Danziger Productions Ltd; *Carry on Sergeant*, © Anglo Amalgamated Film Distributors; *Carry on up the Khyber*, Rank Film Distributors; *Lawrence of Arabia*, © Horizon Pictures; *Local Hero*, © Celandine Films; *Billion Dollar Brain*, © Javera S.A.; *The Reckoning*, © Columbia (British) Productions; *The Wind That Shakes the Barley*, © Oil Flick Films No. 2 LLP/© UK Film Council/© Sixteen Films/© Element Films/© EMC GmbH/© BIM Distribuzione/© Tornasol Films.